MICHIGAN AUTHORS

by

Michigan Association for Media in Education

Second Edition
1980

Library of Congress Cataloging in Publication Data

Michigan Association for Media in Education
Michigan authors

First ed. (1960) by R.M. Hilbert.
1. Authors, American—Michigan—Bio-bibliography.
I. Hilbert, Rachel M., ed. Michigan authors.
II. Title.
PS283.M5M5 1979   810'.9'9774 [B]   78-20829
ISBN 0-933110-00-6

Manufactured in the United States of America

Published by MICHIGAN ASSOCIATION FOR MEDIA
            IN EDUCATION
            401 South Fourth Street
            Ann Arbor, Michigan 48103

TABLE OF CONTENTS

32170

INTRODUCTION

The purpose of this second edition of *Michigan Authors* is to identify as many authors and poets who have contributed to the state's cultural heritage as possible. Michigan poets, originally listed in a separate publication, are now included in this new edition.

INCLUSION CRITERIA:

Space limitations preclude the inclusion of every author who ever wrote about or resided in Michigan. Two criteria for inclusion were established by the Editorial Committee:

(1) significant ties with Michigan either through birth and/or extended residence sufficient to have influenced the author's writing; and

(2) publication of at least one book of prose or poetry with popular appeal to the young people.

No attempt was made to evaluate the quality of the author's works or the worthiness of their publishers. Information on authors listed in the first editions of *Michigan Authors* (1960) and *Michigan Poets* (1964) has been up-dated and included if the writers met the new criteria. Author entries containing an asterisk (*) appeared in the 1960 edition of *Michigan Authors.* These authors also qualified for this edition, but did not respond to our queries for up-dated information.

METHOD:

Identification of published authors with strong Michigan ties was a formidable task. Many author biographical reference works were searched. Regional historical societies and museums, statewide organizations of authors, educators, and librarians, as well as many individuals, were contacted.

After a preliminary screening of names from available sources, the Editorial Committee consulted standard biographical reference works (see "Sources Consulted") to compile the bio-bibliographies of authors qualified for inclusion but known to be dead.

Authors assumed to be living were sent questionnaires to help determine their eligibility for inclusion in this edition. For those meeting the criteria for inclusion, the bio-bibliographies were prepared and the results were checked by the authors themselves for accuracy.

Some authors did not respond to the request for information, and many addresses were invalid. The committee attempted to contact the last families, agents and last known publishers. If no information was available, the author was omitted from the book.

ARRANGEMENT:

The entries are arranged in alphabetical order by the author's last names. Cross references refer the reader from any pseudonyms to the appropriate biographical entries. However, surprisingly few pseudonyms were employed by these authors. Each entry includes name pseudonym(s), birth and death dates where appropriate, parents, marital status, children, education, career, address, writing, work in progress, and a quote from the author. Of importance in a reference work of this type is the bibliography of each author's published work, including title, publisher and date. Wherever any category is omitted, the information was unavailable, the category irrelevant, or it was deleted at the author's request.

The entries vary in completeness because the information provided by the authors or their representatives was not consistent in depth or detail.

ACKNOWLEDGEMENTS

Many people and organizations assisted in the preparation of this edition of *Michigan Authors*. Their help is gratefully acknowledged by the committees with whom they worked.

Special thanks are extended to Rachel M. Hilbert, now retired from librarianship, who was editor of the first edition of *Michigan Authors* and of its supplement *Michigan Poets*. Her generous advice materially aided the committee preparing this edition. Kenneth Vance of the University of Michigan School of Library Science, who served on the editorial committees of the previous publications, also provided helpful insights. Len Thomas, Assistant Coordinator of Educational Services of the Flint Public Schools, and Della Mitchell, Media Specialist, Vicksburg Public Schools, both former members of the MAME Non-Periodic Publications Committee also contributed significantly.

Some other people and organizations who helped are: Reference Librarians, Ann Arbor Public Library; Staff, Baldwin Public Library, Birmingham, Mich.; Marcia Bernhardt, Education Committee Chairperson, Iron County Historical and Museum Society; Annie Brewer, Editor, Gale Research Company; Patrick Butler, Director, Library and Resource Center, Schoolcraft College; Esther B. Bystrom, Director, Marquette County Historical Society; Burton Historical Collection Staff, Detroit Public Library; Detroit Women Writers; Margaret Drake Elliott, former Librarian, Muskegon High School; Dick Hathaway, Head, Michigan History Division, Michigan State Library; Nelda Hinz, Assistant Director, Hoyt Public Library, Saginaw; Staff, Michigan Room, Grand Rapids Public Library; Staff, Henry Ford Centennial Library, Dearborn; Hillsdale Educational Publishers; Howard Hoffman, Archives Specialist, University Archives and Regional History Collection, Western Michigan University; Jean Liebensberger, University of Michigan Information Services; Peggy I. Lugthart, Reference Department, Hoyt Public Library, Saginaw; Michigan Council for the Arts; Eleanor McKinney, Professor, School of Librarianship, Western Michigan University; Fran Murray, Information Officer, Michigan State University News Bureau; John Olson, Librarian, Library and Resource Center, Schoolcraft College; Mary Jo Pugh, Archivist, Bentley Historical Library, University of Michigan; James E. Taylor, former Professor, Business Education, Schoolcraft College; Reference Staff, Graduate Library, University of Michigan; Sandra Yolles, Promotion Manager, Wayne State University Press; and Michigan historical societies and museums, too numerous to mention.

MAME Committees for
MICHIGAN AUTHORS

EDITORIAL COMMITTEE

Donna Taylor (chairperson), Publisher, Green Oak Press, Brighton.
Thomas W. Downen, Associate Professor, School of Library Science, University of Michigan.
Joan E. Duryee, Media Specialist, South Redford Schools.
Bee Green, Director, Library/Media Services, Plymouth-Canton Community Schools.
Diane M. Gunn, Media Consultant, Birmingham Public Schools.
Phyllis R. Kuehn, Media Specialist, Saginaw Public Schools.
Betty Lee, Media Specialist, Dearborn Public Schools.
Beverly C. Rentschler, Elementary Media Coordinator, Walled Lake Consolidated Schools.
Dorothy Ringlein, Media Specialist (retired), Bentley Community Schools.

CONSULTANTS

Rachel M. Hilbert, Library Media Specialist (retired), Livonia Public Schools.
Kenneth E. Vance, Assistant Dean and Professor, School of Library Science, University of Michigan.

NON-PERIODIC PUBLICATIONS COMMITTEE

Jan Mort (Chairperson), Media Specialist, Sturgis Public Schools.
Gary Dell, Director, Media Services, Wayne-Westland Community Schools.
Elaine Didier, Library Consultant, Bureau of School Services, University of Michigan.
James Doyle, Public Services Librarian, Macomb County Community College.
Patricia Slocum, School Library/Media Specialist, Michigan State Library Services.
Marian West, Media Specialist, Plymouth-Canton Community Schools.
Donald J. Wilkening, Consultant, IMC Services, Instructional Media Center, Michigan State University.
Ron Zolton, Director, Instructional Materials Center, Saginaw Intermediate School District.

AARDEMA, VERNA 1911-

Born: June 6, 1911; New Era, Michigan
Parents: Alfred E. and Dora (VanderVen) Norberg
Married: Albert Aardema (deceased); Dr. Joel Vugteveen, Sr., a dentist
Children: Austin A. Aardema, M.D., and Mrs. Paula Dufford
Education: Michigan State University, B.A. 1934
Career: 24 years as an elementary school teacher and 21 years as staff-correspondent for *The Muskegon Chronicle*
Address: 1423 Forest Park Rd., Muskegon, MI 49441

Writings:

Tales From the Story Hat	Coward McCann	1960
The Na of Wa	Coward McCann	1960
Otwe	Coward McCann	1960
The Sky God Stories	Coward McCann	1960
More Tales From the Story Hat	Coward McCann	1966
Tales From the Third Ear	E.P. Dutton	1969
Behind the Back of the Mountain	Dial Press	1973
Why Mosqutoes Buzz in People's Ears (Caldecott Medal winner, 1976)	Dial	1975
Who's in Rabbit's House? A Masai Tale	Dial	1977

Work in Progress: *Ji-Nongo-Nongo Means Riddles*, from Africa, Four Winds; *The Riddle of the Drum* from Tizapan Mexico, Four Winds; *Half-a-Ball of Kenki, an Akan Tale*, Warne.

She says: "I tailor folk tales from another culture to fit American children. All of my books have been African tales, except for *The Riddle of the Drum* which is from Tizapan, Mexico.

"I choose tales, from early sources, and redo them so they will be satisfying and understandable to American children. I study the areas from which they come so that my added bits of background will be authentic—even the ideophones which I use are from authentic sources. But I sometimes shorten them or use a simpler spelling.

"I aim to present stories that black children (and in the case of *The Riddle of the Drum*, the Mexican children) can proudly claim as part of their heritage."

ABBOTT, ALICE see: BORLAND, KATHRYN

ABBOTT, MARGARET EVANS 1896-1976
Born: October 6, 1896, Galesburg, Illinois
Parents: Edward J. and Mary Josephine (Betrand) Evans
Married: O. Lawrence Abbott, a teacher and college professor
Children: Helen M. Draper, Jane E. Hart, John L. Abbott
Education: University of Northern Iowa, B.A. 1924
Career: Teacher and writer

Writings:

Matched Pair (with Lawrence Abbott)	Candor Press	1963
Beyond Now (with Lawrence Abbott)	Candor Press	1968
Poems published in the Diplomat, Chicago Tribune, Denver Post, etc.		

Mrs. Abbott won a number of poetry prizes, including first prize in the Kentucky State Poetry Contest and several in Poetry Society of Michigan contests. She served as President of the Lansing Poetry Club for a year, and as editorial consultant for *Peninsula Poets,* published by the Poetry Society of Michigan for ten years.

ABBOTT, O. LAWRENCE 1900-
Born: July 19, 1900; Conesville, Iowa
Parents: I.S. and Nan (Settlemire) Abbott
Married: Margaret Evans Abbott
Children: Helen M. Draper, Jane E. Hart, John L. Abbott
Education: University of Northern Iowa, B.A. 1923, University of Iowa, M.A. 1928; Michigan State University, Ph.D. 1953
Career: High school teacher, college professor, writer
Address: 508 Charles St., East Lansing, MI 48823

Writings:

Matched Pair (with Margaret Abbott)	Candor Press	1963
Beyond Now (with Margaret Abbott)	Candor Press	1968

He says: "My wife and I won a number of poetry prizes and published poems in many newspapers and magazines."

ABODAHER, DAVID JEROME 1919-
Born: February 1, 1919; Streator, Illinois
Parents: Simon George and Rose (Ayoub) Abodaher
Children: Lynda (Mrs. Robert Henderson); adopted son: Mounir Consul Abodaher

Education: University of Detroit, 1935-36; Notre Dame University, 1936-38

Career: Wrote pulp sport, western and mystery stories and radio dramas for WJR while in school, leaving college to accept staff job at WJR. Wrote for radio: WJR and WLW Cincinnati. Program Manager, WKY, Oklahoma City and WKZO, Kalamazoo, before army service. After army discharge in 1944, Radio Director of Simons-Michelson Advertising and Radio-TV Director of W.B. Doner Advertising. Later with J. Walter Thompson Advertising and Kenyon & Eckhardt. Currently in second employment period with Kenyon & Eckhardt, Detroit office

Address: 20965 Lahser Rd., Apt. 412 Southfield, MI 48034

Writings

Under Three Flags (a biography of Gabriel Richard)	*Hawthorn*	*1965*
Explorer of the Northlands (Daniel Duluth)	*P.J. Kennedy & Sons*	*1966*
Warrior on Two Continents (Thaddeus Kosciuszko)	*Messner*	*1968*
Freedom Fighter (Casimir Pulaski)	*Messner*	*1969*
Rebel on Two Continents (Thomas Meagher)	*Messner*	*1970*
French Explorers of North America	*Messner*	*1970*
Mag Wheels and Racing Stripes	*Messner*	*1974*
Compacts, Subs and Minis: Be Your Own Mechanic	*Messner*	*1976*

Work in Progress: *The Incredible Formula I Race Cars: Great Drivers Who Made Racing History*

He says: "An avid reader, and as proud of my library as of anything I own, I feel deep concern over the lack of reading by too many of today's young people. Which is one reason I never turn down a school invitation to talk writing and the importance of reading, and have thoroughly enjoyed my six or so appearances at the Children's Book Fairs sponsored by the *Detroit Free Press* and the *Port Huron Times Herald.* I am fully convinced that reading is essential for one to be a 'complete' person, that if one does not read—and read a cross-section of all types of literature—he cannot help but be handicapped to some degree in life."

ADAMS, ANGELA see: SMITH, KAY

ADAMS, BETSY 1942-
Pseudonym: Elisabeth Jymes
Born: May 1, 1942; Port Huron, Michigan
Parents: Lorne P. and Dora (Burgar) Adams
Education: University of Michigan, B.S. 1964; Wayne State University, M.S. 1970; Boston University, M.S. 1976
Career: Research Associate in Biophysics, 10 yrs.; Teacher: Creative Writing, Science, English conversation to Japanese students; Science Editor for *Second Growth;* Research Assistant in *Ecological Evolution*
Address: 6480 South State Rd., Saline, MI 48176

Writings:

Losing the Moon 4, 3, 2, 1.	*Mill Creek Press*	*1978*
Histories	*Mill Creek Press*	*1978*

and poems in about 55 magazines and scientific articles in professional journals
Work in Progress: 2 books

She says: "At present I am very deeply involved in seeking and implementing alternatives to the uses of animals in Bio-Medical research and related areas. I am working toward a Ph. D. in Ecological Evolution, while working as a research assistant in this area."

ADAMS, HENRY H. 1917-
Born: March 26, 1917; Ann Arbor, Michigan
Parents: Henry F. and Susan (Hitch) Adams
Married: Catherine S. Adams
Children: Catherine A. Hartman and Henry A.S. Adams
Education: University of Michigan, A.B. 1939; Columbia University, M.A. 1940; Ph.D. 1942
Career: Naval Service during World War II. Retired from Naval Reserve in 1968 with rank of Captain. Cornell University, 1945-51, Instructor in English. U.S. Naval Academy, 1951-68, Asst. Prof., Associate Prof., and Prof. of English and History. Illinois State University, 1968-73, Head, Department of English and Professor
Address: Ferry Farms, Annapolis, MD 21402

Writings:

English Domestic or Homiletic Tragedy	*Columbia U. Pr.*	*1943*
Dramatic Essays of the Neoclassic Age	*Columbia U. Pr.*	*1950*
Techniques of Revision	*Ronald Pr.*	*1951*
United States and World Sea Power (contributor)	*Prentice Hall*	*1955*

Sea Power, a Naval History *(Contributor and Co-editor)*	Prentice Hall	*1960*
1942: The Year That Doomed *the Axis*	McKay	*1968*
Years of Deadly Peril	McKay	*1969*
Years of Expectation	McKay	*1971*
Years of Victory	McKay	*1973*

(Note: the above four books
  constitute a social, political,
  and military history of World
  War II.)		

The War Lords, ed. by Sir
  Michael Carver. (contributed
  biographies of Admiral Nimitz
  and Admiral Sprunace)
	Little, Brown	*1976*

Harry Hopkins: A Biography	Putnam's	*1977*

Work in Progress: Averell Harriman's memoirs of the Truman years. Working with Harriman.

He says: "The study of history and the study of literature can be closely allied, if you take the view that history deals with people. Thus, I have found the transition easy to make, and my professional writing is now completely in the field of history."

ADAMS, JULIA HUBBARD 1892-1975
Born: July 5, 1892; Cambridge, Massachusetts
Parents: Lucius Lee and Frances (Johnson) Hubbard
Married: Platt Adams
Children: Charlotte A. Barber, Nancy Adams, Platt Adams, Jr.
Education: University of Wisconsin, 1910-11
Career: Housewife

Writings:
Memories of a Copper *Country Childhood.*	Self-Published	*1973*

ALKEMA, CHESTER JAY 1932-
Born: July 17, 1932; Martin, Michigan
Parents: Rev. William and Jennie (Vander Meer) Alkema
Education: Calvin College, A.B. 1954; Michigan State University, M.A. 1959; M.F.A. 1961
Career: Teacher, public and parochial schools, 1954-66; Instructor, Assistant & Associate Professor of Art, Grand Valley State College, 1965-present
Address: 3365 Wildridge Dr., N.E., Grand Rapids, MI 49505

Writings:

Creative Paper Crafts in Color	Sterling	1967
The Complete Crayon Book in Color	Sterling	1969
Practical Encyclopedia of Crafts (Co-author)	Sterling	1970
Alkema's Complete Guide to Creative Art for Young People	Sterling	1971
Art for the Exceptional	Pruett	1971
Masks	Sterling	1971
Puppet Making	Sterling	1972
La Palette Des Crayons	Dessain et Tolra	1972
Creations en Papiers de Couleur	Dessain et Tolra	1972
Family Book of Crafts (Co-author)	Sterling	1973
Family Book of Hobbies (Co-author)	Sterling	1973
Crafting With Nature's Materials	Sterling	1973
Monster Masks	Sterling	1973
Tissue Paper Creations	Sterling	1973
Greeting Cards You Can Make	Sterling	1973
Aluminum and Copper Tooling	Sterling	1974
Starting With Papier Mache	Sterling	1974
Vingerpoppen, Sokpoppen, Handpoppen en Stokpoppen	Cantecleer, B.V., De Bilt	1975
Giant Book of Crafts (Co-author)	Sterling	1975
Easy Crafts Book (Co-author)	Sterling	1975
Metalcrafting Encyclopedia (Co-author)	Sterling	1975
Alkema's Scrap Magic	Sterling	1976

and numerous articles in such magazines as: *School Arts, Arts and Activities, Grade Teacher, The Instructor, Design,* and others.

Work in Progress: an encyclopedia—a general treatment of arts and crafts

He says: "In preparing journal articles and books, research is required. But the greatest contribution to my publications is made by my students—who are so creative. They take a suggested idea and move far beyond it, thereby suggesting new possiblities and insights into the use of familiar art techniques and media. The teacher teaches his students and vice versa. This intimate interaction is reflected in all of my publications.

"I continue to photograph student art work and my own art creations. My photographs, in black and white, and in color, now run into the thousands. One single lens reflex camera is always located with black and white film, and a second camera is reserved for color film—always in preparation for another journal article—another book."

Awards: Biography appears in the Michigan State Library, Lansing, in honor of cultural contributions made to the state of Michigan.

Listed in *Who's Who in American Art, The International Directory of Arts,* and *Outstanding Educators of America.*

ALLEN, DURWARD L. 1910-

Born: October 11, 1910; Uniondale, Indiana
Parents: Harley J. and Jennie M. (LaTurner) Allen
Married: Dorothy H. Allen, a homemaker
Children: Stephen R., Harley W., Susan E.
Education: University of Michigan, A.B. 1932; Michigan State College, Ph.D. 1937
Career: Game Research Biologist, Michigan Department of Conservation, 1935-46; Military Service, 1943-45; Biologist, Assistant & Acting Chief, Branch of Wildlife Research, U.S. Fish and Wildlife Service, 1946-54; Professor, Purdue University, 1954-present
Address: 1010 Windwood Lane, West Lafayette, Indiana 47906

Writings:

Michigan Fox Squirrel Management	*Mich. Dept. of Conservation*	*1943*
Pheasants Afield	*Stackpole*	*1953*
Our Wildlife Legacy	*Funk & Wagnalls*	*1954* rev. *1962*
Fasanen og Vildtplejen (a translation of Pheasants Afield	*Danish Game Foundation*	*1955*
Pheasants in North America (Editor)	*Stackpole and Wildlife Management Inst.*	*1956*
The Life of Prairies and Plains	*McGraw Hill*	*1967*
Land Use and Wildlife Resources (Editor)	*National Academy of Science*	*1970*

and approximately 100 articles in such magazines as *Field and Stream, Boys' Life, Sports Afield, Outdoor Life, National Wildlife, Audubon Magazine, Sports Illustrated, Ford Times, Family Circle, Science Digest,* and *National Geographic* and approximately 60 technical papers in scientific journals and conference transactions.

Work in Progress: a book on 18 years of wolf research on Isle Royale (Michigan), to be published in 1978

He says: "When man develops the wisdom to learn from nature, he will know that his most basic problems are biological and enviromental. Without this insight, he will find no order in his social and economic confusion."

Awards: Membership in honor societies: Phi Sigma, Sigma Xi, Seminarium botanicum, Xi Simga Pi; The Wildlife Society. Annual technical publication award, 1945 (for *Michigan Fox Squirrel Management*); The Wildlife Society. Annual conservation education award, 1955 (for *Our Wildlife Legacy* and *Pheasants Afield*); Angler's Club of New York. Medal of honor for service to wildlife conservation, 1956; Indiana "Conservation Educator of the year", 1965; The Wildlife Society, Honorary membership, 1966; Outdoor Writers Association of America, Jade of Chiefs Award & honorary membership, 1968; American Forestry Association, Honorary Vice President, 1968-69; The Wildlife Society, Leopold Memorial Medal, 1969; Northern Michigan University, Honorary Doctor of Human Letters, 1971; Indiana Dept. of Natural Resources, Award of Merit, 1973; Indiana Academy of Science, Lecturer of the Year, 1973-74; Purdue University, Chase S. Osborn Award, for service to wildlife conservation in Indiana 1977.

ALLEN, ELIZABETH 1914-
Married name: Elizabeth Allen Thompson
Born: 1914; Syracuse, New York
Parents: S.W. and Helen (Brown) Allen
Married: J.B. Thompson; Physician
Children: Patricia; James Jr.; Robert
Education: University of Michigan, A.B. 1936, M.A. 1938
Career: Prepared to teach English in secondary school, however English teachers were not in demand during the thirties. Therefore, took crash courses at University Hospital (Ann Arbor) and spent several years in Medical Case Work
Address: 3022 E. 38th Place, Tulsa, OK 74105

Writings:

The In Between	*Dutton*	*1959*
The Loser	*Dutton*	*1963*
The Forest House	*Dutton*	*1967*
You Can't Say What You Think	Dutton	*1968*
Margie	*Dutton*	*1969*
Younger's Race	*Grosset*	*1972*

Work in Progress: *Figures on a Landscape* (short story); *Some Words For Women* (poetry)

She says: "My creative writing interests in college were largely centered on poetry and the short story. It seems strange that my publications have been, at least as far as books are concerned, in the field of 'literature for young people,' and all but one of these books have been novels. The fact that I got very involved with my children's concerns prompted these books.

"Now that my children are grown, I find that I am returning to short stories and poems. I am very interested in writing some truly honest stories about women, and do have a group of stories in progress. I am also writing, and doing some publishing of poems.

"My stories and poems since college have appeared in periodicals that show a fair amount of variety. I also write a weekly column for a feminist monthly newspaper, *Sister Advocate*, published in Oklahoma City, and since I am committed, although non-militant, feminist, I write stories with a feminist slant for confession magazines and have had about ten of these appear.

"I am attending a poetry workshop at the Women's Concerns Center taught by poet Mary MacAnally-Knight. I have several poems in the mail and work on poetry almost daily. You don't get anywhere keeping things in a drawer!"

Honors: Hopwood winner, 1932 and 1936

ALLEN, JAMES B. 1931-
Born: August 7, 1931; Grand Rapids, Michigan
Parents: C. Dewey and Caroline (Butterfield) Allen
Married: Rosemary Allen, a bookseller
Children: Sean and James
Education: University of Michigan, A.B. 1954, M.A., A.B.D. 1973
Career: Bookseller and Writer
Address: 26 Division N., Grand Rapids, MI 49503

Writings:
See the Lighthouse Burning   Peter Quince   1976

Work in Progress: "My first book was autobiographical/ confessional. The second one is more objective, less room for self-pity." *City Aflame*

He says: "I own a bookstore in downtown Grand Rapids, a general bookstore. I write poetry. I read my poetry for the Michigan Council for Arts, and around at colleges. The luminous image is what I'm after to resolve conflict and transform outer ugliness to inner calm and beauty. My poems are utterances to God, saying, 'Change me.'"

Awards: University of Michigan's Avery Hopwood Award for literature, 1972 and 1973

ALTEMESE, ELETHEA see: THOMPSON, JAMES W.

ALTROCCHI, JULIA COOLEY 1893-1972

Born: July 4, 1893; Seymour, Connecticut
Parents: Harland Ward and Nellie (Wooster) Cooley
Married: Rudolph Altrocchi; Professor and Department Chairman—Italian; University of California
Children: John Cooley; Paul Hemenway
Education: Vassar, A.B. 1914
Career: Writer and Lecturer

Writings:

Poems of a Child	Harper	*1904*
Dance of Youth & Other Poems	Sherman French	*1917*
Snow Covered Mountains:		
A Pioneer Epic	Macmillan	*1936*
Wolves Against the Moon	Macmillan	*1940*
Old California Trail	Caxton	*1945*
Spectacular San Franciscans	Dutton	*1950*
Girl with Ocelot, & Other Poems	Humphries	*1964*

Contributor to *Atlantic, Yale Review, Harper's, Poetry,* and others.

Mrs. Altrocchi's summers were spent at a family cottage in Harbert, Michigan. About this summer home she said, "I still own, loving as I do Michigan's scenery, history, and general magnificence."

AMOS, WINSOM 1921-

Pseudonym: Hilary Theron
Born: May 10, 1921; Lansing, Michigan
Parents: Charles and Inez (Kinnebrew) Amos
Married: Oris Amos
Children: Patsy
Education: Ferris State College, B.S. 1951; Michigan State University, 1952; Ohio State University, M.A. 1970
Career: Counselor for on-the-job training for young adults, 1969-70; Supply Cataloger at Defense Construction Supply Center, Columbus, OH
Address: 673 Omar Circle, Yellow Springs, OH 45387

Writings:

Like a Dream (poetry)	Soma Press	*1971*
Oriole to Black Mood (poetry)	Soma Press	*1973*

Work in Progress: *Love Poems: Youth and Young Adult Poems;* a novel; *On-the-Job Training Young Adults.*

He says: "I always try to write with tenderness and force. This is true of *Oriole to Back Mood.* My poetry has appeared recently in several poetry anthologies: *Poetry of Our Time; Journal of Con-*

temporary Poets; Sunshine; Poetry of the Year, Bicentennial Edition; and will appear in *50 Outstanding American Poets During 1977,* J. Mark Press. N.Y. Poem " A Growing Suburb" appeared in Otterbein Community Service Project-Report to Federal Government-Printing Office (book form)-1973. Poem "Sit Perk and Label Me" appeared in *Ohio Adult Education Association Bulletin, 1973.*

"I say to be successful in your own way, but don't forget from where you came. Don't forget us and turn your back."

ANDERSON, DAVID D. 1924-
Born: June 8, 1924; Lorain, Ohio
Parents: David J. and Nora (Foster) Anderson
Married: Patricia Ann Anderson, a Library-Media Specialist
Education: Bowling Green State University, B.S. 1951, M.A. 1952; Michigan State University, Ph.D. 1960
Career: USN, 1942-45; USA, 1952-53; General Motors Institute, 1953-56; MSU, 1956-present; Fulbright Lecturer in American Literature, University of Karachi, Pakistan, 1963-64; Currently Professor of American Thought and Language and Assistant Dean, University College, at MSU
Address: 6555 Lansdown Drive, Dimondale, MI 48821

Writings:

Louis Bromfield	*Twayne*	*1964*
Critical Studies in American Literature	*University of Karachi*	*1964*
Sherwood Anderson	*Holt, Rinehart & Winston*	*1967*
Sherwood Anderson' Winesburg, Ohio	*Barron*	*1967*
Brand Whitlock	*Twayne*	*1968*
The Black Experience (Editor)	*MSU Press*	*1969*
Abraham Lincoln	*Twayne*	*1970*
The Literary Works of Abraham Lincoln (Editor)	*Charles E. Merrill*	*1970*
The Dark and Tangled Path (Co-editor)	*Houghton-Mifflin*	*1971*
Sunshine and Smoke: American Writers and the American Environment (Editor)	*Lippincott*	*1971*
Suggestions for the Instructor	*Lippincott*	*1971*
Robert Ingersoll	*Twayne*	*1972*
MidAmerica I (Editor)	*Midwestern Press*	*1974*
MidAmerica II (Editor)	*Midwestern Press*	*1975*

MidAmerica III (Editor)	Midwestern Press	1976
MidAmerica IV (Editor)	Midwestern Press	1978
American Literary Manuscripts: A Checklist (Co-editor)	U. of Georgia Pr.	1977
Sherwood Anderson's Uncollected Writings (Co-editor)	Paul P. Appel	(sched. for 1978)
Woodrow Wilson	Twayne	(sched. for 1978)
Ignatius Donnelly	Twayne	(sched. for 1979)

Work in Progress: *William Jennings Bryan* for Twayne Publishers

He says: "I have an abiding respect for the art and craft of writing prose."

ANDERSON, LUTHER A.

Born: Ironwood, Michigan
Parents: Peter Edward and Carolina (Gustafson) Anderson
Married: Ethel M. Anderson, a teacher
Education: DePaul College of Commerce, Chicago, B.S.C. 1925; University of Chicago, Ph.B. 1927
Career: Accountant with a hobby of writing. After retiring, full-time writer
Address: 139 South Curry St., Ironwood, MI 49938

Writings:

Hunting, Fishing, and Camping	Macmillan	1945
Hunting the American Game Field	Ziff-Davis	1949
How to Hunt Deer and Small Game	Ronald Pr.	1959
How to Hunt Whitetail Deer	Funk & Wagnalls	1968
How to Hunt American Small Game	Funk & Wagnalls	1969
A Guide to Canoe Camping	Reilly & Lee	1969
Hunting the Uplands With Shotgun and Rifle	Winchester	1977

Articles in *Outdoor Life, Field and Stream, Sports Afield, Fur-Fish-Game.*

He says: "I have been interested in the outdoors all my life, as an angler, hunter, and camper. I do informative work for the most part, writing the how-to-material for both amateur and expert, mostly the former. Have had success in my work, and just keep writing, hoping my work will see the light of day in print. With seven books published, along with articles in the foremost 'Outdoor' magazines, believe I am doing all right, and hope to so continue.

ANDREWS, VICKI see: SMITH, KAY

ANGELO, FRANK 1914-
Born: September 6, 1914; Detroit, Michigan
Parents: Nicolo and Ida (Dugini) Angelo
Married: Elizabeth
Children: Frank Jr., and Andrew Nicholas
Education: Wayne State University, B.A. 1934
Career: *Detroit News,* 1934-41; *Detroit Free Press, 1941-*
Address: *Detroit Free Press,* 321 W. Lafayette St., Detroit, MI 48226

Writings:

Yesterday's Detroit	*E.A. Seeman*	*1974*
Yesterday's Michigan	*E.A. Seeman*	*1976*

ANGUILM, JOHN A. 1912-
Born: January 9, 1912; Rapid River, Michigan
Parents: John and Neil (LaBumbard) Anguilm
Married: Evelyn M.
Children: Evelyn, Sally, Patricia, Mary
Education: High School, St. Ignace, MI
Career: 43 years with Department of Natural Resources: Fire Officer; Conservation Officer; District Supervisor; U.P. Forest Fire Supervisor; Chief, Division of Law Enforcement, Lansing.
Address: P.O. Box 221, Trout Lake, MI 49793

Writings:

Tales and Trails of		
Tro-La-Oz-Ken	*Gerrie Press*	*1976*

He says: "I admire the land and peace."

ANNIXTER, JANE see: STURTZEL, JANE LEVINGTON COMFORT

ANTON, REV. MICHAEL J. 1940-
Born: December 6, 1940; Memphis, Tennessee
Parents: William John Herman and Dorothy Margaret (Eken) Anton
Married: Charlotte Ann Kirsch
Children: Mark William, Philip Michael, Matthew James

Education: St. Paul's College, Concordia, MO, A.A. 1960; Concordia College, Ft. Wayne, IN, B.A. 1962; Concordia Theological Seminary, St. Louis, MO, Master of Divinity, 1966

Career: Pastor, Lutheran Church of the Good Shepherd, Niagara Falls, Ontario, 1966-67; Master Teacher, Niagara College of Applied Arts & Technology, Welland, Ontario, 1967-69; Pastor, Grace Lutheran Church, Hastings, MI 1969-

Address: 239 E. North St., Hastings, MI 49058

Writings:

Three Advent/Christmas		
Chancel Dramas: "From		
Humbug to Heaven"		
"What Are We Going to Do		
With the King?"		
"The Night That Was"	*C.S.S. Publishing Co.*	*1972*
Evangelism Drama:		
"Evangelism in 3-D"	*C.S.S. Publishing Co.*	*1973*
Snoring Through Sermons	*C.S.S. Publishing Co.*	*1974*
Good News for Now	*C.S.S. Publishing Co.*	*1976*

Work in Progress: Collection of chancel dramas

He says: "Each of the items published to date was 'field-tested' in my present parish setting. Because my writing is done as a practical parish help, I have wanted to try it on for size in a real parish before suggesting its use by others. Being involved in publishing has been an avocation for me, but my continuing dream is that of being a full-time writer."

ANTONACCI, ROBERT J. 1916-

Born: January 21, 1916; Toluca, Illinois

Parents: Nicholas and Angela (Materelli) Antonacci

Married: Amaryllis, a Medical Technician

Children: Robert, Jr. and Clarissa

Education: Indiana University, B.S. 1941; University of Michigan, M.S. 1946, Ed D. 1956

Career: Coached and taught Wrestling and Physical Education, University of Michigan 1941, 1945, and 1946 and six summer sessions; 1941-45 special assignment as a physical fitness instructor and administrator, U.S. Navy; Oregon State University, 1953-57; Supervisor, Gary, Indiana School District, 1957-65; Temple University, Graduate Faculty, Philadelphia, PA, 1965-present as professor of health and physical education

Address: 1508 Elkins Ave., Abington, PA 19001

Writings:

Sports Officiating	*A.S. Barnes*	*1948*
Coaches Wrestling Manual	*Self-published*	*1949, 1955, 1963*

Track and Field for Young Champions (Co-author)	McGraw-Hill	1974
Football for Young Champions (Co-author)	McGraw-Hill	2nd ed. 1976
Physical Fitness for Young Champions (Co-author)	McGraw-Hill	2nd ed. 1976
Baseball for Young Champions (Co-author)	McGraw-Hill	2nd ed. 1977
Soccer for Young Champions (Co-author)	McGraw-Hill	1978
Basketball for Young Champions (Co-author)	McGraw-Hill	2nd ed. 1979

and over 30 magazine articles, contributor to 12 school and college textbooks, and manuals and guides in the area of health and physical education curricula.

Work in Progress: *Tennis For Young Champions* (with Dr. Barbara Lockhart), magazines articles, and outlines for two additonal books.

He says: "My goal is to write books that will tell the young readers that engaging in healthy sports and fitness activities will give them a feeling of joy, fun, respect for others, and a sense of fair play. My greatest motivators and critics have been my wife, Amaryllis, daughter Clarissa, and son Bob, Jr., who often remind me of how the playground and elementary school programs helped me as a young boy growing up in Chicago. Many of my best moments occur when talking to young boys and girls during the special library and school-community programs."

Awards: Listed in *Who's Who In the East, Who's Who In the Midwest, National Register of Prominent Americans, Dictionary of International Biography, Royal Blue Book,* etc. School Bell Award, American Medical Association Fellow, American College of Sports Medicine; National award from NEA-AAHPER for promotion of the President's Council on Physical Fitness and Sports Youth Fitness Testing programs; Bishop's Award, Chicago-Gary Area Catholic Youth Organization for contributing to boys and girls sports and fitness literature; YMCA award for service to youth; Producers Award, Program Aids Co., Mt. Vernon, NY, for development of innovative programs in physical education and athletics.

ARBOR, LYNN SCHOETTLE 1943-
Born: August 13, 1943; Ann Arbor, Michigan
Parents: Herb and Gloria (Sexton) Calkins
Children: Susan Elizabeth Schoettle, James Joseph Schoettle
Education: Oakland Community College; 1971-76; Wayne State

University, 1976-77

Career: Assistant editor of *Contemporary Authors, Gale Research,* 1974; Keyliner, M & M Graphics, 1975-77; North American Graphics, 1977-present; Paintings, Habatat Gallery since 1975

Address: 412 N. Connecticut, Royal Oak, MI 48067

Writings:
Grandpa's Long Red
Underwear   *Lothrop Lee & Shephard   1962*
also author of a decorating column in the *Detroit News* 1967-68.

Work in Progress: Currently painting in every spare minute after work. Would like to write another novel (two unpublished so far) but can't find the time.

She says: "My main philosophy is to try (with effort sometimes) not to regret any part of my life. Every choice we make grows out of our needs at the time, though sometimes later we feel we've goofed. We should try to be gentle with ourselves and realize that we can be fragile.

"My major conflict is being torn between writing and painting and not having enough time to devote to either."

ARMOUR, DAVID ARTHUR 1937-
Born: July 12, 1937; Grove City, Pennsylvania
Parents: Arthur S. and Marian (Bowie) Armour
Married: Grace Hendrika Lootsma, a homemaker
Children: Marian Grace, Arthur David, David James, Anne Marie
Education: Calvin College, A.B. 1959; University College, London 1957-58; Northwestern University, M.S. 1963, Ph.D. 1965
Career: Instructor and Assistant Professor, University of Wisconsin, 1963-67; Assistant Superintendent, Mackinac Island State Park Commission, 1967-present
Address: 2330 Northwest Ave., Lansing, MI 48909

Writings:

Massacre at Mackinaw 1763	*Mackinac Island State Park Commission*	*1966*
Treason? at Michilimackinac	*Mackinac Island State Park Commission*	*1967*
Editor. Historical Archaeology	*Society for Historical Archaeology*	*1968-73*

Work in Progress: *At the Crossroads: Michili-Mackinac During the American Revolution.*

ARMSTRONG, TOM 1935-

Born: August 4, 1935; Detroit, Michigan
Parents: Thomas Gordon and Beatrice Clara (Ostrowski) Armstrong
Married: Y. Elaine Armstrong, a bookkeeper
Children: Michael Anthony; Joseph Allen
Education: U.S. Armed Forces Institute: Wayne State extension courses; Schoolcraft College; Creative writing and poetry related courses 1972-present
Career: Product Designer
Address: 11313 Beech Daly, Redford, MI 48239

Writings:

Echoes From Silence	*Jemta Press*	*1977*

Work in Progress: Metaphysical in nature, untitled at present.

He says: "The writing of poetry has become an important part of my life. I have been writing seriously for the last five years, and three of those years have been associated with the Livonia Poetry Workshop, a group of people interested in good creative writing. We participated in poetry readings in public as well as on the radio.

"Photography has also been an important interest of mine for many years. *Echoes From Silence* is a compilation of some of my poetry (haiku and other short forms) and nature-related photography.

"I believe that mankind is a part of a great spirtual reality in which man will eventually achieve high spiritual awareness. I would like my writing and photography to further this spiritual awareness."

ARNOLD, EDMUND C. 1913-

Born: June 25, 1913; Bay City, Michigan
Parents: Ferdinand N. and Anna J. (Begick) Arnold
Married: Viola I. Burtzloff
Children: Bruce Robert Arnold, Bethany Record, Kathleen Loomis
Education: Bay City Junior College, A.A. 1934; Michigan State University, A.B. 1954
Career: Editor, *Frankenmuth (MI) News;* Picture editor,*Saginaw News;* night editor, *Lansing State Journal;* editor, *Linotype, News, NYC;* Director of Trade Relations, Mergenthaler Linotype Co.; Professor and Chairman, Graphic Arts Dept., School of Journalism, Syracuse University; Professor of Journalism, Virginia Commonwealth University. Conducted 200 seminars for American Press Institute, Reston, VA. Designed newspaper format for:

Christian Science Monitor	*Boston Globe*
Today	*Kansas City Star*

Lexington (KY) Leader and Herald	*Chicago Tribune*
Edinburgh Scotsman	*Tornoto Star*
Otaga (New Zealand) Times	*Montgomery Advertiser*
El Mundo, Puerto Rico	*Vanguard (magazine)*
El Universo, Guayaquil, Ecuador	*Lutheran Forum (magazine) etc.*

Consultant to: Southam Business Publications, *St. Petersburg Times, Detroit News, Akron Beacon Journal, Minneapolis,* etc.

Contributing editor to *Canadian Printer & Publisher, Ragan Report, Publishers' Auxiliary,* etc.

Address: 3208 Hawthorne Ave., Richmond, VA 23222

Writings:

Functional Newspaper Design	*Harper & Row*	*1956*
Profitable Newspaper Advertising	*Harper & Row*	*1960*
Feature Photos That Sell	*Morgan & Morgan*	*1960*
Ink on Paper: a Handbook of the Graphic Arts	*Harper & Row*	*1963*
The Student Journalist (with Hillier Krieghbaum)	*New York University Press*	*1964*
Tipografia por Periodicos	*Inter American Press*	*1964*
The ICS series on Graphic Arts	*International Textbook*	*1964*
Student Journalist and the Yearbook	*Richards Rosen*	*1966*
Modern Newspaper Design	*Harper & Row*	*1969*
Editing the Yearbook	*Richards Rosen*	*1973*
Handbook of Student Journalist (with Hillier Krieghbaum)	*NYU Press*	*1977*
Encyclopedia Americana		*Contributing editor*
Random House Dictionary		*Section editor*
Graphic Arts Production	*Contributing editor-over 2,000 articles*	

Work in Progress: *Arnold's Ancient Axions on Typography; Ragan Report*

He says: "I fly some 50,000 miles yearly and conduct at least 50 seminars besides my regular academic schedule at VCU. My theme is the facilitating of communication through the printed word. I am a fervent advocate for TEACHING reading, not concocting excuses why Johnny can't read. I believe that the transmission channels for verbal communication must be clear and efficient or the semantic content will not reach the reader. I believe that the Latin alphabet is a major gift of God and that good book, magazine and newspaper design is as much an art as are painting, sculpture, etc."

Awards: George Polk Memorial Award, 1956; Arthur Hill High School (Saginaw, MI) Honor Alumnus, 1963; Honorary Doctor of Humane Letters, Hartwick College, 1963; Friars Award, U.S.

Army merit, etc. In journalism, the Edmund C. Arnold awards were named for him.

ARNOW, HARRIETTE SIMPSON 1908-

Born: July 7, 1908; Wayne County, Kentucky
Parents: Elias Thomas and Mollie Jane (Denney) Simpson
Married: Harold B. Arnow
Children: Marcella Jane; Thomas Louis
Education: Berea College, 1924-26; University of Louisville, B.S. 1931
Career: Teacher, Housewife, Author
Address: 3220 Nixon Road, Ann Arbor, MI 48109

Writings:

Mountain Path	Covici-Friede	1936
Hunter's Horn	Macmillan	1949
The Doll Maker	Macmillan	1954
Seedtime on the Cumberland	Macmillan	1960
The Flowering of the Cumberland	Macmillan	1963
The Weedkiller's Daughter	Knopf	1970
The Kentucky Trace	Knopf	1973
Old Burnside	University of Kentucky Press	1977

Mrs. Arnow writes novels longhand sitting in the breezeway where she cannot hear the telephone.

She says, (referring to a summer job in a small resort near Petosky), "I found myself in a delightful world of blue water, blue skies, white birches, stump fences, swamps, and with leisure to enjoy it all." *Michigan in Books,* Vol. 11, No. 2, p. 6

Honors: Friends of American Writers Award, 1955; Honorary Degree, Albion College, 1955; Berea College Centinnel Award, 1955; *Women's Home Companion* Silver Distaff Award for "Unique contribution by a woman to American life," 1955; Commendation from Tennessee Historical Commission, 1961; Award of Merit of American Association for State and Local History, 1961; *Tennessee Historical Quarterly* prize for the best article of the year, 1962; Cranbrook Writers Guild Award, 1975

AVERY, BURNIECE SALLY 1908-

Born: June 12, 1908; York, Alabama
Parents: John E. and Elizabeth (Bishop) Crews
Married: Robert H. Avery, retired

Children: Shirley Enid
Education: Wayne State University, B.A. 1961
Career: Teacher, Actress, Writer
Address: 141 Longfellow Ave., Detroit, MI 48202

Writings:

Smouldering	*(a 3-act play)*
As Others See Us	*(a play)*
What Makes Suzy Run	*(a play)*
Walk Quietly Through the Night and Cry Softly	Balamp Pub.

Work in Progress: Short story, and re-writing plays

She says: "I tend to write about people and how they react in various situations. I believe that human beings are more ALIKE than they are different."

Mrs. Avery's autobiography, *Walk Quietly Through the Night and Cry Softly,* has been likened to Alex Haley's *Roots.* Mrs. Avery's plays have been presented by a Detroit television station. For many years an elementary teacher, she is also a talented actress who played in *Member of the Wedding* at Meadow Brook Theater.

AYARS, JAMES S. 1898-
Born: November 17, 1898; Wilmette, Illinois
Parents: Henry N. and Jeannie (Lord) Ayars
Married: Rebecca Caudill, a writer and housewife
Children: James S. Ayars, Jr. (deceased) and Rebecca Jean Ayars Baker
Education: Northwestern University, B.S. 1922; Short periods University of Chicago, Northwestern, Western Michigan University, University of Illinois
Career: Teacher of English and History, 1922-25, Paw Paw, MI High School; critic teacher of same subjects, Western Michigan University, 1925-28; editorial and advertising staff, *Athletic Journal,* Chicago, 1928-37; technical editor and head, Section of Publications and Public Relations, Illinois State Natural History Survey, Urbana; many freelance articles on nature and agricultural subjects, 1937-65; chairman of Committee on Form and Style, Council of Biology Editors, that produced *CBE Style Manual,* 1972; conductor of boy's page in *The Target,* 1930-41; in *Boys Today,* 1941-47
Address: 510 West Iowa St., Urbana, IL 61801

Writings:

Basketball Comes to Lonesome Point	*Viking*	*1952*
Caboose on the Roof	*Abelard-Schuman*	*1956*

Pet Parade	Abelard-Schuman	1960
Happy Birthday, Mom!	Abelard-Schuman	1963
Butterflies, Skippers, and Moths (with M.W. Sanderson)	Whitman	1964
Another Kind of Puppy	Abelard-Schuman	1965
John James Audubon, Bird Artist	Garrard	1966
The Illinois River	Holt, Rinehart & Winston	1968
Contrary Jenkins (with Rebecca Caudill)	Holt, Rinehart & Winston	1969
Track Comes to Lonesome Point	Dutton	1973
We Hold These Truths: From Magna Carta to the Bill of Rights	Viking	1977

He says: "Although I was born in a suburb of Chicago, from the time I was about five years old until I went away to college I lived on a fruit farm four miles east of Paw Paw and thirteen miles west of Kalamazoo, Michigan. I grew up liking and respecting hard work. I sometimes worked for neighbor farmers for $1.00 per day (not hour), $1.25 in haying time. I never learned to work fast or type well. So I must write and rewrite, erase and erase, check and recheck—great wastes of time. Although I spent 28 years on the University of Illinois campus where I edited technical papers in Biology for the Illinois State Natural History Survey, I still have some sentimentality. At the settlement of my mother's estate, I asked for and was given that part of the old farm on which, long before, my father and I had planted white pine seedlings that in the intervening years had forested a once-barren hillside."

Awards: Clara Ingram Judson Award for *The Illinois River*, 1969

BACON, FRANCES ATCHINSON 1903-

Born: March 11, 1903; Holly, Michigan
Parents: John A. and Bertha (Fillingham) Atchinson
Married: Hilary E. Bacon, a consulting engineer
Children: Hillary Edwin Bacon, III and Albion Bennington
Education: Graduate Carnegie Library School, Carnegie Tech., 1924; Special courses University of Michigan, Evansville College, Johns Hopkins University, Indiana State Teachers College
Career: Children's Librarian, Flint, MI, 1921-23; Children's librarian and branch director, Evansville, IN, 1924-27; Assistant to director of Children's work, Enoch Pratt Free Library, Baltimore, MD 1928-35; Founder and director of School of Chimes, 1947-49;

board, 1947-72; Visiting Lecturer in Children's Literature, Goucher College, 1951-55
Address: 5506 Kemper Rd., Baltimore, MD 21210

Writings:

A Book of Giant Stories (with Kathleen Adams)	Dodd	1926
A Book of Princess Stories (with Kathleen Adams)	Dodd	1927
A Book of Enchantment (with Kathleen Adams)	Dodd	1928
There Were Giants (with Kathleen Adams)	Dodd	1929
Turkey Tale	Oxford	1935
Kitty Come Down	Oxford	1944
The Lords Baltimore (with Nan Hayden Agle)	Holt	1962
The Ingenious John Banyard (with Nan Hayden Agle)	Seabury	1966

Work in Progress: History of Kemper Green, small section of Baltimore in which we have lived since 1938.

She says: "I am interested in education of mentally retarded and have been active in this field since 1947. Writing is hard work, very demanding, and requires honesty and a feeling for the children you hope to reach, but very rewarding. Am happy that the little school I founded in 1947 has grown from five children to an enrollment of over three hundred."

BAKER, RAY STANNARD (1870-1946)
Pseudonym: David Grayson
Born: April 17, 1870; Lansing, Michigan
Parents: Joseph Stannard and Alice (Potter) Baker
Married: Jessie I. Beal
Children: James Stannard, Dr. Roger Denio, Rachel B. Natier, Alice B. Hyde
Education: Michigan State University, B.S. 1889; University of Michigan, Law and literature
Career: Reporter, *Chicago Daily Record;* 1892-1897 Manager McClure Syndicate; 1898-1905; Editor and part owner, *American Magazine;* 1906-1915; Special Commissioner, State Department; 1918; Author; Historian

Writings:

Boy's Book of Inventions	Doubleday & McClure	1899
Our New Prosperity	Doubleday & McClure	1900
Seen in Germany	McClure, Phillips	1901

Boy's Second Book of Inventions	Doubleday, Page	1903
Following the Color Line	Doubleday, Page	1908
The Spiritual Unrest	Frederick A. Stokes	1910
What Wilson Did in Paris	Doubleday, Page	1919
The New Industrial Unrest	Doubleday, Page	1920
Woodrow Wilson and World Settlement (3 Volumes)	Doubleday, Page	1922
Woodrow Wilson: Life and Letters (8 Volumes) written under pseudonym; David Grayson	Doubleday, Page	1927-39
Adventures in Contentment	Garden City Pub. Co.	1907
A Day of Pleasant Bread	Doubleday, Doran	1910
Adventures in Friendship	Doubleday, Page	1910
The Friendly Road	Doubleday, Page	1913
Hempfield	Doubleday, Page	1915
Great Possessions	Doubleday, Page	1917
Adventures of David Grayson	Doubleday, Page	1925
Adventures in Understanding	Doubleday, Page	1925
Adventures in Solitude	Doubleday, Doran	1931
The Countryman's Year	Doubleday, Doran	1936
Native American	C. Scribner's & Sons	1941
Under My Elm	Doubleday, Doran	1942
American Chronicle	C. Scribner's & Sons	1945

Of Interest: Baker became acquainted with Woodrown Wilson while editor and part owner of *American Magazine*. This friendship resulted in his being designated to edit the President's papers. The last letter Woodrow Wilson wrote was addressed to him, January 27, 1924; he wrote to his friend asking him to write an official biography: "I would rather have your interpretation than that of anyone else I know."

"Baker, round-featured, with a clipped moustache and rimless glasses, looked more like a businessman than the outdoors person that he was."

Current Biography, 1940

He believed, "When men come really to understand one another—if that time ever comes—war will end, poverty will end, tyranny will end, and this under almost any sort of government, almost any economic system."

The Detroit News, December 22, 1941

Honors: Pulitzer Prize for Biography, 1940 for *Woodrow Wilson: Life and Letters.*

BAKKER, NINA DIKEMAN (deceased)
Born: Hart, Michigan
Married: William
Career: Housewife with hobbies of poetry and painting

Writings:

These Grandchildren: (poems)	*New Athenaeum Press*	*1956*
With Jesus in Nazareth		
God's Organ		
Mrs. Santa Claus		

Her poetry has appeared in 18 magazines and 7 newspapers.

BALD, F. CLEVER (1897-1970)
Born: August 12, 1897; Baltimore, Maryland
Parents: Frederick William and Elizabeth (Krise) Bald
Married: Laura M. McGarth; (2nd wife) Jane R. Howard
Children: Robert E.
Education: Franklin and Marshall College, 1914-1917; University of Aix-Marseille, 1919; University of Michigan, A.B. 1920; Wayne State University, M.A. 1937; University of Michigan, Ph. D. 1943
Career: History teacher, Hudson School (Detroit), 1922-1929; Headmaster, Hudson School, 1929-1932; Professor of History and Government, Detroit Institute of Technology, 1932-1943; Instructor, University of Michigan, 1943 to 1947; Assistant Director, Michigan Historical Collections, University of Michigan, 1943-1960; Professor of History and Director of Michigan Historical Collections, 1960-1967

Writings:

Detroit's First American Decade, 1796-1805	*University of Michigan Press*	*1948*
Michigan in Four Centuries	*Harper*	*1954*
Revised and enlarged		*1961*

BALLARD, JOAN KADEY 1928-
Born: May 16, 1928; Port Huron, Michigan
Parents: P.H. and Amelia (Marks) Kadey
Married: Deane Bruce Ballard, a Minister
Children: Cathy, David, Julia, Susan, Kimberly
Education: Hougton College, Houghton, NY 1946-49; Wheaton College, Wheaton, IL, B.M.E. 1950
Address: 7551 Fairway Blvd., Miramar, FL 33023

Writings:

A Child Prays	*Zondervan*	*1962*

| A Saw A Mother Chicken | Moody | 1963 |
| A Child Asks | Zondervan | 1964 |

She says: "My philosophy in children's literature is contained in Proverbs 22:6 'Train up a child in the way he should go, and when he is old he will not depart from it.' It's a beautiful thing to see a child secure in the knowledge that he is loved by God unconditionally."

BANNER, MELVIN EDWARD 1914-

Born: July 16, 1914; McDonald, Pennsylvania
Parents: Clyde and Marie (Brown) Banner
Married: Patricia, a teacher
Children: Melvina Ford
Education: Flint Junior College, A.A. 1936; University of Michigan, 1950-54, B.A., M.A.; Michigan State University, graduate studies
Career: Teaching; Journalism; Electronics
Address: 1913 Barks St., Flint, MI 48503

Writings:

Urban Renewal and You	City of Flint	1960
Riddles of Felicity	Telescope	1962
Training Brings Opportunities	G.M. Publications	1963
Short Negro History of Flint	M. Banner	1964
Black Pioneer in Michigan		
—Flint and Genesee County-		
Vol. I	Pendell	1973

Work in Progress: *Black Pioneer In Michigan—Vol. II; Reflections in Black*—30 poems; *The Iron Pourer and Other Poems*—36 poems.

BANNON, LAURA (1894-1963)

Born: July 25, 1894; Acme, Michigan
Parents: James William and Carrie (Freeman) Bannon
Education: Western Michigan State College, 2 year course; School of the Art Institute of Chicago, 4 year course and post-graduate work
Career: Teacher, high school in Battle Creek, Michigan; Supervisor, public school art, Mt. Clemens, Port Huron, Michigan, and Racine, Wisconsin; Instructor and Director, Art Institute of Chicago Junior School; Authur and Illustrator

Writings:

Manuela's Birthday	A. Whitman	1939

Gregorio and the White Llama	A. Whitman	1944
Red Mittens	Houghton	1946
Patty Paints a Picture	A. Whitman	1946
Baby Roo	Houghton	1947
Watch Dog	A. Whitman	1948
Billy and the Bear	Houghton	1949
Big Brother	A. Whitman	1950
Horse on a Houseboat	A. Whitman	1951
The Best House in the World	Houghton	1952
Mind your Child's Art (adult non-fic.)	Farrar	1952
When the Moon was New	A. Whitman	1953
The Wonderful Fashion Doll	Houghton	1953
Hat for a Hero	A. Whitman	1954
Burro Boy and His Big Trouble	Abington	1955
The Little Doll Sister	A. Whitman	1955
The Scary Thing	Houghton	1956
Nemo Meets the Emperor	A. Whitman	1957
The Tide Won't Wait	A. Whitman	1957
Jo-Jo, the Talking Crow	Houghton	1958
Whistle for a Pilot	A. Whitman	1959
Katy Comes Next	A. Whitman	1959
The Other Side of the World	Houghton	1960
Hop-High, the Goat	Bobbs-Merrill	1960
The Famous Baby-Sitter	A. Whitman	1960
The Gift of Hawaii	A. Whitman	1961
Hawaiian Coffee Picker	A. Whitman	1962
Who Walks the Attic	A. Whitman	1962
Toby's Friends	A. Whitman	1963
The Contented Horse Trader	A. Whitman	1963
Little People of the Night	Houghton	1963
Twirlup on the Moon	A. Whitman	1964
Make Room for Rags	Houghton	1964

Also illustrated children's books by other authors.

She said: "My greatest single help in writing and illustrating books for children is the circumstance of having come from a large family. All eight of us lived out the noisy ups and downs of childhood on a hill overlooking Grand Traverse Bay, Michigan."

More Junior Authors, Kunitz

Honors: Chicago Society of Typographic Arts award, 1944, for *Gregorio and the White Llama; New York Herald Tribune;* Spring Book Festival honor award, 1953, for *When Moon is New;* Friends of American Writers award, 1960, for *Hop-High, the Goat;* Children's Reading Round Table of Chicago Annual Award, 1962.

BARANET, NANCY NEIMAN 1933-

Born: January 1, 1933; Detroit, Michigan
Parents: Allen and Mayme (Buch) Neiman
Married: Nicholas Baranet, a hospital administrator
Children: Nicholas, Michael, Matthew, Holly
Education: Cooley High School, 1950; Detroit Business Institute, 2 years
Career: Secretary; Writer
Address: 5762 1st St., Plantation, FL 33317

Writings:

The Turned Down Bar	Dorrance	1964
Bicycling	A.S. Barnes	1973

She says: "My best contributions are always about people, although I am an expert in the bicycling field, in both racing and touring."

BARENDRECHT, COR W. 1934-

Pseudonym: Wm. Brecht
Born: October 9, 1934; The Hague, The Netherlands
Parents: C.W. Barendrecht, Sr., and A.v.d. Heijden
Married: Stephanie M. Rooks, a registered nurse
Children: Sharlene
Education: Grand Rapids Junior College, A.A. 1969; Grand Valley State College, B.A. 1971; Graphic Arts, Kent Skills Center, 1977
Career: Free-lance writer
Address: 1530 Valley, N.W., Grand Rapids, MI 49504

Writings:

Somewhere a Child is Crying	Metamorphosis Pr.	1972
In a Strange Land	Being Publication	1974
Crosswise	Houghton College Pr.	1976

also poetry in anthologies, fiction in literature texts, and translation

Work in Progress: A new collection of poetry; a collection of fiction for boys ages 10-14; an adult novel

He says: "My attempt at poetry is to help audiences and/or readers rediscover simplicity of language as a means of literary expression. Deep poetic images can be understood on different levels of meaning, or dimensions of understanding; therefore my poetic attempts aim at finding the common denominator that is able to convey such multiple meanings.

"The strength of my fiction writing, I've been told, is in involving the reader in a particular mood and description, so that the setting of the story greatly contributes toward the building of plot and the resolving of conflict in the denouement.

"I work at writing every day; beginning at 10 a.m. and working until about 3 p.m., taking a break every few hours, and working into the night, usually 10 p.m., but often working until the early morning hours. In the process of writing, re-reading, and editing what has been written, the basic story emerges."

Awards: Dyer-Ives Poetry Award, 1975

BARLOW, RUTH C.

Born: Chicago, Illinois. Summers in New Buffalo, Michigan
Education: Knox College; Western Reserve
Career: Library Assistant, Chicago Public Library; Head Librarian, Children's Department, Flint Public Library; Head Librarian, Children's Library, Fairfield, Connecticut; 1952

Writings:

Fun at Happy Acres	*Crowell*	*1935*
Lisbeth Holly	*Dodd, Mead*	*1947*

She says, "Our summer home, where I spent my first seventeen summers, was in Michigan where we had 45 acres of beautiful sand dunes, woods, blueberries, wild grapes, tall ferns, wild flowers in profusion and friendly wood-folk."

BARNES, HALLY "AL" 1904-

Born: December 8, 1904; Madison, South Dakota
Parents: Rubin Perry and Sadie Dessie (Smith) Barnes
Married: Evelyn
Children: Dennis W.L., JoAnn, Vickie
Education: Athens, Michigan high school, 1 year; Pathfinder School, high school diploma, Traverse City, 1977. "Actually I'm very proud of the fact that I educated myself without the aid of schools and colleges. I taught myself Latin, algebra, geometry, Spanish and a smattering of French.
Career: Writer, photographer, Traverse City *Record Eagle,* 30 years; Retired 11 plus years; Lecturer through the state; Writer; "Haven't firmly decided on a career. Thinking of watchmaking."

Writings:

One Hundred Years from the Old Mission	*Henderson*	*1939*
Vinegar Pie	*Wayne State U. & Harlo Press*	*1959*
Supper in the Evening	*Dorrance & Co.*	*1968*
Let's Fly Backward	*Harlo Press*	*1977*

Work in Progress: "If we have all of our smarts, we don't discuss things we hope to do. We do those things and then surprise people . . . sometimes.''

He says: "I am a nut about writing the truth and researching my projects. My errors in writing have been very few and I apologize for them. I am sick in the gut with half-truth-writing and sensationalism. One of my lectures is 'You can't believe everything you read.' The media is a rabble-rousing mess despite the fact that I gave it so much of my life. My philosophy? It can be found, beginning with the book of Genesis and on through the book of Jude and as much of Revelations as I understand.

"My hobbies are ceramics, stone cutting, polishing, and gem making. In addition, I garden, keep bees, help Mama with the cooking and housework, and do a little fishing, hunting, and wandering. I have been on the move since I retired.

"I have no police record. I have few enemies. I hate no one, but there are some folks I can get along without.''

BATTAGLIA, ELIZABETH LOUISE 1925-
Pseudonym: Bette Battaglia
Born: February 27, 1925; Stantoy, Ohio
Parents: Walter and Marie (Pohlabeln) Wall
Married: Vito, a plant manager
Children: Mark, Bruce, and Maria
Education: Michigan State University, 1975; Grand Rapids Junior College, 1975- (seeking A.A. degree)
Career: Wife, mother, homemaker, poet, writer
Address: 3106 Cascade Rd., S.E., Grand Rapids, MI 49506

Writings:

The Blood of Roses	Dorrance	1968
Palace of Ice	Dorrance	1977

Work in Progress: Novel: Far From the Sun

She says: "I have published many poems in 'little magazines,' newspapers, anthologies . . .also short stories. Am included in Who's Who in American Women, International Who's Who in Poetry, The World Who's Who in Women. I'm a member of the Poetry Society of Michigan.''

BEACY, REX ELLINGWOOD (1877-1949)
Born: September 1, 1877; Atwood, Michigan
Parents: Henry Walter and Eva Eunice (Canfield) Beach
Married: Edith Crater

Education: Rollins College, 1891-1896; Chicago College of Law, 1896-1897; Kent College of Law, 1899-1900

Career: Miner, Nome, Alaska "Gold Rush"; Writer

Writings:

Pardners	Burt	1905
The Spoilers	Burt	1906
The Barrier	Burt/Harper	1908, 1948
The Silver Horde	Burt/Harper	1909
Going Some	Burt/Harper	1910
The Ne'er-Do-Well	Burt/Harper	1911
The Net	Burt/Harper	1912
The Iron Trail	CollierBurt	1913
The Auction Block	Burt	1914, 1927
Heart of the Sunset	Burt/Harper	1915
Rainbow's End	Burt/Harper	1916
The Crimson Gardenia	Burt	1916
Laughing Bill Hyde	Burt	1917
The Winds of Chance	Burt/Harper	1918
Too Fat to Fight	Harper	1919
Oh, Shoot	Garden City Pub.	1921
Flowing Gold	Burt/Harper	1922
Big Brother	Harper	1923
Four in One Adventures	Garden City Pub.	1923
North of Fifty-three	Garden City Pub.	1924
The Goose Woman	Burt/Harper	1925
The Miracle of Coral Gables	Baird-Ward	1926
Padlocked	Harper	1926
The Mating Call	Harper	1927
Don Careless	Harper	1928
Son of the Gods	Harper	1929
Money Mad	Cosmopolitan	1931
Men of the Outer Islands	Farrar	1932
Beyond Control	Farrar	1932
Alaskan Adventures: The Spoilers	Burt/McClelland	1933
The Hands of Dr. Locke	Farrar	1934
Masked Women	Farrar	1934
Wild Pastures	Farrar	1935
Jungle Gold	Farrar	1935
Valley of Thunder	Farrar	1939
Tower of Flame	Bantam	1940
Personal Exposures	Harper	1941
The World in His Arms	Putnam	1946
Woman in Ambush	Putnam	1951

Of Interest: Dubbed the "Victor Hugo of the North"

BEARE, MURIEL ANITA NIKKI (BRINK) 1928-
Born: March 7, 1928; Detroit, Michigan
Parents: Elbert Stanley and Dorothy Margaret (Welch) Brink
Married: Richard Austin Beare, a financial consultant
Children: Sandra Lee Beare
Education: Northwestern Michigan Community College, 1952; University of Miami; Miami-Date Community College, 1970-74; Skidmore College
Career: Free-lance writer; Newspaper reporter and columnist; Project HOPE, Area Director, 1967-69; Assistant Vice-President, I/D Associates, Inc., 1969-71; President, Nikki Beare & Associates, 1971-77
Address: 5900 S.W. 73 Street, Rm. 102, S. Miami, FL 33143

Writings:

Pirates, Pineapples & People;		
Tales & Legends of the		
Florida Keys	Atlantic	*1961*
From Turtle Soup to Coconuts	Atlantic	*1964*
Florida Historical Map	Hurricane House	*1964*
Bottle Bonanza, a Handbook for		
Bottle Collectors	Hurricane House	*1965*

Articles in *Christian Science Monitor, The Scholastic Weekly,* and many national magazines. Wrote for *Miami News, Key West Citizen, Homestead News Leader,* and other Florida newspapers

Work in Progress: *People Power and Practical Politics; A Handbook on Political Campaigning.*

She says: "Over the years, I have learned to utilize my talents effectively and gain personal satisfaction as well as financial remuneration. In addition to my publishing books, I have been a magazine writer, have my own radio show, and produce TV programs and films. Since 1967, I have been active in the women's movement and am a national leader in the National Women's Political Caucus and National Organization for Women."

BECHKO, PEGGY ANNE 1950-
Born: August 26, 1950; South Haven, Michigan
Parents: Edwin L. and Elizabeth (Schleimer) Bechko
Education: Manatee Junior College, 1968-69
Career: Writer
Address: 8324 Midnight Pass Rd., Sarasota, FL

Writings:

Night of the Flaming Guns	Doubleday	*1974*
Gunman's Justice	Doubleday	*1974*
Blown to Hell	Doubleday	*1976*
Dead Man's Feud	Pinnacle Books	*1976*

The Winged Warrior	Doubleday	1977
Blown to Hell (French	Librarie des Champs	
translation)	Elysees	1977

Work in Progress: Comedy western and adventure

She says: "My life's philosophy is 'Live and let live.' "

BECK, EARL CLIFTON 1891-1977

Pseudonym: Doc Beck
Born: April 7, 1891; Hickman, Nebraska
Parents: Cornelius Porter and Louisa (Theade) Beck
Married: Marjorie Mae Miller, an educator
Children: Margymae B. Fairman and Jane Louise Smith
Education: Peru Teachers College, Peru, Nebraska; University of Nebraska, B.A., M.A.; Harvard University, M.A.; George Peabody College, Ph. D.
Career: Public school teacher and adminstrator in Nebraska; College training school in Dillon, Montana; College teacher in Florida, Michigan (head of English Dept. at Central Michigan University), and Alabama

Writings:

Songs of the Michigan	University of Michigan	
Lumberjacks	Press	1941
Lore of the Lumber Camps	University of Michigan	
	Press	1948
They Knew Paul Bunyan	University of Michigan	
	Press	1956
Sounds of the Lake and the		
Forest	Hillsdale	1959

Comments:"My father-in-law, Earl C. Beck, died on March 21, 1977, in Farmington Hills, Michigan. My brief comments do not do justice to the man, his literary efforts, or his contribution to the education of thousands of young people of every race and creed over a period of nearly sixty years. He taught the meek and the mighty, and he entertained many audiences with his lumberjack tales, songs, and performers. He was many things—farmer, cowpuncher, miner, sportsman, athlete, husband, father—and a friend to all who extended a hand of welcome."

Arlies G. Fairman

BEHEE, JOHN 1933-

Born: September 28, 1933; Leavenworth, Kansas
Parents: Burton and Dorothy (Wanstreet) Behee
Married: Judith Hartman, an elementary school teacher

Children: Mark and Anne
Education: Benedictine College, B.S. 1958; Kansas State Teachers College, M.A. 1964; University of Michigan, Ph. D. 1970
Career: Teaching and coaching in Colorado, Kansas, Michigan, and Indiana, 1958-68; Chairman, Physical Education Dept., Tri-State University, Angola, IN, 1968-present
Address: 1004 Springhill Dr., Angola, IN 46703

Writings:

Fielding Yost's Legacy	*Ulrich's Books*	*1971*
Hail to the Victors	*Ulrich's Books*	*1974*
Wave the Flag for Hudson High	*Ulrich's Books*	*1977*

He says: "If I were to spend an hour on his couch, I'm sure my analyst would conclude that the thread that binds my fabric is sport, especially football. It absorbed my energies during those adventuresome teen years, keeping me out of a lot of additional mischief I would certainly have created. It challenged me to strive for perfection. (At 5'4", 134 lbs. cunning on the gridiron was absolutely essential to my self-preservation.) It drew me to such exotic American cities as Antonito, Colorado; Tonganoxie, Kansas; Emporia, Kansas; and Angola Indiana, where I carried the proud and powerful title of 'Coach'. And it has me on 'offense' now, learning to write about the great coaches of all time such as Michigan's Fielding Yost, the plight of black athletes such as those who carried Michigan's name to national and international acclaim, and the little town of Hudson, Michigan, which took a magic carpet ride, returning to earth only after having established a national record by winning 72 straight football games.

"My analyst would probably advise me to 'hang in there, young man. You may never be a writing celebrity, but the fabric is in pretty good shape.'"

BELL, STEVE see: SCHMOCK, HELEN H.

BENAGH, JIM 1937-
Born: October 10, 1937; Flint, Michigan
Parents: William Edward and Christina (Hoiland) Benagh
Education: University of Michigan, 1955-60
Career: Sports editor and head photographer, *Cheboygan Daily Tribune;* Sports staff, *Ann Arbor News;* Sports editor of post newspaper, Fort Knox, KY; Associate editor, *Sport* magazine, 1962-64; Assistant Sports editor, *Newsweek* magazine, 1964-68; Mexican Olympian Committee, 1968; Part-time sports editor, Random House, 1969; Public relations work and writer for Fight of Champions, Inc., 1971; Free-lance writer, 1968-; Sports

feature writer, *Detroit Free Press*, 1976-
Address: 444 E. 82nd, Apt. 7F, New York, NY 10028

Writings:

The Official Encyclopedia of Sports	Watts	*1964*
Tom Harmon's Book of Sports Information	Pratt	*1965*
Pictorial Sports Annual	Hammond	*1967*
Incredible Athletic Feats	Hart	*1969*
Krazy About the Knicks	Hawthorn	*1971*
Watch It! How to Watch Sports on TV	Benjamin	*1971*
Official Ali-Frazier Fight Program	Fight of the Century, Inc.	*1971*
The Great Olympians	StadiaSports	*1972*
ABC's Wide World of Sports Encyclopedia	StadiaSports	*1973*
Walt Frazier; Superguard of Pro Basketball	Scholastic	*1973*
Incredible Football Feats	Tempo Books	*1974*
Incredible Basketball Feats	Tempo Books	*1974*
Incredible Baseball Feats	Tempo Books	*1975*
Incredible Olympic Feats	McGraw-Hill	*1976*
Terry Bradshaw: Super-Arm of Pro Football	Putnam's	*1976*
Teams Get There	Dodd, Mead	*1976*
Go Bird Go!	Dell	*1976*

Approximately 300 magazine articles in such magazines as *Newsweek, Sport, True, Argosy, Money, Boys' Life, Tennis,* etc. Special newspaper articles for the *New York Times, Washington Star,* Gannett News Service, etc. Written entries for *Encyclopedia Americana* and serveral other reference books.

He says: "I was sports editor and head photographer for the *Cheboygan Daily Tribune* while still in high school. I wrote my first story at sixteen. . .On a special three-month assignment for the first Ali-Frazier bout, I did public relations and wrote a special souvenir program for the promoters. I've been to three Olympics, and have covered sports in several countries, including the Soviet Union, England, Germany and Italy."

BENJAMIN, STANLEY L. 1895-
Born: September 19, 1895; Constantine, Michigan
Parents: William H. and Cora Belle (Langton) Benjamin
Married: Lillian M. (Couch) Benjamin, a housewife
Children: Robert S., Edward L., William H., Dorothy Homes,

Norma Cade, Helen Knudtzon
Education: Albion College, A.B. 1924; University of Michigan, M.A.; Eden Seminary, 1958
Career: U.S. Army, 2nd Lieutenant, 1917-18; Superintendent of Schools, Carsonville, South Rockwood, Croswell, Galesburg-Augusta, Indiana River; Minister, First Congregational Church, Cheboygan, MI
Address: 4682 S. Straits Hwy., Indian River, MI 49749

Writings:
Through the Years (poetry)   Harlo   1971

Work in Progress: Family stories (for his grandchildren)

He says: "My poems were written 'just for fun' over a period of more than fifty years.

"I was ordained into the Ministry past the age when most Ministers have retired. After serving thirty-eight years as a school superintendent, I served the Cheboygan Church for nine years."

BERNHARDT, DEBRA E. 1953-
Born: May 9, 1953; Nurnberg Germany
Parents: Harold Olaf and Marcia Ann (Webster) Bernhardt
Education: University of Michigan, B.A. 1975; Wayne State University, M.A. 1977
Career: Co-Director of Research Project on Labor History, Ohio State Historical Society Columbus, Ohio
Address: Rt. 2, Bernhardt, Rd., Iron River, MI 49935

Writings:
Black Rock and Roses: A   *Iron County Historical*
Play of Iron County   *Society*   1976

Work in Progress: *We Knew Different: The Michigan Timber Workers' Strike of 1937*

She says: "*Black Rock and Roses* grew out of over a hundred oral history interviews with miners, muckers, union men, management, boarding house matrons—the inhabitants of an Upper Peninsula iron mining town as the mining reality was rapidly fading away. I sought out the old timers, many of them immigrants, to understand myself through the community I grew up in, believing as William Faulkner said that 'No man is himself; he is the sum of his past.' What I heard revealed so much of importance in language and imagery that the poet in me envied, that I knew it must be shared. I came to see myself as an instrument through which these people, many of whom had never been heard, could speak. The result was *Black Rock and Roses,* which was produced as a bicentennial event in Iron County."

Awards: U. of M. Hopwood Award for "Spring Valley Stories" 1974; Michigan Historical Society Award of Merit for "innovative work as a researcher and writer of the history of Iron County," 1976

BERNHARDT, MARCIA A. 1926-
Pseudonym: M.A. Bernhardt
Born: July 12, 1926; Ingham, Michigan
Parents: Glenn S. and E. Hilda (Eifert) Webster
Married: Harold O. Bernhardt, an educator-historian
Children: Debra E. and Andra E.
Education: Michigan State University, B.A. 1947; University of Wisconsin, 1951; Handelskoskolen, Copenhagen, Denmark, 1953; Northern Michigan University, M.A. 1967
Career: Psychiatric Social Worker, 1947-50; Teacher in Army Education Centers in Germany, 1952-54; English Teacher, 1960-present
Address: Rt. 2, Bernhardt Rd., Iron River, MI 49935

Writings:

They Came . . . to Iron County, Michigan	Dickinson-Iron Intermediate School District	1975
The Jewel of Iron County	Iron County Historical & Museum Society	1976

Work in Progress: Material collected for another folklore book. Material partially organized for book on Iron River—scheduled for Centennial release. Work begun on Landmark II-The Carrie Jacobs Bond Home

She says:"My writing, secondary and often editorial, is supplemented by a strong sense for the need of historical preservation. After several years of continuous writing of press releases, I began to write feature articles for the *Green Bay Press-Gazette* and occasionally for *The Milwaukee Sentinel.* I also worked with students on publications for the Junior Historical Society, co-advising *The Rum Rebellion* supervised the writing and production of three vaudeville type shows in the historical vein and I have edited *Past-Present Prints,* newsletter of the Historical Society for ten years.

"The foregoing experiences, chairmanship of the Iron County Preservation of Historical Sites committee and encouragement from several research grants from the Michigan Council for the Arts have spurred me on to additional writing. This activity is supportive of my work as exhibits coordinator of the Iron County Museum where I must do research before designing new exhibits. A hobby of photography and the recording both in black and white and color of historical sites led to the publication of the photographic essay on the Iron County Courthouse. I also used the slides with students in a creative writing class and we produced four historical sites series for the Bicentennial. I consider myself a journeyman with a driving force to get things down in print before we lose them!"

BERTHELOT, JOSEPH A. 1927-
Born: January 3, 1927; Detroit Michigan
Parents: Joseph Alfred and Eva M. (Atchinson) Berthelot
Education: University of Western Ontario CA, B.A. 1949; Univeristy of Texas, El Paso, M.A. 1955; University of Denver, Ph. D. 1962
Career: Department of English, U.S. Air Force Academy . . . From instructor to full professor, 1958-72
Address: 2505 Monterey Peninsula Dr., Corona, CA 91720

Writings:

Michael Drayton	Twayne	1968
Annual Bibliography of English		
Language & Literature.		
(Contributing editor)	MHRA	1964-71

He says: "I am either the only Michigander, or one of the very few, who has completed a full USAF military career with a full college academic career, while on active duty. Aside from my academic career, I flew well over 3,000 hours in military aircraft, 122 combat missions, and hold the distinguished Flying Cross, Bronze Medal, Meritorious Service Medal, five Air Medals, Air Force Commendation Medal, etc. I am sure that I am the only Michigander who flew and won his combat medals while a full professor on a dean-imposed sabbatical."

BLACK, ALBERT GEORGE 1928-
Born: August 22, 1928; Northville, Michigan
Parents: William and Ruth Black
Married: Mary, an educator
Children: Anne, Alan, Erich
Education: University of Michigan, A.B., A.M.
Career: Teacher, Birmingham, MI Public Schools, 1952-58; Teaching Fellow, English, The University of Michigan 1958-60; Reporter, *Ypsilanti Press,* 1960-61; Assistant Editor, Institute of Science and Technology, The University of Michigan, 1961-62; Instructor, California State University, Long Beach, 1962-64; Assistant Prof. 1964-74; Assoc. Prof. 1974-
Address: P.O. Box 15224, Long Beach, California, 90815

Writings:

Oakland County History		
Readings	Edwards	1959

Michigan Novels	Michigan Council of Teachers	1963
California Campus Reaction to Change: The Student View	Calif. State University	1969
The Vigilant Balance: From Parody to High Seriousness— Studies in English Literature (Co-authored with Mary E. Black)	Calif. State University	1971
Reading in the University	Calif. State University	1973

Founder and Editor of *The Asterisk: A Journal of English Traditions,* 1974

Work in Progress: A novel, a study of Samuel Johnson and work on American semiotics

BLACK, MONTGOMERY see: HOLDEN, (WILLIS) SPRAGUE

BLAIR, OLIVE TINKER 1892-
Born: September 2, 1892; Mancelona, Michigan
Parents: Charles and Emma (Richards) Tinker
Married: Glen B. Blair, deceased
Children: Norma Jean, 4 grandchildren; 4 great-grandchildren
Education: Western Michigan University, 1926
Career: Teacher
Address: Mancelona, Michigan 49659

Writings:

What Next, Gerty!	Commett Press Books	1956
"Johnny's Christmas Dream" (play)	Beckley, Cardy	1943
"By Thy Faith" (play)	Eldridge	1942

BLOUGH, GLENN O. 1904-
Born: September 5, 1904; Montcalm County, Michigan
Parents: Levi and Catherine (Thomas) Blough
Education: Central Michigan University, Teaching Certificate, 1926; University of Michigan: A.B., A.M. 1932; Graduate study: University of Chicago; Columbia University
Career: Eastern Michigan University, 1932-36; Colorado State University, 1937-38; University of Chicago, 1939-42; U.S. Office of Education, 1946-54; University of Maryland, 1956-72. Now Professor Emeritus, University of Maryland
Address: 2820 Ellicott St., N.W., Washington, D.C. 20008

Writings:

Doing Work	Harper	1943
Water Appears and Disappears	Harper	1943
An Aquarium	Harper	1943
The Insect Parade	Harper	1943
The Pet Show	Harper	1945
Useful Plants and Animals	Harper	1945
Animals and Their Young	Harper	1945
Animals That Live Together	Harper	1945
The Monkey with a Notion	Holt	1946
Beno, the Riverburg Mayor	Holt	1948
Methods and Activities in Elementary School Science	Holt	1951
How the Sun Helps Us	Harper	1952
The Tree on the Road to Turntown	McGraw Hill	1953
Not Only for Ducks	McGraw Hill	1954
Wait for the Sunshine	McGraw Hill	1954
Making and Using Elementary Science Material	Holt	1954
Lookout for the Forest	McGraw Hill	1955
When You Go to the Zoo	McGraw Hill	1955
After the Sun Goes Down	McGraw Hill	1956
Animals Round the Year	Harper	1956
Who Lives in This House?	McGraw Hill	1957
Young People's Book of Science	McGraw Hill	1958
Soon After September	McGraw Hill	1958
Discovering Dinosaurs	McGraw Hill	1959
Who Lives in the Meadow	McGraw Hill	1959
Birds in the Big Woods	Harper	1960
Christmas Trees and How They Grow	McGraw Hill	1960
Who Lives at the Seashore?	McGraw Hill	1961
Bird Watchers and Bird Feeders	McGraw Hill	1962
Discovering Plants	McGraw Hill	1963
Discovering Insects	McGraw Hill	1966
Elementary School Science and How to Teach It (with Julius Schwartz)	Winston	1967

Contributor to many magazines, author of series of textbooks.

Work in Progress: Revisions of textbooks

He says: "My initial feeling about natural science developed when I was a small boy living in Montcalm, Michigan. *The Tree on the Road to Turntown* is a Michigan oak. I am an environmentalist and ecologist, and these had their beginnings when I attended college and the University in Michigan. My personal and professional roots are in Michigan.''

Awards: Phil Delta Kappa; Phi Sigma; Diamond Award, University of Maryland; President, National Science Teachers Association, 1957-58; President, National Council for Elementary Science, 1952-53; Honorary doctorate for contribution to education, Central Michigan University; listed in *Who's Who in America.*

BOLT, ROBERT 1930-
Born: August 16, 1930; Grand Rapids, Michigan
Parents: Martin and Tena (Bouma) Bolt
Married: Carolyn A. Bolt
Children: James A., Robert D., Lynn M., Timoth D., and Krisin L.
Education: Calvin College, A.B. 1952; University of Michigan, A.M. 1953; Michigan State University, Ph. D. 1962 .
Career: U.S. Army, Historical Division, 1953-55; Teacher of History: Grand Rapids Christian High, 1955-60; Illinois State University, 1962-65; Calvin College, 1965-
Address: 1819 Ridgemoor Dr., S.E., Grand Rapids, MI 49506

Writings:

Donald Dickinson	Eerdmans	1970

Work in Progress: A work on the religions of the American Presidents

He says: ''I believe that history must be written in an interesting fashion if one expects it to be read by many people. I have published several articles in the *Grand Rapids Press' Wonderland* magazine with that in mind.''

BORDIN, RUTH BIRGITTA 1917-
Born: November 11, 1917; Litchfield, Minnesota
Parents: Emil and Martha (Linner) Anderson
Married: Edward Bordin, a professor of psychology
Children: Martha Hillyard and Charlotte Lin
Education: University of Minnesota, B.S. 1938, M.A. 1941
Career: Archivist, research associate, teacher, writer
Address: 1000 Aberdeen, Ann Arbor, MI 48103

Writings:

Hear Ye My Chiefs		
(Editor & Co-author)	Caxton	1952
The Manuscript Library		
(with R.M. Warner)	Scarecrow	1965
Pictorial History of the	University of Michigan	
University of Michigan	Press	1967

Work in Progress: *A Woman at Work* (Emma Hall and the Reformatory Principle); A History of the W.C.T.U. in relationship to the Woman's Movement

She says: "I shall continue to write, and I hope to write things people will read."

BORLAND, KATHRYN 1916-
Pseundonyms: Jane Land, Alice Abbott
Born: August 14, 1916; Pullman, Michigan
Parents: Paul and Vinnie (Bensinger) Kilby
Married: James Borland, a chemist
Children: James Barton, Susan Lee
Education: Butler University, B.S. 1937
Career: Editor, *North Side Topics,* Indianapolis; Free Lance Writer
Address: R.R. 3, Frankfort, IN 46401

Writings:

Southern Yankees	*Bobbs-Merrill*	*1960*
Allan Pinkerton	*Bobbs-Merrill*	*1962*
Miles and the Big Black Hat	*E.C. Seale*	*1963*
Everybody Laughed	*E.C. Seale*	*1964*
Eugene Field	*Bobbs-Merrill*	*1964*
Phillis Wheatley	*Bobbs-Merrill*	*1968*
Harry Houdini	*Bobbs-Merrill*	*1968*
Clocks from Shadow to Atom	*Follett*	*1969*
The Third Tower	*Ace*	*1974*
Stranger in the Mirror	*Ballantine*	*1974*
Good-Bye to Stony Crick	*McGraw-Hill*	*1975*
Good-Bye, Julie Scott	*Ace*	*1975*
To Walk the Night	*Ballantine*	*1976*

Work in Progress: Historical romance for Doubleday

She says: "Everything I have written has been done with Helen Ross Speicher of Indianapolis as co-author. Friends since childhood, we live 40 miles apart and commute to write together two days a week."

BORTH, CHRISTY (1896-1976)
Christened: Christian Carl Borth
Born: February 17, 1896; St. Louis, Missouri. Came to Detroit at age 15. Died at age 80 in Fenton, Michigan, of influenza complications.
Married: Evangeline Loomis
Education: Formal education ended at sixth grade

Career: Reporter, *The Detroit Free Press*, 1932-37; Established a Detroit Bureau for *Time* magazine, 1937; Free-lance writer, 1938-41; Staff member of the Automobile Council for War Production, 1942-48; Assistant to Managing Director, the Automobile Manufacturers Association, 1948-61 (retired)

Writings:

Pioneers of Plenty	*Bobbs-Merrill*	*1939*
True Steel	*Bobbs-Merrill*	*1941*
Reprinted	*Otterbein Press*	*1966*
Masters of Mass Production	*Bobbs-Merrill*	*1945*
Freedom Arsenal (official history of industry throughout war years)	*Automotive Council for War Production*	*1948*
Mankind on the Move; the Story of Highways	*Washington Automotive Safety Foundation*	*1969*

Mr. Borth was "the unofficial historian of the automobile industry." He was a "walking encyclopedia of automobile legends and anecdotes."

The Detroit Free Press, March 25, 1976

BOTTOM, RAYMOND 1927-

Born: May 23, 1927; Cincinnati, Ohio
Parents: Bert and Tressie (Anderson) Bottom
Married: Linda, a teacher
Children: Elaine and Cheri
Education: Western Kentucky University, B.A. 1951; Eastern Michigan University, M.S. 1960; Wayne State University, Ed. Spec. 1966
Career: Teacher, School Administrator
Address: 120 Ruff Drive, Monroe, MI 48161

Writings:

The Education of Disadvantaged Children	*Parker*	*1970*
Hardwood Hero	*Abingdon*	*1971*

Approximately one hundred published articles; numerous short stories and juvenile fiction; and approximately one hundred poems in general circulation and poetry magazines.

Work in Progress: Final six of eighteen articles prepared for National Research Bureau

He says: "My work is based on those matters I know best—my experiences based on responses and reactions to my world. I followed this suggestion as a beginning writer and happily found it unneccessary to change."

BOUMA, DONALD H. 1918-
Born: February 9, 1918; Grand Rapids, Michigan
Parents: Fred D. and Anna (Breen) Bouma
Married: Ruby W. Bouma
Children: Gary, Jack, Margene Burnett
Education: Calvin College, B.A. 1940; University of Michigan,
  M.A. 1943; Michigan State University, Ph. D. 1952
Career: Teacher, Wyoming Park High School (Grand Rapids)
  1940-43; U.S. Navy, Lt. (j.g.), executive officer fleet mines-
  weeper, 1944-46; Chairman and professor, Dept. of Sociology,
  Calvin Collge, 1946-60; Professor of Sociology, Western
  Michigan University, 1960-present; Visiting Professor University
  of Michigan and Michigan State University
Address: 78 Lake Doster Dr., Plainwell, MI 49080

Writings:

Dynamics of School Integration	Eerdmans	*1968*
Kids and Cops—A Study in Mutual Hostility	Eerdmans	*1969*

Associate Editor, *Intellect Magazine* and more than 30 articles in
professional journals; chapters for several other books

Work in Progress: updating the *Kids and Cops* study to as-
certain whether hostility patterns have changed

He says: "All of life for all of us is roses and thorns. Some have
more roses, others more thorns; but happiness and contentment
grow as we contemplate the roses."

BRABLEC, CARL 1908-
Born: September 24, 1908; Ogden Township, Lenawee County,
  Michigan
Parents: George and Mary (Priby) Brablec
Married: Dorothy (Kanous) an educator
Education: Michigan State Normal College (Eastern Michigan
  University), B.A. 1930; Charles University, Prague,
  Czechosloviakia, 1930-31; University of Michigan, M.A. 1940
Career: Britton, MI, High School Principal, 1932-40; Superinten-
  dent, 1940-44; Clarkston, MI, Superintendent, 1944-47; Roseville
  Public School Superintendent, 1947-70; Board of Regents,
  University of Michigan, 1958-66
Address: 18308 Mesle St., Roseville, MI 48066

Writings:

Tales From the Headlands	Prescott Pr.	*1972*

He says: "*Headlands*. . .is a narrative on the Moravian
(Czech) immigrants who came to the sugar beet fields of

southeastern Michigan and northern Ohio during the period of 1904-14. I was born into this ethnic element and wished some day to tell the story of their progress, outlook, and fusion into American life. A fairly intensive survey of fifty-five representative families provided most of the information respecting the people themselves. My own readings, travel, and studies supply the rest of the book which treats with historical overseas background and the casual and institutional forces which influenced the Moravians, who, incidentally, are more commonly, but less accurately, called 'Bohemians.' Very few were Czechs (Bohemians) although the Moravian is about as different from the Czech as an Iowan is different from a Nebraskan! For instance, the same written language is used and they are the same ethnically. . .only typical European regional standings distinguish them."

Awards: *Tales from the Headlands* received a Michigan Historical Society citation of merit.

BRAMAN, KAREN JILL 1943-

Pseudonym: Kitte Braman
Born: October 23, 1943; Detroit, Michigan
Parents: Verne Tucker and Dorothy (Fletcher) Braman
Education: Dancy Adult Day School, G.F.D. 1968; Highland Park Community College, 1968-70; Detroit Institute of Technology, 1970-73
Career: Child care worker in day care centers; remedial reading teacher; waitress; social welfare worker; library aide; beauty expert, planning to be cosmetologist; a practicing writer who feels it can be fun, as well as necessary to have a second vocation
Address: 2619 Cass, Detroit, MI 48207
Writings:

Poetic Fills and Fancies	*Contemporary Pr.*	*1975*
The Disclosure and Sing to Me		
of Rainbows	*Contemporary Pr.*	*1976*

Work in Progress: *Throbbing Tender*, a book of poetic odes to Elvis Presley

She says: "I have a dual nature as regards my life AND my art. I write half to please myself and half to reach humanity. Self-love is a necessary ingredient in enabling a writer to overcome the obstacles that will inevitably turn up. However, talent is given one with an obligation, and a writer's attitude towards his fellow man is also vital. Any writer who wants only to be a 'free artist' without regard to others, or to using his art for their sake as well as his own, is of a narrow outlook, and his work will reflect this. But I understand how difficult it is to achieve this ideal balance. Perhaps it will take a lifetime."

BRECHT, WILLIAM see: BARENDRECHT, COR. W.

BRAMS, STANLEY HOWARD 1910-
Born: May 14, 1910; Greenville, Michigan
Parents: Samuel S. Fredericka (Fixel) Brams
Divorced
Children: John and James
Education: Columbia University, 1929-31
Career: Advertising writer, 1931-35; free lance correspondent, manager, Detroit bureau, Transradio Press Service, 1936-39; Detroit editor, *The Iron Age,* 1939-46; Detroit bureau manager, McGraw-Hill Publishing Co., 1946-53; Publisher, *Labor Trends,* 1945 to date
Address: 31850 Partridge Lane, Farmington Hills, MI 48018

Writings:

Understanding Collective Bargaining (Contributor)	American Management Association	1958
Remembrances of Things Past	Trends	1976

Work in Progress: Various magazine articles

He says: "I have written for any number of magazines including the best ones—*Reader's Digest, Saturday Evening Post, New Yorker,* etc. Most work, obviously has been in general areas, primarily automotive and labor, rather than fiction—though I wrote fiction in earlier years. I believe the prime function of writing is to communicate something—an idea, a set of facts, an emotion or emotions—and in so doing to demonstrate developement. The best writing is basic writing, because only with basics can the writer reach and affect the largest number of readers."

BRAUN, RICHARD EMIL 1934-
Born: November 22, 1934; Detroit Michigan
Education: University of Michigan, A.B. 1956, A.M. 1957; University of Texas, 1960-62, 1968-69, Ph. D. 1969
Career: University of Alberta, Department of Classics: Lecturer, 1962-63; Assistant Professor, 1963-69; Associate Professor, 1969-76; Professor 1976-
Address: Dept. of Classics, Humanities Centre, University of Alberta, Edmonton, Alberta, Canada, T6G 2E5

Writings:

Children Passing	Univ. of Texas Press	1972
Bad Land	The Jargon Society	1971
The Foreclosure	Univ. of Illinois Press	1972

Sophocles: Antigone Translation
   with commentary   *Oxford University Press*   *1978*
Euripides: Rhesos Translation
   with commentary.   *Oxford University Press*   *1978*

Work in Progress: Translations, with introductions and commentaries, of Persius' *Satires* and of Euripides' *Electra;*completion and revision of two further books of poems, and additions to two more

He says: "The subject matter of poetry should be no more restricted than that of prose, and it should be expounded by a full array of techniques and combinations of techniques. That is, it is up to us to avoid making poetry 'musical,' and to strive toward keeping it a comprehensive, composite art able amply to interpret any or all human experience. The need for 'abstraction' is real, but it is important to manifest this need in the niceties of style, rather than in the restrictions of content; for the latter risks making poetry a *Minor* art."

BRAMAN, KITTE see: BRAMAN, KAREN JILL

BREITMEYER, LOIS FROMM 1923-
Born: 1923
Married: John F. Breitmeyer, Jr.
Education: Degree in science
Address: 250 Cranbrook Road, Bloomfield Hills, MI 48013

Writings:
The Dinosaur Dilemma   *Golden Gate Jr. Books*   *1964*
The Rabbit is Next   *Western Pub.*
   (with Gladys Garner Leithauser on all articles and books)

Contributor to *Jack and Jill* magazine

BRENDTRO, LARRY K. 1940-
Born: July 26, 1940; Sioux Falls, South Dakota
Parents: A. Kenneth and Bernice (Matz) Brendtro
Married: Janna Agena
Children: Daniel Kenneth and Steven Lincoln
Education: Augusta College, B.A. 1961; South Dakota State University, M.A. 1962; University of Michigan, Ph.D. 1965
Career: Child Care Worker, Teacher-School Social Worker, Principal: Cripple Children's Hospital, Sioux Falls, South Dakota, Hawthorn Center, Northville, MI; Psychological Examiner, Haw-

thorn Center; Instructor, Dept. of Education Psychology, University of Michigan; Clinical Teaching Faculty, University of Michigan Fresh Air Camp; Asst. Professor, Dept. of Special Education, University of Illinois, Urbana; President, Starr Commonwealth for Boys, Albion, MI
Address: Starr Commonwealth for Boy's Albion, MI 49224

Writings:

The Other 23 Hours (with A. E. Treischman & James Whittaker)	Aldine Publishing Co.	1969
Positive Peer Culture (with Harry Vorrath)	Aldine Publishing Co.	1974

Editor, *Residential Group Care,* magazine for National Association of Homes for Children

BRINKMAN, MICHAEL W. 1943-
Born: February 23, 1943; Milwaukee, Wisconsin
Parents: John Fredrick Brinkman (deceased) & Phyllis (Trout) Mankin
Married: Lois Fenlon, a homemaker and counselor
Children: Mary Claire, Juliet Marie, Elizabeth Anne, Amy Christine, Jessica Nicole, and Joshua Luke
Education: Indiana State University, A.B. 1964; Loyola University, 1966-68; University of Illinois, 1968; St. Mary's College, M.A.T. 1976; University of Michigan, 1977-working toward Ph. D.
Career: Latin teacher, Dyer Central High School, 1964-66; Merrillville Senior H.S., 1966-68; Alpena Public Schools, 1969-present. Also teaches psychology, world religion, and general business. President, Brinkman Enterprises, 1972-present
Address: P.O. Box 232, Alpena, MI 49707

Writings:

Poetry for Peoples	Campus Press	1970
Verse Diverse	Brinkman Ed. Ent.	1973
In Pursuit of the Tuit: a Concise History	Brinkman Ed. Ent.	1976
The Wordsmith (a vocabulary program)	Brinkman Ed. Ent.	1975
My Own Busy Bee Book (editor)	Brinkman Ed. Ent.	1978

and word games, a musical composition, and a weekly poetry feature in The Alpena News

Work in Progress: *Sonnets: In Pursuit of Life, Classical Latin Meter, A Programed Approach* word games and vocabulary programs

He says: "I write poetry because I am a poet. I am a lover—a lover of mankind in general and individuals specifically. Primarily, my work is either didactic or an impetus to the reader to engage in introspection. I want my readers to disclose themselves to themselves first and foremost; to be honest with themselves; to allow themselves to see themselves as they are, not merely as they would have themselves and others believe they are; to allow themselves to forgive their own faults, and work to change them; and to grow in love, the single most meaningful force and ideal in the universe.

BRINKS, HERBERT J. 1935-
Born: May 25, 1935; Illinois
Parents: Herbert J. and Alyce (Van Kley) Brinks
Married: Ruth E. Kortenhoeven, a techer
Children: Timothy, Steven, Marie, and John
Education: Calvin College, A.B. 1957; University of Michigan, M.A., Ph. D. 1965
Career: Professor of History: Calvin College, 1965-69; Michigan State University, 1969-70; Director of Michigan Historical Society, 1970-71; Professor of History & Archivist, Calvin College, 1971-78
Address: 1440 Adams, S.E., Grand Rapids, MI 49506

Writings:

Guide to Dutch-American Historical Collections (Joint Editor)	Dutch-American Historial Commission	1967
Peter White	Eerdmans	1970
A Michigan Reader: 11,000 B.C. to A.D. 1865 (with C. May)	Eerdmans	1970
Schrijf spoedig Tevug	Boekencentrum	1978

Work in Progress: *Dutch-American Immigration & Americanization*

BROMAGE, MARY COGAN 1906-
Born: October 13, 1906; Fall River, Massachusetts
Parents: James Joseph and Edith (Ives) Cogan
Married: Arthur W. Bromage
Children: Susanna Sarah (Mrs. John Paterson)
Career: Author and Educator
Education: Radcliffe College, B.A. 1928; University of Michigan, M.A. 1932
Address: 2300 Vinewood Blvd., Ann Arbor, MI 48104

Writings:

De Valera and the March of a Nation	Hutchinson & Co., London	1956
	Noonday Pr., NY	1957
	Greenwood Pr.	1976
Churchill and Ireland	University of Notre Dame Pr.	1964
Writing for Business	University of Michigan Pr., reprinted several times	1964
Cases in Written Communication (with Bruce A. Nelson)	Bureau of Business Research, School of Business Administration, The University Michigan	1964
Cases in Written Communication II (with Bruce A. Nelson)	Bureau of Business Research, School of Business Administration, The University of Michigan	1967
	Second printing	1971
	Third printing	1973
	Fourth printing	1977

Work in Progress: Operational Audit Reports

BRONER, E. M.
Career: Associate Professor of English, Wayne State University
Address: English Department, Wayne State University, Detroit, MI 48202

Writings:

Summer is a Foreign Land	WSU Press	1966
Journal/Nocturnal and Seven Stories	Harcourt	1968
Her Mothers	Holt, Rinehart & Winston	1975
Her Mothers	Berkley-Medallion	1976
Her Mothers (French)	Editions de Femmes	1977
A Weave of Women	Holt, Rinehart & Winston	1978

Articles, stories, reviews in MS., Commentary, Midstream, Epoch, Southern Humanities Review, New Letters, Seneca Review, Present Tense, Story Quarterly, Greensboro Review, etc. Play: The Body Parts of Margaret Fuller

She says: "Working artists don't have time for philosophy or 'interesting sidelights.' Working artists have bad tempers and time for work and people to whom they commit themselves."

Awards: Faculty Recognition Award, Wayne State University; Bicentennial Award for play: The Body Parts of Margaret Fuller

BROWN, ELIZABETH L. 1924-

Born: October 12, 1924; Kent County, Michigan
Parents: Charles William and Mable (Fern) Brown
Education: Grand Rapids Junior College, A.A. 1947; Grand Rapids Baptist Bible Institute, 3 years
Career: Executive secretary, employed by Zondervan Publishing House (on 2 occasions) and by Kregel Publications for 2 years; Director: Rights and Permissions, Zondervan Publishing House, Grand Rapids
Address: 0-9161 Kenowa, S.W., Grand Rapids, MI 49504

Writings:

The Candle of the Wicked	*Zondervan*	*1972*
"The Message of the Bells"		
a Christmas program	*Moody Press*	*1960*

Work in Progress: A nature/devotional; a second novel; a book on the importance of the mind in the Christian life

She says: "I have had one or two poems published and my work is currently being looked over for excerpting of more poems in a new magazine, *Faith & Inspiration.*

"As a Christian my philosophy must be relating my Christian beliefs to the rest of my life, and that is what my writing is about. At the moment my writing is only done at odd moments because of my full-time work. Since 1960, I have been employed in the Editorial Department of the above firm and therefore am very closely allied with writing, proofreading, some editing and publishing."

BROWN, GERALD S. 1911-

Born: February 25, 1911; Port Maitland, N.S., Canada
Parents: George E. and Catherine E. (Nicherson) Brown
Married: Dorothy L. Brown, a housewife
Children: Catherine R. Andrejak
Education: Acadia University, Wolfville, N.S. Canada; B.A. 1932 M.A. 1937; University of Minnesota, Ph. D. 1948
Career: Teaching Fellow, University of Minnesota and University of Michigan. Assistant, Associate, Full Professor, University of Michigan
Address: 1720 Hanover Rd., Ann Arbor, MI 48103

Writings:

Canada and the U.S. (with H.L.		
Keenleyside	*Knopf*	*1952*
The American Secretary	*Univ. of Mich. Press*	*1963*
The American Past 2 vols.		
(Ed. with Sidney Fine)	*Macmillan*	*4 editions*
and articles in professional journals		

BRUCKER, CLARA H. 1900-
Born: December 22, 1900; St. Ausger, Iowa
Parents: Emil and Regina (Stroebel) Hantel
Married: Wilber M. Brucker, an attorney
Children: Wilber M. Brucker, Jr.
Education: Drexel Institute, Philadelphia, 1918; Columbia University, A.B. 1930, M.A. 1930
Career: Statistician for General Motors Corp. in New York
Address: 56 Vendome Road, Grosse Pointe Farms, MI 48236

Writings:
To Have Your Cake and Eat It   Vantage   1968
and several magazine articles

Work in Progress: Wilbur M. Brucker's scrapbook

She says: "Because of my busy life collecting my husband's papers for U. of M. Bentley Library in Ann Arbor, and collecting his memorabilia for the Wilber M. Brucker Hall at Ft. Myers, Virginia, I have had little time for writing, but hope soon to continue working on my experiences while Governor's wife of Michigan. I have organized a School of Government in Detroit—was first president and founder, and am still coordinator for programs. To Have Your Cake and Eat It is about our Washington experiences."

Awards: Honored by Northwood Institute (Midland) as one of the distinguished women in 1972

Note: Mrs. Brucker's husband, Wilber M. Brucker, was Governor of Michigan during the years 1931-32. He served in Washington, D.C. as General Counsel for the Department of Defense, and was Secretary of the Army, 1961-66, under President Eisenhower.

BUOR, JOY OLNEY 1918-
Pseudonym: Joy Oleny Mann Lytle
Born: January 23, 1918; Charlevoix, Michigan
Parents: Ira H. and Sylvia (Kemp) Olney
Married: Charles L. Buor, ad advertising salesman
Children: Mrs. Sue Fischer and Mrs. Constance Swanson
Education: Traverse City High School, 1933; Alma College, A.B. 1937; University of Minnesota, 1964; University of Michigan, 1965-67; Michigan State University, 1967-68
Career: Teacher of French, Creative Writing, English, and Journalism
Address: 2234 Marshall Court, Saginaw, MI 48602

Writings:
Snowflakes and Thistles   M & D Publishers   1968
Haiku: Exitement   M & D Publishers   1970

and articles in *Photolith Magazine* and *The Saginaw News*

Work in Progress: a book of children's poetry

She says: "I love rhythm, music and words. Rhythm is a need so basic that it appears everywhere in the universe, from the 'lub-dub' of a healthy heart to the grand rhythms of the tides or the seasons. About words: I like to play with them, to mix and match, and come up with new combinations like 'popcorn moon' or 'eyelash talk!' I love oxymoron and litotes, light and shadow, humor and pathos.

"I believe:
Like a wild flower, love grows where you least expect it. When power enters, compassion abdicates. Anything truly beautiful has a touch of mystery. Some of the fragrance always clings to the hand that gives you roses."

Awards: Winner, Roy W. Hamilton Sonnet Contest, Alma College, 1936; Teacher-of-the-Year Award, Newspaper Fund of the *Wall Street Journal*, 1966 (for Journalism); *Wall Street Journal* Fellowship to the University of Minnesota, 1964, presented by the Newspaper Fund

BURGETT, DONALD ROBERT 1925-
Born: April 5, 1925; Detroit, Michigan
Parents: Elmer W. and Lillian Mae (Bruce) Burgett
Married: Twyla Moonen (Austin) Burgett
Children: Kenneth, Rene, Mark, Gary, Jeffrey
Education: Brighton High School (Adult), grad. 1972
Career: Modernization contractor; Pilot's license on G.I. Bill and still do some flying; Writer
Address: 4848 Vines Rd., Howell, MI 48843

Writing:

Currahee! (about paratroopers in Normandy, World War II)	Houghton Mifflin	1967

Work in Progress: *Seven Roads to Hell! Battle of the Lowlands!* Reprint of *Currahee!* by Bantam under title *As Eagles Screamed* (in a new war series)

He says: "I write the way I speak or talk—so far I have written personal experiences only—I wish to get away from war stories and into adventure and sports.

"I have very strong feelings toward family and loved ones. Do not hold with churches or religion (superstitious hold-over from man's four-legged days.) The best helping hand I have ever found was at the end of my own arm."

BURGOYNE, LEON E. 1916-
Born: 1916; Berrien Springs, Michigan
Education: Western Michigan University, B.S.; University of Michigan, M.A.
Career: Mathematics teacher and Basketball Coach in Michigan schools, until 1951; Drug store owner, St. Joseph, Michigan, 1951-

Writings:

State Champs	*John C. Winston*	*1951*
Jack Davis, Forward	*John C. Winston*	*1953*
Ensign Ronan: a story of Fort		
Dearborn	*John C. Winston*	*1955*

BURGTORF, FRANCES D. 1916-
Born: June 10, 1916; Cleveland, Ohio
Parents: James A. and Genevieve M. (Bloom) Donoghue
Married: Carl E. Burgtorf, U.S. Park Service, U.S. Forest Service, retired
Education: University of Michigan, 1933-35
Career: Housewife, waitress, manager of tourist home, clerk in county health office, Welcome Wagon Hostess, bookmobile driver, substitute teacher
Address: Rt. 1, Box 514, Cheboygan, MI 49721

Writings:

Chief Wawatam, the Story of a		
Hand-Bomber	*Frances D. Burgtorf*	*1976*

She says: "We retired from Washington in 1966 to our new home south of Cheboygan, MI and became interested in local history and Great Lakes shipping lore. After riding on the train ferry, *S.S. Chief Wawatam* as guest of the Captain and Mate, I was asked to write the history of the boat. The men were afraid she would be scrapped before she could be preserved. So I recorded, photographed, researched, and typed for five years to save the *Chief's* history. Now we are busy presenting the book to the libraries, schools, and stores in various areas near her (and hope to get to other states soon.) Meanwhile we are enjoying the many unusual letters from boat buffs, railroads buffs, and *"Chief*-lovers" all over the States, including Hawaii and Alaska . . .we feel that the ol' *Chief* will be well remembered."

BURKE, THETA 1926-
Born: December 15, 1926; Bumpus Mills, Tennessee
Parents: Harvey and Lucy (Woodson) Burke
Education: Austin Peay State University (TN); B.S. 1950; Uni-

versity of Tennessee, M.S.S.W. 1954

Career: Director of social work, Hawthorn Center, Northville, MI, until resignation to devote full time to writing

Address: 742 Stoney Pt. Rd., Suttons Bay, MI 49682

Writings:

I've Heard Your Feelings	*Delafield Press*	*1976*
Sounds of Yourself	*Delafield Press*	*1977*

Work in Progress: half dozen books similar to above—books of children's poetry, song lyrics, etc.

She says: "All my work, I hope, will reflect my philosophy written on the back side of *Sound of Yourself*—'The more truly we learn to express what we are, the greater shall become our faith in our limitless possibilities. We learn that an increasing awareness of our resources, coupled with that action of which we are capable, can lead to a oneness within which allows for the existence of our most basic freedom—that of being ourselves.' "

BURROWS, EDWIN GLADDING 1917-

Born: July 23, 1917; Dallas, Texas

Parents: Millar and Irene (Gladding) Burrows

Married: Beth Elpern, a teacher

Children: (by former marriage) Edwin, Daniel, David

Education: Yale University, B.A. 1938; University of Michigan, M.A. 1940

Career: Mainly in public broadcasting. Manager, WUOM/WVGR, The University of Michigan, Ann Arbor, 1955-70; Director, National Center for Audio Experimentation, Madison, WI, 1970-73; Executive Producer, WUOM/WVGR, 1973-

Address: 1952 Traver Rd., #204, Ann Arbor, MI 48103

Writings

The Arctic Tern (poems)	*Grove Press*	*1957*
Man Fishing (poems)	*Sumac Press*	*1970*
The Crossing (poems)	*New Moon/Humble Hills*	*1976*
Kiva (poems)	*Ithaca House*	*1976*

and 6 broadcast plays produced recently by Canadian Broadcasting Corporation, NCAE, Madison, WI, etc., and poetry published in numerous journals and anthologies, including *Accent, American Poetry Review, Atlantic Monthly,* and many more.

Work in Progress: *The House of August* (poems)

Awards: John Masefield Poetry Award, 1938; Major Hopwood Award in Poetry, 1940; Seven Ohio State Awards, 1953-74; Fellow, Yaddo Foundation, Saratoga Springs, NY 1963, 1966; Borestone Mountain Poetry Award, 1964; First poetry collection, *The Arctic Tern,* was runner-up for the National Book Award.

BURTON, GABRIELLE 1939-
Born: February 21, 1939; Lansing, Michigan
Parents: Clifford James and Helen Dailey Baker
Married: Roger Burton, a psychologist
Children: Maria, Jennifer, Ursula, Gabrielle, Charity
Education: Marygrove College, Detroit, B.A. 1960
Career: Free-lance writer
Address: 174 Le Brun Rd., Eggertsville, NY 14226

Writings:
I'm Running Away From Home
  But I'm Not Allowed to Cross
  the Street   *Know, Inc.*   1972
and articles, essays, poetry, book reviews, etc. for various sources
including *Washington Post* and *New York Times Features Syndicate*

Work in Progress: a novel: *Nearly Time*

BUSH, GEORGE 9125-
Born: April 23, 1925
Married: Margery Burke
Children: Susanna and Richard
Education: Wayne University, B.A. 1947; M.A. 1948
Career: Reporter: *Detroit News, Detroit Free Press, San
  Francisco Examiner;* Executive Editor, Carmel-Pacific Pub-
  lications; Assistant professor of Journalism, University of Minne-
  sota; Associate professor of Journalism, Penn State U.; on
  editorial staffs of *Look and Saturday Evening Post;* since
  1961 *Better Homes and Gardens* editor-at-large, now
  contributing editor
Address: P.O. Box 94, Lumberville, PA 18933

Writings:
Your Sins and Mine (a novel)
  with Parker Smith   *Tower*   1960
The Strange World of Insects *Putnam*   1968
Escape From Addiction for Dr.
  Gordon Bell   *McGraw-Hill*   1970
Future Builders, the Story of
  Michigan's Consumers Power
  Company   *McGraw-Hill*   1973
The Wide World of Wickes, the
  Story of an Unusual Growth
  Company   *McGraw-Hill*   1976
plus articles and/or stories in *American Mercury, The Lamp, Holi-
day, Travel & Leisure, Apartment Life, Vista USA, Skiing, Flying,
Alfred Hitchcoks's Myster Magazine, True,* and others

Work in Progress: History/profiles of Diamond Shamrock Corp., Whirlpool Corp., and Weil Brothers Cotton, Inc.

He says: "If anything makes me a Michigan writer, though certainly not 'author', it's hardly my former, somewhat limited sojourn in the state. Rather, it's that I was exposed in Michigan to some of the people who influenced me most in my youth: the late Dr. Harold Basilius of Wayne University; the late Larry Henderson, night city editor of the *Detroit News* and favorite mentor of succeeding generations of young reporters; Charlie Haun, the former night city editor of the *Detroit Free Press;* and the first real-life author I'd ever met, old friend Glendon Swarthout."

BUTLER, HAL 1913-
Born: January 3, 1913; St. Louis Missouri
Parents: Charles and Estelle Butler
Married: Eleanor, a homemaker
Children: Beverly and Joyce
Education: High School
Career: Freelance writer for more than thirty years, "starting with fiction in the pulps, then on to better magazines and books." Managing editor of *Ford Times Travel Magazine,* 1964-74. Now freelancing exclusively

Writings:

The Harmon Killebrew Story	Messner	1966
The Bob Allison Story	Messner	1967
There's Nothing New in Sports	Messner	1967
Baseball All-Star Thrills	Messner	1968
Stormin' Norman Cash	Messner	1968
Roar of the Road	Messner	1969
Under Dogs of Sport	Messner	1969
The Willie Horton Story	Messner	1970
Millions of Cars	Messner	1972
Sports Heroes Who Wouldn't Quit	Messner	1973
Al Kaline & the Detroit Tigers	Regnery	1973
Baseball's Champion Pitchers	Messner	1974
Abandon Ship!	Regnery	1974
Inferno!	Regnery	1975
Nature at War	Regnery	1976

Work in Progress: Magazine articles

He says: "Having always been something of a sports nut, my first books (as you can see) were on sports. Have branched out a bit with the last three books, which are on ship diasters, fire disasters, and natural disasters—which might mark me as something of a disaster as a writer (no best sellers yet!) Love to write and wouldn't want to do anything else.''

CAESAR, EUGENE LEE 1927-

Pseudonyms: Anthony Stirling, Johnny Laredo
Born: December 10, 1927; Saginaw, Michigan
Parents: Ernest and Eunice (Lee) Caesar
Married: Judy, a dance teacher
Children: Cheryl, Craig, Jeffrey
Education: Central Michigan University, 1945; Case Institute of Technology, Cleveland, 1945; Illinois Institute of Technology, 1946; University of Miami, 1947-49
Career: Free-lance magazine writer, novelist, historian, etc., 1949 to 1968. Education and school-finance consultant, Michigan State Legislature, 1968 to present
Address: 1024 Pickton Dr., Lansing, MI 48917

Writings:

Mark of the Hunter	Sloane	1953
The Wild Hunters	Putnam	1957
King of the Mountain Men	Dutton	1961
Rifle for Rent	Monarch	1963
Incredible Detective	Prentice Hall	1968

Awards: Western Heritage Award, 1961, for *King of the Mountain Men*

CAMPBELL, ANNE 1888-

Married name: Anne Campbell Stark
Born: June 19, 1888; Lynn, Michigan (St. Clair County)
Parents: High J. and Mina (Atkinson) Campbell
Married: George W. Stark; Detroit newspaperman and historiographer
Children: George Winter, Alison Jean Wilson, Richard Campbell
Education: High school education; Wayne State University, Honorary Degree, 1953
Career: Writer of verse for Associated Newspapers of New York from 1922; appeared in *The Detroit News,* Philadelphia *Bulletin, Boston Globe,* and others; Writer, speaker, poet.
Address: Presently residing in Eventide Home, 3643 Park, Detroit, Michigan

Writings:

Companionship and Other Poems	Barse & Hopkins	1924
Back Home	Barse & Hopkins	1926

The Heart of Home	*Winston*	*1931*
Jesus and His Twelve Apostles		
Four Songs from the Lord's Prayer		
Songs from the Beatitudes (with Ward-Stephens)		
The House That Love Built	*Arnold-Powers*	*1940*
Two Heads are better	*Alved*	*1947*

Honors: Honorary member of the Poetry Society of Michigan; Honored by Detroit Federation of Women's Clubs; Silver Anniversary as *Detroit News* Poet, 1922-47; Michigan Mother of the Year, 1953

CAMPBELL, NANCY A. 1930-

Born: December 11, 1930; Charlevoix, Michigan
Parents: Elton C. and Genevieve (Weber) Dagwell
Married: Richard Campbell, employed by Mackinac Bridge Authority
Children: Steven and Eric
Education: Eastern Michigan University, 1948-49; Central Michigan University, B.S., 1952; Graduate work at Wayne State, Michigan State, University of Michigan
Career: Elementary teacher, Farmington; Teacher & Librarian, Mackinaw City Public Schools; Librarian of Mackinaw Woman's Club Public Library
Address: 110 E. Etherington, Mackinaw City, MI 49701

Writings:

Memories of Mackinaw	*Little Traverse Printing*	*1976*

Work in Progress: a book on the maritime history of the area

She says: *"Memories of Mackinaw* was my first endeavor in the field of writing. My chief interest is historic preservation and beautification projects, of which I am involved in several both locally and nationally. My hobbies are reading, painting and piano. Although born in Charlevoix, I have spent my entire life in Mackinaw City, with the exception of two years in Farmington and time spent traveling here and aboard."

CANDLER, JULIE J. 1919-

Born: December 28, 1919; Springfield, Illinois
Parents: Frank and Edith (Rickey) Jennings
Children: Carolyn Candler Solaka, William Robert Candler IV, Rickey Candler Faermark
Education: Wayne State University, 1940-42; University of Michi-

gan, 1942-43

Career: Writer, Dodge News Bureau, 1954; *Birmingham Eccentric,* 1955-60; general news and police reporter, city editor; public relations consultant, Julie Candler & Associates, 1960-present; writer of monthly feature "Woman at the Wheel" in *Woman's Day* magazine, 1964-present; freelance writer; member, National Motor Vehicle Safety Advisory Council, U.S. Department of Transportation, 1974-77; member, board of directors for Action for Child Transportation Safety, 1975-

Address: 430 N. Woodward, Birmingham, MI 48011

Writings:

Woman at the Wheel	Paperback Library	1967

Work in Progress: a novel

Awards: National Safety Council's Public Service Award, 1967 "Headliner of the Year" award, Detroit chapter of Women in Communications, 1967; Evinrude outdoor writing award, 1974; Deep Woods award, 1974; Uniroyal Journalism Safety award, 1974

CANTONI, LOUIS JOSEPH 1919-

Born: May 22, 1919; Detroit, Michigan

Parents: Pietro and Stella (Puricelli) Cantoni

Married: Lucile Eudora Moses Cantoni, a social work supervisor

Children: Christopher Louis and Sylvia Therese

Education: University of California, A.B. 1946; University of Michigan, M.S.W. 1949, Ph. D. 1953

Career: Social Caseworker, Detroit Public Welfare Dept., 1946-49; Rehabilitation Counselor, Mich. Dept. of Ed., 1949-50; Doctoral student, 1950-51; Conference Leader, Psychology Teacher and Counselor, General Motors Institute, Flint, 1951-56; Professor and Coordinator of Vocational Rehabilitation Counseling, Wayne State University, 1965-present

Address: 2591 Woodstock Drive, Detroit, MI 48203

Writings:

A Follow-up Study of the Personal Adjustment of the Subjects Who Participated in the 1939-43 Flint, Michigan Guidance Demonstration	University Microfilms	1953
Placement of the Handicapped in Competitive Employment (Editor)	Wayne State University	1957
University and Field Agency Contributions to the Preparation of Vocational Rehabili-		

tion Counselors Through Field
Voc. Guidance & Rehab.

Instruction (Co-editor)	*Services*	*1958*
Counseling Your Friends (with		
Lucile Cantoni)	*William Frederick*	*1961*
With Joy I Called to You		
(75 poems)	*South & West*	*1969*

Work in Progress: *Gradually the Dreams Change* (75 poems)

He says: "I began writing poems in response to the wonders of a young and growing family. My son, Christopher, and daughter, Sylvia, now in their early twenties, continue their formal schooling. My wife, Lucile, has contributed books and articles in her professional field of social work.

"My first book of poems, *With Joy I Called to You,* explored a variety of themes and forms. Some of the poems in *Gradually The Dreams Change* reach back to the pristine years of my marriage. In the main, however, this second book captures the feelings and outlook of a man moving from his ebullient thirties to his steady-eyed fifties.

"My philosophical perspective is that of a personalist. I have the following views regarding personalism: In this philosophy, the value of persons stands above all other values, and the essence of our lives inheres in the quality of our relationsips with other persons. God is the supreme person and we as humans share in the godhead insofar as our relationships with other persons, including God, approach perfect harmony."

CARLETON, WILL 1845-1912
Christened: William McKendree Carleton
Born: October 21, 1845; near Hudson, Michigan (Lenawee County)
Parents: John Hancock and Celestia (Smith) Carleton
Education: Adora Niles Goodell
Career: Worked for Chicago newspaper; editor and part owner, *Hillsdale Standard;* Editor, *Detroit Weekly Tribune;* Founder and publisher, *Everywhere* magazine, 1894-1912; Hillsdale College 1887-1912; poet and lecturer

Writings:
Poems	Lakeside	1871
Farm Ballards	Harper	1873
Farm Legends	Harper	1875
Young Folks' Centennial		
Rhymes	Harper	1876
Farm Festivals	Harper	1881

City Ballads	Harper	1885
Country Ballads	Dillingham	1887
An Ancient Spell	Clark, Maynard	1887
City Legends	Harper	1890
City Festivals	Harper	1892
Rhymes of Our Planet	Harper	1895
The Old Infant	Harper	1896
Songs of Two Centuries	Harper	1902
Poems for Young Americans	Harper	1906
In Old School Days	Moffat, Yard	1907
The Duke and The King	Globe Literary Bur.	1908
Drifted In	Everywhere Pub. Co.	1908
A Thousand Thoughts from Will Carleton	Everywhere Pub. Co.	1908
The Burglar-Bracelets	Globe Literary Bur.	1908
Arnold and Talleyrand	Globe Literary Bur.	1909
Tainted Money	Globe Literary Bur.	1909
A Thousand More Verses	Everywhere Pub. Co.	1912
Over the Hill to the Poor House and Other Poems	Century	1913
Reprinted	Harper	1927

"As a sentimental recorder of domestic farm life in the Middle West and a cheerfully sympathetic observer of the underprivileged, he reflects both an era and an attitude of American Life."

American Authors 1600-1900, Kunitz

" 'Over the Hill to the Poorhouse' did almost as much for poor folks as Harriet Beecher Stowe's *Uncle Tom's Cabin* did for slavery."

The Detroit News, October 16, 1963

Honors: Carleton, Michigan (Monroe County) named after him. Designated *Michigan Poet;* Will Carleton Day-October 21st- to be celebrated in all Michigan public schools each year. Carleton Highway-from Adrian to Hudson and Hillsdale and Will Carleton Road West from Flat Rock.

CARLI, AUDREY 1932-
Pseudonyms: Beth Craig, Ann Patyn
Born: March 14, 1932; Wakefield, Michigan
Parents: Henry and Helen (Niemi) Johnson
Married: David Carli, a social studies instructor
Children: Debbie, Glenn, Lynn, Lori
Education: Wakefield High School, 1950; Iron County Community School, Creative Writing Certificate, 1963
Career: Free-lance writer; part-time Creative Writing teacher

Address: 807 Jefferson Ave., Box 158, Stambaugh, MI 49964

Writings:

Jimmy's Happy Day	T.S. Denison	*1967*

articles, essays, short stories, published in many magazines

Work in Progress: a book entitled *Loneliness, Good-bye!* (positive ways to cope with loneliness)

She says: "Writing is a powerful need of mine because it is fulfilling to be able to observe spirit-lifting situations and write inspirational articles that may help the troubled. It is also satisfying to gather research on a social, medical, psychological, child care or financial problem and create an article that can help the reader. I also enjoy writing fiction that will entertain, uplift as well as educate the reader.

"An interesting sidelight is that my mail has brought in letters from readers that have inspired me to write the book now in progress, *Loneliness, Good-Bye!* Also, it is satisfying to receive personal comments from a reader who has helped to overcome loneliness or has been helped in some other way."

CARLSON, BERNICE WELLS 1910-
Born: July 21, 1910; Clare, Michigan
Parents: George Bryon and Bernice (Cook) Wells
Married: Dr. Carl W. Carlson, a Chemistry Professor
Children: Christine (Mrs. Paul J. Umberger), Philip Wells Carlson, Marta Carlson
Education: Ripon College, A.B. 1932; Dramatic Art Dept., Wisconsin Conservatory of Music, teacher's certificate, 1928
Career: Lansing, *MI State Journal:* society editor two years, "stringer" 7 years; substitute teacher, Franklin Twp., N.Y., 20 years; volunteer: Girl Scouts, Cub Scouts, retarded children, church groups, etc.; lecturer
Address: Rt. 3, Box 332D, Somerset, NJ 08873

Writings:

The Junior Party Book	*Abingdon*	*1939*
Make it Yourself	*Abingdon*	*1950*
Do It Yourself	*Abingdon*	*1952*
Fun for One or Two	*Abingdon*	*1954*
Act It Out	*Abingdon*	*1956*
Make It and Use It!	*Abingdon*	*1958*
The Right Play for You	*Abingdon*	*1960*
The Party Book for Boys and Girls	*Abingdon*	*1963*
Listen! And Help Tell the Story	*Abingdon*	*1965*
You Know What? I Like Animals	*Abingdon*	*1967*

Play a Part	Abingdon	1970
Let's Pretend It Happened to		
You!	Abingdon	1973
Funny-Bone Dramatics	Abingdon	1974
Picture That!	Abingdon	1977

Co-authored

Ready to Work?	Abingdon	1977
Recreation for Retarded		
Teenagers and Young		
Adults	Abingdon	1968
Play Activities for the		
Retarded Child	Abingdon	1963
Masks and Mask Makers	Abingdon	1962
We Want Sunshine in Our		
House	Abingdon	1973
Water Fit to Use	John Day-Harper	1966-72

Paperback

| Mary Had a Baby | Abingdon | 1975 |

Other Writings:
Chapters for Grolier Topical Encyclopedia and Child Craft; Christmas programs; Magazine articles dealing with family life.

Work in Progress: Related stories and art activities for older children.

She says: "Every type of recreation can help a person develop in all areas of growth; physical, emotional, social, intellectual, and the language arts. I have written a variety of activity books, story books, and non-fiction that can prompt a child to develop imagination, skills, intellectual curiosity, self-reliance, and sensitivity to other people. My interests include the retarded as well as 'normal' person as he progresses from childhood into maturity.

"A great deal of my writing depends on my heritage, my family roots in Michigan, and experiences in the woods, lakes, and fields of the state."

CARLSON, LEWIS H. 1934-
Born: August 1, 1934; Muskegon, Michigan
Parents: Robert LaVine and Margaret Carlson
Married: Simone, a teacher
Education: University of Michigan, B.A., 1957, M.A., 1962; Michigan State University, Ph.D. 1967
Career: Assistant Professor of History, Ferris State College, 1965-68; Assistant & Associate Professor of History, Western Michigan University, 1968-present
Address: 3530 Meadowcroft Dr., Kalamazoo, MI 49007
Writings:

"The Negro in Science," in
Roucek, J.S. and Kiernam, T.
The Negro Impact on West-
Civilization   Philosophical Library   1971
In Their Place: White America
Defines Her Minorities, 1850-
1950 (co-editor with George
Colburn)   Wiley   1972

Work in Progress: *American's Fancy: Spectator Sports in America* (with George Colburn)

CARLSON, WILLIAM SAMUEL 1905-

Born: November 18, 1905; Ironwood, Michigan
Parents: Samuel & Mary (Lamsted) Carlson
Married: Maryjane Rowe
Children: Kristin Rowe
Education: University of Michigan, A.B., 1930, M.S., 1932, Ph. D., 1937; University of Copenhagen, 1931; Columbia University, 1935
Career: High School principal, Wakefield, Michigan, 1933-34; High school principal, East Lansing, Michigan, 1935; Professor and Dean of Admissions and Records, University of Minnesota, 1937-46; President, University of Delaware, 1946-50; President, University of Vermont, 1950-52; President, State University of New York, 1952-58; President, University of Toledo, 1958-72
Address: 131 Bluffview Drive, Belleair Bluffs, Florida 33540

Writings:
Greenland Lies to the North   Macmillian   1940
Student Teachers Handbook
with C.W. Boardman   Burgess   1940
Manual for the Supervising
Teacher   Minneapolis, MN   1940
Report of the Northern Division
of the Fourth University of
Michigan Greenland
Expedition   U. of Mich. Press   1941
Lifelines Through the Arctic   Duell, Sloan, etc.   1962
The Municipal University   Center for Applied
                                Research in Education   1962

Work in Progress: Presently a New York agent has two of my manuscripts—one on the Aleutian campaign, another on the Arctic in Transition; publication uncertain.

He says: "Some years ago on a sledging expedition in Greenland I spent a night at Kigtorsak, a small winter colony, whose director was a combination dictator and sage. He was an old man among

Eskimos; but his watery eyes were penetrating, and with the help of a cane fashioned from a willow he was as spry as a man of twenty. He claimed the ice at Kigtorsak became poor when the Panama Canal was opened and joined the two oceans. Seal hunting on sea ice was destroyed. The director was righteously indignant. Two years earlier he had gone so far as to draw a petition to have the Canal closed. (The petition got as far as God-haven—capital of North Greenland—before being shelved.) Fortunately for me, an American, he did not know the exact location of the Canal, believing it to be in Denmark, and I was able to enjoy his unstinted hospitality."

Honors: Henry Goodard Leach Fellowship of American-Scandinavian Foundation

Honorary LL.D.: Dickinson College, University of Delaware; University of Michigan; Middlebury College; University of Cincinnati

Honorary D. Litt.: University of Toledo

Honorary D. Sc.: Alfred University; Bowling Green State University

Accompanied an expedition to Greenland in 1927, returning in 1930 to spend a winter at the Upernivik Glacier as Fellow, American-Scandinavian Foundation.

CARR, HARRIETT HELEN 1899-

Born: January 1, 1899; Ann Arbor, Michigan
Parents: Paul and Nellie (Loomis) Carr
Education: Michigan State Normal College; University of Michigan; New York University
Career: Reporter and News Editor, *Ypsilanti Daily Press,* 1920-35; Feature writer, *The Detroit News,* 1935-39; Staff Writer, *Michigan Educational Journal,* 1939-40; Editor, *Michigan Vocational Out-Look,* 1940-45; Assistant Director of field services, *Scholastic Magazine,* 1945-63; Full-time writer of fiction; 1963-
Address: 430 Bay NE, St. Petersburg, FL 33701

Writings:

Gravel Gold	Farrar, Straus	1953
Borghild of Brooklyn	Farrar, Straus	1955
Where the Turnpike Starts	Macmillan	1955
Against the Wind	Macmillan	1955
Miami Towers	Macmillan	1956
Sharon	Hastings House	1956
Wheels for Conquest	Macmillan	1957
Valley of Defiance	Macmillan	1957

Confidential Secretary	Macmillan	1958
The Mystery of the Aztec Idol	Macmillan	1959
Young Viking of Brooklyn	Viking	1961
Mystery of Ghost Valley	Macmillan	1962
Rod's Girl	Hastings House	1963
Bold Beginnings	Hastings House	1964

Quote: "The Carr family did not come to America on the Mayflower, but by 1670 they were established in Massachusetts. And almost from that time on they have followed the frontier, from Massachusetts to New York State, on to Michigan, Colorado, North Dakota; to the Pacific coast and back again. Generation after generation they wrote letters. . .they told stories to their children. . .they made friends with the Indians, established trading posts, broke the soil of the plain states, mined gold." From this inheritance she was led to write.

CARRICK, DONALD 1929-
Born: April 7, 1929; Wayne County, Michigan
Parents: Fay and Blanche (Soper) Carrick
Married: Carol Carrick, a writer and mother
Children: Christopher and Paul
Education: Colorado Springs Fine Art Center, 1949; Art Students League, New York City, 1950; Vienna Academy of Art, Austria, 1954
Career: Illustrator and writer
Address: Box 1811, Edgartown, MA 02539

Writings:

The Tree	Macmillan	1971
Drip Drop	Macmillan	1973
The Deer in the Pasture	Greenwillow	1976

Work in Progress: "I've been writing an untitled book for a year, but illustration keeps me from a finish."

He says: "Despite the above, my first interest is as a painter. I've had several one-man shows in New York and abroad—plan another for Fall, 1978. The above are children's books which I both wrote and illustrated. I have illustrated another 26 books written by my wife and several other authors."

CARRIGAN, ANDREW G. 1935-
Born: March 7, 1935; Battle Creek, Michigan
Parents: Robert G., Sr. and Kathyrn (Dinkel) Carrigan
Married: Susan J. Carrigan, an art teacher

Children: R. Jason Carrigan
Education: Western Michigan University, 1953; Olivet College, 1954-56; University of Michigan, B.A., 1961, M.A., 1966
Career: Teacher: Writing poetry, Bible Lit., English, 1973-77; Poet at University of Michigan Residential College
Address: 212 West Henry St., Saline, MI 48176
Writings:

Book 3 (poems)	Sumac Press	1972
Babyburgers (poems)	Street Fiction Press	1975

Work in Progress: To Read to Read (poems)
He says: "Writing is more important than publishing,"

CARSON, ADA LOU 1932-
Born: March 6, 1932; Pittsburg, Pennsylvania
Parents: Morris and Mary (Pitler) Siegel
Married: Herbert L. Carson, a college teacher and writer
Children: William, Rosalyn, Bryan
Education: Bradley University, 1949-51; University of Pittsburgh, B.A. 1953; Teachers College, Columbia University, M.A. 1955; University of Minnesota, 1955-present, Ph. D. candidate
Career: Secretary, Teacher of English and Science at Hillside (NJ) Junior High School; Teacher of Freshman Composition and Freshman Communication at University of Minnesota; Teacher of English, speech, and humanities at Ferris State College; Teacher of American Literature and of Current Best Sellers in Fiction for the Independent Study Division, University of Minnesota. Occasional book reviewer, Grand Rapids Press
Address: Dept. of Language and Literature, Ferris State College, Big Rapids, MI 49307
Writings:

Impact of Fiction (with Herbert L. Carson)	Cummings	1970
Royall Tyler: A Critical Biography (with Herbert L. Carson)	Twayne, U.S. Authors	1978

several articles and study guides
Work in Progress: an edition of Thomas Pickman Tyler's Memoirs of Royall Tyler.
She says: "And gladly would she learn, and gladly teach."

CARSON, HERBERT L. 1929-
Born: October 3, 1929; Philadelphia, Pennsylvania
Parents: Saul and Bertha (Shapiro) Carson
Married: Ada Lou Carson, a teacher and writer
Children: William, Rosalyn, Bryan
Education: University of Pittsburgh; B.A. 1953; Columbia Univer-

sity; M.A. 1955; University of Minnesota; Ph.D. 1959
Career: Served with U.S. Infantry, W.W.II; copy boy for Philadelphia *Inquirer;* worked for Stanley-Warner Motion Pictures, Philadelphia, PA, and Metro Advertising, New York City. Teacher at U. of Minnesota, U. of Nebraska, Youngstown State U.; presently Professor of Humanities, Literature, and Philosophy at Ferris State; Reviewer, *Grand Rapids Press*
Address: J-4; Ferris State College, Big Rapids, MI 49307
Writings:

Steps in Successful Speaking	*Van Nostrand*	*1967*
Impact of Fiction (with Ada		
Lou Carson)	*Cummings*	*1970*
Royall Tyler: A Critical		
Biography (with Ada Lou		
Carson)	*Twayne U.S. Authors*	*1978*

Work in Progress: *George Lillo and the Dream of Democracy*
He says: "Of the making of books there is no end, and much study is weariness of the flesh.' Ecclesiastes"

CARSON, JOHN F. 1920-
Born: August 2, 1920; Indianapolis, Indiana
Parents: Fredric P. and Mary (McKenzie) Carson
Married: Beverly V. (Carlisle) Carson, a teacher
Children: Jacqueline Ann, John F., and Bruce G.
Education: Butler University, B.S., 1948; Indiana University, M.S. 1955, Ph. D., 1966
Career: High School Teacher (English, Biology) 5½ years; High School Principal, 7 years (Gosport-Wayne Township School, 1 yr., North Judson High School, 3 yrs., Taipei, American School, 3 yrs.); Associate Professor, Central Michigan University, 12 years to present
Address: 6691 W. Pickard Rd., Mt. Pleasant, MI 48858
Writings:

Floorburns	*Farrar, Straus & Giroux*	*1957*
The 23rd Street Crusaders	*Farrar, Straus & Giroux*	*1958*
The Boys Who Vanished	*Duell, Sloan & Pearce*	*1959*
The Coach Nobody Liked	*Farrar, Straus & Giroux*	*1960*
The Mystery of the Missing		
Monkey	*Farrar, Straus & Giroux*	*1963*
Court Clown	*Farrar, Straus & Giroux*	*1963*
The Mystery of the Tarnished		
Trophy	*Farrar, Straus & Giroux*	*1964*
Hotshot	*Farrar, Straus & Giroux*	*1965*

Work in Progress: rewrites of a horse story and a basketball story; a possible sequel to *The 23rd Street Crusaders.*
He says: "Writers of books for young readers have more of a responsiblity to their readers than do writers of adult novels, it seems to me. One writes to communicate, to share ideas, to help

the young reader identify himself in values, decisions, and relationships to other people as well as to entertain. A sense of humor adds brightness to life and helps us not to take ourselves too seriously. I feel a personal identity with the protagonists in my stories, and although they are fictitious personalities, they seem very real to me. I hope these characters seem real people to the young readers."

CARTER, JAMES L. 1935-
Born: October 17, 1935; Grand Marais, Michigan
Parents: Forest L. and Cecille (LaCosse) Carter
Education: Acquinas College, B.A., 1961; University of Michigan, 1962-64; Northern Michigan University, M.A., 1967
Career: Teacher, Grand Rapids and Spring Lake, 1961-64; Editorial staff member, *The Mining Journal,* Marquette, MI, 1964-68; Founder and publisher, *The Grand Marais Pilot & Pictured Rocks Review* newspaper, 1970-75; Technical writer, Northern Michigan University, 1968-70; Coordinator, American Indian Program, NMU, 1970-75; Director, NMU Press, 1973-; News Director, NMU, 1975-
Address: 430 E. Michigan, Marquette, MI 49855
Writings:

Voyageurs' Harbor	The Pilot Press	1967
American Voyageur: The Journal of David Bates Douglass (Editor, with Sydney W. Jackman et al)	NMU Pr.	1969
North to Lake Superior: The Journal of Charles W. Penney, 1840. (Editor, with Ernest H. Rankin)	John M. Longyear Research Library	1970
The Grand Island Story (Editor)	John M. Longyear Research Library	1974

plus miscellaneous historical articles in professional journals

Work in Progress: a general history of the Upper Peninsula of Michigan; History of Caribou Island, Lake Superior.

CASE, LEONARD L. 1900-
Born: December 12, 1900; Benzonia Michigan
Parents: William L. and May (Hubbell) Case
Married: Freda Olsen Case
Children: Mrs. Sherman (Marietta) Nelson, William E. Case, Leonard Case, Jr.
Education: Amherst College, 1924-25; Olivet College, A.B. 1927
Career: Private business; Benzie County Magistrate, 85th Michigan Judicial District; Newspaper reporter and freelance writer
Address: 845 Michigan Ave., Benzonia, MI 49616

Writings:

Benzie County—A Bicentennial		
Reader	Cadillac Printing Co.	*1976*

Work in Progress: Continuing weekly column "The Crystal Glazer" appearing in *Benzie County Advisor,* Frankfort, MI

CASTELLANOS, JANE 1913-
Born: August 6, 1913; Lansing, Michigan
Parents: Charles S. and Florence (Sherwood) Robinson
Married: Jose C. Castellanos
Education: University of Michigan, B.A., 1934; Stanford University, M.A., Ph. D., 1938; Mills College, 1940-41
Career: Instructor in French and German, San Francisco College for Women, 1937-39; Instructor, Child Development, Mills College, 1941-50; Instructor, Family Life Ed., Psychology & Counselor, Diablo Valley College, 1950-77
Address: 2950 Brookdale Ct., Concord, CA 94518

Writings:

A Shell for Sam	*Golden Gate*	*1963*
Something New for Taco	*Golden Gate*	*1965*
Tomasito and The Golden		
Llamas	*Golden Gate*	*1968*

She says: "My writing was carried on for my own pleasure. I wrote three other manuscripts, but could not find a publisher. They contained all of the ideas I felt like writing about and which I had the talent to tackle. Since I did not have the talent to write beyond that, the kind of work I would like to have created, I ceased writing."

CATTON, BRUCE 1899-1978
Born: October 9, 1899; Petoskey, Michigan
Parents: George R. and Adella M. (Patten) Catton
Married: Hazel Catton
Children: William Catton
Education: Oberlin College, 1917-20
Career: Newspaper reporter: Cleveland, Boston and Washington, 1920-40; War Production Board, Department of Commerce, Interior Department, 1941-52; Editor, later Senior Editor, *American Heritage Magazine,* 1953-1978

Writings:

War Lords of Washington	Harcourt Brace & Co.	*1949*
Mr. Lincoln's Army	*Doubleday*	*1950*
Glory Road	*Doubleday*	*1951*
Stillness at Appomattox	*Doubleday*	*1953*
This Hallowed Ground	*Doubleday*	*1956*

American Heritage Picture		
History of the Civil War	Doubleday	1958
Grant Moves South	Little Brown & Co.	1960
The Coming Fury	Doubleday	1961
Terrible Swift Sword	Doubleday	1963
Never Call Retreat	Doubleday	1965
Grant Takes Command	Little, Brown & Co.	1968
Waiting for the Morning Train	Doubleday	1972

Work in Progress: The Bold and Magnificent Dream, with William Catton

CHAMBERLAIN, ELINOR 1901-

Born: June 21, 1901; Muskegon, Michigan
Parents: Charles L. and Marie (Lambert) Chamberlain
Married: William R. Kuhns
Children: William C. Kuhns and Mary K. Fancher
Education: University of Michigan, B.A., 1922, M.A., 1951; Columbia University, M.S., 1954
Career: Instructor in English, University of Philippines, 1923-27; Housewife, Novelist, Adapter & Abridger of books published by various publishers; Indexer
Address: 308 N.E. 17 Ave., Ft. Lauderdale, FL 33301

Writings:
Appointment in Manila	Dodd, Mead	1945
Manila Hemp	Dodd, Mead	1947
Snare for Witches	Dodd, Mead	1948
The Far Command	Ballantine	1953
Mystery of the Moving Island	Lippincott	1965
Mystery of the Jungle Airstrip	Lippincott	1967

Work in Progress: a novel, not yet titled

She says: " Writing is work that brings great rewards, but those rewards seldom include much cash. Would-be writers should be warned that they must look for a steady income, at least at the beginning, from some other source."

CHAPIN, KIM 1942-

Born: July 18, 1942; Bay City, Michigan
Parents: Wendell P. and Roberta (Cameron) Chapin
Education: Vanderbilt University, 1960-64
Career: Atlanta Journal, 1964-66; Sports Illustrated, 1966-69, Freelance, 1969-
Address: 3430 N. Lake Shore Drive, Chicago, IL 60657
Writings:

Tennis to Win (with Billie Jean		
King)	Harper & Row	*1970*
Billie Jean (with Billie Jean		
King)	Harper & Row	*1974*

CHAPUT, DONALD CHARLES 1933-

Born: December 19, 1933; Houghton County, Michigan
Parents: Arthur and Mamie-Louise (Remillard) Chaput
Married: Antoinette Young
Children: Ben and Ed
Education: Suomi College, Hancock, MI, 1953; Northland College, Ashland, WI, B.A., 1957; Michigan State University, M.A., 1958
Career: Instructor, Elgin (IL) Community College, 1964-66; Editor and research director, Michigan Historical Commission, 1966-71; Senior Curator of history, Natural History Museum, Los Angeles, 1972-present
Address: 2130 N. Craig St., Altadena, CA 91001
Writings:

Hubbell: A Copper Country		
Village	*author*	*1969*
Michigan Indians: A Way of		
Life Changes	*Hillsdale*	*1970*
The Cliff: America's First Great		
Copper Mine	*Sequioa Press*	*1971*
Francois X. Aubry: Trader, Trail-		
maker and Voyageur in the		
Southwest, 1846-1854	*Arthur H. Clark Co.*	*1975*

Work in Progress: "French Nobility at Mackinac," Mackinac Island State Park Commission, to appear in 1978

He says: "I have had a lifelong interest in the Indians and French in the greater Great Lakes region, as well as the fur trade, missions, exploration, and military affairs."

CHERWINSKI, JOSEPH 1915-

Born: December 3, 1915; Green Bay, Wisconsin
Education: Public schools of Muskegon and Lansing college and city evening courses
Career: State employee with Michigan State Library since 1941; Began as a page; now member of general reference staff; Poetry judge for numerous organizations, including Poetry Society of Texas
Address: 1207 Walsh St., Lansing, MI 48912
Writings:

| *No Blue Tommorrow* | *Kaleidography* | *1952* |

A Land of Green	Eerdman's	1960
Don Quixote With a Rake	Humphries	1964
A Breath of Snow	Branden	1969
The Staggering Man	Branden	1975

plus poems published in *The Christian Science Monitor, The New York Times, Ladies' Home Journal, Good Housekeeping, Poet Lore, The Lyric, Kansas City Star, Portland Oregonian, Denver Post, Epos, Flame, Prairie Schooner,* etc.; Poems in several anthologies, including *The Reading of Poetry,* Allyn & Bacon, 1963; *The Diamond Anthology, Poetry, Society of America,* A.S. Barnes, 1971.

Work in Progress: *Collected Poems*

He says: "Wrote a poem used on the Michigan State Highway Map in 1972 to illustrate a series of photographs of Michigan. Not signed because state law forbids.

"My position at the State Library utilizes my familiarity with poetry and general literature. Member Lansing Poetry Club, Poetry Society of Michigan, and Poetry Society of America. Editor, 1953-75, *Penninsula Poets,* organ of Poetry Society of Michigan."

Awards: Poetry prizes from *Kaleigography,* Dallas, Texas; Poetry Society of Michigan; Poetry Society of America; *North American Mentor,* Iowa; *The Lyric,* Virginia; Special citation ($100) from *The Lyric 1970,* for contributions to poetry over the years

CHESHAM, SALLIE KEELER 1917-

Born: June 28, 1917; Detroit, Michigan
Married: Col. A. Howard Chesham, a Salvation Army officer
Children: David and Julie (Mrs. Alan Kennedy)
Education: Northwestern University
Career: Salvation Army officer
Address: 24 John A. Andrew St., Jamaica Plain, MA 02130

Writings:
Born to Battle	Rand McNally	1965
Walking With the Wind	Word	1969
Today Is Yours	Word	1972
Trouble Doesn't Happen Next		
Tuesday	Word	1972

plus more than 700 feature articles, stories, booklets, brochures, poems, books, plays, pageants.

Work in Progress: *The Cobham Story* and *Peace Like A River*

She says: "I believe creativity is God. 'Ask and ye shall receive; seek and ye shall find; knock and it SHALL be opened unto you!' "

Awards: Chicago Poetry Award, 1971 for *Walking With The*

Wind; Chicago Publishers Award, 1973, for *Trouble Doesn't Happen Next Tuesday;* Meritorious service plaque: "Outstanding and dedicated service, Chicago Near North UPC" 1976

CHRISTIE, TREAVOR L. 1905-1969
Born: March 3, 1905; San Francisco, California
Father: Robert Christie
Married: Dorothy F. Christie, currently a free-lance proofreader
Children: Joyce W., now Mrs. Albert G.S. Stewart and Michael R.S. Christie
Education: Michigan State College
Career: Reporter, *The Shanghai Post, New York Herald Tribune,* Associated Press, *Newsweek* magazine; with Office of War Information during World War II; later travel editor of *The Paris Herald,* joined the Marshall Plan working on travel development, also served in Beirut for the Point IV Program

Writings:

Legacy of a Pharoah	*Lippincott*	*1966*
Recapturing America's Past	*Lippincott*	*1967*
Antiquities in Peril	*Lippincott*	*1967*
Etched in Arsenic	*Lippincott*	*1968*

plus articles in such magazines as *Saturday Review, Ford Times, Science Digest, Rudder, etc.*

Mrs. Christie says: "My husband resided in Michigan for about 10 years—from age 12 to 22."

CHRISTINA-MARIE see: UMSCHEID, CHRISTINA-MARIE

CHRYSLER, C. DONALD 1925-
Pseudonym: Don Chrysler
Born: March 10, 1925; Talmadge, Michigan
Parents: Freeman and Geraldean (Chalmers) Chrysler
Married: Merle, a housewife
Children: Donald, Arthur, William
Education: Grand Rapids School of the Bible & Music, 1949-52; Wayne State University, B.A., 1959, M.A., 1963
Career: Pastor, Coopersville Bible Church; Elementary Principal, Grandville Public Schools
Address: 2191 Melvin S.W., Wyoming, MI 49509

Writings:

On Course to the Stars	*Kregel Publications*	*1968*
The Story of the Grand River	*Grace Publications*	*1975*

Work in Progress: *This Generation,* a book on prophecy
He says: "My first experience in writing was in 1963 when I wrote *The History of the Chrysler Family 1711-1963.* Had I known at the

time, I would have entitled it *Roots* and made a fortune. In 1966 I was asked by the Grand Rapids Historical Commission to write a chapter on the Grand River for their proposed new history book. I completed the work in 1967, and it was incorporated in their book *The Story of Grand Rapids.*

"My philosophy of writing is best reflected in *On Course To The Stars,* where I took the every technical and complex world of an astronaut in the space program and made it readable and understandable to the lay reader.

"I am very much involved in my church, school and many other organziations. I consider myself very fortunate and happy in this busy life."

CIANCIOLO, PATRICIA JEAN
Born: Chicago, Illinois
Parents: Michael and Lottie Cianciolo
Education: University of Wisconsin, Milwaukee, M.A. Ed.; Ohio State University, Ph. D.; Cardinal Stritch College, Ph. B.
Career: Elementary teacher, Milwaukee, WI Public Schools; University teacher, Marquette University, Ohio State University, University of Hawaii, Michigan State University, University of Nevada, and in Overseas Graduate Education Program: London, Lakenheath, Rome, Puebla, Mexico, Japan, Okinawa, The Philippines, Indonesia
Address: 4206 Wabaningo Rd., Okemos, MI 48864

Writings:

Children's Literature-Old and New (collaborator)	National Council of Teachers of English	1964
Literary Time Line in American History (Co-author)	Doubleday	1969
Study for Educational Psychology (Co-author)	Wadsworth	1967
Toward Perfection in Learning (collaborator)	Pendell	1969
Reading Ladders for Human Relations (collaborator)	National Council of Teachers of English	1972
Authors & Illustrators of Children's Books; Writings on Their Lives and Works (Contributor)	Bowker	1972
Picture Books for Children	American Library Association	1973
Forum for Focus: Language Arts in the Elementary School (with Robert E. Emans & Martha King)	National Council of Teachers of English	1973

Laidlaw Reading Program		
(Children's literature Consul-		
tant)	River Forest, IL	1975
Illustrations in Children's Books	Brown	1970, 1976
Adventuring With Books	National Council of	
(Editor)	Teachers of English	1977

plus films, sound filmstrips, and many magazine articles

She says: "I enjoy reading and studying literature and through my teaching and writing hope to help others enjoy it too."

CLACK, ROBERT WOOD 1886-1964

Born: June 9, 1886; Clear Lake, Iowa
Parents: William Rollinson and Sarah Ada (Wood) Clack
Married: Edith Gordon
Children: Gordon, Constance, Douglas, Llywellyn, Roderick, Wayne
Education: Grinnel College, A.B. 1907; University of Chicago, M.A. 1908; University of Michigan; Peking Union Language School; Peking Union Theology Seminary
Career: Instructor, high school, 1908-10. Professor, mathematics, Chihli Provincial College, China, 1910-13. Foreign secretary of the International Committee of YMCA and founded Paotingfu YMCA, 1913; General Secretary, YMCA, Paotingfu, China, 1912-23; Executive Secretary of the International Famine Relief Committee of Central Chihli, in the Great Famine of 1920-21; Professor of mathematics and astronomy, Alma College, 1924-54; Ordained to ministry, Congregational Church, 1924; Served repeatedly as President of the Michigan Mathematical Association, and as President of the Michigan State Registrar's Association; Life membership in Poetry Society of Michigan, Secretary and Vice President for a number of years, 1930-64.

Writings:

From Bamboo Glade and Lotus		
Pool	Banner Press	1934
Celestial Symphonies: A Study		
of Chinese Music	Gordon Press	1976
Millenniums of Moonbeams: An		
Historical Anthology of		
Chinese Classical Poetry,		
3 volumes	Gordon Press	1978
The Soul of Yamato: An Histori-		
cal Anthology of Japanese		
Poetry, 2 volumes	Gordon Press	1978
The Herd Boy and the Weaver		
Maid: A Collection of Chinese		
Love Songs Translated into		
English Verse	Gordon Press	1978

Honors: Phi Beta Kappa, 1907; Versecraft Poetry Manuscript Award, for a collection of translations of Chinese poetry, 1934; Honorary degree, D. Sc., Alma College, 1952

CLARK, JAMES STANFORD 1906-
Born: June 15, 1906; Sivas, Turkey
Parents: Charles and Ina Van Lou (Clawson) Clark
Married: Irene B. Clark
Children: Douglas and Judith Joslyn
Education: Oberlin College, A.B., 1928; Harvard University, A.M.,1932
Career: High School and college training
Address: 1939 Cumberland Rd., Lansing, MI 48906

Writings:

Retreat and Return	*Carlton Press*	*1974*

He says: "This small bone of poems (mostly in meter and rhyme) is based on the theme of Lake Huron- its character and moods- written while the author was observing 'Nature' over many years when living in a cottage adjacent to Sanilac County Park.

"Retreat and Return tries to convey an idea- the fleeting escape of city man from the urban 'fold' into the relative freedom of nature, here to the Michigan shores of Lake Huron. In this lyric-descriptive poetry, I personify certain elements of the immense Lake."

CLARK, WALTER, H., JR.
Born: Pittsfield, Massachusetts
Married: Francelia Clark, a student
Children: Alison
Education: Swarthmore College, B.A., 1954; Harvard University, A.M.T., Ph. D., 1957-65
Career: Teacher, Department of English, University of Michigan
Address: 122 Chapin St., Ann Arbor, MI 48103

Writings:

19 Poems	*Little Square Review Press*	*1967*
View From Mount Paugus	*Abattoir Editions*	*1976*

Work in Progress: *Campus*

CLELAND, CHARLES E. 1936-
Born: February 2, 1936; Kane, Pennsylvania

Parents: Charles and Margaret (Mason) Cleland
Married: Nancy Nowak
Children: Elizabeth, Joshua, Elena
Education: Denison University, B.A., 1958; University of Arkansas, M.S., 1960; University of Michigan, M.A., Ph. D., 1960-64
Career: Curator of Anthropology at MSU Museum from 1964 to present; also Professor of Anthropology and Racial and Ethnic Studies
Address: The Museum, Michigan State University, East Lansing, MI 48824

Writings:

The Paleozoology and Ethnozoology of the Upper Great Lakes	Museum of Antropology, University of Michigan	1966
A Brief History of Michigan Indians	Division of Michigan, History, Mich. Dept. of State	1975
Culture Change and Continuity: Essays in Honor of James B. Griffin	Academic Press	1976

CLINE, CHARLES WILLIAM 1937-

Born: March 1, 1937; Waleska, Georgia
Parents: Paul Ardell and Mary Montarie (Pittman) Cline
Children: Jeffrey Charles Cline
Education: Reinhardt College, A.A., 1957; Cincinnati College-Conservatory of Music, 1957-58; George Peabody College, B.A., 1960; Vanderbilt University, M.A., 1963
Career: Assistant professor of English, Shorter College, Rome, GA, 1963-64; Instructor in English, West Georgia College, Carrollton, 1964-68; Instructor in English and resident poet, Kellogg Community College, Battle Creek, MI, 1969-; Manuscript procurement editor for Fiedler Co., Grand Rapids, MI
Address: 3529 Romence Rd., Kalamazoo, MI 49002

Writings:

Forty Salutes to Michigan Poets (editor)	Poetry Society of Michigan	1975
Crossing the Ohio (poems)	Golden Quill Press	1976

Work in Progress: *A Snow Journal* (second volume of poems) and a third book of poems

He says: "Experiencing the northern winter for the first time was a catalyst for my poetry writing, which started as an occasional pursuit and became serious in 1972. My creative energy still peaks during the winter months. Writing poetry is a means to balance intellect with emotion in an imaginative framework and to envelop statement through carefully selected images. A sidelight: I have combined my musical training with writing to produce a recital of poems and piano music that reflect each other; this program has been given several public performances along with the standard poetry reading."

CLINTON, D. 1946-
Born: August 29, 1946; Topeka, Kansas
Parents: John J. and Natalie (Matthews) Clinton
Married: Jacqueline Fay Clinton, a nurse researcher
Children: Melissa Elizabeth Sobin
Education: Southwest College, Winfield, KS; B.A., 1968; Wichita State University, M.A., 1972; Bowling Green State University, M.F.A., 1975
Career: Educator, through university writing classes & through the National Endowment of Arts (Poetry in the Schools Project); editor, poet, and arts administrator
Address: 1562 Jones Drive, Ann Arbor, MI 48105

Writings:

The Conquistador DOG Tests	*New Rivers Press*	*1976*
Inca Memoirs	*New Rivers Press*	*1978*

Work in Progress: A long historical "lyric novel" encircling the lives of Dona Marina and a conquistador named Hernan Cortez

He says: "I am presently being absorbed into the great Maya, Aztec, and Inca Empires and I feel it is important for someone to retell these great stories and tales which few North Americans have ever given considerable thought to. So a projected five-year project has me researching, processing into a contemporary vernacular, and re-telling these 'American' literatures. Perhaps in a few years I will cross the Rio Grande River and begin work with North American tribes, acting as a kind of 'wide translator' of their stories, but until I run out of stories to the south, I imagine to wander around Mexico, Central American and Peru for a long time. I am hoping to work as 'adapter and chronicler' at the same time."

CLOUTIER, HELEN H. see: SCHMOCK, HELEN H.

COFFEE, ARTHUR B. 1897-
Born: November 3, 1897; Saginaw County, Michigan
Parents: William and Louisa (Stanton) Coffee
Married: Leah B., a school teacher

Children: Byron, Brent, Joyce
Education: Central State University, 1926-28
Career: Reared on farm, mostly Genesee County; Army, 1st War, salesman and teacher until retirement; then author
Address: 1098 Daffodil Dr., Pontiac, MI 48054

Writings:

Grandpa Tells It Like It Was	Vantage	1971
Our Yesterdays	Independent Printing Co.	1973
Remembering	Independent Printing Co.	1975

Work in Progress: Collecting pictures of old times for possible books

He says: "Very little has been written about the 'good old days' before the 1st World War, and that is the time of my books, so that present children and those to come may read of them as written by those who lived them.

"No generation in the history of the earth has lived through as many world-shaking events as our own. None has survived as many tremendous wars. . .We have lived through it all, and survived; survived and revolutionized every phase of life. . .We began with the horse and buggy, and now are searching for the stars. . .We have survived, and still have hope that the new generation will equal or pass our own accomplishments, and avoid our mistakes."

COGGAN, BLANCHE B. 1895-

Born: 1895; cattle ranch in Colorado
Parents: Adam Frederick and Emma Viola (Moore) Brown
Married: Charles F. Coggan
Children: 3 sons; 1 daughter
Education: Majored in Music, Psychology and Education; Michigan State University, M.A.
Career: Writes articles, poems, lyrics for songs, plays and stories

Writings:

When God Quit: a story of the days after the bombs	Greenwich Book Pub.	1955
Out of the Past—Into the Future (play)	Greenwich Book Pub.	1956
The Soul Turner: a handful of stars (based on diary of pioneer bride)	(Ann Arbor)	1961
Prior Foster, Pioneer Afro-American Educator	(Lansing)	1969

contributed poetry and articles to many magazines

COHEN, SAM 1922-

Born: February 13, 1922; Detroit, Michigan
Parents: Joseph and Bella (Epstein) Cohen
Education: Wayne State University, B.A. 1949, M.A. 1954
Career: Writer, poet and playwright
Address: 19211 Tracey, Detroit, MI 48235

Writings:

Wilhelm Reich Theatrically	Self-Published	1974
Poems From the Prison of Western Civilization	Self-Published	1975
Sex and the State—and Other Essays	Self-Published	1977

Work in Progress: Thelma-And Other Short Stories

He says:"Whatever is easier
　　　Is often not breezier,
　　　Whatever secure
　　　Is often not sure,
　　　Whatever stable
　　　Is often a fable
　　　Be snug
　　　And gone is the run!
　　　Reach that knoll
　　　And lose a piece of soul!
　　　'Cause everything
　　　　　　　has
　　　　　　　　a price!"

COLLINS, ELSIE M. 1904-

Born: March 22, 1904; Ely, Minnesota
Parents: Andrew and Sophia (Dahlgren) Lehto
Married: Joseph George Collins, an expressman
Children: Kathleen Ellen
Education: Northern Michigan University, B.A., 1930; Eastern Michigan University and Wayne University, 1950s and 60s
Career: Began teaching in 1923, Aura School, L'Anse Twp., MI; Principal, Ogemaw County Normal, 1930-32; Principal, Missaukee County Normal, 1932-33; elementary 1933-35; English teacher, Romulus MI, 1943-45 and 1952-68
Address: Rt. 1, Box 100-B, Aura, MI 49906

Writings:

From Keweenaw to Abbaye	Globe Printing, Inc.	1975

She says: "The reward for having written From Keweenaw to Abbaye has been in discovering that it has stimulated ethnic pride among Finns in the Upper Peninsula. There is power in the printed word. I recommend that my readers add to their reading lists Maxine Seller's *To Seek America — A History of Ethnic Life In The U.S.* (Jerome S. Ozer, 340 Tenafly Rd., Englewood, NJ 07631). From this work they will learn that immigrants of all nationalities, even in colonial times, suffered from the prejudices of those who had preceded them to America. It is time that succeeding generations seek causes other than nationality for their feelings of inadequacy or inferiority.

"My good fortune was having healthy immigrant Finnish parents who taught their children to work and take pride in their Finnish heritage, without which they could not be patriotic and productive citizens of the U.S."

COMFORT, WILL LEVINGTON 1878-1932
Born: January 17, 1878; Kalamazoo, Michigan
Parents: Silas H. and Jane (Levington) Comfort
Married: Adith Duffie-Mulholland
Children: Jane Levington Comfort Sturtzel, Michigan author; John Duffie; Tom Tyrone
Education: Detroit Public Schools
Career: 5th U.S. Cavalry, Spanish-American War; 1898; War Correspondent-Philippines and China, *Detroit Journal, 1899; Reporter, Russia and Japan, 1904; Baseball player; Writer*

Writings:

Trooper Tales	*Street & Smith*	*1899*
Lady of Fallen Star Island	*Street & Smith*	*1902*
Routledge Rides Alone	*Lippincott*	*1910*
She Buildeth Her House	*Lippincott*	*1911*
Fate Knocks at the Door	*Lippincott*	*1912*
The Road of Living Men	*Lippincott*	*1913*
Sport of Kings	*Lippincott*	*1913*
Down Among Men	*George H. Doran*	*1913*
Fatherland	*George H. Doran*	*1914*
Midstream	*George H. Doran*	*1914*
Red Fleece	*George H. Doran*	*1915*
Lot and Company	*George H. Doran*	*1915*
The Last Ditch	*George H. Doran*	*1916*
Child and Country	*George H. Doran*	*1916*
The Hive	*George H. Doran*	*1918*
The Shielding Wing	*Small, Maynard*	*1918*
Yellow Lord	*George H. Doran*	*1919*
Son of Power	*Doubleday, Page*	*1920*
This Man's World	*Doubleday, Page*	*1921*
The Public Square	*Appleton*	*1923*
Somewhere South in Sonora	*Houghton Mifflin*	*1925*

Samadhi	*Houghton Mifflin*	*1927*
Apache	*Dutton*	*1931*
The Pilot Comes Aboard	*Dutton*	*1932*

It was said: "the romantic in Comfort was always tending to crowd out the realist, and increasingly so as he grew older."

Arnold Mulder, *Michigan History,* September, 1951

COOK, BERNADINE F. 1924-

Born: September 6, 1924; Saginaw, Michigan
Parents: Luke and Evelyn Estella (Rand) Smith
Married: George Cook, Jr. a railroad brakeman
Children: George Daniel, Joan Lousie Hylton, Marcie Ann Blair, Lise Dawn Pettyjohn, Brian Lee
Education: Bay City Central High School, 1942
Career: Writer; part-time local news correspondent, feature story writer and reporter; worked in TV sales office; did TV commercials, copy writing & proof reading in advertising agency; public information officer for Saginaw County Mental Health Services; free-lance writer
Address: 10625 E. Garrison Rd., Durand, MI 48429

Writings:

Little Fish That Got Away	*Wm. R. Scott*	*1956*
Curious Little Kitten (also in Japanese)	*Wm. R. Scott*	*1956*
Looking for Susie	*Wm. R. Scott*	*1959*

Work in Progress: "If" Little People's Press

She says: "Many people seem surprised when they learn I do not have any college education. I have many times lamented the fact that I had no opportunities for such. When speaking to youngsters, I encourage them to go to college if they can. But I also tell them their goals can still be unlimited, and even with only high school, they can be successful at their chosen fields if they work toward their dreams and learn from everything about them. My philosophy? To do what I can, as well as I can, and make no apologies for those things I can't do. To keep and use my sense of humor, and not take life too seriously, but with deep appreciation for each day."

COOK, WILLIAM WALLACE 1867-1933

Pseudonym: John Milton Edwards
Born: April 11, 1867; Marshall, Michigan
Parents: Charles Ruggles and Jane Elizabeth (Bull) Cook

Married: 1st. Anna Gertrude Slater; 2nd. Mary A. Ackley
Education: Public schools in Ottawa, Kansas; Lafayette, Indiana; and Cleveland, Ohio
Career: Court reporter; Journalist

Writings:

Diamond Dick, Jr's Call Down	Street & Smith	1896
His Friend the Enemy	Dillingham	1903
Wilby's Daw	Dodd, Mead	1904
A Quarter to Four	Dillingham	1909
The Fiction Factory	The Editor Co.	1912
Around the World in Eighty Hours	Chelsea House	1925
Plotto	Ellis Pub.	1928

"He was known as a fabricator of serials for pulp magazines . . . lived in rural grandeur on a Kalamazoo Avenue estate at town's end (Marshall). Cook was an amazing writer—he could turn out ten thousand words of clean copy a day. Once a week he would be seen in the evening, jauntily swinging his cane, on the way to the mailbox at the Michigan Central depot, there to deposit a fat envelope containing his obligatory shipment to Street and Smith. The town was quite proud of him."

Reuben W. Borough, *Michigan History,* June, 1964

COOPER, CHARLES ARTHUR 1906-1972
Born: March 17, 1906; Two Harbors, Minnesota
Parents: Charles and Alvina (Perkins) Cooper
Married: Margaret Johnson Cooper
Children: Margaret K. Dobler, Philip Charles
Education: University of Michigan, M.D., 1930
Career: Medical Doctor; practiced in the Copper Country of the Upper Peninsula of Michigan, at Painesdale, Freda, the Quincy mine above Hancock, and Stambaugh.

Writings:

We Pass This Way	Exposition Press	1950

He was a school board member for fourteen years; wrote newspaper articles; started a Kiwanis Club and wrote a monthly news bulletin; as well as being very active in Upper Peninsula medical programs.

COOPER, SYLVIA 1903-
Pseudonym: Sylvia Paul Jerman
Born: 1903; New York, New York

Parents: Lee Ashley and Virginia (Fitz Randolph) Grace
Married: John Arnold Cooper
Children: Sylvia (Mrs. H.T. Fitch), Virginia (Mrs. R.M. McFarland), Anthony, Maud Danger
Education: Radcliffe College
Career: Hearst newspapers and *Cue* magazine
Address:1660 Apple Lane, Bloomfield Hills, Michigan 48103

Writings:

Prelude to Departure	*Harper*	*1933*
Set Free	*H. Smith*	*1934*
Attention: Miss Wills (with three books written under Sylvia Paul Jerman)	*Harcourt*	*1938*
Thunder Stone	*Simon & Shuster*	*1955*
Self-Made Man	*Random House*	*1960*

COPE, DAVID EDGE 1948-
Born: January 13, 1948; Detroit, Michigan
Parents: Robert and Jean (Hamilton) Cope
Married: Susan
Children: Annie
Education: University of Michigan, A.B., 1974
Career: A series of manual labor jobs; editor of *Big Scream/NADA Press*
Address: 696 48th St., S.E., Grand Rapids, MI 49508

Writings:

The Clouds	*Free Press*	*1974*
The Stars	*NADA Press*	*1975*
Go	*NADA Press*	*1976*
A Need for Tenderness	*NADA Press*	*1977*

Work in Progress: A book of essays; a book of poems

He says: "My work is personal, to some extent auto-biographical. I am not given to explaining it via elaborate theory or esthetics. I am interested in rhythm, tonality, and an exact description of experience.

CORBETT, RUTH 1912-
Born: January 24, 1912; Northville, Michigan
Parents: Howard J. and Rhoda (Fuller) Corbett
Married: Roy Brent, an actor
Children: Jana Loi Paton
Education: Cranbrook Academy, Bloomfield Hills, MI, 1932-33; Meinzinger Foundation Art School, Detroit, 1938-39; The

Magazine Insitute, New York City, 1954-56; Famous Writer's School, Westport, CN, 1967-69

Career: 22 years in retail & national advertising accounts; Detroit studios; also copywriting; 18 years in Universal Pictures advertising & publicity; personality profiles, nostalgia articles

Address: 25681 Sun City Blvd., Sun City, CA 92381

Writings:

Daddy Danced the Charleston	A.S. Barnes	1970

Work in Progress: *Diary of a Hill-Hugger*—a woman's misadventures buying a hill house in Sherman Oaks, CA. *Some of My Best Friends are Birds*—observations after living surrounded by birds. *A Vision or a Sight?* Writing and illustrating how every woman can usually look better than she does.

She says: "Writing and art have always been complusive expressions of life as I lived and saw it. Several times I've unsuccessfully tried to stop them, but became twitchy along with an empty feeling for which there's no known antidote except to get back into the throes.

"I believe our art, in whatever form, and books should truthfully mirror life not only for us who identify with it, but clearly show future generations what those archaic oldtimers were up to way back in the 1970's. More than that—the entire 20th century!

"Perhaps some of the facts concerning *Daddy Danced the Charleston* might be interesting. I began gathering the material as early as 1922 simply because I loved to cut pictures from magazines, some of which dated back to 1915. The idea to write and illustrate a large book incorporating the material collected for many years didn't come until the 1960's. It was a labor of love and tears for six years, and although I was by then a Californian, much of the credit for 'getting the show on the road' is due *The Detroit News, The Detroit Times & The Detroit Free Press* as well as many other Michigan publications. I drew heavily on my storehouse of memories, happy and sad, of the life I had in Michigan after having lived not only in Northville, but Plymouth, Ypsilanti, Ann Arbor, Saline, Pontiac and finally Detroit. No matter where my pen is applied to paper, I'm very much a Michigan writer and artist!"

COTTON, PHEBE E. 1911-

Born: January 15, 1911; adopted Lupton, Michigan

Parents: A. Lawrence and Elizabeth (Tomlinson) Dunlap

Married: Raymond L. Cotton, a farmer

Children: Donald Cotton, Glenn Cotton, Margaret Ritenburgh, Beth Priest, & Jane Werner

Education: Marion College, Marion, IN, 1928-30; Central State

College, Mt. Pleasant, MI, Life certificate, 1931
Career: Taught 4th grade at Haslett, MI, for 3 years; Raised 5
children and has taken part in community activities
Address: Rt. 2, Box 340, Kalkaska, MI 49646

Writings:

History of Excelsior Township	Leader & Kalkaskian	1968
History of Orange Township	Leader & Kalkaskian	1971
Historical Atlas of Kalkaska County	Johnson & Clark	1974

Work in Progress: *Phebe In Wonderland,* portraying the way of
life at Lupton, MI during her "growing up" years

She says: "Doing these books has given me lots of personal
satisfaction because I have wanted this information, local people
find the books of real interest, and many of the Michigan colleges
and universities are using my books as source material in their
history departments.

"After publishing *History of Excelsior Township,* I was surprised
and happy to receive an award of merit from the Historical Society
of Michigan. This gave me incentive to do another township,
which involved researching all available old records of Orange
Township and its country schools and churches.

"I was asked to do other townships but decided this was not feasi-
ble, so instead wrote an historical atlas of the whole county. I
received excellent cooperation and help from the county register-
of-deeds and the United States Postal Records Department.
Scores of persons loaned old pictures and maps for copying. I was
able to find senior citizens with good memories and lots of time,
enabling them to fill in the plats of villages recorded in the
courthouse.

"In the three documented books there are 336 pictures, 55 maps,
several documents and dates and postmaster's names relevant to
24 post offices which have been in Kalkaska County."

Awards: Michigan Historical Society, Award of Merit, for
History of Excelsior Township

COURLANDER, HAROLD 1908-
Born: September 18, 1908; Indianapolis, Indiana
Parents: David and Tillie (Oppenheim) Courlander
Married: Emma, a housewife and painter
Children: Erika Wolfson, Michael Courlander, Susan Courlander
Education: University of Michigan, B.A. 1931; Columbia Univer-
sity; special non-credit work with the Archive of Primitive Music;
1938-40

Career: Writer; during the depression years, 1933-38, farmed with family near Romeo, Michigan; at times news analyst for the U.S. Information Agency (VOA), writer-editor for the U.N. Department of Publications, speech-writer for the U.S. Mission to the U.N., etc.

Address: 5512 Brite Dr., Bethesda, MD 20034

Writings:

Swamp Mud	Blue Ox Press	1936
Home to Langford County	Blue Ox Press	1938
Haiti Singing	Univ. of N. Carolina Pr.	1939
The Caballero (Novel)	Farrar and Rinehart	1940
Uncle Bouqui of Haiti	Morrow	1942
The Cow-Tail Switch and Other West African Stories (with George Herzog).	Holt	1947
The Fire on the Mountain and Other Ethiopian Stories (with Wolf Leslau)	Holt	1950
Kantchil's Lime Pit and Other Stories from Indonesia	Harcourt, Brace	1950
Ride With the Sun	Whittlesey House	1955
Terrapin's Pot of Sense	Holt	1957
The Hat-Shaking Dance and Other Ashanti Tales From Ghana	Harcourt Brace	1959
Shaping Our Times, What the United Nations is and Does	Oceana	1960
The Tiger's Whisker and Other Tales from Asia and the Pacific	Harcourt Brace	1959
On Recognizing the Human Species	One Nation Library	1960
The Drum and the Hoe, Life and Lore of the Haitian People	Univ. of Calif. Pr.	1960
The Big Old World of Richard Creeks (novel)	Chilton	1962
The King's Drum and Other African Stories	Harcourt Brace Jovanovich	1962
Negro Folk Music, U.S.A.	Columbia Univ. Pr.	1962
The Piece of Fire and Other Haitian Tales	Harcourt Brace Jovanovich	1964
Religion and Politics in Haiti. (with Remy Bastien)	Institute for Cross-Cultural Research	1966
The African (novel)	Crown	1967
Olode the Hunter	Harcourt Brace Jovanovich	1968
People of the Short Blue Corn	Harcourt Brace Jovanovich	1970
The Fourth World of the Hopis	Crown	1971

Tales of Yoruba Gods and Heroes	Crown	1973
The Son of the Leopard	Crown	1974
A Treasury of African Folklore	Crown	1975
A Treasury of Afro-American Folklore	Crown	1976
The Mesa of Flowers (novel)	Crown	1977
Big Falling Snow, the Life, Times and Recollections of a Tewa-Hopi Indian	Crown	1978

Work in Progress: The transciption and annotation of Hopi texts (traditions, explanations and recollections) recorded 1968-77 on the Hopi reservation, for publication in 1979.

He says: "I have always written only about things that greatly interest me, whether as non-fiction or fiction. I suppose my writings about Afro-Americans, Haitians, Africans, Indonesians and other people are motivated by a desire to know not what is different in the thinking and traditions of various cultures, but what is the same. To quote myself *(On Recognizing the Human Species)*:'All societies build their institutions and their way of life out of the common materials of the earth and their common human impulses. . .Between one group of people and another, regardless of their particular solutions of the problems of living, it is impossible to distinguish varying degrees of human nature. Just below the surface the manners and customs lies our common identity.' "

COURT, WESLI see: TURCO, LEWIS

CRAIG, BETH see: CARLI, AUDREY

CRATHERN, ALICE TARBELL 1894-1973
Born: 1894; Boston, Massachusettes
Education: Mount Holyoke, Western Reserve University, M.A. 1928, Ph.D. 1936; London University, 1 year
Career: Teacher, Eastern High School (Detroit); also sponsor of school paper "The Indian,"; Instructor, Western Reserve University, 1937-retirement

Writings:
In Detroit Courage Was the Fashion	Wayne State University Press	1953

Dr. Crathern retired to South Hadley, Massachusetts.

Honors: March Teacher-of-the-Month by the Detroit Teachers
Association

CRAWFORD, LINDA 1938-
Born: August 2, 1938; Detroit, Michigan
Parents: Arthur R. and Mary Elizabeth (Forshar) Crawford
Education: University of Michigan, B.A., M.A., 1961
Career: Journalist, *Chicago Tribune,* 1961-67
Address: 149 Sixth St., Greenport, NY 11944

Writings:
In a Class by Herself	Scribner's	1976
Something To Make Us Happy	Simon & Schuster	1978

CRUM, HOWARD ALVIN 1928-
Born: July 14, 1928; Mishawaka, Indiana
Parents: Earl Earnest and Eunice Eva (Crain) Crum
Married: Helen Irene (McCarthy) Crum
Children: Mary Eunice and Roger Joseph
Education: Western Michigan University, B.S., 1947; University
of Michigan, M.S., Ph. D., 1951
Career: Research Associate, Stanford University, 1951-53; Assis-
tant Professor, University of Louisville, 1953-54; Curator,
National Museum of Canada, 1954-65; Professor, University of
Michigan, 1965-present; Curator, University Herbarium, 1965-
Address: 735 Dartmoor, Ann Arbor, MI 48103

Writings:
Mosses of the Great Lakes Forest	Univ. Herbarium	1972
Mosses of the Great Lakes Forest	Univ. Herbarium	1976

Work in Progress: *Mosses of Eastern North America*
(2 volumes, to be published by Columbia University Press, 1979)

CRUSE, HAROLD WRIGHT 1919-
Born: March 8, 1919; Petersburg, Virginia
Parents: Hanson S. and Kate (Wright) Cruse
Children: Patricia Cruse Maudesly
Education: Peabody High School, Petersburg, 1937; College
courses in Historical Research Methodology
Career: U.S. Army, 1941-45; Journalist; Free-lance writer; Film
Technician; Historical Researcher; Theater Technician; Com-

munity Social Action Organizer
Address: 1904 Anderson, Ann Arbor, MI 48104

The Crisis of the Negro		
Intellectual	*Morrow*	*1967*
Rebellion or Revolution?	*Morrow*	*1968*

Work in Progress: A book on Black Politics in the Seventies

He says: "Being an aspiring writer plus university professor is a difficult chore."

"CRYSTAL GAZER" see: **CASE, LEONARD**

CULBERTSON, JOHN M. 1921-
Born: August 25, 1921; Detroit, Michigan
Parents: Glen A. and Lydia (Hawley) Culbertson
Married: Frances Mitchell, a psychologist
Children: John D., Joann D., Lyndall G., and Amy L.
Education: University of Michigan B.A., 1946, M.A., 1947, Ph. D., 1956
Career: Economist, Board of Governors of the Federal Reserve System, 1950-57; University of Wisconsin, 1957-, Professor of Economics since 1962
Address: 5305 Burnett Dr., Madison, WI 53705

Writings:

Full Employment or Stagnation?	*McGraw-Hill*	*1964*
Macroeconomic Theory and		
Stabilization Policy	*McGraw-Hill*	*1968*
Economic Development: An		
Ecological Approach	*Knopf*	*1971*
Money and Banking	*McGraw-Hill*	*1972*
		2d ed. 1976
Public Finance and Stabilization		
Policy: Essays in Honor of		
Richard A Musgrave (Editor		
with Warren Smith)	*North Holland*	*1974*

Work in Progress: *Empirical Economics and Economics and Philosophy*

CUMMINGS, JEAN 1930-
Born: April 19, 1930; Charles City, Iowa
Parents: William K. and Eathel (Gibson) Carr

Married: Dwain W. Cummings, D.O., a surgeon
Children: Bruce, Beth, Brenda
Education: Carleton College, Northfield, MN, 1948-49; University of Iowa, 1949-51; Drake University, B.A., 1953
Career: Homemaker, secretary, medical assistant. Member of Muskegon County Library Board
Address: 4211 S. Brooks Rd., Muskegon, MI 49444

Writings:

Why They Call Him Buffalo Doctor	Prentice-Hall	*1971*

Work in Progress: *Shinglebolt,* a fiction young adult novel set in Muskegon, MI during lumbering days. *Alias The Buffalo Doctor,* a sequel to the book listed above

She says: "Our family hobby of raising and tending our herd of American buffalo keeps us busy and provides constant learning experiences. My husband, children and I do research with buffalo and at present we are working on an anti-cancer vaccine for humans using buffalo. Sometimes it's very scientific and sometimes a dusty, frightening rodeo."

CURWOOD, JAMES OLIVER 1878-1927

Born: June 12, 1878; Owosso, Michigan
Parents: James Moran and Abigail (Griffen) Curwood
Married: (2nd wife) Ethel Greenwood
Children: (by 1st wife) Viola Van Lautt and Carlotta Marshall (by 2nd wife) James Oliver Curwood, Jr.
Education: University of Michigan, 1898-1900
Career: Reporter and editor, *Detroit News-Tribune;* 7 years Writer; Canadian Government (explored Hudson Bay Country) Freelance writer

Writings:

Courage of Captain Plum	*Bobbs-Merrill*	*1908*
The Wolf Hunters	*Bobbs-Merrill*	*1908*
The Gold Hunters	*Bobbs-Merrill*	*1909*
Reprinted	*Triangle*	*1944*
The Great Lakes; the Vessels that Plough Them	*Putnam*	*1909*
The Danger Trail	*Bobbs-Merrill*	*1910*
Reprinted	*Triangle*	*1944*
God's Country	*Doubleday, Page*	*1915*
Reprinted	*Triangle*	*1940*
Philip Steel of the Royal Northwest Mounted Police	*Bobbs-Merrill*	*1911*
The Honor of the Big Snows	*Bobbs-Merrill*	*1911*
Flower of the North	*Grosset & Dunlap*	*1912*

Isobel	*Grosset & Dunlap*	*1913*
Kazan	*Bobbs-Merrill*	*1914*
Reprinted	*Grosset & Dunlap*	*1941*
The Hunted Woman	*Doubleday, Page*	*1916*
Baree, son of Kazan	*Doubleday, Page*	*1917*
The Beloved Murderer	*Winthrop Press*	*1914*
The Grizzly King	*Doubleday, Page*	*1916*
The Courage of Marge O'Doone	*Doubleday, Page*	*1918*
Nomads of the North	*Doubleday, Page*	*1919*
The River's End	*Grosset & Dunlap*	*1919*
Reprinted	*Triangle*	*1946*
The Valley of Silent Men	*Grosset & Dunlap*	*1920*
Reprinted	*Grosset & Dunlap*	*1943*
Back to God's Country	*Grosset & Dunlap*	*1920*
The Flaming Forest	*Grosset & Dunlap*	*1921*
Reprinted	*Triangle*	*1946*
The Gold Snare	*Grosset & Dunlap*	*1921*
The Alaskan	*Grosset & Dunlap*	*1923*
Reprinted	*Triangle*	*1943*
The Country Beyond	*Grosset & Dunlap*	*1925*
Reprinted	*Triangle*	*1943*
A Gentleman of Courage	*Grosset & Dunlap*	*1924*
The Ancient Highway	*Cosmopolitan*	*1925*
Swift Lightning	*Grosset & Dunlap*	*1926*
The Black Hunter	*Grosset & Dunlap*	*1926*
The Glory of Living (autobiog.)	*Hodder & Stoughton*	*1928*
The Plains of Abraham	*Doubleday, Doran*	*1928*
The Croppled Lady of Peribonka	*Doubleday, Doran*	*1929*
Green Timber	*Doubleday, Doran*	*1930*
Son of the Forests	*Doubleday, Doran*	*1930*
Falkner of the Inland Seas	*Grosset & Dunlap*	*1931*
The North-Country Omnibus	*Grosset & Dunlap*	*1936*

Of Interest: "Curwood Castle" (Curwood's studio) was made a public memorial in Owosso. Located on the banks of the Shiawassee River, its architecture was Norman style.

He was a decendent of Captain Marrayat, the novelist.

He had a keen interest in conservation. He founded the first conservation movement in the State of Michigan. January 1, 1927, he was named Chairman, Game, Fish & Wildlife Committee of the Conservation Department of the State of Michigan. He was also named Head of the Izaak Walton League (an international group dedicated to natural resources conservation). He developed what he chose to call a "Creed of the Wild":

"To hunt and fish is the first great law of nature. Everything 'hunts and fishes,' from man to the weakest of the creatures and things which he destroys. It is ordained that the ashes of destruction shall give birth to life, and that in killing, if it is within the immutable bounds prescribed by nature, there is rejuvenation; but to adventure beyond those limitations, until killing becomes a lust, is to invite destruction of the balance of those laws of nature which makes existence possible.

"I believe that many generations, if not centuries, will pass before man arrives at a point where he will view all manifestations of life as so nearly a kin to his own that he will cease to slaughter for pleasure."

Curwood died at the age of 48 from a poisonous spider bite.

CUSHMAN, DAN 1909-
Born: June 9, 1909; Marion, Michigan
Parents: Sumner Davis and Rose Ann (Blaisdell) Cushman
Married: Betty Lou Loudon, an accountant
Children: Mary Lou Iverson, Robert Loudon, Stephen James, and Matthew George
Education: University of Montana, B.S. 1935
Career: Newspaper writer, prospector, geologist, chemist, radio announcer and writer, photographer, magazine writer, novelist, historian

Writings:

The Commanche John Stories	Macmillan	1952
Stay Away, Joe	Viking	1953
The Silver Mountain	Appleton Century	1957
The Old Copper Collar	Ballantine	1957
Goodbye, Old Dry	Doubleday	1959
The Grand and the Glorious	McGraw-Hill	1963
The Great North Trail	McGraw-Hill	1966
Cow Country Cook Book	Stay Away Joe Pub.	1967
Montana—The Gold Frontier	Stay Away Joe Pub.	1973
Plenty of Room and Air	Stay Away Joe Pub.	1975

Work in Progress: A novel entitled *Rusy Trons—A Rob Roy of the Plains* and a long novel of the west

He says: "My grandfather, William Wilkins Cushman, from the state of Maine, was shipwrecked 'in a terrible tempest' on the Michigan shore while on his way to Wisconsin. Undaunted he borrowed shoes and an axe and went up to Muskegon from Big Rapids and for the remainder of his life engaged in lumbering, mainly in the Middle Branch area, but toward the end in the Upper Peninsula.

"My father was born in Middle Branch, my mother nearby, both graduated from Ferris Institute, had three children, I the youngest. My father followed the boom towns, a footloose entrepreneur of cheerful establishments (all within the law), and my early years were spent in the Copper Range, the Iron Range, various lumber towns, finally in Box Elder, Montana, where the Indian lands had been thrown open for settlement, and beyond. We even got back to Michigan, to Ann Arbor, where my father was associated with 'The Orient.'

"For Michigan readers, my *The Grand and the Glorious* should be of interest, as it was the only book I ever wrote with that background. . ."

Awards: *The Grand and the Glorious* was chosen by The National Association of Independent Schools as one of the year's 10 best adult books for pre-college readers, 1963; *The Silver Mountain,* 1957 Western Writers' prize for the best historical novel of the year

DAIN, FLOYD RUSSELL 1910-
Born: November 20, 1910; Hamburg, New York
Parents: Burton Roy and Effie Alzada (Wolfe) Dain
Married: Carolyn (Slaby) Dain, Housewife
Children: Kathleen Ann
Education: Wayne State University, A.B. 1934; Wayne State University, M.A. 1943; University of Michigan, Graduate Work— 1960's
Career: Teacher, Detroit Public Schools, 1937-66; Special Instructor, Wayne State University, 1950-66; Professor, History Dept., Central Michigan University, 1966-present; Freelance writer
Address: 565 Hiawatha Drive, Mt. Pleasant, MI 48858
Writings:

Detroit and the Westward Movement	Wayne University Press	1951
Detroit: The Story of Water Transportation	Wayne University Press	1951
Every House a Frontier	Wayne Univeristy Press	1956
Education in the Wilderness	Michigan Historical Com.	1968
A Silver Spire (co-author)	Enterprise Printers	1971

Work in Progress: Sequel to *Every House a Frontier,* tentatively entitled, *On, On To Michigania*

He says: "I enjoy teaching and writing Michigan history. I believe that a person is especially fortunate to be able to tie an avocation to vocation. Over the years, I have probably promoted Michigan by means of the classroom to approximately 15,000 students. This is my 41st year of teaching—and I hope to do several more."

DALRYMPLE, DOROTHY 1910-
Born: December 13, 1910; Kalamazoo, Michigan
Parents: Charles and Lottie (Wilson) Carroll
Married: Loren Dalrymple, grocery store owner and farmer
Education: Otsego High School, '28
Career: Office work; Managed husband's grocery store, 25 years;
Freelance writer
Address: 808 Riverview, Plainwell, MI 49080

Writings:
As It Was in Otsego   Minit Man Printer, Otsego   1976
Work In Progress: The Kalamazoo River: Its Assets and Liabilities

She says: "Did much local history research with old newspapers.
Assembled my book to tie in with Otsego Bicentennial Committee
projects. Collected or copied all available pictures and old post
cards, and invited a friend, Archie Nevins, to add some of his personal experiences in Otsego during the 1910-20 era. My book is a
detailed chronological history of Otsego beginning with the first
settler in 1831. I am still interested in local history and still doing
research."

DANNER, MARGARET ESSE 1915-
Born: 1915; Chicago, Illinois
Parents: Caleb and Namoi Danner
Married: Otto Cummingham
Children: Namoi Washington
Education: Chicago YMCA, 1943; Roosevelt College, 1944;
Northwestern University, 1945; Loyola University, 1946
Career: Staff Member, Art Center, Chicago, Illinois; Assistant
Editor, Poetry Magazine, 1956; Poet-in-Residence, Wayne State
University, 1959-60; Founder & Director, Boone House Cultural
Center, Detroit; Virginia Union University, 1968-72; Poet-in-
Residence, LeMoyne-Owen College, 1972-76
Address: 626 E. 102nd Place, Chicago, Il 60628

Writings:
To Flower   Hemphill   1963
Poem Counterpoem (co-
authored)   Broadside   1966
Impressions of African Art   Broadside   1968
Iron Lace   Poets Press   1970
The Down of the Thistle   Country Beautiful   1976
Poems in many periodicals, including:
Chicago Magazine
Negro Digest
Negro History Bulletin
Negro Story

Poetry Magazine
Quicksilver
Talisman
Voices
Poems in anthologies:

Beyond the Blues	ed. Rosey E. Pool	1962
Black Poetry	ed. Dudley Randall	1969
For Malcom	eds. Dudley Randall and	
	Margaret G. Burroughs	1967
To Gwen With Love	eds. Patricia L. Brown, Don L.	
	Lee, Francis Ward	1971
The Black Poets	ed. Dudley Randall	1971
Afro-American Poetry	ed. Bernard W. Bell	1972
Black Writers of America	eds. Richard Barksaale and	
	Kenneth Kinnamon	1972
The Poetry of Black America	Harper & Row	1973
Understanding the New Black		
Poetry	Morrow	1973
Broadsides: Broadside #22	Broadside	1968

Miss Danner has read her poetry in colleges and universities through the United States, England, France, and West Africa.

She says: ''I believe that creativity is one of the gifts from the force for Good. Attempting to develop my individual expression of this force is my activity.''

Awards: John Hay Whitney Fellowship; American Writers Award; Harriett Tubman Award; Native Chicagoan Literary Award; American Society for African Culture Fellowship; Midwestern Writers Award

DARING, HOPE see: JOHNSON, ANNA

DAVEY, JOHN see: RICHEY, DAVID JOHN

DAVIS, VERNE (THEODORE) 1889-1973
Born: August 14, 1889; Michigan
Parents: Theodore Thornton and Mary (De Frienne) Davis
Married: Minnie Kathrine (Bara) Davis
Children: Phyllis Eileen (Davis) Briody
Education: University of Valparaiso, 1908-10; International Correspondence School

Career: Supt. of Construction, U.S. Bureau of Reclamation, 1916-25; Texas Power and Light, 1925-31; and with various private firms, the last with Vinnell Co., Calif., 1958-60; Writer

Writings:

The Time of the Wolves	Morrow	1962
The Gobbler Called	Morrow	1963
The Runaway Cattle	Morrow	1965
The Devil Cat Screamed	Morrow	1966
The Orphan of the Tundra	Weybright & Talley	1968

Mr. Davis was born in the Michigan lumber woods. He taught school and worked in other fields before entering the construction business. He was a wonderful nature lover, and could distinguish all the song birds that came to his vicinity. He once stated that he read everything he could find pertaining to birds and animals.

DE ANGELI, MARGUERITE 1889-

Born: March 14, 1889; Lapeer, Michigan
Parents: Shadrach George and Ruby (Tuttle) Lofft
Married: John Dailey de Angeli
Children: John, Arthur, Harry E., Nina, and Maurice Bower
Education: Public Schools, Lapeer, Michigan, and Philadelphia, PA
Career: Concert and Church soloist, 1906-20's; Illustrator of Articles for *Country Gentlemen;* Writer and Illustrator of books, 1935-

Writings:

Ted and Nina Go to the Grocery Store	Doubleday	1935
Ted and Nina Have a Happy Rainy Day	Doubleday	1936
Henner's Lydia	Doubleday	1936
Petite Suzanne	Doubleday	1937
Skippack School	Doubleday	1938
A Summer Day with Ted and Nina	Doubleday	1940
Thee, Hannah!	Doubleday	1940
Elin's Amerika	Doubleday	1941
Copper-Toed Boots	Doubleday	1943
Yonie Wondernose	Doubleday	1944
Turkey for Christmas	Westminster	1944
Bright April	Doubleday	1946
Jared's Island	Doubleday	1947
The Door in the Wall	Doubleday	1949
Just Like David	Doubleday	1951
Marguerite de Angeli's Book of		

Nursery and Mother Goose		
Rhymes	Doubleday	1954
Black Fox of Lorne	Doubleday	1956
The Old Testament	Doubleday	1960
Marguerite de Angeli's Favorite		
Hymns	Doubleday	1963
The Goose Girl	Doubleday	1964
The Old Testament	Doubleday	1967
Better at the Old Price: The		
Autobiography of Marguerite		
de Angeli	Doubleday	1971

Marguerite de Angeli's childhood interests: drawing, painting, writing, singing, carried over into her adult life. Her love of family life also found its way into her books. Her pictures and books depict the happy, pious, gentle features of her character. Many of her books are of minority groups and foreign born, and show a child working to attain some degree of maturity set by the parents.

Awards: Junior Literary Guild Selection for *Bright April*, 1946; John Newbery Award for *The Door in the Wall*, 1950; Distinguished Daughter of Pennsylvania, 1958

DE FLUENT, AMELIE see: GALLUP, LUCY

DE JONG, MEINDERT 1906-
Born: March 4, 1906; Wierum, Friesland, Netherlands
Parents: Raymond and Jenny (DeJong) DeJong
Married: Beatrice (DeClaire) DeJong, homemaker
Children: five step-children
Education: Calvin College, A.B. 1928; University of Chicago, studies
Career: Writer
Address: 504 Lake Drive, Allegan, MI 49010

Writings:
The Big Goose and the Little		
White Duck	Harper & Row	1938
	new edition	1963
Dirk's Dog Bello	Harper & Row	1939
The Cat That Walked a Week	Harper & Row	1943
Good Luck Duck	Harper & Row	1950
The Tower By the Sea	Harper & Row	1950
Smoke Above the Lane	Harper & Row	1951
Hurry Home, Candy	Harper & Row	1953
Shadrach	Harper & Row	1953

The Wheel on the School	Harper & Row	1954
The Little Cow and the Turtle	Harper & Row	1955
The House of Sixty Fathers	Harper & Row	1956
Along Came a Dog	Harper & Row	1958
The Mighty Ones: Great Men and Women of Early Bible Days	Harper & Row	1959
The Last Little Cat	Harper & Row	1961
Nobody Plays with a Cabbage	Harper & Row	1962
The Singing Hill	Harper & Row	1962
Far Out the Long Canal	Harper & Row	1964
Puppy Summer	Harper & Row	1966
Journey from Peppermint Street	Harper & Row	1968
A Horse Came Running	Macmillan	1970
The Easter Cat	Macmillan	1971
The Almost All-White Rabbity Cat	Macmillan	1972

He says: "The separate world of the child is a brief world because it is a world of wonder. Come into an afternoon of a child and into the simple wonder of the curl of smoke out of a chimney, or the agony of seeing a crippled bird wing-dragging across a lawn, or the loveliness seen in the curl of a sleeping cat that needs to be cradled in small arms and held tight. Or if that is too pleasant, the eternity of twenty minutes of a child's life as he waits before a closed door, desolate, alone and bereft.

"What separates this world from the adult world is wonder. But where does wonder go? In a few brief years it is stultified into adulthood. Few seem to realize that it is precisely that wonder and that intensity of sensation (which are lost in adult stultification) that the child must draw on in order to grow and gain acceptance, assurance and security.

"Certainly, in terms of adult experience, the child's world and the world of children's literature are limited worlds. But it is in that very limitation that the writer for children finds his joy and his challenge and his untrammeled creativity. Braque said it right for painting; I say it after him for children's literature: 'Limitation of means determines style, engenders form and new form, and give impulse to creativity.' "

Awards: Aurianne Award, 1953; Child Study Award, 1953; Newbery Award, 1954 (American Library Association); Deutcher Jugendbuchpreis, 1957; Deutcher Judgendbuchpreis, 1959; Hans Christian Anderson Medal, 1962 (first American to win); Regina Medal Award, 1972 (Catholic Library Association); Calvin College Distinguished Alumni Award, 1975

DeJong books have been translated into 20 foreign languages.

DE KRUIF, PAUL HENRY 1890-1971

Born: March 2, 1890; Zeeland, Michigan
Parents: Hendrik and Hendrika J. (Kremer) de Kruif
Married: Eleanor (Lappage) de Kruif
Children: Hendrik and David
Education: University of Michigan, B.S. 1912; University of Michigan, Ph.D. 1916
Career: Assistant Professor, University of Michigan, 1916-17; Researcher, Pasteur Institute, Paris, 1918; Associate in pathology, Rockefeller Institute, N. Y., 1920-22; Freelance Writer, 1922-71

Writings:

Civilization in the United States: an Inquiry by Thirty Americans (Contributor)	Harcourt	1922
Our Medicine Men	Century	1922
Microbe Hunters	Harcourt	1926
Hunger Fighters	Harcourt	1928
Seven Iron Men	Harcourt	1929
Men Against Death	Harcourt	1932
Yellow Jack (with Sidney Howard)	Harcourt	1933
Why Keep Them Alive? (with wife Rhea de Kruif)	Harcourt	1936
Toward A Healthy America	Public Affairs Committee	1939
Activities of the National Foundation for Infantile Paralysis in the Field of Virus Research	Nat'l Foundation	1939
Health is Wealth	Harcourt	1940
Kaiser Wakes the Doctors	Harcourt	1943
The Male Hormone	Harcourt	1945
Life Among the Doctors (with Rhea de Kruif)	Harcourt	1949
A Man Against Insanity	Harcourt	1957
The Sweeping Wind, a Memoir	Harcourt	1962

Collaborator on medical background for *Arrowsmith,* by Sinclair Lewis

Regular contributor to Curtis Publishing Co. magazines, including *Country Gentlemen, Ladies' Home Journal,* 1925-71; *Reader's Digest,* contributing editor, 1940-1971; contributor to other magazines.

Dr. de Kruif was former consultant to Chicago Board of Health, Michigan State Health Department.

The Microbe Hunters and *The Hunger Fighters* both were best sellers; the former being printed in 18 languages. *Yellow Jack* was made into a motion picture by MGM, 1938 and produced on radio by the Theatre Guild, 1946; *Fight For Life* was made by Columbia, 1940; "Dr. Ehrlich's Magic Bullet," based on *The Microbe Hunters,* was filmed by Warner Bros., 1940.

DELP, MICHAEL 1948-
Born: December 21, 1948; Greenville, Michigan
Parents: William and Frances (Kipp) Delp
Education: Alma College, B.A. 1971; Western Michigan University, 1975; Central Michigan University, 1976
Career: Alternative Education Teacher; Teacher, Grayling High School (Mich.), 1971-present; Freelance writer
Address: P.O. Box 167, Grayling, MI 49738

Writings:

A Dream of the Resurrection	*Cold Mountain Press*	*1976*
The Third Coast: An Anthology		
of Contemporary Michigan	*Wayne State*	
Poetry (Selected poems)	*University Press*	*1976*

Poems in various "little" magazines.

Work in Progress: *River: Lines from the Journal of a Michigan Winter; The Notebooks of Alva Stoner* (prose poem novel)

He says: "My writing draws its energy from the physical and spiritual environment of Michigan. I try to be aware that writing is more than a physical process, and is really the process of looking for and surprising yourself.

"To me writing is a conscious disordering of the senses, a fever, something you do because you have to."

Mr. Delp has been associate editor of *Skywriting Magazine* and is presently working on the Michigan Creative Writing Project.

DETZER, KARL 1891-
Pseudonym: Michel Costello, Wm. Henderson, Leland Woods
Born: September 4, 1891; Fort Wayne, Indiana
Parents: August and Laura (Goshorn) Detzer
Married: Clarice (Nissley) Detzer, writer
Children: Karl, Jr. and Mary Jane (Detzer) Moench
Education: Fort Wayne High School
Career: Ft. Wayne, Indiana, Reporter, 1909-16; Indiana National Guard, Mexico Border, 1916-17; Capt., Infantry, U.S. Army, WW I; Amer. Div. of Criminal Invest., 1919-20; Advertising Writer, Chicago, 1920-23; Screenplay writer, director, Hollywood, 1934-36; Colonel, U.S. Army, General Staff Corps, 1944-

46; Roving Editor, *Readers' Digest,* 1937-76
Address: 617 N. Lake, Leland, MI 49654

Writings:

True Tales, DCI	*Bobbs Merrill*	*1925*
The Marked Man	*Bobbs Merrill*	*1927*
The Broken Three	*Bobbs Merrill*	*1929*
Pirate of the Pine Lands	*Bobbs Merrill*	*1929*
Contrabands	*Bobbs Merrill*	*1936*
Carl Sandburg, Study in		
Personality	*Harcourt Brace*	*1941*
The Mightiest Army	*Readers' Digest*	*1945*
Army Reader (Editor)	*Bobbs Merrill*	*1945*
Culture Under Canvas	*Hastings House*	*1958*
Myself When Young	*Funk & Wagnalls*	*1968*

Many anthologies; 145 articles for *Readers' Digest;* many short stories for popular magazines.

Work in Progress: Full length book.

Mr. Detzer was Publisher, *Weekly Leelanau Enterprise-Tribune,* 1947-51; Special Adviser, Military Government, Berlin, Germany, 1948; Member, Michigan State Corrections Council, 1948-49; Chairman, Michigan Citizens Committee for Reorganization of State Government, 1950-51; President, Leland (Mich.) Harbor Corp., 1963-70; and is now retired on a life pension from *Readers' Digest,* 1976.

His screenplay, *Car 99,* was based on the Michigan State Police.

Awards: Honorary member, International Association of City Managers; Honorary member, Michigan State Police

DE VIEW, LUCILLE 1920-
Born: December 9, 1920; Detroit, Michigan
Parents: John and Viola (Jonske) Starkey
Children: Hardy de View and Robin Pappas
Education: Wayne State University, 1938-41
Career: Newspaper writer-editor; Advertising & Public Relations
  Agency owner; Staff Writer, *Detroit News;* Freelance writer
Address: 2165 Burns, Detroit, MI 48214

Writings:

Up North: A Contemporary		
Woman's Walden	*Indian Village Press*	*1977*

Work in Progress: Novel, poetry

She says: "As a journalist and columnist my specialties are feminist issues and the family. I believe in problem-solving journalism which sheds light on human dilemmas and needs and offers soltuions and hope. As a creative writer of poems and fiction, I probe for universal truths about the human condition and say in story or verse what often cannot be said in the confines of a news feature story."

DE VRIES, CARROW 1906-

Born: July 6, 1906; Oveisel, Michigan
Parents: Igar R. and Maggie (Hoeksema) De Vries
Married: Billie (Schulz) De Vries
Children: Carrol De Vries
Education: Holland High School, graduated 1923; University of Michigan, 1924-25
Career: House painter, Bank Boy; Grunter; Michigan State Policeman; Steel Mill Guard; Chief of Plant Protection; Farmer; Writer
Address: R.R. 3, A-4695 142 Ave., Holland, MI 49423

Writings:

Passing Butterflies	S. Nishiguchi Art Pubs.	1967
Moment of Flower and Leaf	S. Nishiguchi Art Pubs.	1967
Hawthorn	Prairie Press	1967
An Alphabet Book of Haiku & Tanka	Cartwright's Old Time Printshop	1973
100 Haiku	Cartwright's Old Time Printshop	1976

Work in Progress: *Conversational Pieces* (collection of poems)

He says: "I teach for free in many of the schools in Holland, Michigan, including the High School both American Poetry and Haiku and Tanka; also in many of the surrounding schools. I attended the Sherwood Anderson Centenary at Michigan State University where I read a poem about him."

In August, 1977, Mr. De Vries was interviewed for an hour. The resulting tape is now in the Center for Midwestern Literature, Michigan State University, and is called: *An Oral History of Sherwood Anderson.*

DEWEY, THELMA (ABBOTT) 1908-

Born: July 21, 1908; Williamston, Michigan
Parents: Guy and Jessie (Jeffres) Abbott
Children: Miriam
Education: Michigan State Normal, 1928; Michigan State University, B.A. 1933; Western Michigan University
Career: Teacher, Jr. High, Holt, Michigan, 3 years; Clerical work,

State & Federal Offices, 15 years; Librarian, Jr. High, Lansing, Michigan, 12 years
Address: 1626 Alpha, Lansing, MI 48917
Writings:

Coffers of My Heart	Self	*1953*

Number of freelance articles in *The State Journal* and *Michigan Christian Advocate.*

DILES, DAVID L. 1931-
Born: October 14, 1931; Middleport, Ohio
Parents: Lisle D. and Lucille (Bowman) Diles
Children: Beverly and David Lisle
Education: Ohio University, A.A. 1951
Career: News-Sports writer, 1946-51; Correspondent, Associated Press, 1950-61; Sports Director, WXYZ-TV & Radio, 1961-72; Radio commentary, WJR Radio, 1973-74, WDEE Radio, 1975-78; Sports commen tator, WCAR Radio, 1978-present; Commentator, ABC-TV Sports (Wide World of Sports), 1962-present
Address: 29510 Kings Pointe Court, Farmington Hills, MI 48018

Writings:

Duffy	Doubleday	*1974*
Nobody's Perfect	Dial Press	*1975*
Twelfth Man in the Huddle	Word	*1976*
Archie	Doubleday	*1977*

Work in Progress: *Dr. Feelgood,* the curious life and times of Dr. Max Jacobson, New York physician, whose license was revoked for giving amphetamines to patients.

He says: "I'd rather write one book that sold 10,000 copies than do one television show watched by 50 million viewers. As for other personal comments, I leave those pretty much to others—my own view of myself is admittedly full of prejudice, but I'm not as good nor as nice as the public relations people would have you believe, nor as bad nor incompetent as my detractors might think."

DIVINE, FLOY (SHERMAN) 1881-
Born: January 11, 1881; Grand Ledge, Michigan
Parents: Warren and Mary (Guilford) Sherman
Married: Leroy C. Divine, farmer
Children: Marjorie, Haldon, Arthur L., LaCorda M.
Education: Grand Ledge High School, 1900; Michigan State University, 6 years Home Economics Extension

Career: Real Estate sales, 20 years
Address: 7460 Parkstone Lane, Birmingham, MI 48010

Writings:

The Things I Love	*Review and Herald Publishing Assoc.*	*1974*

She says: "Music was my first love. I played and taught piano, and composed several songs.

"My first poems were published at age fifteen, by Grand Ledge, County and State newspapers. I did not begin a serious study of poetry until, as a widow, I had moved to Lansing, and there joined the Lansing Poetry Club; where the friendly criticism was most helpful.

"I do believe that 'love is the heart of every Christian grace'—as I said in my poem 'Charity'."

DONER, MARY FRANCES 1893-

Born: July 29, 1893; Port Huron, Michigan
Parents: James and Mary Jane (O'Rourke) Doner
Education: Western High School, Detroit; St. Clair High School, Mich., graduate 1911; Studied music at Cathedral Conservatory, Detroit; St. Andrew's Fifth Avenue Church, N.Y.; City College of the City University of New York; and York University; Studied journalism at Columbia University
Career: Staff writer, Dell publishing Co., 1924-32; Music reporter, *Herald-Traveller,* Boston; Magazine writer and novelist; Teacher of creative writing, Boston Center for Adult Education, 1943-45; and Ludington, Michigan, West Shore Community College, 1972-
Address: 210 N. Lewis St., Ludington, MI 49431

Writings:

The Dancer in The Shadow	*Chelsea House*	*1930*
The Dark Garden	*Chelsea House*	*1930*
The Lonely Heart	*Chelsea House*	*1930*
Fool's Heaven	*Chelsea House*	*1932*
Broken Melody	*Chelsea House*	*1932*
Forever More	*Chelsea House*	*1934*
Let's Burn our Bridges	*Alfred H. King*	*1935*
Child of Conflict	*Chelsea House*	*1936*
Gallant Traitor	*Penn Publishing*	*1938*
Some Fell Among the Thorns	*Penn Publishing*	*1939*
The Doctor's Party	*Penn Publishing*	*1940*
Chalice	*Penn Publishing*	*1940*
Not By Bread Alone	*Doubleday, Doran*	*1941*
Glass Mountain	*Doubleday*	*1942*

O Distant Star!	*Doubleday*	*1944*
Blue River	*Doubleday*	*1946*
Ravenswood	*Doubleday*	*1948*
Cloud of Arrows	*Doubleday*	*1950*
The Host Rock	*Doubleday*	*1952*
The Salvager	*Ross & Haines*	*1958*
The Shores of Home	*Bouregy*	*1961*
While the River Flows	*Bouregy*	*1962*
The Wind and the Fog	*Bouregy*	*1963*
Cleavenger vs. Castle: A Case of Breach of Promise and Seduction	*Dorrance*	*1968*
Return a Stranger	*Bouregy*	*1970*
Thine Is the Power	*Bouregy*	*1972*
Not By Appointment	*Bouregy*	*1973*
The Darker Star	*Bouregy*	*1974*
Pere Marquette: Soldier of the Cross (booklet for Pere Marquette Society)		*1969*

Contributor of nearly 300 short stories and novelettes to pulp magazines in earlier years; later contributor to *Toronto Daily Star* and other Canadian newspapers, and to periodicals, including *Woman's Home Companion, Woman Today, Charm, Modern Priscilla, Chatelaine.*

Work in Progress: A documentary for Albion College.

Ms. Doner's books generally are based in the Great Lakes area; a number of them have been transcribed into braille, and *The Host Rock* was broadcast as a radio serial by American Broadcasting Co. The Librairie Hachette in Paris, France, featured *The Wind and The Fog.* Her books are listed in *The Royal Blue Book,* London, England (1968). She is listed in *The Authors' and Writers' Who's Who* (Burke's Peerage, England); and in six of Marquis' *Who's Who* (1960-1975).

DOUGLAS, LLOYD CASSEL 1877-1951
Born: August 27, 1877; Columbia City, Indiana
Parents: Rev. Alexander Jackson and Sarah Jane (Cassel) Douglas
Married: Bessie I. (Porch) Douglas
Children: Bessie I. and Virginia Vorys
Education: Wittenberg College, Ohio, B.A. 1900, M.A. 1903; Hamma Divinity School, B.D. 1903; Fargo College, N. Dak., D.D. 1920
Career: Minister, 1903-33; Writer and Lecturer
Writings:

An Affair of the Heart	Summit	1922
Magnificent Obsession	Houghton Mifflin	1929
Forgive Us Our Trespasses	Houghton Mifflin	1932
Precious Jeopardy: A Christmas Story	Houghton Mifflin	1933
Green Light	Houghton Mifflin	1935
White Banners	Houghton Mifflin	1936
Home For Christmas	Houghton Mifflin	1937
Disputed Passage	Houghton Mifflin	1939
Doctor Hudson's Secret Journal	Houghton Mifflin	1939
Invitation to Live	Houghton Mifflin	1940
The Robe	Houghton Mifflin	1942
Time to Remember	Houghton Mifflin	1951

Rev. Douglas spent 30 years in the ministry, after which he retired to devote full-time to writing.

Magnificent Obsession was made into a motion picture twice, in 1935 and in 1954. *The Robe* was made into a motion picture in 1953.

During his ministry, Rev. Douglas was pastor of the Congregational Church in Ann Arbor, Michigan, for several years.

DOWDY, HOMER E. 1922-

Born: July 16, 1922; Flint, Michigan
Parents: Homer G. and Gladys (Russell) Dowdy
Married: Nancy (Showalter) Dowdy
Children: Margaret, Rebecca, Barbara, David, Jennifer, Susan
Education: Wheaton College, A.B. 1947
Career: Newspaper reporter and editor; Freelance writer; Foundation vice president, Mott Foundation
Address: 3021 Westwood Parkway, Flint, MI 48503

Writings:

Building a Christian Home (Co-authored with Henry Brandt)	Victor Books	1961
Christ's Witchdoctor	Harper & Row	1963
The Bamboo Cross	Harper & Row	1964
Out of the Jaws of the Lion	Harper & Row	1965
Christians Have Troubles, Too (Co-authored with Henry Brandt)	Revell & Co.	1968

He says: "My books have tried to portray the excitement—yet tranquility—of God's working in the lives of people, whether in the Amazon, Vietnam, Congo, or America."

DRAKE, ALBERT DEE 1935-

Born: March 26, 1935; Portland, Oregon
Parents: Albert Howard and Hildah Leone (Lotten) Drake
Married: Barbara Ann Drake, writer/teacher
Children: Moss Christopher, Monica Durrell, Barbara Ellen
Education: Portland State College; University of Oregon, B.A. 1962; University of Oregon, M.F.A. 1966
Career: Research Assistant, Oregon Research Institute, 1964; Research Assistant, English Dept., University of Oregon, 1965; Teaching Assistant, English Dept., University of Oregon, 1965-66; Assistant Professor, English Dept., Michigan State University, 1966-70, Associate Professor, 1970-; Freelance writer
Address: 1790 Grand River, Okemos, MI 48864

Writings:

Michigan Signatures (Editor)	Quixote Press	1969
3 Northwest Poets	Quixote Press	1970
The Postcard Mysteries & Other Stories	Red Cedar Press	1976
Tillamook Burn	The Fault Press	1977
In the Time of Surveys	White Ewe Press	1978

Chapbooks:

Riding Bike	Stone Press	1973
By Breathing In & Out	3 Rivers Poetry Press	1974
Returning to Oregon	The Cider Press	1975
Cheap Thrills	Peaceweed Press	1975
Roadsalt	The Bieler Press	1976

In addition, fiction, poetry and prose in more than 200 magazines, and his work is included in many anthologies.

Work in Progress: *One Summer* (novel); an untitled book of stories; a group of related poems

He says: "I'm especially interested in various kinds of short fiction—from 2 to 50 pages. I've been writing and publishing stories for 15 years, but most of these, whether traditional or experimental, average 15 pages. But a story needn't be that length any more than a TV program needs to be 27 or 54 minutes. A lot can be done in 3-4 paragraphs—a return to the parable, perhaps. On the other hand, a story of, say, 50 pages can be fun; it allows development of characters, description, related themes, etc. Too long for magazine editors, too short for book publishers, it is a 'pure' form and I find myself liberated while working within its bountiful latitudes.

"Writing is hard work; a writer has it tougher than any tradesman, and with less monetary rewards. But I maintain writers aren't born—they emerge and develop. If someone really wants to write, and he works at it, he'll get published."

Awards: National Endowment for the Arts ($5,000) 1974; Coordinating Council of Literary Magazines grants 1972, 1975

Other Literary Involvment: Michigan Poets in the Schools; Readings/Workshops: Hope College, Olivet College, Michigan State University, Oakland University, Eastern Michigan University, etc.

Editor: *Happiness Hold Tank* (1970-present); *Stone Press* (1968-present)

DRAKE, BARBARA 1939-

Born: April 13, 1939; Abilene, Kansas
Parents: J.W. and Monica (Lorson) Robertson
Married: Albert Drake, writer/teacher
Children: Moss, Monica, Barbara
Education: University of Oregon, B.A. 1961; University of Oregon, M.F.A. 1966
Career: Teaching Assistant, English Dept., University of Oregon, 1961-62 and 1964-66; Textbook writer; Instructor, Dept. of American Thought and Language, Michigan State University, 1974-77; Assistant Professor, Dept. of American Thought and Language, Michigan State University, 1978-; Freelance writer
Address: 1790 Grand River, Okemos, MI 48864

Writings:

Concepts in Literature (Co-editor) Textbook Series	Holt, Rinehart & Winston	1969-1974
Love at the Egyptian Theatre	Red Cedar Press	1978

Chapbooks:

Narcissa Notebook	Stone Press	1973
Field Poems	Stone Press	1975

Work in Progress: Poetry—individual poems and collection.

She says: "My writing deals very much in every day subjects and the common American landscape, including freeways and shopping centers, the life of the family and the natural world as it appears to us, busy within the structures of our own human encampment; I think my poetry offers images which are quite recognizable and accessible."

DRISCOLL, JACK 1946-

Born: March 7, 1946; Holyoke, Massachusetts
Parents: John and (   ) Driscoll
Education: University of Massachusetts, M.F.A., 1972
Career: Insurance photographer; Real estate investor; Carpenter; Logger; Teacher, high school and college

Address: P.O. Box 29, Interlochen, MI 49643

Writings:

Home Grown	*Peaceweed Press*	*1972*
The Language of Bone	*Spring Valley Press*	*1978*

Poems published in several dozen magazines including *North West Review, Poetry Northwest, Chelsea, Three Rivers Poetry Journal, Kansas Quarterly, Shenandoah,* and *New York Quarterly.*

Work in Progress: *Diving Under the Ice,* book of poems

He says: "Broadly speaking, my poems deal with the impossibility of maintaining human relationships. For example, in a series of poems ("Searching for Love") two people (let's call them husband and wife) are continually visited by a third who turns out to be the force that either pushes them apart or pulls them back together. In fact, this third person may not even be a separate identity but rather a part of each of them experiencing change. Sometimes we find a reconciliation, sometimes not. If not, we find characters in reclusion sorting out their lives. If so, we find a new set of rules by which to live, at least for a little while."

DUNBAR, WILLIS FREDERICK 1902-70

Born: June 9, 1902; Hartford, Michigan
Parents: Willis H. and Nettie M. (Seabury) Dunbar
Married: Carita C. (Clark) Dunbar
Children: Patricia (Dunbar) Gregg and Robert Douglas
Education: Kalamazoo College, Michigan, B.A. 1924; University of Michigan, M.A. 1932; Univeristy of Michigan, Ph.D. 1939
Career: History Instructor and Instrumental Music Director, St. Joseph High School, 1924-28; History Professor, Kalamazoo College, 1928-43; Dean, Kalamazoo College, 1938-42; Program and Public Affairs Director, WKZO Kalamazoo and WJEF Grand Rapids, 1943-51; History Professor Western Michigan University, 1951-69; Chairman, History Dept., Western Michigan University, 1960-69; Writer

Writings:

Centennial History of Kalamazoo		
College (Co-authored)		*1933*
Michigan Through the Centuries		*1955*
Kalamazoo and How It Grew		*1959*
The Michigan Record in Higher		
Education		*1963*
A History of the Wolverine		
State	*Eerdmans*	*1965*
All Aboard! History of Railroads		
in Michigan	*Eerdmans*	*1965*
Life of Lewis Cass	*Eerdmans*	*1965*

Michigan Historical Markers
   (Editor)   *Mich. Hist. Comm.*   *1967*
How it Was in Hartford   *Eerdmans*   *1968*
Numerous articles in educational and historical journals.

Dr. Dunbar was a frequent lecturer on subjects of local, state and regional interest. He was adviser on Public Affairs to the Fetzer Broadcasting Co., with regular news commentaries and public affairs programs on WKZO, WJEF and WKOZ-TV.

In 1951 he was elected to the Kalamazoo City Commission as Vice-Mayor, and was re-elected in 1953 and again in 1955. He was also Michigan State Historical Commissioner for 20 years, and President of the Michigan Historical Society. Dr. Dunbar also was on the board and an officer of many civic organizations.

Awards: Award of Merit, American Association for State and Local History, 1960; Kalamazoo College, LL.D, 1965; Western Michigan Univ. Alumni Association's Distinguished Faculty Award, 1968

DUNNING, (ARTHUR) STEPHEN (JR.) 1924-
Born: October 31, 1924; Duluth, Minnesota
Parents: Arthur Stephenson and Juila (Hunter) Dunning
Married: Florence Jane (Danielson) Dunning, Counselor, young people
Children: Steven, Elizabeth, Julie, Sarah
Education: Carleton College, B.A. 1949; University of Minnesota, B.S. and M.A. 1951; Florida State University, Ph.D. 1959
Career: High school teacher in Minnesota, Florida, New Mexico; College teacher at Duke University, Northwestern University, and University of Michigan; Writer
Address: 517 Oswego St., Ann Arbor, MI 48104

Writings:

Courage (Co-author)	*Scholastic*	*1960*
"Reflections on a Gift of Watermelon Pickle..."and Other Modern Verse (Co-editor)	*Scott, Foresman*	*1966*
"Some Haystacks Don't Even Have Any Needle" and Other Complete Modern Poems (Co-editor)	*Scott, Foresman*	*1969*
Mad, Sad & Glad (Editor)	*Scholastic*	*1970*
Poetry (Co-author)	*Scholastic*	*1970*
Superboy/Supergirl (Co-author)	*Scholastic*	*1971*
Story (Co-author)	*Scholastic*	*1973*
Poetry II (Co-author)	*Scholastic*	*1974*
Literature for Adolescents:		

*Teaching Poems, Stories,
Novels, and Plays (Co-author)* Scott, Foresman   1975
*The Real World English Pro-
gram, 12 books, Junior High
English*   Scholastic   1978

He says: "I am new to, but deeply interested in, writing poems. A beginner, but making progress and having some luck. Poems in the past year have been accepted by twenty five 'little magazines.' "

DYE, REX J. 1899-
Born: September 12, 1899; Boyne Falls, Michigan
Parents: Jacob and Gracie (Sullivan) Dye
Married: Alice Dye
Children: Rex, Hugh, Douglas
Education: University of Michigan; I.C.S. Electrical Engineering and Commercial Art; Academy of Fine Arts, Chicago; Emerson Institute of Efficiency; LaSalle Extension Insitute of Accounting
Career: Retail Sales and Advertising; Newspaper reporter and editor; Real Estate Promotion, 1925-75
Address: 23587 Novi Rd., Northville, MI 48167

Writings:
*A Study of Market Depletion
Capitalism in a Changing World*   1974
*Lumber Camp Life in Michigan
(Co-authored with father,
Jacob Dye)*   Exposition   1975
*The Hospital/Medical Racket
and You*   Exposition   1975

Work in Progress: *Mind/Life/Energy Field Theory; 35mm and Minox Photography; Half Century of Real Estate Promotion in Metro Detroit; Economics,* a book containing my correspondence with professors of economics, economists and others.

DYER, WAYNE W. 1940-
Born: May 10, 1940; Detroit, Michigan
Parents: Melvin Lyle and Hazel (Vollick) Dyer
Married: Susan Elizabeth Dyer, teacher of the deaf
Children: Tracy Lynn
Education: Wayne State University, B.S. 1965; Wayne State University, M.S. 1966; Wayne State Univeristy, Ed. D. 1970
Career: Resource Teacher/Counselor, Pershing High School Detroit, 1965-67; Director, Guidance & Counseling, Mercy High School, Farmington, MI, 1967-71; Instructor, Wayne State Uni-

versity, 1969-71, Summer School, 1970-73; Staff Consultant, Mental Health Association of Nassau County and Nassau County Department of Drug & Alcohol Addiction, 1973-75; Assistant Professor, St. John's University, Jamaica, NY, 1971-74; Staff Consultant, Drug Information and Service Center, Board of Cooperative Educational Services, Dix Hills, NY, 1972-74; Trainer & Staff Consultant, Guidance & School Psychological Personnel, Half Hollow School District, Huntington, NY, 1973-75; Teaching Staff & Adjunct Consultant, North Shore University Hospital, Cornell University, 1974-75; Staff Consultant, Detroit Hospital Drug Treatment Program, Herman Kiefer Hospital, 1974-75; Associate Professor, St. John's University, 1974-77; Private Counseling, Therapy Practice, Huntington, NY, 1973-present

Address: The Shore Club, Tower House C, 1905 N. Altantic Blvd., Ft. Lauderdale, FA 33305

Writings:

Counseling Effectively in Groups (Co-authored with John Vriend)	Educational Technology Pubs.	1973
Counseling Techniques That Work: Applications to Individual and Group Counseling (Co-authored with John Vriend)	American Personnel and Guidance Assoc. Press	1974
Your Erroneous Zones	Funk & Wagnalls	1976
Pulling Your Own Strings	Crowell	1978

Many articles for both popular magazines and professional journals.

Work in Progess: *Raising "Erroneous Zoneless" Children*

He says: "You are the sum total of the choices you make—don't let anyone dictate your life, and recognize that you can CHOOSE to be happy, excited and alive in any life-situation, as well as choosing anger, guilt, depression or anxiety—being healthy emotionally means making the healthy choices."

Dr. Dyer has not only regularly appeared on several radio and TV shows, he has also hosted some; and has had many speaking engagements in such varried places as Vienna University. University of Hawaii, and in Acapulco, Mexico.

Awards: Distinguished Lecturer Award, College of Education, Wayne State Univ., 1978; Anthony Wayne Award, College of Education, Wayne State Univ., 1978

EAST, BEN 1898-

Born: July 18, 1898; Holly, Michigan
Parents: Darwin and Cora (Dorn) East
Married: Helen East
Children: David East and Barbara (East) Pope
Education: Holly High School, 1916
Career: Outdoor Editor of Booth Newspapers, 1926-46; Midwest Field Editor of *Outdoor Life Magazine,* 1947-66; Senior Editor of *Outdoor Life,* 1966-70; Field of *Outdoor Life,* contributing basis, 1970-present
Address: 10025 School Lot Lake Drive, Holly, MI 48442

Writings:

Narrow Escapes and Wilderness Adventures	*Outdoor Life BookDivision*	*1960*
Survival	*Outdoor Life Book Division*	*1967*
Danger	*Outdoor Life Book Division*	*1970*
The Silence of the North	*Crown Publishers*	*1972*
The Last Eagle	*Crown Publishers*	*1974*
The Ben East Hunting Book	*Outdoor Life Book Division*	*1974*
This Was the North	*Crown Publishers*	*1975*
The Bears of North America	*Outdoor Life Book Division*	*1977*

Ben East has had a distinguished career in illustrated travel and adventure lectures, 1938-51. He appeared at National Geographic Society, Maryland Academy of Science, Philadelphia Academy of Science, Philadelphia Geographic Society, Chicago Geographic Society, American Museum of Natural History, Explorers Club (of which he is a member), and George Pierrot's World Adventure Series, as well as many others. He has lectured to audiences as small as 12 in number and as large as 70,000.

EBELT, ALFRED 1904-
Born; February 28, 1904; Bay City, Michigan
Parents: Julius and Marie (Van Driessche) Ebelt
Married: Mabel (Winquist) Ebelt
Children: Alan and Alic (Ebelt) Dunn
Education: Western High School, Bay City, Mich.
Career: Inspection Supervisor, Chevrolet Motors, Bay City, 1925-45; Owner, Cabin resort, Ogemaw, 1945-56; Supervisor, Foster Twp., 1952-74; Chairman, Ogemaw Co. Board of Supervisors, 1961-74; Freelance writer
Address: 4155 Grass Lake Rd., Rt. 3, West Branch, MI 48661

Writings:

Back Through Many Doors	*Harlo Press*	*1965*
Shoulder the Sky	*Valkyrie Press*	*1975*

Work in Progress: Just writing and submitting verse to various magazines.

He says: "I am a compulsive writer, not an author by design. Inspiration for my work comes suddenly, at most anytime of the day or night. I never sit down and force myself to write, the words come easily and with a minimum of revision.

"My work is marked by alliteration, possibly influenced by Swinburne. My preferences in poetry lean toward Housman, Hardy, Yeats, and the American poet Edward Arlington Robinson. My philosphy includes both tranquility and curiosity."

EBERLY, CAROLE 1943-
Born: December 15, 1943; Detroit, Michigan
Parents: Paul and Mary (Sintay) Walaskay
Married: John Eberly
Children: Jessica
Education: Michigan State Unviersity, B.A., 1966
Career: Reporter, *Charlevoix Courier,* 1966-68; Senate Reporter, United Press International, Lansing, Mich., 1968-73; Freelance writer, *Detroit Free Press, National Enquirer,* various Michigan newspapers, 1973-present
Address: 430 N. Harrison, E. Lansing, MI 48823
Writings:

Michigan Cooking...and Other Things	*CME Publishing*	*1977*
Michigan Puzzles	*Shoestring Press*	*1978*
101 Apple Recipes	*Shoestring Press*	*1978*

Work in Progress: Career book for women, Anthology of Michigan writing, Political novel.

She says: "My only philosophy about writing is I just keep writing—day in and day out, hour after hour. I love to write. I have to write. My fingers go numb if I'm away from the typewriter more than two days at a stretch.

"I formed my own publishing companies, CME Publishing and Shoestring Press, in 1977 with an $800 loan and a lot of optimism. In 1978, the companies will make more than $20,000 in profit, which proves self-publishing can be financially—as well as emotionally and mentally—rewarding. I do everything from writing the first drafts to layout to promotion to distribution. I'm having a great time with it and have found much support for my venture and books throughout the country. I can't say enough for self-publishing—obviously."

EBNER, HANS, JR. 1944-
Born: September 20, 1944; Washington, D.C.

Parents: Hans and Margaret Marie (Care) Ebner
Marital status: Single parent
Children: David and Mark
Education: Macomb County Community College, A.G.S., 1974; Wayne State University
Career: Technical Writer, Detroit Edison, Michigan; Freelance writer
Address: 3635 Nottingham, Detroit, MI 48224

Writings:

Ten Years of Sad Rain	*Realities*	*1975*
	2nd printing	*1976*
Wordmaster	*Realities*	*1977*

Work in Progress: *Pieces of Silver*—a novel about Vietnam

He says: "I make a living from technical writing and editing. However, I've published over a hundred poems, and have had both short fiction and non-fiction printed. I've been working on *Pieces of Silver* for over four years and am now finished with it. It's a novel based on my personal experiences as a soldier in Vietnam. The soldiers who come back are still fragmented, and literature is one of the methods that we can employ to get ourselves together again.

"In 1977, I gave a 30 minute public reading of my poetry at Detroit Public Library. I would like to give more readings."

ELLIOTT, MARGARET DRAKE 1904-
Pseudonym: Ag-Kaa-Noo-Ma-Gaa-Qua
Born: August 31, 1904; Breckinridge, Michigan
Parents: Wilkie M. and Rhoda M. (Waggoner) Drake
Married: Paul Arthur Elliott (deceased), journalist
Education: Albion College, A.B. 1924; University of Michigan M.S. 1925; Michigan State University; San Jose State College, California
Career: Biology teacher, Muskegon Community Schools; Ravenna Public Schools; Reeths-Puffer Community Schools; Albion College; Bay View University; Librarian, Muskegon High School; Field Naturalist; Freelance writer; Lecturer
Address: 1530 Nelson St., Muskegon, MI 49441

Writings:

ABC of Herbs		*1950*
Christmas Again (Co-authored with husband)	*Earle Press*	*1963*
Round and Round-A Year	*Earle Press*	*1967*
Happy Thoughts (Haiku and Senryu)	*Earle Press*	*1969*
Little Things (for children)	*Earle Press*	*1970*

Phoenix Feathers	*Earle Press*	*1974*
ABC of Indian Herbs		*1974*
Poppy Petals (poems of		
Southern Calif.)	*Earle Press*	*1977*

400 poems and verses in anthologies, newspapers and magazines. 36 juvenile stores, 3 children's plays, 2 pageants. Outdoor articles for 15 Michigan newspapers, *Muskegon Chronicle* (1932-present), *Ozark Gardens* (1952-77), *Herbs Reporter* (1977-present). *The Muskegon Sportsman* (1972-present). Freelance articles in *Hobbies, Grit, Michigan Out of Doors, Prospector Michigan Christian Advocate,* etc.

Work in Progress: Collection of poems about herbs; Collection of prose articles on Michigan outdoors and/or herbs.

She says: "I never get lonesome, I have a vast amount of memories and they crowd in around me. You can't help looking back.

"I've learned that material things are not important, but my friends and faith are. I'd rather be out with the rabbits and 'possums'. My philosophy of nature includes everything with humanity. That's why all my hobbies fit into one another.

"Many poets feel the more obscure the better, but I see no point in writing if the reader does not know about what you are writing."

Margaret Eilliot has also taught classes and conducted workshops in herbs, their culture and uses; reading for fun; creative writing; the world of Haiku, and was a guest speaker at the Deep South Writers Conference, Lafayette La.

She was President of the Poetry Society of Michigan (1950-55) and is presently editorial consultant to the Society. She is the orginator and chairman of the Muskegon Poetry Appreciation Group, as well as a charter member and present Chairman of Writers, Creative Writing Group meeting regularly since 1931.

She was a student and champion of American Indians long before their plight aroused widespread interest. In honor of her interest she was adopted as a member of the Ottawa Indian Tribe, and given the name "Ag-Kaa-Noo-Ma-Gaa-Qua," which means "Friendly Teaching Lady."

ELLISON, JAMES WHITFIELD 1930-
Born: May 15, 1930; Lansing, Michigan
Parents: Chester W. and Clara (Von Weber) Ellison
Married: Debbra Lynn Ellison, a dancer
Children: Owen W.
Education: University of Michigan, B.A. 1951
Career: Senior Editor, *Psychology Today* magazine

Address: 230 Central Park West, 4-D, New York, NY 10024

Writings:

I'm Owen Harrison Harding	*Doubleday*	*1955*
The Freest Man on Earth	*Doubleday*	*1958*
Master Prim	*Little, Brown*	*1968*
Descent	*McCalls*	*1970*
The Summer After the War	*Dodd Mead*	*1972*
Proud Rachel	*Stein & Day*	*1975*

Work in Progress: Novel to be published in 1979

ELLISON, MAX 1914-

Born: March 21, 1914; Bellaire, Michigan
Parents: Roy and Margaret (Fuller) Ellison
Divorced:
Children: Edith, Margaret, John, Roy, Andrew
Education: Bellaire Public Schools
Career: Writer, Poetry Reader
Address: Box 424, Bellaire, MI 49615

Writings:

The Underbark	*Conway House*	*1969*
The Happenstance	*Conway House*	*1972*
Double Take	*Conway House*	*1973*
The Blue Bird	*Conway House*	*1977*
Poems by Max Ellison	*Conway House*	*1977*

He says: "I have read poetry—my own and that of other poets—in college, universities, and public schools in 22 states. This is my way of opening up the world of poetry to students."

EL-MESSIDI, KATHY 1946-

Born: January 23, 1946; Detroit, Michigan
Parents: Thomas Emil Groehn and Helen Margaret Schreck
Married: Dr. Adel El-Sayed Ali El-Messidi, petroleum engineer
Education: University of Michigan, B.A., 1967; Southern Oregon College, M.A., 1970; University of Oklahoma; Ph. D., 1976
Career: Reporter, copygirl, apprentice, freelance writer, public relations writer, feature program producer; Graduate teaching assistant, American History, University of Oklahoma, 1973-76; Freelance public relations and journalism, 1977; Communications Director, Bovay Engineers, Inc., 1978-
Address: 716 Lochmoor Blvd., Grosse Pointe, MI 48236

Writings:

Grosse Pointe, Michigan: Race Against Race	*Michigan State University Press*	*1972*

Work in Progres: *The Bargain* (The Development, Meaning of the 1948 GM-UAW Contract)

She says: "Michigan has great inspiration for me. My dad fostered a love of writing in me when he helped me produced my first newspaper, *The Merriweather Messenger,* on Merriweather Road, Grosse Pointe, Michigan. At eight and nine years of age I was printing "All the News That's Fun to Print" (our motto) about my neighbors. My years at Crystalaire Camp and at the University of Michigan found me writing a journal of my reflections, so I can look back on them and remember my wonderful native state wherever I go.

"My book grew from my experiences as a *Grosse Pointe News* reporter. I took the police beat when the first black family moved into the community in 1966. For my doctoral dissertation, upon which my current manuscript is based, I researched General Motors and UAW files in Detroit."

ELWART, JOAN POTTER 1927-
Born: August 27, 1927; Detroit, Michigan
Parents: J.F. Douglas and Thirza (Markham) Potter
Married: Dean J. Elwart, City Engineer, Dearborn, Michigan
Children: Elizabeth Schlaff, Marylou Potts, Dean M., Ann, Amy
Education: Marygrove College, B.A.; University of Detroit; Wayne State University
Career: Elementary school teacher, Garden City and Dearborn, Michigan; Freelance writer, researcher, lecturer and public relations person; Conducts writing workshops for Michigan colleges, secondary and elementary schools, for the Michigan Council for the Arts; Lecturer, Writers' Conference, Oakland University, Michigan
Address: 333 Fort Dearborn Avenue, Dearborn, MI 48124

Writings:

In, On, Under, Through	*Whitman Publishing*	*1965*
The Five Star General	*Whitman Publishing*	*1965*
Animals Babies	*Whitman Publishing*	*1966*
Santa's Surprise Book	*Whitman Publishing*	*1966*
Hey! Let's Go	*Whitman Publishing*	*1966*
Daisy Tells	*Steck-Vaughn Co.*	*1966*
Nina the Nurse	*Whitman Publishing*	*1967*
Right Foot, Wrong Foot	*Stech-Vaughn Co.*	*1968*
Santa's Surprise Book (reprint)	*Golden Press*	*1971*
What Hides Inside	*Rand McNally*	*1972*

Contributed one story to *The Real Book of First Short Stories,* Randy McNally, 1973. Contributed Chapter 13 to *How to Make Money From Your Sparetime by Writing,* Simon Schuster, 1971. Articles in *Parents Magazine, Catholic Digest, Writer's Digest, Detroit News Magazine,* etc.

Work in Progress: Short poetry, Childcraft; Where's the Fire?, Imperial International Learning; *Achieve Communicating,* Sandy Corporation; Biography of Horace and John Dodge, Sun Press, with Jean Madden Pitrone

She says: "Writing for me is a marvelous and necessary process in which I preserve 'important' moments in life that otherwise might be lost—and then share these moments with someone I care about—the reader.

"The 'important' moment may be the excitement of a child discovering the joys of clattering down the street in Coke-can shoes, or it may be the joy of discovering, in the memory of an elderly relative, a wonderfully dramatic scene in which three tough and powerful business tycoons wrestle for control over the million-dollar company they all have built.

"I think it is important to communicate not only ideas and themes, but some human insights. It is the writers' obligation—and pleasure—to enhance the readers' interest and joy in living. Words—in stories or poems—whether for a child or an adult, should in some way contribute to the reader's *Joie de Vivre.*"

ELWELL, STILLMAN J. 1894-1977
Born: February 3, 1894; Leonard, Michigan
Parents: Frand Minnie (Clack) Elwell
Married: Mary O. Elwell, retired reading teacher
Education: Leonard High School, 1909
Career: Farmer, Supervisor, Dryden Twp., Mich., 1963-70
Address: 5811 Hollow Corner Road, Dryden, MI 48428

Writings:

Furrows	*Self*	*1940*
Windows of Thought	*Simon & Schuster*	*1971*
These Things I Love	*Naylor Company*	*1975*

He says: "The good things in life are all around us—if only we will look for them. (As he said in one of his poems: 'I've got a million dollars, but of course it ain't in cash.')

"I began in my late twenties, just writing silly rhymes for fun, but one day I thought maybe I could write a serious poem. It's just a way of life for me, that's my enjoyment."

His wife says that his poem "Goodness in Man," sums up his philosophy: "...Look for God in man, however, And you'll hear the songbirds sing; See the glory and the beauty God has placed in everything!"

Stillman Elwell gained a reputation as an after-dinner speaker, giving homely little talks about ordinary things, like changing a tire, winding up reciting one of his poems.

EMSHWILLER, CAROL FRIES 1921-
Born: April 12, 1921; Ann Arbor, Michigan
Parents: Charles C. and Agnes (Carswell) Fries
Married: Edmund Emshwiller, independent film & video artist
Children: Eve, Sue and Peter
Education: University of Michigan, B.A., 1945 (Music) University of Michigan, B.A., 1949 (Design)
Career: MacDowell Colony; New York State Creative Artist Public Service grant; Writer, TV narrations for *Net & Narrator:* Freelance writer
Address: 43 Red Maple Dr., Wantagh, NY 11793

Writings:
Joy in Our Cause   *Harper & Row*   *1974*
also short stories published in literary and science fiction magazines.

Work in Progress: more short stories

She says: "I'm interested in experimenting with form. I like to combine 'poetic' structures and methods into the short story length. Also I'm interested in exploring feminine psychological and sexual views, sets, experiences.

"Writing and bringing up three children has been hard. Also (typical mother) I haven't had a room of my own through most of my writing career."

ERNO, RICHARD BRUCE 1923-
Born: May 11, 1923; Boyne City, Mich.
Parents: Richard Gabriel and Edith (Stafford) Erno
Married: Edith Joyce (Van Sickle) Erno
Children: Deborah, Bruce, Richard, Christopher, Joanna, Janice
Education: Michigan State University, B.A., 1950; University of Denver, M.A., 1951; University of Minnesota, Ph. D., 1953
Career: English Instructor, McCook Jr. College, 1953-55; English Instructor, George Washington Univ., 1955-57; Professor, English, Arizona State Univ., 1957-present
Address: 1107 E. Broadmor Dr., Tempe, AZ 85282

Writings:
My Old Man   *Crown Publishers*   *1955*
The Hunt   *Crown Publishers*   *1960*

The Catwalk	*Crown Publishers*	*1965*
Johnny Come Jingl-o	*Crown Publishers*	*1967*
Billy Lightfoot	*Crown Publishers*	*1969*
An Ultimate Retreat	*Crown Publishers*	*1971*

Work in Progress: *A Knife for Jennifer*

He says: "All my books are works of love—love for the characters, for those characters' struggles, and for the art required to render those people and their lives eternal and unchanging."

ETTINGER, ROBERT C.W. 1918-
Born: December 4, 1918; Altantic City, NJ
Parents: Alfred and Rhea (Chaloff) Ettinger
Married: Elaine (Mevis) Ettinger, College teacher
Children: David A. and Shelly B.
Education: University of Michigan, 1936-37; Wayne State University, B.S., 1951, M.S., 1953, M.A., 1954
Career: Teaching Physics, Highland Park College
Address: 24041 Stratford, Oak Park, MI 48237

Writings:
The Prospect of Immortality	*Doubleday*	*1964*
Man Into Superman	*St. Martins Press*	*1972*
(several foreign language editions of each)		

Work in Progress: A novel and a textbook

He says: "I am the President of Cryonics Association and of Cryonics Institute. *The Prospect of Immortality* first introduced Cryonics (freeze the newly dead for storage and eventual revival, repair, and rejuvenation). About 28 have been frozen, to date. A facility is being constructed in Michigan."

FARLEY, CAROL 1936-
Pseudonym: Carol McDole
Born: December 20, 1936; Ludington, Michigan
Parents: Floyd and Thressa (Radtke) McDole
Married: Dennis Scott Farley, U.S. Army Officer
Children: Denise, Elise, Roderick Jeannette
Education: Western Michigan University, Teaching Certificate 1956; Michigan State University, Study in Communications 1968-69
Career: Writer
Address: 605 E. Melendy Street, Ludington, Michigan 49431

Writings:
Mystery of the Fogman	*Watts*	*1966*

Sergeant Finney's Family	Watts	1969
The Bunch on McKellahan		
Street	Watts	1971
The Garden is Doing Fine	Atheneum	1975
Loosen Your Ears	Atheneum	1977
Settle Your Fidgets	Atheneum	1977

Work in Progress: A book written by a young girl who has moved to Seoul, Korea with her military family. The book consists of letters she writes back to her good friend in Washington, D.C.

She says: "If one imagines that life is a bowl of cherries, then two things make up the whipped cream on the top: a good question and a good laugh. As a writer, I know I can depict the worms, stems, leaves, pits, and bugs in this imaginary concoction, but I prefer to leave those areas to others—in my work, I want to create more whipped cream.

"Although I'm well aware of the agony and misery in life, I believe that laughter and curiosity can make all things bearable. By the time I was thirteen years old, I had lost three of the people I loved most—my father, my stepbrother, and a best friend. Theirs deaths left me puzzled and wary. What value had life if it could so easily be snatched away? I spent my teen years searching for answers. I haunted churches, devoured books, and, because of a foolish idea that surely they ought to know more because they'd been around longer, I quizzed all the elderly people I could lasso.

"Gradually, I discovered two facts: nobody had any real answers to my questions, and few people had ever even considered the questions. Those people who had pondered the unknowables, however, were the ones who had the most zest for life, the ones who were, to my mind at least, the most interesting. Much to my amazement, I found, too, that they seemed to laugh the most.

"And so I write books that I hope will prod readers into thinking a little more about the how and why of life, and, by pondering, maybe get to see the humor of it too. I certainly don't have the answers, but I feel real joy comes from the quest for them. Usually I try to have elderly characters in my tales because they add the finest flavor to the whipped cream."

Awards: Franklin Watts Mystery Metal, 1966; Golden Kite from Society of Children's Book Writers, 1975; Award from Child Study Association/Wel-Met., 1975; Juvenile Award from Friends of American Writers, 1975

FENNER, CAROL 1929-
Born: September 30, 1929; Almond, New York
Parents: Andrew Jackson Fenner and Esther V. Rowe Fenner

Married: Jiles Brantley Williams, Major, USAF, ret.

Career: Freelance writer; author of children's literature; Public Relations Specialist, 1971 to the present; Copy Director for small Michigan agency, 1968-71; resided in Philippines where she taught swimming and wrote, 1965-67; Assistant to Director of Public Relations, Girls Scout National Headquarters Staff, 1964-65; Assistant Editor, *McCalls Corporaion,* 1962-64; Editorial Director, Polycor Company Inc., NYC

Address: 190 Rebecca Road, Battle Creek, MI 49015

Writings:

Tigers in the Cellar	*Harcourt, Brace*	*1963*
Christmas Tree on the Mountain	*Harcourt, Brace*	*1966*
Lagalag, the Wanderer	*Harcourt, Brace*	*1968*
Gorilla, Gorilla	*Random House*	*1973*
The Skates of Uncle Richard	*Random House*	*1978*

Work in Progress: *The Most Beautiful Horse; Flight of the Bird Kite; Tales of the Unicorn; Grama's Girl; Phyllis' Dream*

She says: "I am self taught, both as a writer and illustrator. In other words, my formal education ended when I graduated from high school in 1948. For myself, I learn better and more deeply on my own. I am strongly self directed and would not recommend discontinuing formal education to anyone who isn't. I did have formal training both as an actress (Herbert Berghof & Curt Conway in New York) and a modern dancer (New Dance Group with McKayle, Burton, Weidman, etc.) I have performed professionally on television and the stage."

Awards: *Gorilla, Gorilla* won a Christopher Award in 1974 for best science book for 1973. It was nominated for Newbery Medal, was on the ALA Notable Books for 1973 and the NSTA's Outstanding Science Trade Books for Children 1973.

FENNIMORE, KEITH J. 1917-
Born: November 20, 1917; Parma, Michigan
Parents: Frank H. and Beatrice (Robinson) Fennimore
Married: Jean Joy (Livingston) Fennimore, educator
Children: James L. and Robert K.
Education: Albion College, Michigan, A.B., 1939; University of Michigan, M.A., 1940; Michigan State University, Ph. D., 1956
Career: Director of Education, Starr Commonwealth for Boys, Mich., 1941-42; English Instructor, Kemper Jr. College, 1942-45; Instructor, University of Illinois, 1945-46; Professor of English, Albion College, 1946-78; Dean, Bay View Summer College, 1961-69
Address: 511 Perry St., Albion, Mich. 49224

Writings:

Booth Tarkington: Man and		
Novelist	*Twayne (USAS series)*	*1974*
The Heritage of Bay View	*Eerdmans*	*1975*

Work in Progress: *The Fiction of our Forefathers: The American Short Story in the 18th Century*

He says: "As my teaching career draws to a close, I find increased interest in exploring neglected areas in our national literature and regional history. One way to protect the future is to preserve the past, hence my concern for sustaining public support for matters of archival or antiquarian interest. As the Michigan story unfolds, I hope to contribute my chapters."

FITTING, JAMES E. 1939-

Born: January 18, 1939; Detroit, Michigan
Parents: Edward and Lora (Nunneley) Fitting
Married: Mary Ellen (Rein) Fitting
Children: Sean, Chris, Erik, Tim
Education: Michigan State University, B.A., 1960; University of Michigan, M.A., 1962, Ph. D., 1964
Career: Assistant Professor, University of Michigan, 1964-68; Associate Professor, Professor, Case Western Reserve Univ., 1968-72; State Archeologist of Michigan, 1972-75; Planner & Department Mgr., Commonwealth Associates, 1975-78
Address: 209 E. Washington Ave., Jackson, MI 49201

Writings:

The Archeology of Michigan: A		
Guide to the Prehistory of the		
Great Lakes Region	*Natural History Press*	*1970*
The Development of North	*Pennsylvania State*	
American Archeology	*Univ. Press*	*1973*

Work in Progress: Study of the French and Indian contact in Michigan in the 17th century.

He says: "I am a lifelong resident of Michigan and am fascinated with its past. While I have carried out anthropolocial and historical research in 22 states and three foreign countries, Michigan is the most exciting of them all."

FITZPATRICK, DOYLE C. 1908-

Born: March 9, 1908; St. Johns, Michigan
Parents: Rutherford Hayes and Jessie Mable (Irving) Fitzpatrick
Married: Phyllis Jean (Millward) Fitzpatrick

Children: Leland Chace, Colleen (Fitzpatrick) Lackey, Susan (Fitzpatrick) Alverson, Marsha (Fitzpatrick) Huston
Education: Michigan State University
Career: Owner, Sales Promotion Company; Vice President, Industrial Display Corp.; Supervisor of Art, General Motors, Olds Div.; 1942-73 (Retired)
Address: Box 84, St. James (Beaver Island), MI 49782

Writings:

The King Strang Story	National Heritage	1970

He says: "I am actively interested in American History, and have devoted years to the study of Strangite Mormon phenomena. We live at Beaver Island all year round on property once owned by 'King' Strang."

FITZSIMMONS, THOMAS 1926-
Born: October 21, 1926; Lowell, Mass.
Parents: William and Irene (Courtois)
Married: Karen (Hargreaves)
Children: Sean, Ian
Education: Fresno State College, 1947-49; Sorbonne/Institut de Science Politique, France, 1949-50; Stanford University, B.A. 1951; Columbia University, M.A., 1952
Career: Consultant, Office of Sec. of Defense, 1952; Writer/Editor, *New Republic Magazine,* 1952-55; Research Chairman, 1955-56, Director of Research, 1956-58, and Director/Editor, 1958-59, HRAF Press, Yale; Assistant Professor, American University, 1955-59; Assistant Professor, Associate Professor; Professor, Oakland Univ., 1959-present; Visiting Professor/Poet in Residence, Tokyo Univ. of Education, Keio Uni versity, and Japan Women's University, 1973-75
Address: Dept. of English, Oakland University, Rochester, MI 48063

Writings:

RSFSR	HRAF Press, Yale	1957
USSR	HRAF Press, Yale	1960
This Time, This Place	Press Zero	1969
Downinside (Co-authored)	Press Zero	1969
Morningdew	Press Zero	1970
With the Water	New Voices Press	1971
Mooning	Red Hanrahan Press	1971
Meditation Seeds	Stone Marrow Press	1971
Ghazals of Ghalib	Columbia U. Press	1971
Japanese Poetry Now	Schocken (N.Y.)	1972
Birds in Big Red Overshoes	Press Zero	1973
Playseeds	Pilot Press	1973

The Big Huge	KT Did Press	1975
The House of My Friend	KT Did Press	1976
Trip Poems	KT Did Press	1977

He says: "I like to get poetry out of books, onto the breath (voiceweaves), into space (eyeweaves). See poetry as an energizing and healing motion that can activate capacities for harmony and respect."

FORD, RICHARD CLYDE 1870-1951

Born: May 17, 1870; Calhoun Co., Michigan
Parents: Charles A. and Meranda Elizabeth (Floyd) Ford
Married: Grace A. (Gogshall) Ford
Children: Ann (Ford) Signor and Richard
Education: Albion College, B.A. 1894, Ph. M. 1897; University of Freiburg, Munich, Ph.D. 1900; University of Mont Pellier, France
Career: Teacher, Methodist Mission School, Singapore, Michigan; Superintendent, White Cloud, Mich. Schools; Dept. Head, Modern Lang., Northern Michigan Univ., 1901-03; Dept. Head, Modern Lang., Eastern Michigan Univ., 1904-40; Writer
Writings:

Scheffel as a Novelist	(Munich, Germany)	1901
Elementary German for Sight Translation	Ginn	1904
John D.Pierce, Founder of the Michigan School System (co-authored)	Scharf Tag Label & Box Co.	1905
The Conspiracy of Pontiac (a translation)		1913
The White Captive, a Tale of the Pontiac War	Rand McNally	1915
Sandy MacDonald's Farm, a Tale of the Mackinaw Fur Trade	School Services	1929
Heroes and Hero Tales of Michigan	E. M. Hale	1930
Red Man or White, A Story of Indian Life in the Northwest	Lyons & Carnahan	1931

Dr. Ford was an active member of the State Historical Board for many years and was President of the Michigan Historical Society at the time of his death.

Awards: He was made a member of the local Indian tribe.

FOX, CONNIE see: FOX, HUGH

FOX, FRANCES MARGARET 1870-1959

Born: June 23, 1870; South Farmington, Massachusetts
Parents: James and Frances S.M. (Franks) Fox
Education: Michigan Female Seminary
Career: Secretary; Writer

Writings:

Farmer Brown and the Birds	Page & Co.	1900
Betty of Old Mackinaw	Page & Co.	1901
What Gladys Saw; A Nature Story of Farm and Forest	W.A. Wilde	1902
The Little Giant's Neighbours	Page & Co.	1903
Little Lady Marjorie	Page & Co.	1904
Mother Nature's Little Ones	Page & Co.	1904
Brother Billy	Page & Co.	1905
How Christmas Came to the Mulvaneys	Page & Co.	1905
The Rainbow Bridge	W.A. Wilde	1905
The Country Christmas	Page & Co.	1907
Carlota, A Story of the San Gabriel Mission	Page & Co.	1908
Seven Christmas Candles	Page & Co.	1909
Seven Little Wise Men	Page & Co.	1910
Mary Anne's Little Indian, and Other True Stories for Children	A. Flanagan	1913
Doings of Little Bear	Rand McNally	1915
Adventures of Sonny Bear	Rand McNally	1916
The Kinderkins	Rand McNally	1918
The Adventures of Blackberry Bear	Moffat, Yard & Co.	1918
Little Bear at Work and at Play	Rand McNally	1920
Ellen Jane	Rand McNally	1924
Little Bear Stories	Rand McNally	1924
Nan's Christmas Boarder	Page & Co.	1924
Janey	Rand McNally	1925
Little Bear's Ups and Downs	Rand McNally	1925
Sister Sally	Rand McNally	1925
Angeline Goes Traveling	Rand McNally	1927
Uncle Sam's Animals	Century	1927
Little Bear's Ins and Outs	Rand McNally	1928
Nancy Davenport	Rand McNally	1928
Nannette	P.F. Volland	1929
Washington, D.C., The Nation's Capital	Rand McNally	1929
The Wilding Princess	P.F. Volland	1929
The Magic Canoe	Laidlaw Bros.	1930
Fairy Man with the Wet Potato Heart	Eldridge Entertainment	1933

Flowers and Their Travels	Bobbs Merrill	1936
Little Bear's Playtime	Rand McNally	1936
Little Toad	Viking	1938
Little Mossback Amelia	Dutton	1939
They Sailed and Sailed	Dutton (also Hale)	1940
Legend of the Christ Child	Sneed & Ward	1941
The Little Cat That Could Not Sleep	Dutton	1941
Quakers Courageous	Lothrop, Lee & Shepard	1941
True Monkey Stories	Lothrop, Lee & Shepard	1941
Gay Legends of the Saints	Sneed & Ward	1942

Most of her writing was done in Mackinaw City, Michigan. During the winter she resided in Washington, D.C., where she worked in the Library of Congress.

FOX, HUGH 1932-
Psuedonym: Connie Fox, Gabriel Tallafierro, Angele Poitiers
Born: February 13, 1932; Chicago, Illinois
Parents: Hugh and Helen (Mangan) Fox
Married: Nona Fox, writer
Children: Hugh, Cecilia, Marcella, Margaret, Alexandra
Education: Loyola University, Chicago, B.A., 1954, M.A., 1955; University of Illinois, Urbana, Ph. D., 1958
Career: Instructor Loyola University, Los Angeles, 1958-68; Fulbright Hays Fellow, University of Hermosillo, Mexico, 1961; Fulbright Hays Fellow, Instituto Pedagogico, Caracas, Venezuela, 1964-66; John Carter Brown Library Fellowship, Brown University, 1968; Pan American Union Grant; U. of Buenos Aires, Argentina, 1970; Lecturer, United States Information Service, Spain, 1976; Founding Director COSMEP (Committee of Small Magazine Editors and Publishers); Associate Professor, Dept. of American Thought and Language, Michigan State University, 1968- present
Address: 526 Forest, Lansing, MI 48823

Writings:

The Industrial Ablution (Co-author)	Ghost Dance Press	1972
Handbook Against Gorgons (Co-author)	Ghost Dance Press	1972
The Invisibles	The Smith	1976
The Gods of the Cataclysm	Harper's Magazine Press	1976
First Fire: S. American Indian Myths	Anchor Books	1978

Work in Progress: Second Coming, a novel about feminism and androgyny; The Messianic Eye, an encyclopedic look at film theory—the beginnings to the present

He says: "I used to think I was a victim of a corrupt, superficial publishing-media world that had no space/time for quality. Then I helped found COSMEP (Committee of Small Magazine Editors and Publishers) which now numbers, 1,400 press-magazine-personal members. Now I think THIS alternative, 'underground' world has become the center of artistic life in the U.S., and I feel that Madison Avenue is peripheral and hopelessly outdated."

FOX, JEAN M. (living)
Born: Norwood, Ohio
Parents: Floyd and Ruth (Edwards) McGriff
Married: Orville T. Fox, attorney (deceased)
Children: John, Joanne, Susan
Education: Indiana University, A.B., 1937, M.A., 1942
Career: Editor and publisher, *Southfield Sun,* 1958-74; Founder, editor and publisher, *Farmington Forum,* 1967- 74; Founder, editor and publisher, Novi *Sun-Forum,* 1971-74

Writings:

Windows of Old Mariners	Lone Pine Press	1976
Farmington's Centennial Families	Farmington Hills Hist. Comm.	1978

Work in Progress: Book of poetry, series of sketches on Men of Farmington

She says: "Writing which is to be read and have an impact on mankind must be of the type to chronicle or inspire man's search for his highest abilities and achievement. The average man's life is too much of a reality—in literature he should be challenged to become his best self. Modern writers of pessimism and 'reality', when it tends to degrade, will be, in the long run, as forgotten as yesterday's newspaper."

FOX-LOCKERT, LUCIA 1928-
Pseudonym: Lucia Fox
Born: March 29, 1928; Lima, Peru
Parents: Fabricio and Enriqueta (Zevallos) Ungaro
Married: Clinton Lockert, Bibliographer
Children: Hugh, Marcella, Cecilia
Education: Universidad de San Marcos, Lima, Peru, B.A., 1950; Washington University, St. Louis, Mo., M.A., 1955; University of Illinois, Ph. D., 1958
Career: Colegio Nacional de Mujeres Rosa de Sta. Maria, Lima, Peru, 1950-53; Centro Venezolano Americano, 1962-64; Univer-

sity of California, Northridge, 1966-68; Michigan State University, 1968-present

Writings:

Latin America In Evolution	*Superspace Edition*	*1974*
Mosaicos (English edition)	*Old Marble Press*	*1974*
Assemblage: Lucia Fox in		
Translations	*Superspace Edition*	*1977*

Dozen books in Spanish, and poems in several anthologies.

Work in Progress: *Women Novelists in Spain and Latin American* (tentative title)

She says: "I have a long struggle going on all the time. My Spanish, Catholic, Conservative backgroud is questioned all the time by my New Self: International, Zen Buddhist and liberal way of life. As you can see after one divorce, I am far from being the traditional woman I was. Still, my Indian identity—my country was the Incan Empire—my intellectual search and my contemplative nature make it difficult for me to adjust to any particular way of life. I search for my own. At the present I am writing a collection of poems entitled: *Legends of an Indian Princess.* In this book I am trying to clarify that what is essential and transcendental in the middle of all changes and faces of life."

FRANCK, HARRY, ALVERSON 1881-1962

Born: June 29, 1881; Munger, Michigan
Parents: Charles Adolph and Lillie E. (Wilsey) Franck
Married: Rachel Whitehill (Latta) Franck
Children: Harry Alverson Jr., Katherine Latta (Franck) Huettner, Patricia Wilsey (Franck) Sheffield, Charles William, Peter Whitehill
Education: University of Michigan, A.B., 1903; Columbia University; Harvard University; Studied abroad
Career: Teacher, Central High School, Detroit, 1903-04; World traveler, 1904-05; Teacher, Bellefonte Pa., 1906; Teacher, Browning School, New York City, 1906-08; Dept. Head, Tech High School, Springfield, Mass., 1908-11; World traveler alternating with teaching

Writings:

Three Hoboes in India	*Century*	*1910*
A Vagabond Journey Around		
the World	*Century*	*1910*
Four Months Afoot in Spain	*Century*	*1911*
Zone Policeman 88	*Century*	*1913*
Things As They Are in Panama	*T.F. Unwin*	*1913*
Tramping Through Mexico,		
Guatemala, and Honduras	*Century*	*1916*

Vagabonding Down the Andes	Century	1917
Working My Way Around the World	Century	1918
Vagabonding Through Changing Germany	Harper & Bros.	1920
Roaming Through the West Indies	Century	1920
Working North from Patagonia	Century	1921
Wandering in Northern China	Century	1923
Wandering in China	T.F.Unwin	1924
Glimpses of Japan and Formosa	Century	1924
Roaming Through Southern China	Century	1925
East of Siam	Century	1926
All About Going Abroad	Brentano's	1927
China: A Geographical Reader	F.A. Owen	1927
The Japanese Empire	F.A. Owen	1927
Mexico and Central America	F.A. Owen	1927
The Fringe of the Moslem World	Century	1928
South America	F.A. Owen	1928
I Discover Greece	Century	1929
Marco Polo, Jr.	Century	1929
A Scandinavian Summer	Century	1930
Foot-Loose in the British Isles	Century	1932
Trailing Cortez Through Mexico	Stokes	1935
A Vagabond in Sovietland	Stokes	1935
Roaming in Hawaii	Stokes	1937
Sky Roaming Above Two Continents	Stokes	1938
The Lure of Alaska	Stokes	1939
The Pan American Highway from the Rio Grande to the Canal Zone	Appleton-Stokes	1940
Rediscovering South America	Lippincott	1943

Mr. Franck was a Lieutenant in the AEF, 1918-19 and a Major in the U.S. Army Air Corps, 1942-47. He died April 17, 1962, and is buried in Arlington National Cemetery.

FREDRICKS, EDGAR J. 1942-
Born: June 27, 1942; Holland, Michigan
Parents: Russel and Audrey (Beckman) Fredricks
Education: Calvin College, B.A. 1964; Western Michigan University, M.A. 1967, M.A. 1968
Career: Michigan State Representative, 54th District
Address: 392 West 35th Street, Holland, MI 49423

Writings:

MacArthur: His Mission and Meaning	Whitmore Publishing	1968

FROSTIC, GWEN 1906-

Born: April 26, 1906; Sandusky, Michigan
Parents: Fred W. and Sara (Alexander) Frostic
Education: Eastern Michigan University, Teacher's Certificate, 1926; Western Michigan University, Course Work, 1927-28
Career: Teacher, Artist, Writer, Publisher
Address: 5140 River Rd., Benzonia, MI 49616

Writings:

My Michigan	Presscraft Papers	1957
A Walk with Me	Presscraft Papers	1958
These Things Are Ours	Presscraft Papers	1960
A Place on Earth	Presscraft Papers	1962
To Whose Who See	Presscraft Papers	1965
Wingborne	Presscraft Papers	1967
Wisps of Mist	Presscraft Papers	1969
Beyond Time	Presscraft Papers	1971
Contemplate	Presscraft Papers	1973
The Enduring Cosmos	Presscraft Papers	1976
Interlochen, an Unfinished Symphony	Presscraft Papers	1977

Her work is a combination of art and writing. "It is not the story of Michigan that you would find in the history books. . .not the facts and figures of industry or business. . .not as a tourist would record the beauty of its lakes and hills. . .but simply as a series of thoughts that may make you take Michigan in your heart," from *My Michigan.* To put into words that people may relate to, the message of the green world-its insects-its birds and all life upon this earth that my lead to new insights of mankind's inter-relationship with the rhythms of the cosmos.

Awards: Eastern Michigan University, Doctor of Laws, 1965; Western Michigan University, Doctor of Humanities, 1971; Michigan State University, Doctor of Fine Arts, 1973; Alma College, Doctor of Literature, 1977; Sarah Chapman Francis Literary Award, 1972 (Garden Clubs of America)

FULLER, GEORGE NEWMAN 1873-1957

Born: November 17, 1873; Barry Co., Michigan
Parents: Dr. Reuben A. and Delia (Coulter) Fuller
Married: Helene (Custine) Fuller

Education: University of Michigan, A.B., 1905; Harvard University; Yale University; University of Michigan, Ph. D., 1912

Career: Teacher, rural schools; Principal, L'Anse public schools, 1896-1900; Principal, Nashville (Mich.) public schools, 1900-01; Dept. Head, Montana State Normal College, 1905-1909; Michigan Historical Commission, Lansing, 1913-14; Instructor, University of Michigan, 1914-15; Director, Michigan Historical Commission, 1916-46

Writings:

Economic and Social Beginnings of Michigan	Wynkoop Hallenbeck Crawford	1916
Democracy and the Great War	Supt. of Public Instruction	1918
Historic Michigan, Land of the Great Lakes	Nat'l Historical Assn.	1924
Michigan in the World War (Co-authored with Charles Hanford Landrum)	Michigan Historical Comm.	1924
Michigan, a Centennial History of the State and Its People	Lewis	1939

Dr. Fuller continued the series of annual publications known as the *Michigan Historical and Pioneer Collections.* It survives today as the quarterly publication, *Michigan History* magazine.

FULLER, IOLA see: McCOY, IOLA FULLER

GALLUP, LUCY 1911-
Pseudonym: Amelie DeFluent
Born: July 30, 1911; Dundee, Michigan
Parents: Albert R. and Maude (Haines) DeFluent
Married: Louis O. Gallup, a retail store owner and building contractor (retired)
Education: Western Michigan University, A.B., 1934; M.A. in Library Science, 1958
Career: Librarian—reference, children's public and school—in the Kalamazoo Public Library; the Goshen, Indiana Public Library; the New York Public Library; the Sturgis Public Library; Kalamazoo Central High School; and the White Pigeon Community Schools
Address: Daybreak Hill, Route 3, Sturgis, Michigan 49091

Writings:

Spinning Wings	Morrow	1956
Independent Bluebird	Morrow	1959

Work in Progress: A book based upon a journal kept of an unusual summer's experience with a purple martin, a young bird from the flock that occupied the Gallup's martin house at Daybreak Hill, their home near Sturgis. This is the first material in several years that Mrs. Gallup has attempted to put into publishable form.

She says: "Shortly after the publication of *Independent Bluebird,* I took a school library job and its demands claimed all my attention, though I must admit I did considerable traveling in the summers, often on nature study and bird tours. I am interested in many things besides writing, and believe in living life on a basis of broad interests. Someone has said that librarians are generalists rather than specialists; I think that is very true in my case. There are so many facets and aspects to life, so many things at which to try one's hand, that to devote myself entirely to one thing would be to miss too much. At the same time, I write all the while, as part of my way of life. It sharpens my own awareness and deepends experiences."

GALT, THOMAS FRANKLIN JR. 1908-
Psuedonym: Tom Galt
Born: July 29, 1908; Wequetonsing, Michigan (officially, Little Traverse Township)
Parents: Thomas Franklin and Clarace G. (Eaton) Galt
Married: Florella
Education: Harvard University, B.A., 1932
Career: Writer; Taught ethics at Ethical Cultural School, New York City, 1938-45
Address: P.O. Box 417, Wellfleet, Massachusetts 02667

Writings:

Volcano	*Scribners*	*1946*
How the United Nations Works-		
Revisions appeared in 1955		
and 1965	*Crowell*	*1947*
Peter Zenger, Fighter for		
Freedom	*Crowell*	*1951*
The Story of Peace and War	*Crowell*	*1952*
Revised edition published as		
Peace and War, Man Made	*Beacon*	*1963*
The Rise of the Thunderer	*Crowell*	*1954*
Seven Days from Sunday	*Crowell*	*1956*

Poems published in 35 magazines including: *Virginia Quarterly Review, Lyric, Open Places,* and *Southwest Review*

Mr. Galt has also written numerous poems in Japanese. He says that the following one "expresses a good deal of my philosophy":

Round like an apple,
It turns,
My country.

His name in Japanese is Tomi-

GALT, TOM see: GALT, THOMAS FRANKLIN JR.

GARRELS, ROBERT MINARD 1916-
Born: August 24, 1916; Detroit, Michigan
Parents: John C. and Margaret Ann (Gibney) Garrels
Married: Cynthia A. (Hunt)
Children: Joan G. Beitin, James C. Garrels, Katherine G. Garrels
Education: University of Michigan, B.S., 1937; Northwestern University, M.S., 1939; Ph. D., 1941
Career: From instructor to associate professor of geology, Northwestern University, 1941-52; Geologist, United States Geological Survey, 1952-55; Associate professor of geology, Harvard University, 1957-65; Chairman of the department of geological sciences, Harvard University, 1963-65; Henri Speciale Professor of science, University of Brussles, Belguim, 1962-63; Professor of geology, Northwestern University, 1965-69; Professor, Scripps Institution of Oceanography, 1969-71; Professor of geology, University of Hawaii, 1971-74; Professor of geology, Northwestern University, 1974-present
Address: Department of Geological Sciences, Northwestern University, Evanston, Illinois 60201

Writings:

Textbook of Geology	*Harper*	*1951*
Mineral Equilibria (co-author with C.L. Christ)	*Harper*	*1959*
Solutions, Minerals, and Equilibria	*Freeman, Cooper*	*1965*
Evolution of Sedimentary Rocks (Co-author with F.T. Mackenzie)	*Norton*	*1971*
Water the Web of Life (Co-authored with Cynthia Hunt)	*Norton*	*1972*
Chemical Cycles and the Global Environment (Co-authored with Cynthia Hunt and F.T. Mackenzie)	*Kaufmann*	*1973*

Awards: M.A. (honorary), Harvard University, 1955; Arthur L. Day Medal, Geological Society America, 1966; D.Sc. (honorary), University of Brussles, 1969; U.M. Goldschmidt Medal, Geochemical Society, 1975; D.Sc. (honorary), University Louis Pasteur, Strasbourg, 1976

GEORGAKAS, DAN 1938-
Born: March 1, 1938; Detroit, Michigan
Parents: Xenophon and Sophia Georgakas
Education: Wayne State University, B.A., 1960; University of Michigan, M.A., 1961
Career: Teacher—Detroit Public Schools, 1960-64; Overseas School of Rome, Italy, 1965; LaGuardia Community College, Long Island City, New York, 1973-;Writer

Writings:

Z Anthology of Poetry (editor)	Smyrna Press	1969
And All Living Things Their Children (poetry)	Shameless Hussy Press	1972
The Broken Hoop: The History of Native Americans from 1600-1890, from the Atlantic Coast to the Plains	Doubleday	1973
Red Shadows: The History of Native Americans from 1600-1890, from the Desert to the Pacific Coast	Doubleday	1973
Detroit—I Do Mind Dying: A Study in Urban Revolution, co-author with Marvin Surkin	St. Martin	1975

Writer for "Folkways Greek Record"; Associate Editor, Cineaste, 1968-74

Awards: Fulbright research grant, Greece, 1963

GERBER, DAN 1940-
Born: August 12, 1940; Grand Rapids, Michigan
Parents: Daniel F. and Dorothy (Scott) Gerber
Married: Virginia Hartjen Gerber
Children: Wendie Gerber, Frank Gerber and Tamara Gerber
Education: Michigan State University, B.A., 1962
Career: In corporate sales for two years; Professional race driver for five years; Taught high school for two years; Poet in Residence, Thomas Jefferson College, 1969; Poet in Residence, Michigan State University, 1970; Lecturer for two years in various colleges and secondary schools for the National Endowment and Academy of American Poets

Address: P.O. Box 39, Fremont, Michigan 49412

Writings:

The Revenant (poems)	*Sumac Press*	*1971*
Departure (poems)	*Sumac Press*	*1973*
American Atlas (novel)	*Prentice-Hall*	*1973*
Out of Control (novel)	*Prentice-Hall*	*1974*
Indy: The World's Fastest Carni-		
val Ride (non-fiction)	*Prentice-Hall*	*1977*

Work in Progress: *Last Day in the Field* (novel); A new collection of poems; Magazine pieces

He says: "Most of what I write is what is dictated by my experience. In that sense, I fell more like a stenographer or a radio receiver than a creator. I almost never have a sense of, 'I did it.' "

GIANAKARIS, C.J. 1934-
Born: 1934; Morenci, Michigan
Parents: John and Anna (Parry) Gianakaris
Married: Ann Gianakaris, a teacher
Children: Elizabeth Gianakaris
Education: University of Michigan, B.A., 1956, M.A., 1957; University of Wisconsin, Ph. D., 1961
Career: Assistant professor and associate professor of English, Illinois State University, 1961-66; Associate professor and full professor of English, Western Michigan University, 1966-present; Visiting professor, University of Missouri-Columbia, Summer 1974
Address: 1020 Eldridge Drive, Kalamazoo, Michigan 49007

Writings:

Antony and Cleopatra (edition)	*William C. Brown*	*1969*
Plutarch	*Twayne*	*1970*
Foundations of Drama	*Houghton Mifflin*	*1975*

Work in Progress: A book of Peter Shaffer; and studies on Shakespeare and Ben Jonson

Dr. Gianakaris is also the co-founder and still the co-editor of the international, interdisciplinary quarterly, *Comparative Drama.*

GILBERT, EDITH 1917-
Born: September 2, 1917; New York City
Parents: Otto and Ethel (Liebman) Wiesinger
Married: Julius Gilbert
Education: Beverly Hills High School, Beverly Hills, California,

1935; University of California at Los Angeles; Sawyer's School of Business, Westwood, California; Center for Creative Studies, Detroit Michigan
Career: Writer of books and newspaper articles; Consultant-tabletop designer; business and industry
Address: Jet'iquette, 510 Michigan Avenue, Charlevoix, Michigan 49720

Writings:

All about Parties	Hearthside Press	1968
Let's Set the Table	Jet'iquette	1972
Summer Resort Life: Tango		
Teas and All!	Jet'iquette	1976
Tabletop: The Right Way	Jet'iquette	1976

GILLETTE, VIRGINIA M. 1920-
Pseudonym: J. Sloan McLean (in collaboration)
Born: January 27, 1920; Detroit, Michigan
Parents: Philip W. and Mable A. (Wheelock) Sloan
Married: William R. Gillette, a staff engineer
Children: Susan, William, Sarah, Mary, Philip
Education: Attended Elmira College (1938-39) and the University of Michigan (1939-40)
Career: Housewife and mother; Staff member, Oakland University Writer's Conferences; Teacher of adult education classes in creative writing
Address: P.O. Box 41, Algonac, Michigan 48001

Writings:

The Aerie, a modern Gothic		
novel written in collaboration		
with Josephine Wunsch	Nash Publishing Corp.	1974
Numerous short stories		

Work in Progress: Two novels in collaboration with Wunsch under the pseudonym J. Sloan McLean; One novel under own name; Short stories on assignment to *English Magazine*

She says: "I am a late bloomer, starting to try and learn how to write when my youngest child entered school. Doing mainly short stories until the past few years. Now trying romantic suspense novels. I believe it is hard work, persistence and luck. Also, the old-fashioned virtues. I have been fortunate enough to have over two hundred stories published and one novel. I hope for many more."

GILPIN, ALEC R. 1920-
Born: April 23, 1920; Detroit, Michigan

Parents: Archie and Clara (Watson) Gilpin
Married: C. Kathleen (Kinney)
Children: Andrew R. and Jean E.
Education: University of Michigan, B.A., 1941, M.A., 1946, Ph. D., 1950
Career: Michigan State University—instructor; assistant professor; associate professor; and professor
Address: 405 S. Rogers; Mason, Michigan 48854

Writings:

The War of 1812 in the Old Northwest	Michigan State University Press	1948
The Territory of Michigan: 1805-1837	Michigan State University Press	1970

Work in Progress: Dr. Gilpin says: "I am doing research for another book but it will be several years before I finish it."

GIRARD, HAZEL BATTEN 1901-

Born: December 8, 1901; Batten's Crossing, near Glennie, Michigan
Parents: John W. and Johanna (Alexander) Batten
Married: Joseph J. Girard (deceased), a teacher
Children: Victor M. and Marvin Eugene
Education: University High School, Ann Arbor
Career: Freelance writer and photographer—*Michigan Farmer, Detroit Free Press, Detroit Times, Bay City Times, American Home, Colliers, Nature Magazine, Outdoors Magazine, Field and Stream, Popular Photography* and *U.S. Camera;* Photographs syndicated for several years by Freelance Photographers Guild
Address: 1019 Fletcher Street, Owosso, MI 48857

Writings:

A Giant Walked among them: Half-Tall Tales of Paul Bunyan and His Loggers with illustrations by Marvin Eugene Girard, the author's son	Marshall Jones	1977
Blow for Batten's Crossing: A Backwoods' Odyssey	Glendon	1978

Work in Progress: Co-author with Marvin Eugene Girard on a book of light verse, *Once Upon a Rhyme*

She says: "I like writing that treks along without the seeming labor pains of creation. I dislike pompous, academical writing as if the author is suffering from the terminal, dread fear of split infinitives. I have been very fortunate in that editors leave my writing intact, exactly as submitted to them. I was once told by Malcolm M.

Bingay (venerable editor of the *Detroit Free Press*) that I wrote with cadence, with a proclivity for choosing words with 'ear appeal.' I simply like writing that 'picks up its heels' and get trekking down the printed page."

GIRARD, MARVIN EUGENE 1924-
Born: August 3, 1924; Glennie, Michigan
Parents: Joseph Jerome and Hazel (Batten) Girard
Married: Virginia (Kohl)
Children: Giselle Colette Girard
Education: Owosso High School 1943
Career: Theatrical performer and entertainer in theatres, circuses, wild west shows, rodeos and fairs
Address: 1217 Pearce Street, Owosso, Michigan 48867

Writings:

These, My Singing Words: A Collection of Poetry	*Golden Quill Press*	*1976*
A Giant Walked Among Them: Half-Tall Tales of Paul Bunyan and His Loggers by Hazel B. Girard (contributed poems and illustrations)	*Marshall Jones*	*1977*
Blow for Battens Crossing: A Backwood Odyssey (contributed poems)	*Glendon*	*1978*

Poems published in *Horseman Magazine, Canada Rides Magazine, Make it with Leather Magazine,* and *The Detroit Free Press.* Drawings and cartoons in many national publications.

Work in Progress: Co-author with Hazel B. Girard on a book of light verse, *Once Upon a Rhyme*

He says: "I've been writing along in my own poetic groove for years, feeling that my kind of words would somehow find an audience out there in that small world of poetry readers. I have always believed that being able to communicate was the real art of poetry—the ability to pattern simple language into something all people would understand. I employ the use of informal English in all of my writing. I have had a life-long love affair with the idiom of the cowboy, the lumberjack, and the people of the of the circus, roustabouts and performers alike. I've written some of my western poems in common cowboy dialect and feel very much at home in that form.

"Although I have written a great deal of free verse, I still enjoy working the most traditional poetic forms. My poems cover a wide variety of subjects, but I am best known for my western and circus pieces. If they smack of authenticity, it is only because I spent a lot of years as a featured juggler and trick roper in circuses and wild west shows. I am writing about what I know best."

Awards: Elected to membership in The Poetry Society of America; Two poems, *Keeper of the Pines* and *Big Mitten Thoughts,* introduced into the Michigan State Legislature in 1971 for consideration as the official state poem of Michigan

GIROUX, JOYE SMITH 1930-
Born: May 31, 1930; Iosco County, Michigan
Parents: Joseph Earl and Olive Birdie (Jenkins) Smith
Married: Philip Earl Giroux (deceased)
Children: Helen Joye and Patricia Renee
Education: Central Michigan University, A.B. 1952; Graduate work at Wayne State University, University of Michigan, Michigan State University, and Central Michigan University
Career: French and English teacher-Almont High School in Almont, Michigan; South Lake High School in St. Clair Shores, Michigan; and Big Rapids High School in Big Rapids, Michigan
Address: 825 Cherry Avenue, Big Rapids, Michigan 49307

Writings:

A Grain of Sand, No More (Poetry)	Pairie Poets	1976
Where Lies the Dream	Wayside Press	1976
Four Women. . .Getting on With It	Wayside Press	1977

Work in Progress: Expected inclusion in an eight poet anthology, *Wayside 8 Poets,* being planned by Wayside Press; An illustrated poetry collection, *The Whispering of Leaves*

She says: "I find the creative process an individual, and highly personal thing, an experience that varies with every effort. Often, for me, a poem will write itself: it springs full blown from my mind, needling only to be set on paper. Occassionally, however, an idea will dance tantilizingly just beyond my reach and a dozen attempts will fail to capture it fully. Always though, there is the conviction that the thought or emotion MUST find expression—that the poem WILL be written; and always there is a sense of completion when it assumes its final form.

"The most valuable gift any writer possesses is his individuality, that unique quality that sets his work apart from every other writer's. It is well for a young poet to be exposed to good peotry while learning technique, but it is a mistake for him to imitate another's style slavishly. The first, and best, piece of advice every poet should follow is to be himself."

GLAZER, SIDNEY 1905-
Born: November 1, 1905; Quincy, Michigan
Parents: Max and Mildred (Thal) Glazer
Education: Wayne State University, A.B. 1927; University of Michigan, A.M. 1929, Ph.D. 1932
Career: Assistant, department of history, University of Michigan, 1928-30; Instructor, department of history, Wayne State University, 1930-38; Assistant professor (1938-48), associate professor (1948-55) and professor (1955-76), department of history, Wayne State University; Professor emeritus, department of history, Wayne State University, 1976-
Address: The Radisson Cadillac Hotel; Detroit, Michigan 48226

Writings:

Michigan: From Primitive Wilderness to Industrial Comwealth (co-author)	*Prentice-Hall*	*1948*
Industrial Detroit: Men at Work	*Wayne State University Press*	*1951*
Rejected Amendments to the Michigan Constitution, 1910-1961	*Michigan Constitutional Convention Preparatory Committee*	*1961*
The Middle West	*Bookman Associates*	*1962*
Detroit-A Study in Urban Development	*Twayne Associates*	*1965*

Contributor of reviews and articles to professional journals.

Dr. Glazer served as a member of the Michigan Civil War Centennial Observance Commission from 1963-66. He is also a member of the Organization of American Historians, American Historical Assoication, Michigan Historical Association, and Phi Beta Kappa.

GOLD, HERBERT 1924-
Born: March 9, 1924; Cleveland, Ohio
Parents: Samuel S. and Frieda (Frankel) Gold
Married: divorced
Children: Ann and Judith
Education: Columbia College, B.A. 1946; Fulbright Scholar, University of Paris, Sorbonne; Columbia University, M.A. 1948
Career: Writer; Lecturer in philosophy and literature, Western Reserve University, 1951-53; Member of English Department, Wayne State University, 1954-59; Visiting professor: Cornell University , 1958; University of California, Berkeley, 1963; Harvard Summer School, 1964

Writings:

Birth of a Hero (novel)	*Viking*	*1951*
The Prospect Before us (novel)	*World*	*1954*

The Man Who Was Not With It		
(novel)	*Little*	*1956*
Paperback edition	*Avon*	*1974*
The living Novel, ed. by Gran-		
ville Hicks (contributor)	*Macmillan*	*1957*
Fiction of the Fifties: A Decade		
of American Writing, editor		
(stories)	*Doubleday*	*1959*
The Optimist (novel)	*Little*	*1959*
Love and Like (stories)	*Dial*	*1960*
Therefore Be Bold (novel)	*Dial*	*1960*
Stories of Modern America, co-		
editor with David L.		
Stevenson	*St. Martins*	*1961*
The Age of Happy Problems	*Dial*	*1962*
First Person Singular: Essays for		
the Sixties	*Dial*	*1963*
Salt (novel)	*Dial*	*1963*
Fathers: A Novel in the Form of		
a Memoir	*Random*	*1967*
The Great American Jackpot	*Random*	*1969*
Biafra Goodbye	*Twowindows Press*	*1970*
The Magic Will: Stories and		
Essays of a Decade	*Random*	*1971*
My Last Two Hundred Years	*Random*	*1972*
Swiftie the Magician (novel)	*McGraw Hill*	*1974*
The Young Prince and the		
Magic Cone	*Doublday*	*1973*
Waiting for Cordelia	*Arbor House*	*1977*

Awards: Guggenheim fellowhip, 1957; Ohioana Book Award for *The Man Who Was Not With It,* 1957; National Institute of Arts and Letters grant in literature, 1958; Ford Foundation fellow, 1960

GOLDBERG, E. MARSHALL 1931-

Born: December 19, 1931; North Adams, Massachusettes
Parents: Jack and Ida Goldberg
Married: Dr. Melinda Hirsch
Children: Brett, Carey, Sandra, Jeffrey, Dara
Education: University of Rochester, A.B. 1952; Tufts Medical School, M.D. 1956
Career: Physician-currently Full Professor Medience, Michigan State College of Human Medicine and Full-Time Chief of Medi-ence, Hurley Hospital, Flint, Michigan
Address: c/o Hurley Medical Center, Sixth Avenue and Begole, Flint, Michigan 48502

Writings:

The Karamanov Equations (novel) (re-issued by Pinnacle Publishing Corp. in 1975 as a paperback under the title A Deadly Operation	*World*	*1972*
The Anatomy Lesson (novel)		

GOLDFEDER, CHERYL see: PHAZ, CHERYL SUZANNE

GOLDSMITH, DAVID H. 1933-
Born: April 13, 1933; Chicago, Illinois
Married: Vicki
Children: Rachel and Jocelyn
Education: Bowling Green University, B.A., 1958; M.A., 1961, Ph. D. 1970
Career: 1964-68—Assistant Professor, State University of New York, Buffalo; 1970-present—Professor, Northern Michigan University
Address: 324 E. Prospect, Marquette 49855

Writings:

Kurt Vonnegut: Fantasist of Fire and Ice	*Popular Press*	*1972*

Work in Progress: A book on contemporary American Novelists

Awards: Fulbright-Hays Exchange Professor, Taipei, Taiwan, 1973-74

GOREN, JUDITH 1933-
Born: April 5, 1933; Detroit, Michigan
Parents: Herman and Evelyn (Apple) Wise
Married: Robert Goren, an attorney
Children: Gary, Steven, Nancy
Education: Wayne State University, B.A., 1954; M. Ed., 1972
Career: Personal-growth counselor with adults, mostly in group settings but also individually, using a blend of transactional analysis, gestalt awareness, and body-work; Teacher of adult education classes in personal-growth areas and creative writing; Consultant in personal-growth areas and creative writing for various school systems; Listed with Michigan Council for the Arts Creative Writers in Schools Programs, 1975-present; High School English teacher in the 1950's Professional affiliation: Detroit

Women Writers
Address: 21525 W. 13 Mile Road, Birmingham, Michigan 48010

Writings:

Coming Alive (poetry)	*Stone Press*	*1975*
Poetry included in the following anthologies:		
Echoes from the Moon	*Hot Apples Press*	*1976*
Moving to Antarctica	*Dustbooks*	*1975*
Anthology of Women Poets	*Dremen Press*	*1971*

Work in Progress: More poetry

She says: "My work with people and my work as a poet are becoming more and more integrated. Both begin with my being in touch with what is inside myself, and then molding that knowledge in a way that will touch someone else. To me that is the essence of what poetry is about, and I see therapy done well as another kind of poetry, using intuition creatively and knowing exactly what words are right."

GORMAN, SANTINA 1903-
Born: September 21, 1903; Mansfield, Michigan
Parents: John and Santina (Betti) Cederna
Married: Michael Gorman (deceased)
Children: Mrs. A. Rigodanzo and Joanne Gorman (deceased)
Education: Stout-Menomonie, Wisconsin; Teaching Certificate 1923
Career: Home economics teacher for six years; Adult education teacher for one year; Girl Scout Troop leader for four years
Address: Box 123, Stambaugh, Michigan 49964

Writings:

Poems	*Reporter Publishing Co.*	*1966*

Mrs. Gorman enjoys creative stitchery, sewing, knitting, crocheting, painting, and writing poetry. About her philosophy, she says, "To live one day at a time trusting in God. Be a good example to others. Live and let live."

GOULART, FRANCES SHERIDAN 1938-
Born: March 3, 1938; Detroit, Michigan
Parents: Earl Joseph and Helen Monica (Lennon) Sheridan
Married: Ronald J. Goulart, writer of science fiction
Children: Sean Lucien and Steffan Eamon
Education: Southwestern High School Detroit, Michigan 1956; Attended Wayne State University for one and one-half years,

majoring in languages; and the New School for Social Research in New York City

Career: Writer; Lecturer and adult education instructor; Founder and director of the Potsanjammer School of Natural Cooking of Fairfield County

Address: 232 Georgetown Road, Weston, Connecticut 06883

Writings:

The Mother Goose Cookbook	*Price, Stern, Sloan*	*1970*
Bum Steers: How to Make Your Own Mock Meats	*Chatham Press*	*1975*
The Ecological Eclair: A Book of Sugarless Treats	*Macmillan*	*1975*
Bone Appetit: Natural Petfood Recipes	*Pacific Search*	*1976*

Work in Progress: *The Liberated Loaf* (about wonder breads and miracle spreads); *Twenty Carrots: The Vegetarian Weight Loss Cookbook. With Nothing But a Pack of Cards* (about children's card games); *Rin Tin Thin: The Dieting Dogs Cookbook*

In her spare hours, Mrs. Goulart is a long distance runner with many titles and trophies to her credit. She also swims, plays tennis, and cycles 4,000 miles yearly.

GRACE, BETTY

Born: Marshall, Michigan

Parents: James W. and Rose (Hogan) Grace

Education: Marshall High School diploma; County Normal (1 year)

Career: Teacher (3 years in rural schools); Writer

Writings:

The Cat with the Green Whiskers	*Pageant Press*	*1955*
Numerous articles in magazines and newspapers		

Betty Grace was one of nine children. Her father, a business man, believed that girls should study music, so she learned to play the violin. Her first stories were published in a Detroit paper while she was a student in high school. Upon her mother's death, she ended her teaching career to stay home and care for her younger brothers and sisters. In her own words, "I started creating stories for my brothers and sisters; the circle widened. She later lived in Albion, Detroit, and Los Angeles; and then returned to live in Marshall.

GRAY, DOROTHY see: GUCK, DOROTHY (GRAY)

GRAYSON, DAVID see: BAKER, RAY STANNARD

GREEN, JAMES J. 1902-
Born: September 19, 1902; Allegan, Michigan
Parents: Frank H. and Rhoda (Arnold) Green
Married: Gertrude D. Green
Children: James F. and Doris Marie
Education: Western State Teachers College; Certificate 1924
Career: Managing city news stand writing
Address: 357 Monroe Street, Allegan, Michigan 49010

Writings:

All Aboard for the Allegan Fair	*Wise Printing*	*1975*
Railroads Come and Go in		
Allegan County	*Wise Printing*	*1976*
All the World's a Stage	*Wise Printing*	*1976*
Fire! Fire! Fire!	*Wise Printing*	*1977*
Numerous magazine articles.		

He says: "At the present time I am writing mainly on the American Indian and other historical items."

Awards: Allegan Community Council Award, 1962; Meritorious Award of the Grand Chapter R.A.M. of Michigan, 1970; Allegan County Liberty Bell Award, 1974

GREEN, MARY MOORE 1906-
Born: March 17, 1906; Romulus, Michigan
Parents: George and Letitia (Bush) Moore
Married: Wendell Green
Children: George, James, Robert
Education: Wayne High School diploma; Eastern Michigan University
Career: Teacher

Writings:

About Apples from Orchard to		
Market	*Melmont*	*1960*
Three Feathers: The Story of		
Pontiac, co-author with Irma		
Johnson	*Follett*	*1960*

GREEN, PHYLLIS 1932-
Born: June 25, 1932; Pittsburgh, Pennsylvania
Parents: Victor G. and Phyllis (Sailer) Hartman

Married: Robert B. Green, insurance executive
Children: Sharon and Bruce
Education: Westminster College, B.S. in Education 1953; University of Pittsburgh, M. Ed. 1955
Career: Elementary school and special education teacher; Summer theatre actress; Band vocalist; Author, poet and playwright
Address: 130 Quarterdeck Drive, Madison, Wisconsin 53705

Writings:

The Fastest Quitter in Town	*Addison-Wesley*	*1972*
Nantucket Summer (this book begins in Livonia, Mich., and then proceeds to Nantucket)	*Thomas Nelson*	*1974*
Ice River (later translated into Danish)	*Addison-Wesley*	*1975*
Mildred Murphy, How Does You Garden Grow?	*Addison-Wesley*	*1977*
Wild Violets	*Thomas Nelson*	*1977*
Grandmother Orphan	*Thomas Nelson*	*1977*

Work in Progress: Two novels for young adults—*Michael* (tentative title), to be published by Thomas Nelson in 1978; *Walkie-Talkie* (set in Livonia, Michigan), to be published by Addison-Wesley in 1978; and *Nicky's Imperfect Orange,* to be published by Addison-Wesley in 1979. Full-length stage play

She says: "I try to set my novels in places we have lived or places where we like to vacation. I write my stories in spiral notebooks with either a pencil or pen. I mark dates on the manuscript to show how much I have written a certain day. These orginal manuscripts can be seen in the Detroit Women Writers collection in the Burton Historical Society Room of the main Detroit Public Library.

"I lived in Michigan for six years and all the books listed above were written during that time except *Walkie-Talkie,* which was begun in Michigan and finished when we moved here to Wisconsin.

"My creative writing teacher was Mr. Lawrence Hart of San Rafael, California."

GREENE, MERRITT W. 1897-? (deceased)
Born: April 22, 1897; Buffalo, New York
Parents: W.P. and Nora (Smith) Greene
Married: Helen (Michaels) Greene
Children: Merritt William Greene, Jr.
Education: Jonesville High School, diploma, 1916; Hillsdale College
Career: Actor and playwright (about 40 full-length plays); Insurance salesman; Dramatic coach at Hillsdale High School (Michi-

gan); Radio newscaster; Freelance writer; Newspaper worker and county seat correspondent for United Press International, *The Detroit Free Press, The Jackson Citizen-Patroit,* and *The Toledo Blade*

Writings:

The Land Lies Pretty	*Hillsdale Educational Publishers*	*1959*
Curse of the White Panther	*Hillsdale Educational Publishers*	*1960*
Forgotten Yesterdays	*Hillsdale Educational Publishers*	*1964*

GREINKE, ERIC 1948-

Born: July 15, 1948; Grand Rapids, Michigan
Parents: Harold and Alice (Hill) Greinke
Married: Pam Greinke, an artist
Education: Grand Valley State College (Arts and Sciences); B.A., 1972
Career: Seaman in the United States Coast Guard; Publisher, writer and editor; High school creative writing teacher; Book reviewer for the *Grand Rapids Press;* Currently involved in the Michigan Poets in the Schools Program and working toward a Master of Psychology degree
Address: P.O. Box 2662, Grand Rapids, MI 49501

Writings:

Masterpiece Theater	*Pilot Press Books*	*1975*
The Broken Lock: New and Selected Poems (illustrated by Pam Greinke)	*Pilot Press Books*	*1976*
10 Michigan Poets (editor)	*Pilot Press Books*	*1972*
The Drunken Boat and Other Poems from the French of Arthur Rimbaud (translator)	*Free Books, Inc.*	*1976*

Work in Progress: *The Transpersonal Self: A Holistic Paradigm* (psychology)

He says: ''I am interested in discovering potentials of human nature, especially regarding creative therapeutic applications of art, especially poetry. My work as an alternative educator at City High School in Grand Rapids and with the Michigan Poets in the Schools Program has led me toward an understanding of mental health and growth.''

GRICE, JULIA A. 1940-

Born: May 28, 1940; Battle Creek, Michigan
Education: Albion College, B.A., 1962
Career: Freelance writer for ten years
Address: c/o Lenniger Literary Agency, 437 Fifth Avenue, New York, New York 10019

Writings:

Lovefire	*Avon Books*	*1977*
Emeraldfire	*Avon Books*	*1978*

Work in Progress: *Aurora Wind and Daughters of the Flame,* two historical novels awaiting publication; and an historical novel of the early American theater

She says: "I have five published books and one reneged-upon book (accepted but not published) before my first novel finally sold . . . news which should be encouraging to all new writers."

Ms. Grice has served as president of the Detroit Women Writers, a group of professional women writers.

GRINGHUIS, DIRK see: GRINGHUIS, RICHARD H.

GRINGHUIS, RICHARD H. 1918-1974
Pseudonym: Dirk Gringhuis
Born: September 22, 1918; Grand Rapids, Michigan
Parents: Leonard J. and Ruth (Perry) Gringhuis
Married: Helen L. Wiard
Children: Richard L. Gringhuis
Education: American Academy of Art, Chicago, 1940
Career: Freelance illustrator, 1942-60; Director, Hope College Art Department, 1947-52; Art editor, *Children's Health,* Lansing, Michigan, 1952-66; Abrams Planetariums, 1963; Muralist, Mackinac Island Park Commission, 1955-74; Associate Professor and curator of exhibits, museum, Michigan State University, 1964-74; Writer, producer and teacher, weekly television show, *Open Door to Michigan* (station WMPB), 1965-74
Address: Mrs. Wilard: 875 Victor Avenue, Apt. 107, Ingelwood, California 90302

Writings:

Hope Haven	*Eerdmans*	*1947*
Here Comes the Bookmobile	*Albert Whitman*	*1948*
Big Mac	*Macmillan*	*1956*
Tulip Time	*Albert Whitman*	*1951*
The Young Voyageur	*McGraw Hill*	*1955*
Revised edition	*Mackinac Island State Park Commission*	*1973*

The Eagle Pine	Hillsdale	1958
The Big Hunt and the Big Dig	Dial Press	1960
Rock Oil to Rockets	Macmillan	1960
Saddle the Storm	Bobbs Merrill	1962
In Scarlet and Blue	Dial Press	1963
Of Cabbages and Cattle	Dial Press	1962
Of Ship and Fish and Fishermen	Albert Whitman	1963
Mystery at Skull Castle	Reilly & Lee	1964
From Tall Timber	Albert Whitman	1964
Open Door to the Great Lakes	Hillsdale	1966
Stars in the Ceiling	Meredith Press	1967
Giants, Dragons and Gods	Meredith Press	1968
Lore of the Great Turtle	Mackinac Island State Park Commisssion	1970
The Great Parade	Hillsdale	1970
Werewolves and Will o' the Wisp	Mackinac Island Park Commission	1974

Mrs. Wilard says: "Dirk was a romantic and lived each book he wrote and illustrated. He loved history, particularly Michigan history. It was his desire that both children and adults could know some of their heritage and enjoy it. The past for Dirk was always a very alive and exciting time. Dirk was also an authority on American and French and British revolutionary uniforms. In addition, he did the murals for Fort Mackinac and Fort Michillimackinac as well as the mural for the East Lansing Library."

GROSS, STUART D. 1914-

Born: February 2, 1914; Vincennes, Indiana
Parents: Charles A. and Winifred (MacGillvary) Gross
Married: Vernice Gross
Children: Amy Gross Grzisiak and Mary Gross Daenzer
Education: Hope College, Holland, Michigan, B.A. 1936
Career: News reporter, City Editor, the *Saginaw News,* 1936-67; Director of Community Affairs, Assistant to the President, Saginaw Valley State College, 1967-present
Address: 315 Kennely Road, Saginaw, Michigan 48603

Writings:
Indians, Jacks, and Pines	Pendell Press	1962
Trouble at the Grass Roots	Pendell Press	1971
Stolen Christmas Star	Carlton Press	1976

Work in Progress: *Madam President* (fiction); *Where There's a Will* (history of higher education in the Saginaw Valley); *On the Saginaw* (historical novel based on the Saginaw lumber era)

He says: "I have started research on a book that will deal with lumbering era of Michigan, particularly around Saginaw which was the Lumber Capitol of the World in the late 19th century. Lumber in Michigan created more wealth than all the goal mined in California to 1900, and not too much has been written about it. I have some fresh material that is exciting.

"As a reporter for the *Saginaw News,* I won the Michigan School Bell Award for education reporting, and also was honored by the Education Writers of America. I also did a stint as a news photographer, and won a prize in The Island Daily Press Association photographic competition. I was city editor when the college asked me to take over its public relations department, and held that position until 1976 when I became assistant to the president.

"I have another 'published' effort, but very limited circulation. I wrote *You Can't Wear Blue Socks to the Wedding,* highlights of living with a wife, two daughters, several dogs, many cats, and many laughs. The circulation was limited to three copies—one to each of my women."

GROSSMAN, MARTIN 1943-
Born: June 15, 1943; Chicago, Illinois
Parents: Leon and Esther Belle (Immerman) Grossman
Married: Julia L. Grossman, Career Librarian
Children: Sarah Esther Grossman
Education: Lakeview High School, 1961; Michigan State University, B.A., 1969; University of Oregon, M.F.A., 1972
Career: English teacher, Kellogg Community College, 1973-74; Instructor in English and creative writing, Western Michigan University, 1974; Director, Videotape Writers Project/Television Services, Western Michigan University, 1977-
Address: 511 Campbell Street, Kalamazoo, Michigan 49007

Writings:
The Arable Mind	Blue Mountain Press	1977
Into the Book	Tree Books	1977

Work in Progress: A new book of poems

He says: "Since 1971 I have edited *Skywriting,* a literary magazine that has won a number of awards and grants. My poems, essays, and stories have been published widely in nationally recognized magazines, including *The American Poetry Review, The Antioch Review, The Agni Review, Pebble, The Dragonfly, The Northwest Review, Center, Abraxas, Response, The Charlton Review, The Lowlands Review, Red Weather,* and *The Midatlantic Review.* In 1976 I moderated the Panel on Literary Magazines and Small Presses at the Michigan Poetry Conference."

GUCK, DOROTHY (GRAY) 1913-

Pseudonym: Dorothy Gray
Born: May 17, 1913; Grand Rapids, Michigan
Parents: Walter E. and Margaret (Plaat) Gray
Married: Milton Edmund Guck, a United States Forest Ranger (deceased)
Children: Tom, Mick, and Mrs. Mary Crenshaw
Education: University of Wisconsin, 1930-34; Western New Mexico College, 1953-58
Career: Wife of forest ranger; Junior high school teacher of English and social studies; U.S. Postal Clerk; U.S. Forest Service office clerk
Address: Box 515, Nogal, New Mexico 88341

Writings:

Danger Rides the Forest	Vanguard Press	1969
Smokey Bear Pageant	U.S.D.A. Forest Service	1958
Cowboy Camp Meeting, 3rd ed.	Southwest Camp Meeting Association	1973

Work in Progress: Completed but not yet published are one teen-age adventure novel, two Colonial romance novels, and one contemporary romance novel; Another contemporary romance novel

She says: "I graduated in the same class as Gerald Ford from South High of Grand Rapids. He received a cup for the boy graduated who had achieved the most in four years, I received it for the girl. In our senior year, I ran on the same political election ticket as Jerry—he for president of the class—I for vice president. He was defeated, I was elected. We have remained in contact with each other over the years.

"I wrote the first published stories of the rescue of Smokey Bear from Captain forest fire, and was designer and chairman in charge of building the Smokey Museum at Captain.

"For years, I wrote fact articles for newspaper and magazine publication; was a reporter; wrote and told nature stories for children two years for PBS Radio; and did a weekly newscast for a commercial station. However, fiction is my genre now. I believe that fiction should be an entertaining escape from the real world around us and lean toward romantic all-ends-well plotting. My 21 years in Michigan gave me a well-rounded education, happy memories, and a continued zest for life."

Awards: Achievement Award from the United States Forest Service, 1959; Zia Award by New Mexico Press Women for Creative Writing, 1965

GUEST, EDGAR ALBERT 1881-1959

Born: August 20, 1881; Birmingham, England
Died: August 5, 1959; Detroit, Michigan
Parents: Edwin and Julia (Wayne) Guest
Married: Nellie (Crossman)
Children: Janet Guest Sobell and Edgar A. Guest, Jr. ("Bud")
Education: Grammar and high schools in Detroit, Michigan
Career: Newspaperman—with the *Detroit Free Press* from 1895 until his death; Poet and writer of humorous sketches
Address: c/o Mrs. Janet Guest Sobell; 4625 Lakeshore Road; Lexington, Michigan 48450

Writings:

Just Folks	*Reilly and Lee*	*1917*
Over Hers, and a Path to Home	*Reilly and Lee*	*1918*
When Day Is Done	*Reilly and Lee*	*1921*
All That Matters	*Reilly and Lee*	*1922*
The Passing Throng	*Reilly and Lee*	*1923*
Rhythms of Childhood	*Reilly and Lee*	*1924*
The Light of Faith	*Reilly and Lee*	*1926*
Harbor Lights of Home	*Reilly and Lee*	*1928*
The Friendly Way	*Reilly and Lee*	*1931*
Life's Highway	*Reilly and Lee*	*1933*
Collected Verse	*Contemporary Books*	*1934*
All in a Life Time	*Arno*	*1938*
Today and Tomorrow	*Reilly and Lee*	*1942*
Living the Years	*Reilly and Lee*	*1949*
Selected Poems	*Contemporary Books*	

Edgar Guest's family left England and came to Detroit when he was ten years old. During his career with the *Detroit Free Press* he wrote numerous verses and humorous sketches. He was frequently referred to as "The Poet of the Plain People."

GUEST, JUDITH 1936-

Born: March 29, 1936; Detroit, Michigan
Parents: Harry Reginald and Marion Aline (Nesbit) Guest
Married: Larry Lee
Education: University of Michigan, B.A. 1958
Career: Teacher for three years; Newspaper reporter; Writer
Address: 4600 W. 44th, Edina, Minnesota 55424

Writings:

Ordinary People	*Viking*	*1976*
Paperback edition	*Ballantine*	*1977*

Work in Progress: A second novel, tentatively titled *Second Heaven*

In an article published by the *Detroit Free Press,* Judith Guest calls writing "My escape, my terror, my compulsion, my life." About seven years ago she began writing seriously and submitted a short story for a *Reader's Digest* contest. There were one hundred prizes and her story received 60th place. Her next short story was the beginning of her highly-acclaimed first novel, *Ordinary People.* She says, "After I finished my short story, I realized I wasn't ready to put the characters down, that I had more to say about them. So, I thought, I'll write something about what happened to them before and what happened after. And before I knew what I was doing, I was writing a novel." Ms. Guest, who has lived in Michigan most of her life, moved with her family to suburban Minneapolis three years ago. Her great uncle was Edgar Guest, the last Michigan poet.

GUSTIN, LAWRENCE R. 1937-
Born: May 26, 1937; Flint, Michigan
Parents: Robert S. and Doris M. (Irving) Gustin
Married: Rose Mary (Murphy)
Children: Robert L. and David M.
Education: Michigan State University, B.A., 1959
Career: Sports editor, editorial page editor, *Michigan State University State News,* 1957-59; Lansing correspondent, United Press International, 1959; Michigan sports editor, UPI, 1960; *Flint Journal:* sports writer, 1960-63; copy editor, 1964; business writer, 1965; education writer, 1966; City Hall reporter, 1967-69; automotive editor, 1969-76; political writer, 1976-77; assistant metro editor, 1977-
Address: 1438 Country View Lane, Flint, Michigan 48504

Writings:

Billy Durant—Creator of General Motors	*Eerdmans*	*1973*
Flint Journal Picture History of Flint	*Eerdmans*	*1976*

HADLEY, THOMAS ERLE
Born: September 20, 1903
Parents: Clyde and Emily Honor (Lamb) Hadley
Married: Constance Arlene (Cook)
Children: Thom Erle Hadley II and Constance Hadley
Education: University of Michigan, B.S. in architecture, 1925
Career: Architect; Conservationist and lecturer on conservation for the National Audubon Society; Writer

Writings:

Happy Valley: Poetic Interpreta-		
tions of Nature	*Harlo Press*	*1966*
Songs of Nature (poems)		
Cosmic Crumbs (poems)		

Mr. Hadley has also contributed to Walt Disney's *Nature's Half Acre;* filmed and edited J.L. Hudson's *Zoolandia;* and has written for the Michigan Conservation Department.

HAGAR, HENRY B. 1926-

Born: September 12, 1926; Ashland, Kentucky
Parents: John F. and Henryetta (Brandebury) Hager
Married: Laura Price, a teacher
Children: John Price Hager and Jenny Ellen Brandebury Hager
Education: Yale University, 1947-51
Career: Army Air Force, 1945-46; Advertising—since 1970 with Young and Rubicam, Detroit; Part-time teacher of writing at Wayne State University and at the University Center for Adult Education in Detroit
Address: 5841 Wing Lake Road, Birmingham, Michigan 48010

Writings:

Fireball (novel)	*Doubleday*	*1963*

Work in Progress: Two novels

HAHN, DOROTHY 1935-

Born: April 15, 1935; Muskegon, Michigan
Parents: James Henry and Virginia Elinora (Spooner) Jones
Married: Fred Hahn, an engineer
Children: Susan, Shirley, Fred Jr., Joseph, Michael, and David
Education: Numerous courses at Muskegon Community College Orchard View, 1976
Career: Founder and officer of the Muskegon Seaway Scribes in 1966 (currently secretary/treasurer); Founder of the Midwest Michigan Chapter of the National Writers Club (served as Area/ Regional Co-Director and Communications, 1976; Coordinated area writers workshops, 1970-72; Writer of numerous articles, radio scripts and radio copy; Assistant editor of *Michigamme Review,* 1967
Address: 2339 Ducey Avenue, Muskegon, Michigan 49442

Writings:

Roots and Wings	*Sprint Print*	*1977*

Work in Progress: Researching astrology, dream interpretation and ESP. Gathering new poems for another book

She says: "I have been married for 25 years, have six children, and have lived at the same address for 22 years. My earlier poems were written between changing diapers and guiding children toward maturity. I settled down to serious writing in 1975 and began winning contests. With only three children at home, I am doing some 'growing up' too. I used to write only when the spirit moved me. Now I work at writing, setting aside three hours a day to learn new forms. Poetry is very challenging and as varied as life. I began having my work published at age 15, but it was strictly for fun. Now, It's for fun AND profit—and for the joy of accomplishment!" Mrs. Hahn is listed in *International Who's Who In Poetry.*

Awards: 2 first places in the Poetry Society of Michigan, 1975-76; Second place in *Jean's Journal,* 1976; First place in *Jean's Journal,* 1976; Fifth honorable mention, National Federation of State Poetry Societies, 1976; Special mention, *Encore* contest, 1976; Third prize, Poetry Society of Michigan, 1977; Two prize-winning poems included in a text for poets, *Beyond Verse to Poetry,* 1977; First prize in the Serious Quatrain Category of the Poetry Society of Michigan, 1978.

HAINES, DONAL HAMILTON 1886-
Born: 1886; Kalamazoo, Michigan
Education: University of Michigan, A.B.
Career: Newspaper reporter and free-lance writer; Assistant professor of journalism, University of Michigan

Writings:

The Return of Pierre	Holt	1912
The Last Invasion	Harper	1914
Clearing the Seas; or The Last of the Warships	Harper	1915
The Dragon-flies; A Tale of Flying Service	Houghton	1919
Sky-line Inn	Houghton	1919
Fighting Blood; A Tale of Kitchener's Campaign in the Soudan	Houghton	1927
The Transportation Library of the University of Michigan; Its History and Needs	University of Michigan	1929
The Southpaw	Farrar & Rinehart	1931
Toss-Up	Farrar & Rinehart	1932
Triple Threat	Farrar & Rinehart	1933
Team Play	Farrar & Rinehart	1934
Sporting Chance	Farrar & Rinehart	1935

David and Jonathan	*Farrar & Rinehart*	*1936*
Blaine of the Backfield	*Farrar & Rinehart*	*1937*
Advanced Short Story	*University of Michigan*	*1938*
Creative Writing	*University of Michigan*	*1938*
Langford's Luck	*Farrar & Rinehart*	*1939*
Pro Quarterback	*Farrar & Rinehart*	*1940*
Luck in All Weathers; Personal Adventures in Hunting and Fishing	*Farrar & Rinehart*	*1941*
Shadow on the Campus	*Farrar & Rinehart*	*1942*
The Fortress, A Story of Hillton Academy	*Farrar & Rinehart*	*1945*

HALL, CAROLYN VOSBURG 1927-

Born: July 22, 1927; Fenton, Michigan
Parents: Guy M. and Doris (Bourns) Vosburg
Married: Clarence A. Hall, an engineer
Children: Randall Ross, Claudia Lee, and Garrett Alan
Education: Cranbrook Academy of Art, B.F.A. 1949, M.F.A. 1951
Career: Teacher; North Dakota State College, the Detroit Institute of Arts, and the Bloomfield Art Association; Designer of convention and window displays; Art critic for the *Birmingham Eccentric* newspaper, 1963-73; Freelance designer—commissions in art; 22 one-person art shows and many other exhibitions
Address: 20730 Kennoway, Birmingham, Michigan 48010

Writings:

Switched and Stuffed Art	*Doubleday*	*1974*
I Love Popcorn	*Doubleday*	*1976*
I Love Ice Cream	*Doubleday*	*1976*

Work in Progress: *Complete Book of Machine Sewn Crafts*—to be published in 1979 by Van Nostrand Reinhold.

She says: "I always wanted to . . . be an artist, write books, have a husband and family, travel, learn about anything and everything . . . and win at tennis. With good fortune, supportive parents, and a high energy level I've been able to do them all up to 'learn about everything.' I look forward to continuing to try that and as for tennis—5 out of 6 isn't bad."

HAMILTON, FRANKLIN WILLIARD 1923-

Born: November 22, 1923; Benton, Illinois
Parents: James A. and Georgia B. (Dowell) Hamilton
Married: Betty Jean Spellmeyer, a registered nurse
Children: Douglas James and Karen Joyce

Education: Southern Illinois University, B.A. 1949, M.A. 1949; Kansas State Teachers College, M.S. 1955; University of Kansas, Ed.D., 1961

Career: English instructor; Hiwassee College, Madisonville, Tennessee, 1951-52; College of Emporia, Emporia, Kansas, 1953-55; Illinois State University, Normal, Illinois, 1955; University of Kansas, Lawrence, Kansas, 1960-61; Mott Community College, Flint, Michigan, 1956-present; Journalist, Editor, *Huron Review*

Address: c/o Walden Press, 423 South Franklin Avenue, Flint, Michigan 48503

Writings:

Leaf Scar (poetry)	*Brookside Press*	*1965*
Thoreau on the Art of Writing		
(literary criticism)	*Walden Press*	*1967*
Love Cry (poetry)	*Brookside Press*	*1970*

Contributor of poetry to numerous periodicals, including: *American Bard, Poetry and Drama Magazine, Odyssey, Saturday Review, Pegasus, Artesian, New Athenaeu, Trace, College English, Cardinal Poetry Quarterly, Bitterroot,* and *Manhattan Review.*

HAMOD, SAM

Born: February 1; Gary, Indiana

Parents: Sam and Zina (Habhab) Hamond

Children: David and Laura

Education: Northwestern University, B.S. 1957, M.A. 1960; University of Iowa, Ph. D., 1973

Career: University of Iowa, 1966-71; University of Wisconsin, 1971-72; University of Pittsburgh, 1972-73; Writer in Residence; Television writer for *Happy Days* and *The Odd Couple,* 1973-74; *"Poetry in the Schools"* for Michigan Council for the Arts, 1975-77; University of Michigan, Flint, 1975-present

Address: 2035 W. Mt. Morris Road, Mt. Morris, Michigan 48458

Writings:

The Holding Action	*Sea Mark Press*	*1969*
The Famous Boating Party	*Cedar Creek Press*	
After the Funeral of Assam		
Hamady	*Perishable Press*	*1971*
Surviving in America (with		
Anselm Hollo and Jack		
Marshall)	*Cedar Creek Press*	*1971*
The Famous Blue Mounds		
Scrapbook	*Perishable Press*	*1972*
The Famous Boating Party II	*Cedar Creek Press*	*1973-74*

Inclusion in several anthologies including:

Settling America	Macmillan	1974
Traveling America	Macmillan	1977
Poems Here and Now	Morrow	1976

Work in Progress: *Moving,* a book of poems to be published in fall 1977; *Love Poems,* to be published in 1978

He says: "I'm interested in quality of work, not quantity. Also, publication is far down my list of priorities. As much as possible, I include whatever local geography is available. The past few years, Michigan has been the scene of a lot of my work. Then again, all places are related as are all people if your spirit is right, then the writing just flows. I also enjoy teaching a variety of things: writing, history, folklore—it all blends together after a while."

HARRISON, REBECCA (MRS. JOHN ARTHUR) see: NEWTH, REBECCA

HARRISON, JIM 1937-
Born: December 11, 1937; Grayling, Michigan
Parents: Winfield and Norma (Walgren) Harrison
Married: Linda King
Children: Jamie and Anna
Education: Michigan State University, B.A. and M.A. in comparative literature 1956-62
Career: Teacher, S.U.N.Y. at Stonybrook for two years; Writer
Address: Lake Leelanau, Michigan 49653

Writings:
Plain Song	Norton	1965
Locations	Norton	1968
Wolf (novel)	Simon and Schuster	1970
Outlyer	Simon and Schuster	1970
A Good Day to Die (novel)	Simon and Schuster	1972
Letters to Yesenin	Sumac	1975
Farmer (pastoral novel set in Michigan in the 1950's	Viking	1976

Work in Progress: Two novels and a new book of poems

He says: "I grew up in northern Michigan. Both my mother's and father's families were farm families from Osceola and Mecosta Counties. I grew up within that framework. It's whatever you get your juice from, your ideas form. My ideas seem to be rural in nature." Harrison lives with his family on a farm in northern Michigan where he does his writing in an old granary on the property.

Awards: $2,500 award from the Michigan Foundation of the Arts; Grant from National Endowment for the Arts; Guggenheim Fellow

HART, JOHN E. 1917-

Born: February 16, 1917; Barnard, Kansas
Parents: Harriss L. and Anna M. (Hunter) Hart
Married: Mary Helen (Negus), an art consultant
Education: Kansas Wesleyan, A.B. 1938; Syracuse University, M.A. 1942, Ph.D. 1954
Career: Teaching fellow, Syracuse University, 1940-42; Instructor, Cincinnati University, 1946-49; Guest teacher at Odenwaldschule, Heppenheim, Germany, and lecturer at Padagogisches Institute, Darmstadt, Judgenheim, Germany, 1950-51; Assistant professor, Albion College, 1954-60; Associate professor, Albion College, 1960-65; Professor, Albion College, 1965-
Address: 412 Fitch Street, Albion, Michigan 49224

Writings:

History of 334th Field Artillery	U.S. Dept. of the Army	1946
Floyd Dell	Twayne	1971

Contributor to:

The Red Badge of Courage: Text and Criticism-Richard Lettis and others, editors	Harcourt	1960
The Red Badge of Courage: An Annotated Text, Background and Sources-Sculley Bradley and others, editors	Norton	1962
Myth and Literature, John Vickery, editor	University of Nebraska Press	1966
The Red Badge of Courage: Analytic Notes and Review	American R.D.M.	1966
Merrill Studies in "The Scarlet Letter"-Arlin Turner, editor	C.E. Merrill	1970

New England Quarterly, Modern Fiction Studies, and other publications.

Poetry included in:

New Directions Anthology James Laughlin, editor	New Directions	1942

Work in Progress: A full critical study of Albert Halper; and studies of aspects of the work of Galsworthy, Sinclair Lewis, and Oscar Wilde.

HATCHER, HARLAN HENTHORNE 1898-
Born: September 9, 1898; Ironton, Ohio
Parents: Robert E. and Linda (Leslie) Hatcher
Married: Anne (Vance)
Children: Robert Leslie and Anne Linda
Education: Ohio State University, A.B. 1922, M.A. 1923, Ph.D 1927, LL.D. 1952
Career: Ohio State University, Professor of English; University of Michigan, Dean of the College of Literature, Science, and Arts; Vice-president of the University; President of the University; Professor of English, 1951-68; President Emeritus of the University of Michigan, 1968-; Author and consultant, 1968-
Address: 841 Greenhills Drive; Ann Arbor, Michigan 48105

Writings:

Versification of Robert Browning	Ohio State University	1928
Tunnel Hill	Bobbs-Merrill	1931
Patterns of Wolfpen	Bobbs-Merrill	1934
Creating the Modern American Novel	Farar & Rinehart	1935
Central Standard Time	Farrar & Rinehart	1937
The Buckeye Country	Kinsey	1940
The Great Lakes	Oxford	1944
Lake Erie	Bobbs-Merrill	1945
The Western Reserve	Bobbs-Merrill	1949
A Century of Iron and Men	Bobbs-Merrill	1950
Giant from the Wilderness	Cleveland	1955
Pictorial History of the Great Lakes	Crown	1963
Persistent Quest for Values	Missouri University	1966

Editor of the following:

The Ohio Guide	WPA	1940
Modern Continental, British, American Dramas (3 volumes)	Harcourt	1941
A Modern Repertory	Harcourt	1953
Modern American Dramas	Harcourt	1941
Revised edition	Harcourt	1949

Contributor of short stories, essays and articles to various magazines and journals.

HATHAWAY, BAXTER 1909-
Born: December 4, 1909; Cincinnati, Ohio
Parents: William B. and Etta I. (Fee) Hathaway
Married: Sherry Kitchen
Children: Hannah H. Colen, William K. and James B. Hathaway
Education: Kalamazoo College, B.A. 1935; University of

Michigan, M.A., Ph.D. 1935-40
Career: Writer, scholar and teacher at the University of Michigan, University of Montana, University of Wisconsin, and Cornell University (1946-76) Editor of *Epoch* for 29 years; Current editor of *Cornell Review*
Address: 419 Wyckoff Avenue, Ithaca, New York 14850

Writings:

The Stubborn Way (novel about Michigan)	Macmillan	1937
The Age of Criticism	Cornell University Press	1962
Marvels and Commonplaces	Random House	1968
Transformational Syntax	Ronald	1969

Work in Progress: *Life and Times of Sperone Pseroni*

Awards: Hopwood Awards (University of Michigan) in poetry and fiction, 1937

HAUSHALTER, FRED L. 1893-
Born: January 13, 1893; Akron, Ohio
Parents: Milton W. and Ida A. Haushalter
Married: Elizabeth H. (Biram)
Children: Wayne J. Haushalter, Esther A. Allen, Elma J. Ague
Education: Ohio State University, B.E.E. 1917, E.E. 1926
Career: Served in World War I as First Lieutenant, 56th Engineers, in command of Anti-aircraft-Searchlight Unit; Assistant Engineer of tests, B.F. Goodrich Tire and Rubber Company, 1918-28; Rubber Products development engineer, B.F. Goodrich Tire and Rubber Company, 1928-43; Rubber Consultant to Ordnance Tank Automotive Center (Detroit), 1943-45; Automotive engineer on all rubber applications, Firestone Tire and Rubber Company (Detroit) 1945-1958; Chairman of Ordnance-Industry Tank Track Committee for three years during the Korean War; Consulting engineer, 1958-74
Address: 461 Gypsy Lane, Northwood Apt. 68, Youngstown, Ohio 44504

Writings:

Rules for Safe Driving and How Your Tires May Save Your Life	Vantage Press	1971
Inventors I Have Known	Exposition Press	1973

Also: 17 technical articles published in various technical journals over a period of 35 years

Work in Progress: *What is Truth?,* a book about truth as it applies to politicians and leaders of nations; A Sherlock Holmes story, *The Mystery of the Cup*

He says: "Having passed my 85th birthday on January 13th (I was born on Friday the 13th and consider myself very fortunate in having quite good health) I get great satisfaction and comfort in reading such books as Paul Tillich's *The Eternal Now* and the three volumes of sermons of Frederick Robertson of Brighton, England. I read the *New York Times* daily to keep up to date with world affirs and, being a member of the Research Society of the Sigma Xi, receive bi-monthly the *American Scientist.* I also keep reading at my eleven volumes written by Will Durant and his wife, just to see how history in many ways keeps repeating itself. However, I am still an optimist about the future state of the world." Mr. Haushalter also holds 35 patents on various rubber products. His "most important patent was a device which grounded the steel pin of rubber-bushed tank tracks to the steel track block. This device eliminated the static electrical discharges at the sprockets and insured radio reception between tanks in battle." He received a citation for Meritorious Civilian Service for his device from the Chief of Ordnance, Army Service Forces.

Awards: Plaque for Best Book on Patents from the Philadephia Patent Lawyers Association for *Inventors I Have Known,* 1973

HAVIGHURST, WALTER, 1901-

Born: November 28, 1901; Appleton, Wisconsin
Parents: Freeman A. and Winifred Aurelia (Weter) Havighurst
Married: Marion Boyd Havighurst (deceased)
Education: University of Denver, A.B. 1924; Columbia University, A.M. 1927
Career: United States Merchant Marine, 1921-22 and 1925-26; Member of Department of English, Miami University, 1928-29; Writer and contributor to *Saturday Review, American Heritage,* and *The American West*
Address: Shadowy Hills Drive, Oxford, Ohio 45056

Writings:

Pier 17	Macmillan	1935
The Upper Mississippi	Farrar & Rinehart	
The Winds of Spring	Macmillan	1940
The Long Ships Passing	Macmillan	1942
Land of Promise	Macmillan	1946
Signature of Time	Macmillan	1949
Vein of Iron	World	1959
The Heartland	Harper and Row	1962
Voices on the River	Macmillan	1964
The Forts of Mackinac	Prentice Hall	1966
River to the West	Putnam	1970

He says: "As a youthful seaman on Great Lakes freighters I

developed an interest in the history of transportation on American waterways. That interest, still continuing, has led to the writing of most of my books. I am especially drawn to Upper Michigan and the entire Lake Superior country. The best literary sources I have found for an understanding of that region are represented in my anthology *The Great Lakes Reader,* Macmillan 1966."

HECHT, WARREN JAY 1946-

Born: December 31, 1946; Brooklyn, New York
Parents: Abraham and Evelyn J. (Birnbaum) Hecht
Married: Christine Holowicki
Education: The City College of New York, B.A. 1969
Career: Editor; Street Fiction Press, Inc.; Director of the Creative Writing Program in the The Residential College of the University of Michigan
Address: c/o Street Fiction Press, 201 E. Liberty, Ann Arbor, Michigan 48104 or c/o The Residential College, University of Michigan, Ann Arbor, Michigan 48109

Writings:

Babyburgers (co-author with Andrew B. Carrigan)	*Street Fiction Press*	*1975*

Editor of two ongoing series published by Street Fiction Press: *Anon* and *The Periodical Lunch Collection.*

HEDRICK, ULYSSES PRENTISS 1870-1951

Born: January 15, 1870; Independence, Iowa
Died: 1951
Parents: Benjamin Franklin and Mary Cathering (Myers) Hedrick
Married: Amy Willis Plummer
Children: Catherin Layton, Penelope Rodney, and Ulysses Prentiss
Education: Michigan Agricultural College, B.S. 1893, M.S. 1895; Hobart College, D.Sc. 1913; Utah Agricultural College, LL.D. 1939
Career: Assistant horticulturist, Michigan Agricultural College, 1893-95; Professor of botany and horticulture, Oregon Agricultural College, 1895-97; Professor of botany and horticulture, Utah Agricultural College, 1897-99; Professor of horticulture, Michigan Agricultural College, 1899-1905; Horticulturist, 1905-30; and Director, 1938-59, New York Agricultural Experiment Station

Writings:
Apple Districts of New York with Varieties for Each, co-

author with N.O. Booth and O.M. Taylor	New York State Agricultural Experiment Station	1906
The Grapes of New York, co-author with N.O. Booth, O.M. Taylor, R. Wellington, and M.J. Dorsey	J.B. Lyon	1908
The Plums of New York, co-author with W.R. Wellington, O.M. Taylor, W.H. Alderman and M.J. Dorsey	J.B. Lyon	1911
The Cherries of New York, co-author with G.H. Howe, O.M. Taylor, C.B. Tugergen, and R. Wellington	J.B. Lyon	1915
The Peaches of New York, co-author with G.H. Howe, O.M. Taylor and C.B. Tubergen	J.R. Lyon	1917
Fruits for the Home Grounds	Macmillan	1919
Revised edition	Macmillan	1924
Sturtevant's Notes on Edible Plants (editor)	J.B. Lyon	1919
The Pears of New York, co-author with G.H. Howe, O.M. Taylor, S.H. Francis, and H.B. Tukey	J.B. Lyon	1921
Cyclopedia of Hardy Fruits	Macmillan	1922
Second edition	Macmillan	1938
The Small Fruits of New York, co-author with G.H. Howe, O.M. Taylor, Alwin Berger, G.L. Slate and Olav Einset	J.B. Lyon	1925
Systematic Pomology	Macmillan	1925
Reprinted	Macmillan	1939
Peas of New York	New York State Agricultural Experiment Station	1928
A History of Agriculture in the State of New York	New York Agricultural Society	1933
Beans of New York	New York State Agricultural Experiment Station	1934
Fruits for the Home Garden	Oxford University Press	1944
Paperback edition	Dover	1973
Grapes and Wines from Home Vineyards	Oxford University Press	1945
The Land of the Crooked Tree	Oxford University Press	1948
A History of Horticulture in American to 1860	Oxford University Press	1950

Numerous pamphlets and bulletins on horticultural subjects

Of special interest to Michigan residents is *The Land of the Crook-*

ed Tree, found on old maps as L'Arbe Croche on the northern tip of the lower peninsula of Michigan. The book is set in the 1870's and 1880's. According to Dr. Hedrick, it is" . . . not an autobiography, although it is brazenly personal from beginning to end." It is dedicated: "To the memory of my parents, pioneers in the land of the crooked tree."

HELLIE, ANN 1925-
Born: June 16, 1925; Williamsport, Pennsylvania
Parents: LaVerne H. and Ruth (Stewart) Shea
Married: Charles W. Hellie, president of Graphics Company
Children: C. Micheal, Stephen, Mary Elizabeth, John
Education: Bucknell University, B.A. 1946; West Chester State; University of Michigan
Career: Editorial Thesis preparation, Xerox, 1963-64; Department Manager, Jacobson's, 1973-76; Executive Vice President, Graphic Communications Inc., 1976-; Freelance writer, 1960-
Address: 2909 Brockman Blvd., Ann Arbor, Michigan 48104

Writings:

The Box of Important Things	*Western Publishing*	*1968*
Once I Had a Monster	*Western Publishing*	*1970*
Brian and the Long, Long Scarf	*Lerner (Carolrhoda)*	*1973*

Work in Progress: A picture book, *The Terrible Something New;* a children's novel, *Balderdash;* and a historical novel, *Dark Festival*

She says: "I am a tiny bit German, a little bit English, and a whale of a lot Irish. Therefore, tall tales come more easily to me than factual ones. One line in a favorite book, Charles Reade's *The Cloister and the Hearth,* expresses my philosophy very nicely: 'Look into your own heart and write.!' "

HEMINGWAY, ERNEST MILLER 1899-1961
Born: July 21, 1899; Oak Park, Illinois
Died: July 2, 1961; Ketchum, Idaho
Parents: Clarence Edmonds Hemingway, M.D. and Grace (Hall) Hemingway
Married: Hadley (Richardson) in 1919 (divorced 1926); Pauline (Pfeiffer) in 1927 (divorced, 1940); Martha (Gellhorn) in 1940 (divorced in 1946); Mary (Welsh) in 1946
Children: John Hemingway (mother: Hadley (Richardson) Hemingway); Patrick Hemingway and Gregory Hemingway (mother: Pauline (Pfeiffer) Hemingway)

Education: Oak Park (Illinois) Public Schools, high school diploma 1917

Career: Journalist, novelist and short-story writer; Cub reporter for Kansas City *Star;* Reporter and ambulance driver in World War I; European correspondent for the Toronto *Star;* Paris correspondent for Heart's Syndicated News Service; Newspaper correspondent in Spain during the Spanish Civil War; Correspondent for *Collier's* during World War II

Writings:

Three Stories and Ten Poems	Scribner	1923
In Out Time	Scriner	1924
The Torrents of Spring	Scribner	1926
The Sun Also Rises	Scribner	1926
Men without Women	Scribner	1927
A Farewell to Arms	Scribner	1929
Death in the Afternoon	Scribner	1932
Winner Take Nothing	Scribner	1933
The Green Hills of Africa	Scribner	1935
To Have and Have Not	Scribner	1937
The Fifth Column and the First Forty-nine Stories	Scribner	1938
For Whom the Bell Tolls	Scribner	1940
Across the River and into the Trees	Scribner	1950
The Old Man and the Sea	Scribner	1952
A Moveable Feast	Scribner	1964
Island in the Stream	Scribner	1970

Awards: Pulitzer Prize in 1953 for *The Old Man and the Sea;* Nobel Prize for Literature in 1954

Ernest Hemingway is one of the most famous authors associated with Michigan. Although he was born and raised in Oak Park, Illinois, Hemingway spent long summers with his family at their cottage on Walloon Lake near Petoskey, Michigan. This part of his life is vividly depicted in *At the Hemingways,* a book written by his sister, Marceline Hemingway Sanford.

HENRY, VERA
Born: Forest, Ontario
Parents: Hugh T. and Myrtle (Gammon) Johnson
Married: James Alexander Henry (deceased)
Children: James Hugh and Kevin Michael
Career: Associate editor, Writer's Digest School; Writer
Address: 915 E. Fifth, Royal Oak, Michigan 48067

Writings:

A Lucky Number	Lippincott	1957
Mystery of Cedar Valley		
Paperback title: Portrait		
In Fear	Thomas Bouregy	1964
Ong the Wild Gander	Lippincott	1966

She says: "Writing is the most exciting and challenging job in the whole world and it always surprises me a little that anyone wants to do anything else. I particularly enjoy working with new writers and meeting them at conferences. Michigan is a rich, fertile state for the creative mind. No one living here should ever run out of story ideas. I've just completed writing the short story correspondence course for Writers Digest. I'm also working on short stories and finishing a novel."

HEWARD, WILLIAM L. 1949-
Born: November 22, 1949; Michigan City, Indiana
Parents: Joe W. and Helen M. (Jensen) Heward
Married: Jill C. Dardig
Education: Western Michigan University, B.A. 1971; University of Massachusetts, Ed. D. 1974
Career: Assistant Professor, Faculty for Exceptional Children, Ohio State University, 1975-present; Research Assistant, Northwest Regional Media Center for the Deaf, University of Massachusetts, 1972-74; Instructor, Media Specialists Program, University of Massachusetts, 1972-74; Player-Manager, Indianapolis Clowns Baseball Club, 1971-75
Address: 1094 F Fountain Lane, Columbus, Ohio 43213

Writings:

| Some Are Called Clowns: A Season with the Last of the Great Barnstorming Baseball Teams (joint author with D.V. Gat)—(re-issued as a paperback by Warner Books, 1975) | Crowell | 1974 |
| Sign Here: A Contracting Book for Children and Their Parents (joint author with J.C. Dardig) | Behaviordelia | 1976 |

Work in Progress: Two books—*Parenting the Exceptional Child,* to be published by Behaviordelia in 1978; and *Phyllis Goes to College: An Introduction to Behavior Analysis,* to be published by Wadsworth in 1979.

He says: "Professional interests include working with parents of exceptional children, research into the use of educational technology, e.g., Visual Response System, to improve the learning of handicapped persons, and the analysis of sport behavior."

Awards: Waldo-Sangren Scholar, Western Michigan University, 1970-71; Listed in *Contemporary Authors, 1975; Dictionary of International Biography, volume 13; The International Authors,* and *Writers Who's Who, Eighth Edition.*

HILBERRY, CONRAD 1928-
Born: March 1, 1928; Melrose Park, Illinois
Parents: Clarence B. and Ruth (Haase) Hilberry
Married: Marion Bailey, a teacher
Children: Marilyn Hilberry Day, Jane and Ann Hilbery
Education: Oberlin College, B.A. 1949; University of Wisconsin, M.S. and Ph. D. 1950-54
Career: Teacher- DePauw University, Greencastle, Indiana, 1954-61; Assistant-Associated Colleges of the Midwest, 1961-62; Teacher-Kalamazoo College, 1962-present
Address: 1601 Grand Avenue, Kalamazoo, Michigan 49007

Writings:

The Poems of John Collop (edition)	Univ. of Wisconsin Press	1962
Struggle and Promise: A Future for Colleges (with Morris Keeton and others)	McGraw-Hill	1968
Encounter on Burrows Hill (poems)	Ohio Univ. Press	1968
Rust (poems)	Ohio Univ. Press	1974
The Third Coast: Contemporary Michigan Poets (an anthology edited with Herbert Scott and James Tipton)	Wayne State Univ. Press	1976

HILL, JACK 1896-
Born: May 25, 1896; Vaasa, Finland
Married: Vera (Wilen)
Children: Dr. Jack Warren Hill
Education: Self-educated after the age of 14
Career: Laborer-road work, mining and farming
Address: c/o Marcia Bernhardt, Education Committee Chairman, Iron County Historical Society, Rt. 2, Iron River, Michigan 49935

Writings:

The History of Iron County	Reporter Publishing Co.	1955
The History of Iron County,		

Ms. Bernhardt provides the following information, written for the *Green Bay Press Gazette:* " 'History has always been one of my weak points . . . To combine ideas and express them on paper for the information and enjoyment of others is one of the most satisfying of all hobbies.' The speaker was octogenarian Jack Hill, Iron County's scholarly historian. Jack was born in Vaasa, Finland, the third son of four, and came to the United States at the age of six. Life in the new land was not easy and Jack recalled helping his father on road building projects and right of way clearing when he was young. The family had been left motherless three years earlier and no one really encouraged him to continue his formal education. Following service in World War I he returned to Stambaugh, Michigan, and married the former Vera Wilen. The Hills have lived all but the first years of their lives together on the same farm. In the late 1920's Jack worked for the township on the highways and served as road commissioner. Perhaps this led to his interest in public records. Later he worked with the Civilian Conservation Corps program and in the mines.

"It was in the early thirties that his interest in history flowered. In time, as the notes and information accumulated, he was struck with the idea of how important it is to 'learn more about local history and the activities of our forebearers and then to compile the material into somewhat chronological order.' Notes and information mounted for over twenty years. This ultimately led to the publication of *The History of Iron County.* "

HILLERT, MARGARET 1920-

Born: January 22, 1920; Saginaw, Michigan
Parents: Edward C. and Lee Ilva (Sproull) Hillert
Education: Bay City Junior College, A.A. 1941; University of Michigan, R.N. 1944; Wayne State University, A.B. 1948
Career: Primary school teacher in Whittier School, Royal Oak, Michigan, 1948-present
Address: 31262 Huntley Square E., Apt. 1224, Birmingham, Michigan 48009

Just Beginning-to-Read Series:

Three Little Pigs	*Follett*	*1963*
Three Goats	*Follett*	*1963*
Three Bears	*Follett*	*1963*
Funny Baby	*Follett*	*1963*
Yellow Boat	*Follett*	*1966*
Magic Beans	*Follett*	*1966*
Little Runaway	*Follett*	*1966*

Birthday Car	Follett	1966
Snow Baby	Follett	1969
Circus Fun	Follett	1969
House for Little Red	Follett	1970
Cinderella at the Ball	Follett	1970
Little Puff	Follett	1973
Come Play with Me	Follett	1975
Happy Birthday, Dear Dragon	Follett	1977
What Is It?	Follett	1978
Play Ball	Follett	1978
The Golden Goose	Follett	1978
The Cook House	Follett	1978

Writings:

Farthern Than Far (poetry)	Follett	1969
I Like to Live in the City (poetry)	Golden Gooks	1970
Who Comes to Your House (poetry)	Golden Books	1973
The Sleepytime Book (poetry)	Golden Books	1975
Come Play with Me (poetry)	Follett	1975

Hundreds of poems for both adults and children in such periodicals as The Lyric, Western Humanities Review, Christian Science Monitor, Poet Lore, Horn Book, and Woodsrunner; and in such anthologies as Michigan Hot apples, Forty Salutes to Michigan Poets, and Echoes of the Moon.

Work in Progress: Four booklets of verse; and *I'm Special. . .So Are You,* recently sold to Hallmark.

In *Pass the Poetry, Please* (Citation 1972), Ms. Hillert says: "I can't give you a glib one-line definition of poetry such as many I have seen. Poetry has been an undefined but definite part of my life, and I don't think I chose to write it at all. I have been writing it ever since the first one I did when I was eight years old, which seems to indicate it has always been a part of my nature. I read widely, from the poetry stacks in the library when I was growing up—and still do to some extent. I'm not one of those people who can say, 'Today I'll write a poem.' I may go without writing anything for some time as a consequence, but once I get the grain of an idea, the thing must be worked through, sometimes for days, weeks, or months. Things don't usually come to me whole and full blown. It intrigues me to work generally, but not always, with traditional forms but in fresh ways . . ."

HODGES, ELMA J. 1910-
Born: June 29, 1910; Merijavri, O.L., Finland
Parents: Nestor W. and Liisa J. (Koivisto) Ahlstrom

Married: Lester A. Hodges, a machinist (retired)
Children: Dr. Ronald W. Hodges
Education: Gwinn High School, Michigan 1928
Career: Housewife and mother
Address: 2611 Pleasant Grove Road, Lansing, Michigan 48910

Writings:
Goatsbeard and Other Poems   *All-Starr Publishing*   *1976*

Work in Progress: Another book of poems

She says: "I am a regular member of the Lansing Poetry Club and the Poetry Society of Michigan. I joined the Poetry Club in 1966 and have been writing poetry steadily ever since. I am more of a nature poet than any other type. I enjoy reading traditional and modern poetry also.

"In 1973 and 1974 I worked on the Poetry Society of Michigan Youth Contest in the Lansing area. In 1975 I served as Co-chairman and judge locally in the Lansing area for the Youth Contest. I appeared on a local television program in regard to the Youth Contest; and have also given poetry readings."

HOLDEN, (WILLIS) SPRAGUE 1909-1973
Pseudonym: Montgomery Black
Born: January 3, 1909; Grand Rapids, Michigan
Parents: Charles Wayne and Marie (Sprague) Holden
Married: Shelia (Edna) Richart
Education: Grand Rapids Junior College, diploma 1927; University of Michigan, B.A. 1930; Columbia University, M.A. 1932
Career: Sports writer, *Grand Rapids Herald,* 1926; College correspondent for Michigan papers, 1926-29; Staff writer, *Time Magazine,* New Hork, 1930; Reviewer, managing editor, *San Francisco Argonaut,* 1932-36; Editorial writer, Akron (Ohio) *Beacon Journal,* 1936-40; Professor of Journalism, Wayne State University, 1946-73; Founder and Chairman of Wayne State University's Journalism Department, 1949-73; Book reviewer: *Detroit Sunday News,* 1969-72 and Journalism Quarterly, 1968-71; Editor, *Detroit in Perspective: A Journal of Regional History,* 1972-73

Address of Mrs. Holden: 28150 Westbrook Court, Farmington Hills, Michigan 48018

Writings:
Australia Goes to Press   *Wayne State University*
    (Australian edition, 1962)   *Press*   *1961*

Chapters in several books including:
The Speaker's Resource Book:

| Newspapers of the U.S.A. | Scott Foresman | 1964 |
| The Asian Newspapers' Reluc-tant Revolution | Iowa State University Press | 1971 |

Numerous articles, feature stories and sketches in newspapers, professional journals and popular magazines

Mrs. Holden says: "We lived and traveled in all five states of Australia, as well as the Northern Territory and Tasmania; we also traveled in 47 of our 50 states and in 21 other countries. Mr. Holden lectured in universities other than Wayne State University—Columbia, Minnesota, Missouri, Illinois, New Mexico, and the University of California at Berkeley are some that I remember. He wrote every day of the 40 years we were together. All of his manuscripts, correspondence and published works are in the Archives of The Walter Reuther Library of Labor and Urban Affairs at Wayne State University in Detroit."

Awards: Fulbright Grant to study Australian metropolitan daily newspapers, 1956-57; Fulbright Grant and Ford Foundation Grant to study the industrial arbitration-conciliation system of Australia, 1966; 29th Arthur Norman Smith Lecturer in Journalism at the University of Melbourne, the first American to be so honored.

HOLLI, MELVIN G. 1933-
Born: February 22, 1933; Ishpeming, Michigan
Parents: Walfred M. and Sylvia (Erickson) Holli
Married: Betsy (Biggar)
Children: Susan and Steven
Education: Northern Michigan University, B.A. 1957; University of Michigan, M.A. 1958, Ph. D. 1966
Career: National Woodrow Wilson Fellow, University of Michigan, 1957-58; Teacher, Flat Rock (Michigan) Public Schools, 1958-59; Curator of Manuscripts, University of Michigan, 1961-63; Assistant to Professor of History, University of Illinois, Chicago Circle, 1965-
Address: 1311 Ashland Avenue, River Forest, Illinois 60305

Writings:

Reform in Detroit: Hazen S. Pingree and Urban Reform (Urban Life in America series)	Oxford University Press	1969
Detroit (Documentary History of American Cities series)	Franklin Watts	1976
The Ethnic Frontier; Group Survival in Chicago and the Midwest (Co-author with Peter d' A. Jones)	William B. Eerdmans	1977

Work in Progress: *The Ethnic Challenge In Urban America,* to be published by William B. Eerdmans in 1980

He says: "I am interested in writing about urban and midwestern themes. The rich social and human history of the midwest is just now being recovered. I hope to make some contribution to its preservation and dissemination."

HOPF, ALICE L. 1904-
Pseudonym: A.M. Lightner (for fiction)
Born: October 11, 1904; Detroit, Michigan
Parents: Clarence and Frances (McGraw) Lightner
Married: Ernest J. Hopf, an artist
Children: Christopher Hopf
Education: Westover School, 1920-23; Vassar College, 1924-27
Career: Writer
Address: 136 West 16th Street, New York, NY 10011

Writings:
Fiction and Science Fiction-

Doctor to the Galaxy	Norton	*1965*
The Galactic Troubadours	Norton	*1965*
The Space Plague	Norton	*1966*
The Rock of Three Planets	Putnam	*1963*
The Planet Poachers	Putnam	*1965*
The Space Olympics	Norton	*1967*
(Paperback edition)	Tempo	*1972*
The Space Ark	Putnam	*1968*
The Walking Zoo of Darwin Dingle	Putnam	*1969*
The Day of the Drones	Norton	*1969*
(Paperback edition)	Bantam	*1970*
The Thursday Toads	McGraw	*1971*
Wild Traveler: The Story of a Coyote	Norton	*1967*
Star Dog	McGraw	*1973*
Gods or Demons?	Four Winds	*1973*
The Space Gypsies	McGraw	*1974*

Natural Science and Nature Stories-

Earth's Bug-eyed Monsters	Norton	*1968*
Butterfly and Moth	Putnam	*1969*
Misplaced Animals	McGraw	*1975*
Monarch Butterflies	Crowell	*1965*
Carab: The Trap-door Spider	Putnam	*1970*
Biography of an Octopus	Putnam	*1971*
Biography of a Rhino	Putnam	*1973*
Wild Cousins of the Dog	Putnam	*1973*

Misunderstood Animals	McGraw	1973
Biography of an Ant	Putnam	1974
Biography of an Ostrich	Putnam	1975
Biography of an Armadillo	Putnam	1976
Wild Cousins of the Cat	Putnam	1975
Biography of an American Reindeer	Putnam	1976

Work in Progress: Two books scheduled for publication in the fall of 1977 and one in early 1978

She says: "Somehow I got into writing children's books. Not what I envisaged in the beginning. But I like children. I also like animals, and my nonfiction is mostly about nature subjects and animals. I should say that my chief philosophy is conservation and ecology. I am APPALLED to hear that Michigan wants to shoot wolves! Shameful! The Detroit Public Library was founded by my father. His name is engraved on the marble in the entrance."

Awards: National Association of Science Teachers Best Science Books for. . .*Biography of a Rhino,* 1972; *Misunderstood Animals,* 1973; *Wild Cousins of the Cat,* 1975; *Biography of an Armadillo* and *Biography of an American Reindeer,* 1976

HORVATH, BETTY FERGUSON 1927-
Born: May 20, 1927; Jefferson City, Missouri
Married: John Anthony Horvath, a retired teacher
Children: Sally Hope, Polly Lynne, John Charles
Education: Attended Phillips University in Enid, Oklahoma
Career: Writer for various radio stations
Address: 2340 Waite Avenue, Kalamazoo, Michigan 49008

Writings:

Hooray for Jasper	Franklin Watts	1966
Jasper Makes Music	Franklin Watts	1967
Will the Real Tommy Wilson Please Stand Up	Franklin Watts	1969
The Cheerful Quiet	Franklin Watts	1969
Be Nice to Josephine	Franklin Watts	1970
Not Enough Indians	Franklin Watts	1971
Small Paul and the Bully of Morgan Court	Ginn and Company	1971
Jasper and the Hero Business	Franklin Watts	1977

She says: "I have been waiting all my life for somebody to ask me what my philosophy is, and now that you HAVE, I don't know what to say! It's composed of bits and pieces such as 'The good guys always win!' and 'When you think you can't hang on any longer, HANG ON A LITTLE LONGER!' and on the thoughful little gems of that calibre. As for 'interesting sidelights', here's a couple: Daniel Boone is my great-great-great-great grandfather; and I was born on the day that Lindbergh made his historic flight. I have only two comments about my creative work: I do the best I can, and yes, of COURSE I wish it were better.''

HOWARD, ELIZABETH see: MIZNER, ELIZABETH HOWARD

HULBERT, WILLIAM, DAVENPORT 1869-1913
Born: October 12, 1869; Mackinac Island, Michigan
Parents: Francis Robbins and Diantha Hulda (Gillett) Hulbert
Career: Teacher at Allenville near St. Ignace; Writer about and student of outdoor life and natural history

Writings:

Forest Neighbors	*Row Peterson*	*1915*
White Pine Days on the	*The Historical Society*	
on the Tahquamenon	*of Michigan*	*1949*

Numerous articles and stories about nature published in such journals as *McClures Magazine, The Youths' Companion, Frank Leslie's Popular Monthly, The Outlook, Metropolitan Magazine, Outing, American Magazine, Country Life in America,* and the *Atlantic Monthly.*

William Davenport Hulbert wrote about nature and the Michigan wilderness, particularly the area of the Tahquamenon. Because he had been handicapped by infantile paralysis, he could not participate in the vigorous lumbering activities of his father and brothers. As a result, Hulbert developed a keen interest in the plant and animal life of Michigan, as well as in the loggers and settlers who came to the Michigan wilderness. An early death at age 45 deprived Hulbert of the national recognition as a nature writer which would probably have come his way had he lived longer.

In 1949 nine of Hulbert's stories were collected and published by the Historical Society of Michigan as *White Pine Days on the Tahquamenon.* They were edited by the author's brother, Richard C. Hulbert.

Information for the above was taken from *Michigan Authors,* 1964; and from the "Preface" to *White Pine Days on the Tahquamenon.*

HULL, HELEN ROSE 1888?-1971
Born: 1888(?); Albion, Michigan

Died: July 15, 1971
Parents: Warren Charles and Louise (McGill) Hull
Education: Michigan State University, A.B.; University of Michigan, M.A.; University of Chicago, Ph. D. 1912
Career: Instructor in English, Wellesley College, Wellesley, Massachusetts, 1912-14; Instructor, Assistant Professor, Associate Professor, Professor of English, Columbia University, 1914-58; Professor emeritus of English, Columbia University, 1958-71

Writings:

Quest	Macmillan	1922
Labyrinth	Macmillan	1923
The Surry Family	Macmillan	1925
Islanders	Macmillan	1927
Copy (introduction to this collection)	Appleton	1927
The Art of Writing Prose (Co-author with Mabel L. Robinson and Roger S. Loomis)	R. Smith	1930
The Art of Writing Prose— revised edition	Farrar	1936
The Asking Price	Coward	1930
New Copy, 1931 (introduction to this collection)	Columbia University Press	1931
Creative Writing (Co-author with Mabel L. Robinson)	American Book	1932
Heat Lightning	Coward	1932
Hardy Perennial	Coward	1933
Morning Shows the Day	Coward	1934
Uncommon People (short stories)	Coward	1936
Candle Indoors	Coward	1936
Frost Flower	Coward	1939
Through the House Door	Coward	1940
Experiment: Four Short Novels	Coward	1940
A Circle in the Water	Coward	1943
Mayling Soong Chiang (biography of Madame Chiang Kai-shek)	Coward	1943
Hawk's Flight	Coward	1946
Octave, a Book of Stories	Coward	1947
The Writer's Book (Editor)	Harper	1950
	Barnes & Noble	1956
Landfall	Coward	1953
Wind Rose	Coward	1958
Writer's Roundtable (Editor with Michael Drury)	Harper	1959
A Tapping on the Wall	Dodd	1960
Close Her Pale Blue Eyes	Dodd	1963

Contributor of short stories, novelettes, serials to various magazines

Awards: Guggenheim Fellowship for travel and study abroad, 1930; Dodd, Mead award for the best suspense novel written by a college professor for *A Tapping On the Wall,* 1960

HUMPHREYS, J.R. 1918-
Born: June 7, 1918; Mancelona, Michigan
Parents: Harold and Blanche (Beam) Humphreys
Married: Peggy F.
Education: University of Michigan, A.B. 1940
Career: Member of the faculty of Columbia University; Chairman, Writing Department, School of General Studies; since 1946
Address: 70 LaSalle Street, New York, NY 10027

Writings:

Vandameeer's Road (novel)	Scribner	1946
The Dirty Shame (novel)	Dell	1955
The Lost Town and Roads of America	Doubleday	1961
The Last of the Middle West	Doubleday	1966
The Lost Towns and Roads of America, revised edition	Harper & Row	1967
Subway to Samarkand (novel)	Doubleday	1977

Awards: Guggenheim Fellow in Field of the Novel

HYDE, DAYTON O. 1925-
Born: March 25, 1925; Marquette, Michigan
Parents: Frederick and Rhoda (Williams) Walton
Married: Gerda
Children: Dayton, Virginia, Marsha, John, and Taylor
Education: Cate School, 1943; University of California at Berkeley, B.A. 1950
Career: Cattle rancher, writer and conservationist
Address: Box 234, Chiloquin, Oregon 97601

Writings:

Sandy, the Story of a Sandhill Crane	Dial	1968
Yamsi	Dial	1971
Cranes in the Corral	Dial	1972
The Last Free Man	Dial	1973
Raising Wild Ducks in Captivity (Editor)	Dutton	1974
Strange Companion	Dutton	1975

Work in Progress: Two more books

He says: "I believe that man is just another species in slow genetic transfiguration. We do not have dominion over other species but rather responsibility for their welfare."

Awards: The 1975 Dutton Animal Book Award for *Strange Companion*

JACKSON, C[AARY] PAUL 1902-
Psuedonym: Colin Lochlons, Jack Paulson
Born: 1902; Urbana, Illinois
Parents: Caary and Goldie (Harding) Jackson
Married: Orpha Cook
Children: Betty Jackson Soodek, Paul L. William L., Mae L.
Education: Western Michigan University, B.A., 1929; University of Michigan, M.A., 1943
Career: High school teacher and coach, Van Buren County (Mich.), 1922-27, Kalamazoo (Mich.) Public Schools, 1929-51; Writer of books for boys, 1951-

Writings:

All Conference Tackle	Crowell	*1947*
Tournament Forward	Crowell	*1948*
Rose Bowl All-American	Corwell	*1949*
Rookie First Baseman	Crowell	*1950*
Rose Bowl Line Backer	Crowell	*1951*
Dub Halfback	Crowell	*1952*
Clown at Second Base	Crowell	*1952*
Little Leaguer's First Uniform	Crowell	*1952*
Saint in the Midget League	Crowell	*1953*
Spice's Football	Crowell	*1955*
Bud Plays Junior High Football	Hastings	*1957*
Two Boys and a Soap Box Derby	Hastings	*1958*
Little League Tournament	Hastings	*1959*
Bud Plays Junior High Basketball	Hastings	*1959*
Bud Baker, T-Quarterback	Hastings	*1960*
World Series Rookie	Hastings	*1960*
Bullpen Bargain	Hastings	*1961*
Pro Hockey Comeback	Hastings	*1961*
Bud Baker, Racing Swimmer	Hastings	*1962*
Pro Football Rookie	Hastings	*1962*
Tommy, Soap Box Champion	Hastings	*1963*
Little Major Leaguer	Hastings	*1963*
Chris Plays Small Fry Football	Hastings	*1963*
How to Play Better Baseball	Hastings	*1963*

Pee Wee Cook of the Midget League	Hastings	1964
Super Modified Driver	Hastings	1964
Bud Plays Senior High Basketball	Hastings	1964
Fullback in the Large Fry League	Hastings	1965
Minor League Shortstop	Hastings	1965
Junior High Freestyle Swimmer	Hastings	1965
Rookie Catcher with the Atlanta Braves	Hastings	1966
Midget League Catcher	Follett	1966
Bantam Bowl Football	Hastings	1967
Bud Baker, High School Pitcher	Hastings	1967
Tim, the Football Nut	Hastings	1967
How of Fame Flankerback	Hastings	1968
How to Play Better Basketball	Crowell	1968
Second Time Around Rookie	Hastings	1968
Big Play in the Small League	Hastings	1968
Haunted Halfback	Follett	1969
Pennant Stretch Drive	Hastings	1969
Baseball's Shrine	Hastings	1969
Stepladder Steve Plays Basketball	Hastings	1969
Pass Receiver	Hastings	1970
Rose Bowl Old Pro	Hastings	1970
Bud Baker, College Pitcher	Hastings	1970
Tom Mosely, Midget Leaguer	Hastings	1971
Halfback	Hastings	1971
Fifth Inning Fadeout	Hastings	1972
Eric and Dud's Football Bargain	Hastings	1972
How to Play Better Football	Crowell	1972
Beginner under the Backboards	Hastings	1974

(Under name Caary Jackson)

Shorty Makes the First Team	Follett	1950
Shorty at Shortstop	Follett	1951
Shorty Carries the Ball	Follett	1952
Shorty at the State Tournament	Follett	1955
Buzzy Plays Midget League Football	Follett	1956
Stock Car Racer	Follett	1957
The Jamesville Jets	Follett	1959
A Uniform for Harry	Follett	1962
Seashores and Seashore Creatures	Putnam	1964
Midget League Catcher	Follett	1966
Haunted Halfback	Follett	1968

(Under name Caary Jackson, with wife, Orpha B. Jackson)

Star Kicker	McGraw	*1955*
Hillbilly Pitcher	McGraw	*1956*
Basketball Clown	McGraw	*1956*
Puck Grabber	McGraw	*1957*
Freshman Forward	McGraw	*1959*
The Short Guard	McGraw	*1961*
High School Backstop	McGraw	*1963*
No Talent Letterman	McGraw	*1966*

(Under Pseudonym Colin Lochlons)

Stretch Smith Makes a Basket	Crowell	*1949*
Squeeze Play	Crowell	*1950*
Three and Two Pitcher	Crowell	*1951*
Triple Play	Crowell	*1952*
Barney of the Babe Ruth League	Crowell	*1954*

(Under Pseudonym Jack Paulson)

Fourth Down Pass	John C. Winston	*1950*
Match Point	Westminster	*1956*
Side Line Victory	Westminster	*1957*

JACKSON, H[AROLD] C[HARLES] L[EBARON] 1894-1954

Born: February 18, 1894; North Hatley, province of Quebec, Canada

Died: October 18, 1954

Parents: Archibald and Nellie (LeBaron) Jackson

Married: Gretchen (Dold)

Children: Harold C.L., Daniel Dold

Education: University of Michigan, B.A., 1918

Career: Writer and columnist for *The Detroit News* from April 28, 1930 until his death

Writings:

Grand Circus Park, U.S.W.	Arnold-Powers	*1938*
The Paper Bag and Other Stories	Arnold-Powers	*1941*
Longs and Shorts	Arnold-Powers	*1942*
Ups and Downs	Arnold-Powers	*1943*
Left Hand Up and Other Stories	Arnold-Powers	*1944*
'Round Corners	Arnold-Powers	*1945*
Back to Vertical, and Other Stories	Arnold-Powers	*1946*
It Happened in Detroit	Conjure House	*1947*
Dogs, Cats and People	Conjure House	*1949*

Also among H.C.L. Jackson's writings was *The Detroit News* column, "Listening in on Detroit" (1930-54); and the Christmas story, "The Little Girl in the Yellow Dress."

JACOBSON, DANIEL 1923-
Born: November 6, 1923; Newark, New Jersey
Parents: Samuel and Mary (Siegel) Jacobson
Married: Iris, a counselor
Children: Lisa, Darryl, Jerrold
Education: New Jersey State College (Montclair) B.A., 1947; Columbia University, M.A., 1950; Louisiana State University, Ph. D., 1954
Career: High school social studies teacher, 1948-49; Instructor, University of Kentucky, 1952-55; Instructor, Brooklyn College, 1955-57; Associate Professor and Professor, New Jersey State College (Montclair), 1957-65; Professor, Michigan State University, 1965-present
Address: 1827 Mirabeau Drive, Okemos, Michigan 48864

Writings:

The Story of Man	*Home Library Press*	*1963*
The First Americans	*Ginn*	*1969*
The Hunters	*Franklin Watts*	*1974*
The Fishermen	*Franklin Watts*	*1975*
The Gatherers	*Franklin Watts*	*1977*

Numerous journal articles.

Work in Progress: *The Farmers,* to be published by Franklin Watts

He says: "I have been engaged in American Indian studies for over 25 years. It has been my intention to take the very best in theory, knowledge and research in the social science displines—particularly to geography and anthropology— and to relate them to the writing of works for junveniles. I can say with relish that it has been a labor of love."

JERMAN, SYLVIA PAUL see COOPER, SYLVIA

JOHNSON, ANNA (1860-1943)
Pseudonym: Hope Daring
Born: July 11, 1860; Bradford County, Pennsylvania; at age seven moved to Hastings, Michigan
Parents: George T. and L. Jane (Van Vechten) J. Johnson
Education: Albion College, honorary graduate
Career: Teacher in district school for several years; Writer

Writings:

Paul Crandal's Charge	American Tract Society	1900
To the Third Generation	American Tract Society	1901
Agnes Grant's Education	Jennings & Pye	1902
Entering into his Own	American Tracy Society	1903
The Furniture People	G.W. Jacobs	1903
An Abundant Harvest	Jennings & Graham	1904
The Appointed Way	Griffith & Rowland	1905
Madeline, the Island Girl	Jennings & Graham	1906
Father John	American Tract Society	1907
The Virginian Holiday	American Tract Society	1909
Valadero Ranch	American Tract Society	1911
The Gordons	American Tract Society	1912
Paying the Price!	American Tract Society	1914
Sowing and Reaping		1922
The Woods in the Home	Whitman	1927

Miss Johnson lived all her life in Hastings, where she was active in the affairs of the Methodist Church. Her stories have been compared to the *Elsie Dinsmore* series.

JOHNSON, RICHARD see: RICHEY, DAVID JOHN

JOHNSTON, ARNOLD 1942-

Born: May 31, 1942; Cambuslang, Scotland
Parents: James Reid and Eliza (Arnold) Johnston
Married: Kristin Lucille Tyrell, a librarian
Education: Wayne State University, Ph.B., 1963; University of Delaware, M.A., 1966; Ph.D., 1970
Career: Writer of criticism, poetry, fiction, and drama; Associate Professor of English, Western Michigan University, 1966-present
Address: 1012 N. Fletcher, Kalamazoo, Michigan 49007

Writings:

The Witching Voice (a play about Robert Burns)	Western Michigan University Press	1973

Work in Progress: 3 plays (two full-length and a one-act), poetry, and short fiction

He says: "My graduate training was scholarly; my work since has been what people—for want of a better term—call creative. My work, particularly *The Witching Voice,* is influenced by my own Scottish background. I enjoy teaching creative writing courses and conducting workshops in the Michigan Arts Council's Creative Writers in the Schools Program. My playwriting is affected—I hope for the better—by the fact that I do considerable acting; I like my stage work to be entertaining without insulting an audience's intelligence. I sing professionally on occasion, and incessantly for my own enjoyment, and I think that has its effect on my writing, too."

JONES, IRIS EILEEN 1932-
Pseudonym: Iris Sanderson Jones
Born: February 8, 1932; Winnipeg, Canada
Parents: John Emile and Flora (Patterson) Sanderson
Married: Michael Owen Jones, an engineer
Children: David Ralph, Eric Michael
Career: Freelance writer and organizational consultant; Adviser: Michigan Council for the Arts; Writer in Residence, Michigan Creative Writers Project
Address: 22170 West Nine Mile Road, Southfield, MI 48034

Writings:

Early North American Dollmaking	*101 Productions/ Scribner's*	*1976*

Several hundred features in national and regional magazines and newspapers

JONES, IRIS SANDERSON see: JONES, IRIS EILEEN

JORDON, MILDRED ARLENE 1918-
Pseudonym: Millicent
Born: March 18, 1918; Houghton Lake, Michigan
Parents: Truman S. and Maude E. (Calkins) Howe
Married: W. Walter Jordan
Children: Neil A. Carrick and David D. Jordan
Education: Houghton Lake High School, 1933
Career: Homemaker; Election Chairman for township and local school elections; Organist for local church; Author of weekly column in *Houghton Lake Resorter*
Address: Houghton Lake, Michigan 48629

Writings:

Quiet Walks with Millicent Volume I	*Houghton Lake Resorter*	*1972*
Quiet Walks with Millicent Volume II	*Herald House*	*1974*
Volume III	*Herald House*	*1975*

Work in Progress: *Quiet Walks with Millicent Volumes IV* and *V;* Contributions to Herald House for *Daily Bread,* an annual devotional book; Children's stories and meditational material, poetry or prose for weekly column in *Houghton Lake Resorter.*

She says: "A strong belief in a Supreme Being and a sense of kinship with our Creator, found especially in nature, prompted me to begin writing. Many facets of nature lend themselves to analogies of real life situations and serve to provide insight to life's meaning. I desire to share in this way to help others grasp these truths. Personal relationships take on added depth and meaning also. I am interested in photography. In making up the illustrations for my books of poetry I have found that they serve admirably to convey the meaning of the poems used. Occasionally I use one along with my weekly column. My grandchildren are willing subjects and they have often provided inspiration for a column."

JYMES, ELIZABETH see: ADAMS, BETSY

KAMINSKI, MARGARET 1944-
Born: March 16, 1944; Detroit, Michigan
Parents: John Joseph and Gertrude (Malak) Kaminski
Education: Wayne State University, B.F.A. and M.S.L.S. 1962-68
Career: Presently working at Detroit Public Library where career has included public relations work, radio programs and radio interviews with authors, wrote press releases and programs, etc. Travel slide shows for library senior citizen programs and work in editing *Moving Out,* a feminist literary magazine for the last 8 years.
Address: 5053 Commonwealth, Detroit, MI 48208

Writings:

Martinis	White Light Press	1975
10 Michigan Women Poets (ed.)	Glass Bell Press	1975
La Vita De La Mujer	Fallen Angel Press	1976
Moving to Antarctica (ed.)	Dustbooks	1976

Listings: *Contemporary Authors, Who's Who in the Midwest and Who's Who of American Women.*

She says: "I feel that now, besides my own poetry and journals, *Moving Out* and Glass Bell Press are my most important creative efforts. The first is a feminist literary magazine and the second is my publishing company for women's books of poetry; I've published several in the last 4 years, and feel committed to publishing and editing women's work. I also enjoy travel and have visited South America, Mexico, Yucatan, Europe. I find my travels in the U.S. and abroad to be an inspiration for my writing. I am also interested in photography, backpacking, art (my mother goddess collection from around the world), yoga and music."

KELIHER, EVAN C. 1931-
Born: June 30, 1931; Detroit, Michigan
Parents: Evan C., Sr. and Ann (Johnson) Keliher
Married: Patricia, a librarian
Children: Alan Michael, David Evan and Brian Samuel
Education: Wayne State University, randomly from 1952 to 1972,
  B.S., M. Ed. and Ed. D.
Career: Twenty-odd years in the trenches of the Detroit Public
  Schools as a sometime teacher, bouncer, first-aid man and
  victim.
Address: 6164 Coolidge, Dearborn Hts., MI

Writings:
New Africa High: A Low
  Comedy   *published by me*   *1976*

Work in Progress: A stunning new novel which will take the literary world by storm and enrich me beyond my wildest dreams.

He says: "I deplore tyrants and tyranny in all its forms and I do not
suffer fools gladly. I believe fervently in democracy in spite of all its
inadequacies and realize that most of the nations on this planet
would not have allowed a book such as mine to see the light of day.

"I'm also convinced that universal public education in America is a
charade and that it must be re-evaluated and re-structured if it is to
be a viable force in the future."

KELLAND, CLARENCE BUDDINGTON 1881-1964
Born: Portland, Michigan
Education: Detroit College of Law
Career: Newspaper work, magazine editor, writer

Writings:

Mark Tidd	*Harper*	*1913*
The American Boy's Workshop	*McKay*	*1914*
Into His Own	*Harper*	*1915*
Mark Tidd, Editor	*Harper*	*1917*
Dance Magic	*Harper*	*1919*
Highflyers	*Harper*	*1919*
Conflict	*Harper*	*1920*
Scattergood Baines	*Harper*	*1921*
The Steadfast Heart	*Harper*	*1923*
Contraband	*Harper*	*1923*
Hard Money	*Harper*	*1930*
Gold	*Harper*	*1931*
Jealous House	*Harper*	*1934*
Roxana	*Harper*	*1936*
Mr. Deeds Goes to Town	*Barker*	*1936*

Arizona	Harper	1936
The Valley of the Sun	Harper	1939
Scattergood Baines Returns	Harper	1940
Silver Spoon	Harper	1940
Scattergood Baines Pulls the Strings	Harper	1941
Death Keeps a Secret	Harper	1956

Best remembered for his character "Scattergood Baines," Mr. Kelland was vice-president and director of Phoenix (Arizona) Newspaper, Inc. at the time of his death. He worked for *The Detroit News* until becoming editor of the magazine *American Boy.* His first novel appeared in 1913, and his last in 1960. He wrote about 60 novels and over 200 short stories. "Scattergood" ran as a serial in *The Saturday Evening Post.* He spent one year overseas during World War I as director of publicity for the Y.M.C.A. Active in Republican politics, he served as national and later as state committeeman. *Speaking Easy* and *Mr. Deeds goes to Town* were stories of his made into movies.

KELLY DAVE see: KELLY, DAVID M.

KELLY, DAVID M. 1938-
Psuedonym: Dave Kelly
Born: June 23, 1938; Grand Rapids, Michigan
Parents: Earl P. and Margaret (Weisel) Kelly
Married: Sylvia Neahr, writer-teacher
Children: Jordy, Colette, Willow
Education: Michigan State University, B.A., 1961; Michigan State University, M.A., 1962; University of Iowa, M.F.A., 1966
Career: Director of Creative Writing, State University at Genesco; 2 times Fellow, National Endowment for the Arts; Fellow, New York State Council on Arts; *Suny* Faculty Fellow in Poetry
Address: P.O. Box 53, Geneseo, New York 14454

Writings:
The Night of the Terrible Ladders	Hors-Commerce Press	1966
Summer Study	Runcible Spoon	1969
Dear Nate	Runcible Spoon	1969
All Here Together	Lillabulero Press	1969
Instructions for Viewing a Solar Eclipse	Wesleyan University Press	1972
At a Time: A Dance for Voices	Basilisk Press	1972
Did You Hear They're Beheading Bill Johnson Today?	The Stone Press	1974

The Flesh-Eating Horse and		
Other Songs	Bartholomew's Cobble	1976
In These Rooms	Red Hill Press	1976
Poems in Season		1977

Work in Progress: Two collections of poetry

He says: "I work primarily in poetry, prose poetry, and some in prose (about 10 published stories). I believe one shows what one represents philosophically and aesthetically in one's work, probably most recent works, and what is shown should not be trusted not to change in one's next work."

KICKNOSWAY, FAYE 1936-
Born: December 16, 1936; Detroit, Michigan
Parents: Walter and Mable Lousie (Standish) Blair
Children: Kevin Leo and Lauren Beth
Education: Wayne State University, B.A., 1967; San Francisco State University, M.A., 1969
Career: Poet, fiction writer, children's book writer, graphic artist, illustator, fine artist and teacher
Address: c/o John Woolman School, 12585 Jones Bar Rd., Nevada City, California 95959

Writings:

O. You can Walk on the Sky?		
Good.	Capra Press	1972
Poem Tree	Red Hanrahan Press	1973
A Man is a Hook. Trouble	Capra Press	1974
The Cat Approaches	Alternative Press	1977
Bellfish	Oyster Press	1977

Work in Progress: *The Violence of Potatoes. He said. She said.*

She says: "Teaching has opened many new experiences in my own work. Poetry is a magical device, a work of shamans. Personal transformation is its reward. Poetry is discovery and is visual, can change into air and exist at that and be satisfying."

KING, CYNTHIA 1925-
Born: August 27, 1925; New York, New York
Parents: Adolph and Elsie (Oschrin) Bregman
Married: Jonathan King, Professor of Architecture
Children: Gordon B., Austin A., Nathaniel B.
Education: Bryn Mawr College, 1943-44; University of Chicago, 1944-45; New York University School of Continuing Education, 1964-67
Career: Assistant Editor and Managing Editor, Hillman Periodicals,

New York City, 1946-50; Managing Editor, Fawcett Publications, 1950-54
Address: 2659 Englave Drive, Ann Arbor, MI 48103

Writings:

In the Morning of Time	*Four Winds Press*	1970
	Scholastic-Starline	
	Editon (paper)	1973
The Year of Mr. Nobody	*Harper & Row*	1978

Work in Progress: Young adult novel, some poetry for children

She says: "I write fiction for children and for adults; a recently completed novel is currently with my agent. Whatever I write is an exploration of a character, an idea, a conflict, a concept. I feel this process of discovery, translated into language as beautiful and appropriate as I can make it, is what holds my interest as I write. To read a good book, like any experience, should make a person just a little bit different. Or as Abott, the young hero of my recent book for children, says, 'You never know what you'll find in the woods.'"

KING, PEGGY CAMERON 1909-
Born: September 3, 1909; Ontario, Canada
Parents: Angus E. and Ada Isabel (Millar) Cameron
Married: Harry M. King, an engineer
Children: Patricia Mullett, Garrison King, Susan Rabick
Education: University of Toronto, B.A., 1932; Ontario College of Education, Education & Arts, 1933
Career: 2 years teaching high school in Ontario; 4 years substitute teaching in Dearborn, Michigan; 5 years teaching adult classes in Writing for Publication; Freelance writing since 1959, about 400 articles in magazines and newspapers.
Address: Rt. 2, Box S-76, Stephens City, Virginia 22655

Writings:

Ladies, Please Come to Order	*Grosset & Dunlap*	1968
Ladies, Let's Travel	*Grosset & Dunlap*	1970

Work in Progress: Sundry

She says: "Writing is an ALONE business since the creative process requires concentration. But writing is not a LONELY business. The writer is nourished and inspired by his human contacts and experiences."

KIRKLAND, CAROLINE (STANISBURY) 1801-1864
Born: 1801; New York, New York

Career: Writer

Writings:

A New Home—Who'll Follow?	Originally published in 1839. Republished by Putnam	1953
Forest Life	C.S. Francis	1842
Western Clearings	Wiley and Putnam	1846
Spenser and the Faery Queen	Wiley and Putnam	1847
Holidays Abroad	Baker and Scribner	1849
The Evening Book	Charles Scribner	1852
Garden Walks with the Poets	G.P. Putnam	1852
The Book of Home Beauty	G.P. Putnam	1852
A Book for the Home Circle	Charles Scribner	1853
The Helping Hand	Charles Scribner	1853
Autumn Hours	Charles Scribner	1853
Personal Memoirs of George Washington	D. Appleton	1857
The School-Girl's Garland	Charles Scribner	1864

Caroline Kirkland was born in New York City, but later moved to Geneva, then to Detroit, where the family conducted a seminary. From there, they became some of the earliest settlers of Pinckney, Michigan, where her brother was the first postmaster. Mrs. Kirkland was vigorous and realistic in her writings about the Michigan Frontier, so much as that she was deeply resented by her neighbors. During her last years she was identified with numerous organizations for social welfare. In 1843 she returned to New York to live. She died suddenly in 1864; among the pallbears at her funeral were William Cullen Bryant and Nathaniel Parker Willis.

KLAITS, BARRIE 1944-
Born: July 2, 1944; Biloxi, Mississippi
Parents: Harold and Ruth (Ross) Gelbhaus
Children: Frederick and Alexander Klaits
Education: Barnard College, 1962-65, A.B., 1966; University of Minnesota, 1965-66
Career: "I have published two articles in professional paleontogical journals after doing research on fossil rhinoceroses at the Museum of Natural History in Paris. I enjoy teaching "Geology in the National Parks" and traveling to prepare for it."
Address: 4317 Lanette, Pontiac, Michigan 48054

Writings:

Animals and Man in Historical Perspective	Harper and Row	1974
When You find A Rock	Macmillan	1976

Work in Progress: Warm-Blooded Dinosaurs, The City that

turned to Stone, Who Really Discovered America?

She says: "With a background in science, and motherhood my current forum, it is only natural that I look to the schools as the environment for self-expression. I like to toss kernels of ideas to gifted students and watch them tranform them into books or individual projects. I like the mixed classroom where there lurk talents that I have never possessed. These I like most of all, and I try to turn them to the advantage of blossoming writers in the group. The Creative Writers in Schools program of the Michigan Council for the Arts has made it possible for me to work in the classroom."

KONKLE, JANET EVEREST 1917-
Born: November 5, 1917; Grand Rapids, Michigan
Parents: Charles A. and Minnie (Koegler) Everest
Married: Arthur Jackson Konkle, a mechanic
Children: Kraig Everest, Jil Marie, Dan Jackson
Education: Grand Rapids Junior College, 1935-37; University of Michigan, 1937-38; Western Michigan University, B.S., 1939
Career: Teacher: Alexander School, 1939-41; Dickinson School, 1952-53; West Leonard School, 1953-60; Collins School, 1960-61; Hillcrest School, 1961-
Address: 1360 Oakleigh, N.W., Grand Rapids, Michigan 49504

Writings:

Once There was a Kitten	Childrens Press	1951,62
The Kitten and the Parakeet	Childrens Press	1952
Christmas Kitten	Childrens Press	1953, 1964
Easter Kitten	Childrens Press	1955
Tabby's Kittens	Childrens Press	1956
J. Hamilton Hamster	Childrens Press	1957
The Sea Cart	Abingdon Press	1961
	E.M. Hale	1964
Susie Stock Car	Jack and Jill and Childcraft Ency.	1964
Schoolroom Bunny	Childrens Press	1965
The Raccoon Twins	Childrens Press	1972

She says: "In addition to my writing, I am an avid photographer. I became interested in writing when I saw a photo-illustrated book for children at the library. My children were young and I went to the downtown library and brought armloads of books home to read to them. A photo-illustrated book about a cat inspired me and *Once There was a Kitten* was born. I had the cat and kittens, the children, and the camera know-how so I tried writing and my first attempt was accepted for publication. If it hadn't been accepted, I probably would have 'give up' and not attempted writing again.

The *Sea Cart* resulted from a trip to the Gaspé, Canada. The dog carts, children sailing boats, men cleaning fish on the beaches inspired me. At the present time I travel every summer and sometime during the spring vacations. I have visited Spain, Morocco, England, France, Yugoslovia, Turkey, Scotland, Mexico, Austria, Switzerland, and Germany. I have taken many slides of these visits. I hope to continue my travels and my writing."

KORFKER, DENA 1908-

Born: April 6, 1908; Grand Rapids, Michigan
Parents: Henry William and Dina (DeHaan) Korfker
Education: Western State Teacher's College; Teacher's Life Certificate, 1927; Calvin College, A.B., 1943
Career: Teacher, writer
Address: 1720 Plymouth Rd., S.E., Grand Rapids, MI 49506
Writings:

Can You Tell Me?	Zondervan Publishing House	1950, 1971
Question Children Ask	Zondervan	1951
My Bible ABC Book	Zondervan	1952
Ankie Comes to America	Zondervan	1953
The Story of Jesus for Boys and Girls	Zondervan	1953
My Picture Story Bible	Zondervan	1960
My Favorite Picture Bible Stories	Zondervan	1961
Good Morning, Lord	Baker Book House	1973
Mother of Eighty	J.C. Choate Publications	

Work in Progress: *Shepherd of my People* (a book for adults and children about the life of Jesus)

She says: "I taught in the same school I attended as a child. I had the Zondervan children in my classroom. I asked them to publish a Bible story book but they had just published one. They asked me to write the books answering questions children ask. One book led to another. I had no intention of becoming an author and never dreamed I would have more than a quarter million books in print. The book I am trying to get published is the only one I was not asked to write. As soon as I retired, I spent two years in research before I wrote it. I never enjoyed writing anything as much as I did that book. I hope I will be able to get it published. I am now busy telling Bible stories to sick children in the play room at one of our city hospitals. Many times one of the books gives sick children quite a thrill."

Awards: *Angie Comes to America* won first prize in Zondervan's Juvenile Fiction Contest in 1953. An award plaque for being chosen the Children's Author for their first Quarter Century of Publishing.

KROUSE, CHARLES 1940
Born: June 19, 1940
Married: Sandra, a social worker
Education: Ball State University, B.S., 1959-68
Career: Self employed sign painter
Address: 1369 Linwood, Holland, MI 49423

Writings:

Spider Bite & Other Poems	Windmill Press	1976
A Fool's Bubble	Windmill Press	1976

Work in Progress: Untitled collection of Poems; two novels (one finished, one in progress); Untitled collection of sketches & stories

KUBIAK, WILLIAM J. 1929-
Born: May 29, 1929; Grand Rapids, Michigan
Parents: Joseph and Gertrude Kubiak
Married: Barbara, a nurse (divorced)
Children: Heidi, Robin, Joseph, Anthony
Education: Davenport College
Career: U.S. Army, 1951-52; Artist for Grand Rapids Press, 1954-
Address: 539 Michigan St. N.E., Grand Rapids, MI 49503

Writings:

Great Lakes Indians	Baker Book	1970

Work in Progress: Researching individual Indian tribes of this area.

He says: "You must have an interest in the subject, a thorough knowledge of the subject matter, an average amount of talent, a lot of hard work and a will to accomplish your goals."

LA GRONE, CLARENCE OLIVER 1906-
Born: McAlester, Oklahoma
Education: Howard University, University Of New Mexico (A.B. in education with majors in fine arts and sociology)
Career: Sculptor; writer

Writings:
Footfalls
They Speak of Dawns

Oliver La Grone was the first Negro American to be enrolled at Cranbrook Art Academy, where he studied sculpture under Carl Milles. He has held one man sculpture shows in Michigan and New Mexico. Mr. La Grone also studied art and special education at Wayne State University. He conducts private classes in sculpture for adults and children. He lectures and reads poetry, "his own and the Negro's." Mr. La Grone's poetry and sculpture reflect his early years of struggle and variety of hard, physically taxing jobs, as well as the discipline of study.

LAND, JANE see: BORLAND, KATHRYN

LANE, RONNIE, M 1949-
Born: August 13, 1949, Blytheville, Arkansas
Parents: Billy M. and Myrtle F. (Robirds) Lane
Married: Jill (Collins), Poet-Musician
Children: Sara Diane and Matthew William
Education: Grand Rapids Junior College, 1967-70; Grand Valley State College (T.J.C. & CAS), 1971-72
Career: Writer, printer & publisher
Address: Box 1267, Grand Rapids, Michigan 49501

Writings:

Empty Cups	*Metamorphosis Productions*	*1970*
Carnage (Short stories)	*Pilot Press*	*1972*
The Greatest Show on Earth	*Pilot Press*	*1975*
Man Unleashed Upon the		
Universe	*Free Books Inc.*	*1976*

Work in Progress: *Amnesty for the Unborn* (poetry); *Forest of Bones* (novel)

He says: "I also edit *Windows in the Stone.* My publishing company, Free Books Inc., is the extension of my philosophy. I think education should not be sold so my books are free. My aim on the philosophical—metaphysical level is the make people aware that while they are both good and evil, they are basically GOOD not evil: but moreover that they are always in control whenever they decide one way or the other."

LANKIN, DOROTHY see: WITTON, DOROTHY

LARDNER, WILMER RINGOLD (RING) 1885-1933

Born: March 6, 1885; Niles, Michigan
Parents: Henry and Lena Bogardus (Phillips) Lardner
Married: Ellis Abbott
Children: John Abbott, James Phillips, Ring W., David Ellis
Education: Niles, Michigan Armour Institute
Career: Writer

Writings:

Bib Ballads		*1915*
You Know Me Al	*Scribners*	*1916*
Gullible's Travels	*Bobbs-Merrill*	*1917*
Treat 'Em Rough	*Bobbs-Merrill*	*1918*
My Four Weeks in France	*Bobbs-Merrill*	*1918*
Own Your Own Home	*Bobbs-Merrill*	*1919*
The Real Dope	*Bobbs-Merrill*	*1919*
The Young Immigrunts	*Bobbs-Merrill*	*1920*
The Big Town	*Bobbs-Merrill*	*1921*
Symptoms of Being 35	*Bobbs-Merrill*	*1921*
How to Write Short Stories	*Scribners*	*1924*
What of It?	*Scribners*	*1925*
The Love Nest and Other Stories	*Scribners*	*1926*
The Story of a Wonder Man	*Scribners*	*1927*
Round Up	*Scribners*	*1929*
June Moon (with G.S. Kaufman)	*Scribners*	*1930*
Lose with a Smile	*Scribners*	*1933*
The Portable Ring Lardner (Edited by Gilbert Seldes)	*Viking*	*1946*
Shut Up, He Explained (Edited by Babette Rosmond and Henry Morgan)	*Scribners*	*1962*
The Ring Lardner Reader (Edited by Maxwell Geismar)	*Scribners*	*1963*

Ring Lardner attended school in Niles, Michigan, then enrolled at Armour Institute, Chicago, Illinois. He soon found writing his career rather than engineering. Lardner began working as a reporter on the *South Bend* (Indiana) *Times.* He became a sports writer and worked on papers in Chicago, Boston, and St. Louis. He became a writer for the Bell Syndicate in 1919. He also conducted a column in the *New York Tribune.* In 1911, he married Ellis Abbott and they had four sons; one, John Lardner, was a well-known author, sports writer and war correspondent, who died in New York City, on March 24, 1960.

LAREDO, JOHNNY see: CAESAR, EUGENE LEE

LARRIE, REGINALD R. 1928-
Born: September 5, 1928; Detroit, Michigan
Parents: Robert R. and Dora R. Larrie
Married: Margaret
Children: Debra, Reginald, Raymond
Education: Detroit College of Business, 1970; Wayne County Community College, 1973-74; Upper Iowa U., 1975-77
Career: Instructor of African-American History, Wayne County Community College; Taught graduate classes for Wayne State University in Germany (1972)
Address: 1401 S. Beatrice, Detroit, MI 48217

Writings:

Corners of Black History	*Vantage Press*	*1972*
Black Experiences in Michigan History	*Michigan Historical Commission*	
Ethnic Groups in the City (a chapter co-authored with Margaret Larrie)	*D.C. Health and Company*	

Awards: City of Detroit Distinguished Service Award; Montgomery Ward Bicentennial Award; Several Awards and honors from most of Michigan's sports car club; 15 Year Service Award from Boy Scouts of America

LARSON, AMADA WILJANEN 1910-
Born: September 17, 1910; Dorsey, Michigan
Parents: John and Selma (Kuivila) Wiljanen
Married: Divorced
Education: Northern Michigan University, A.B. 1936; University of Michigan, M.A., 1952
Career: Teacher, school principal
Address: 1103 Northrop St., Marquette, Michigan 49855

Writings:

Finnish Heritage in America	*Delta Kappa Gamma Society*	*1976*

She says: "Delta Chapter of the Delta Kappa Gamma Society, an honor society for key women teachers, of what I am a member, sponsored a project on Finnish heritage for the Bicentennial. Because I had spent a lifetime working with children; because I was retired and had time; and, because of my Finnish background, I accepted the task of writing the book, *Finnish Heritage in America,* as part of a teaching module for upper elementary grades. It was a very rewarding experience.

"The book was distributed free to all Upper Peninsula elementary schools. The adult demand was such that a second printing of 5,000 was authorized. This book has had circulation in more than half of the United States and in half a dozen foreign countries.

"Aside from its use in the schools and libraries of the Upper Peninsula, the book has also been used in the media centers of several downstate metropolitan school districts. Copies are in the Northern Michigan University library. The book has served students not only in the Finnish classes but other courses as well."

LAWRENCE, MILDRED E. 1907-
Born: November 10, 1907; Charleston, Illinois
Parents: DeWitt and Gertrude (Jefferson) Elwood
Married: Clarence A. Lawrence, newspaperman (deceased)
Children: Leora Mary (Mrs. James T. Schermerhorn)
Education: Flint Junior College, A.A., 1926; Lawrence University, B.A., 1928; Yale University, M.A., 1931
Career: Newspaper society editor, reporter, music, art, and book reviewer; Writer.
Address: 1044 Terrace Blvd., Orlando, FA 32803

Writings:

Susan's Bears	Grosset & Dunlap	1947

The following published by Harcourt, Brace:

Peachtree Island	1948
Sand in Her Shoes	1949
The Homemade Year	1950
Tallie	1951
Crissy at the Wheel	1952
One Hundred White Horses	1953
Dreamboats for Trudy	1954
Island Secret	1955
Indigo Magic	1956
Good Morning, My Heart	1957
Along Comes Spring	1958
The Questing Heart	1959
The Shining Moment	1960
Forever and Always	1961
Starry Answer	1962
Girl on Witches' Hill	1963
Drums in My Heart	1964
No Slipper for Cinderella	1965
The Treasure and the Song	1966
Reach for the Dream	1967
Inside the Gate	1968

Once at the Weary Why	*1969*
Gateway to the Sun	*1970*
Walk a Rocky Road	*1971*
Touchmark	*1975*

Several of the above in paperback in English and Dutch and two of them in German hardback. *Peachtree Island* is in Braille and *No Slipper for Cinderella* was a talking book. *Touchmark* was a *Junior Literary Guild* selection.

Work in Progress: Research in several different fields for both children and adults.

She says: "I have been especially interested in regional writing, since we have lived and visited a good many fascinating places—a peach orchard on a Lake Erie island, an automobile town (Flint) sprung from a village of wagonmakers, the North Carolina mountains, New Mexico and others. I feel that by knowing the mores of various sections of the country, children will feel more at home in our increasingly complex and changing world. I have been fortunate in earning a living in a way that I love, and I hope some of the fun has been passed on to my readers."

LAWSON, H. LOWE see: LAWSON, HORACE L.

LAWSON, HORACE L. 1900-
Pseudonym: John A. Summers, H. Lowe Lawson
Born: December 25, 1900; Detroit, Michigan
Parents: Dr. Horace G. and Helen (Lowe) Lawson
Married: Marjorie (Congdon) Lawson, housewife
Children: Ann, Helen, and Lorna
Education: Utica High School (Michigan), 1916-19, graduated; eight summers at Indiana University Writers Conferences
Career: Magazine article writer, 1923-77 (spare time); *Detroit Free Press,* 1920-46; editor and publisher, *Jonesville Independent,* 1946-48; Hillsdale College, 1948-66; historian, 1966-70
Address: 303 Scenic Drive, Hillsdale, Michigan

Writings:
Pitch Dark and No Moon	T.Y. Crowell	*1958*
	Warne & Co., Ltd.	
	London, England	*1959*

4,110 articles in class and business magazines under five names, over 54 years

Work in Progress: Book, non-fiction: *A Study in the Supernormal,* based on 50 years of psychic investigation

He says: "Other publications in which my biographical material appeared included: *International Authors & Writers Who's Who,* 1977; *Directory of International Biography,* 1974; *The Writers Directory,* 1971 and 1973; *Michigan Authors,* 1960 and *Contemporary Authors,* 1963."

LAWTON, ETHEL CHAPIN 1903-
Pseudonym: The Poetry Lady
Born: July 23, 1903; Battle Creek, Michigan
Parents: Earl W. and Alice Lenore (Corliss) Chapin
Married: James Pearce Scanlan, retired
Children: Rev. Leon R. Lawton and Elaine Stonestreet
Education: Country school and Battle Creek High
Career: Free Lance Advertising; Wrote and broadcasted Children's program 1941; and Children's record "The Little Christmas Tree" 1960
Address: 243 Creek View Drive, Battle Creek, Michigan 49017

Writings:

Poetry for Children		*1937*
New Lines for Men		*(2nd ed) 1943*
Wings Over Waubascon	*Embossing Printers, Inc.*	*1968*

Work in Progress: 2nd book of poetry for children, another for adults and my autobiography

She says: "Writing since I was twelve when I had my first poem printed. God gave me my talent and He gives me the words faster than I can write them down. My greatest joy is writing for others what they are unable to express. I am psychic."

LEE, JOHN ROBERT 1923-1976
Born: December 26, 1923; Petoskey, Michigan
Parents: Chester and Beryl (Niles) Lee
Married: Susan (Dye) Lee
Children: Elizabeth, Jennifer, Leslie
Education: Central Michigan, B.A., 1947; University of Michigan, M.A., 1954; Stanford University, Ed. D., 1957

Writings:

Readings on Elementary Social Studies: Emerging Changes	*Allyn & Bacon*	*1970*
Teaching Social Studies in the Secondary School	*The Free Press*	*1973*
Teaching Social Studies in the Elementary School	*The Free Press*	*1974*
Investigating Man's World:		

Family Studies; Local Studies;
Metropolitan Studies   Scott Foresman   *1970*
Heroes of the Revolution (8 Bio-
graphies); Events of the Revo-
lution; Cities of the Revolu-
tion   *Children's Press*   *1976*

Author of numberous scholarly articles as well as over a hundred films and filmstrips.

Remarks: As he stated in the introduction to Dr. Lee's best book, he believed that "Above all else, making wise choices is the quality of a teacher."

LEE, TOM L. 1950-
Born: March 7, 1950; Grand Rapids, Michigan
Parents: Howard H. and Yvonne (Sperry) Lee
Education: Grand Rapids Junior College, 1968; Grand Valley State College, 1972
Career: Author, journalist, editor, communications consultant
Address: 3506 Burton Ridge S.E., Grand Rapids, MI

Writings:
Black Portrait of an African
  Journey   Eerdmans   *1972*
Other Voices   N.A.E.C.   *1975*
The African (forthcoming)   *1978*

Author of articles on scientific speculations and cultural subject areas for various publications.

Work in Progress: *Great Kings of Africa*

He says: "Having lived and traveled extensively in Europe and Africa, I am forced to confront life, particularly in my writing, from a broadly-based view and perspective. Nominee, 1972, Pulitzer Prize in Journalism. Did not receive the prize, however. Listed in *Contemporary Authors,* volumes 65-68 (1977). Featured in October, 1972 issue of *Ebony Magazine.*

LEFLER, IRENE WHITNEY 1917-
Born: May 29, 1917; Hominy Falls, West Virginia
Parents: Hughie Mac Jamison and Mary Magdalene Whitney
Married: James C. Lefler, deceased
Children: Mary Ellen Wilson, James Marvin and John Garland Lefler
Education: Oakland Community College; Applied Sciences, 1972-75

Career: Clerical worker, housemother for Starr Commonwealth, puppeteer, lecturer, writing instructor, storyteller, licensed practical nurse
Address: Box 292, Pontiac, MI 48056

Writings:
Bessie Bee   *Southern Publishing Ass'n. 1972*
(This book, though for juveniles, is being used on the OCC campus in the Biology Department).

Work in Progress: *Rugged Trail to Guyandotte* (true story about Shawnee Indians of West Virginia); *Annie Ant* (second in Nature Series requested by Southern Publishing Ass'n.); Possibly a book about the typhoid epidemic Alaska in 1925

She says: "I take my work very seriously. I think children should get more true-to-life stories than all of the fantasy fed to them. I expect to get a state and city grant to take educational puppet programs into schools and hospitals, writing and producing my own scripts on tape. I want to help both children and senior citizens with my puppet theater, which is known as *Religious and Educational Puppets, Featuring 'The Cracker Jacks.'*

"I feel that if what I write does not educate or inform the reader about life, I have spent my time in vain in writing the story. I want my writing to inspire, educate and inform the reader. I love the research involved in putting together stories and hope my young readers can reap the results by feeling rewarded for having read my work. My greatest reward is a child's remark, 'Mrs. Lefler, when is your next book coming out—I really like your stories.' "

LEGLER, PHILIP 1928-
Born: March 7, 1928; Dayton, Ohio
Parents: Ellis Peter and Mary Legler (both deceased)
Married: Martha, Professor of English
Children: David, Barbara and Amy
Education: Denison University, B.A., 1951; University of Iowa, M.F.A., 1953
Career: Have taught at Ohio University, Illinois Wesleyan University, Sweet Briar College, and other colleges in Missouri and New Mexico. Northern Michigan University since 1968
Address; 128 E. Magnetic, Marquette, MI

Writings:
A Change of View	*U. of Nebraska Press*	*1964*
The Intruder	*U. of Georgia Press*	*1972*
Listen to Me: An Anthology of	*Northern Michigan U.*	
Upper Peninsula	*Press*	*1976*
High School Writing, edited by		

Johnson, Legler, Webster,
Vande Zande

Work in Progress: *Peninsula Poems*

He says: "Since 1956 have published poems in many magazines,
such as *Poetry, Prairie Schooner, Poetry Northwest, Choice,
Southwest Review, Nation, Commonweal, American Scholar, Antioch Review, Chelsea, Quarterly Review of Literature, Paris
Review, Ontario Review,* appear in 9 anthologies, latest of which is
The Third Coast: Contemporary Michigan Poetry. Have also read
poetry on National Public Radio's 'All Things Considered'; have
been listed for many years as a participating poet in the MCA's
Writers-in-the-Schools project."

LEITHAUSER, GLADYS GARNER 1925-

Born: February 11, 1925; Detroit, Michigan
Parents: Herbert N. and Carrie (Speer) Garner
Married: Harold E. Leithauser, Attorney
Children: Lance, Mark, Brad, and Neil
Education: Wayne State University, B.S., 1946, M.A., 1969, Ph.
D., 1977
Career: Worked as a research associate in Zoology and Biochemis-
try, Detroit Institute of Cancer Research, 1960-66; graduate
work and part-time instructorship, Department of English,
Wayne State University, 1966-present
Address: 122 Elm Park, Pleasant Ridge, Michigan

Writings:

The Dinosaur Dilemma	*Golden Gate Junior Books*	*1964*
The Rabbit is Next (written	*Western Publishing Co.*	
with Lois F. Breitmeyer)	*(Little Golden Books)*	*1978*

Work in Progress: Juvenile picture books and novels; and
academic articles on Bertrand Russell.

LEONARD, ELMORE 1925-

Born: October 11, 1925; New Orleans, Louisiana
Parents: Elmore and Flora (Rive) Leonard
Married: Divorced
Children: Jane Freels, Peter, Christopher, William, Katherine
Education: University of Detroit, Arts Degree, 1950
Career: In advertising 1949-60. Began writing and selling fiction in
1951. Left advertising agency to go on his own in 1961.
Address: 211 E. Merrill, Birmingham, Michigan

Writings:

The Bounty Hunters   *Novels published by Houghton*

The Law at Randado	Miflin, Ballantine, and Dell	
Escape from Five Shadows	between 1953 and 1957	
Last Stand at Saber River		
The Tall T	Motion picture based on AR-GOSY novelette	
3:10 to Yuma	Motion picture based on DIME WESTERN short story	
Hombre	Ballantine Books	1961
The Big Bounce	Gold Medal	1969
The Moonshine War	Doubleday/Dell	1969
Valdez in Coming	Gold Medal	1970
Forty Lashes Less One	Bantam	1972
American Flag	Original screenplay	1973
Joe Kidd	Original screeplay	1973
Mr. Majestyk	Original screenply, novel published by Dell	1974
Fifty-Two Pickup	Delacorte/Dell	1974
Swag	Delacorte/Dell	1976
Unknown Man No. 89	Delacorte/Dell	1977
The Hunted	Dell	1977
The Switch	Bantam	June, 1978
Juvenal	To be published by Bantam in 1978-79	
Jesus Saves	Teleplay to be produced for NBC	
Seascape	To be published by Bantam in 1979	

He says: "I'm doing now what I've always wanted to do, write novels and motion picture screenplays full time, and I can't imagine doing anything else."

LesSTRANG, JACQUES 1926-

Born: June 13, 1926; Pittsburgh, Pennsylvania
Parents: Jacques and Ada Marie (Mehaffey) LesStrang
Married: Barbara Louise (Hills)
Children: Christian, David, Diane, *Linda, Michelle, *Paul Stephen (*Stepchildren)
Education: George Washington University, A.A., 1949; University of Michigan, A.B., 1951
Career: Formerly president of international marketing firm; currently Senior Editor, publisher, writer
Address: Harbor Island, Glen Lake, Maple City P.O., MI 49664

Writings:

Seaway	Superior Publishing Co.	1976
Seaway	Book-of-the Month Club non-fiction alternate	For release in early 1978

The Lake Carriers Co.   Superior Publishing Nov. 1, 1977

Work in Progress: *They Built a Seacoast; Rivers*

He says: "We moved to Harbor Island two years ago from Ann Arbor. The island is heavily wooded and here I have built a studio. It's small, about 15 acres, and we have about half of it. For a writer, it's the most idyllic spot on earth.

"We choose a quiet, low profile which provides for us a life style which incorporates complete freedom and total control of every aspect of our lives. We shun personal and TV appearances, book promotion tours, and the like, in favor of our less-travled path."

LETHBRIDGE, ALICE 1921-

Born: February 14, 1921; Berwyn, Nebraska
Parents: Ted T. and Mary B. (McEvoy) Skinner
Married: Hugh Lethbridge, a veterans' counselor
Children: Mrs. Joan Colton, Hugh Jr., Kevin, Mary A., and Paul
Education: Mercy College of Detroit, B.S., 1946
Career: Homemaker, reporter and feature writer
Address: 3914 Donnelly St., Flint, MI 48504

Writings:

Halfway to Yesterday	Genesee County Historical Society	1974
Well Do I Remember	Berwyn-London Publishers	1976

Work in Progress: History of women in Flint and Genesee County; Ethnic history of Flint

She says: "Have hopes for publishing a book on my own family history, with the kind of ancedotes that will make it readable and appealing long after I'm gone. At present, I specialize in local history articles for the Journal and am writing a series on 'Houses with a Heritage,' to illustrate our architecture and raise consciousness regarding preservation."

LEWIS, DAVID LANIER 1927-

Born: April 5, 1927; Bethalto, Illinois
Parents: Donald F. and Edith (Jinkinson) Lewis
Married: Yuri Lewis
Children: Kim, Leilani, Sumiko, Lance
Education: University of Illinois, B.S. 1948; Boston University, M.S. 1952; University of Michigan, M.A., Ph.D. 1953-59
Career: Reporter, *Edwardsville* (Illinois) *Intelligencer,* 1948; Bureau Chief, State Editor, *Alton* (Illinois) *Telegraphy,* 1948-51;

Press Relations Representative, Borden Company, 1952; Press Relations Representative, Industrial Arts Awards Supervisor, Ford Motor Company, 1950, 1952-55; Writer, General Motors Corporation, 1959-65; Professor, University of Michigan, 1965-
Address: 2588 Hawthorn, Ann Arbor, Michigan 48104

Writings:

The Public Image of Henry Ford: An American Folk Hero and His Company	Wayne State University Press	1976

Work in Progress: Biography of Edsel Ford; also a book on the impact of the auto on courtship and romance

LEWIS, FERRIS E. 1904-
Born: December 20, 1904; Lewiston, Michigan
Parents: Thomas E. and Lenora A. Lewis
Married: Eldora M. Lewis, retired
Children: Virginia and Mary Kathryn
Education: College of the City of Detroit (Wayne State University); A.B., 1927; University of Detroit, M.A., 1931
Career: Dearborn Public Schools and Henry Ford Community College, 42 years
Address: 223 W. Lincoln, Boyne City, Michigan 49712

Writings:

Our Own State	1st edition 1932, 13th revised edition 1971
My State and Its Story	1st editon 1927, 16th revised edition 1972
Michigan Yesterday and Today	1st edition 1956, 8th edition 1975
Handbook for the Teaching of Michigan History	1st edition 1958, revised 1964 (out of print)
State and Local Government in Michigan	1st edition 1960, 6th revised edition 1974

(All books published by the Hillsdale Educational Publishers)

LIGHTBODY, DONNA MAE 1920-1976
Born: September 7, 1920; Flint, Michigan
Parents: Don R. and Edna Doris (Surner) Larkin
Married: Donald W. Lightbody, retired
Children: Rene D. Hunter
Education: Russell Sage College, 1937-40; Wayne State University, B.B.L.S., M.S.L.S., 1965-69
Career: WAAC and WAC in World War II; secretary; elementary

school librarian; media associate, Coronet Flims; author of children's crafts' books; founder (with others) of International Guild of Craft Journalists

Writings:

Let's Knot, a Macrame Book	*Lothrop, Lee & Shepard*	*1972*
Introducing Neddlepoint	*Lothrop, Lee & Shepard*	*1973*
Easy Weaving	*Lothrop, Lee & Shepard*	*1974*
Hooks and Loops	*Lothrop, Lee & Shepard*	*1975*
Braid Craft	*Lothrop, Lee & Shepard*	*1976*

Comments: Interests included sports, reading, photography, genealogy research, stamp collecting, and such crafts as macrame, weaving, needlepoint, crocheting, and wood craving. How did she find time? She said, "In talking to people I find so many new areas to explore that somehow I make time." About working on a book she wrote, "So I'll start driving myself—nobody else will. Working on your own is a chore-my neighbors think I'm loafing, I know. Only another writer can understand."

LIGHTNER, A. M. see: HOPF, ALICE L.

LIMBACHER, JAMES L. 1926-
Born: November 30, 1926; St. Marys, Ohio
Parents: F.J. and Edith (Smith) Limbacher
Education: Bowling Green State University, B.A.,M.A., 1945-53; Indiana University, M.S. in Ed., 1953-55; Wayne State University; M.S. in L.S., 1969-72
Career: Michigan Librarian of the Year, 1974; Script writer Indiana University Radio and Television; Audio-Visual Librarian, Dearborn Dep't. of Libraries, 1955-present; Star of "Shadows on the Wall," "The Screening Room" and three other TV series
Address: 21800 Morley Ave., Apt. 1201, Dearborn, MI 48124

Writings:

Using Films	*Ed. Film Library Assoc.*	*1967*
Four Aspects of the Film	*Brussel & Brussel*	
	(Land's End)	*1968*
A Reference Guide to Audio-Visual Information	*R.R. Bowker*	*1972*
Feature Films on 8 and 16	*R.R. Bowker*	*Biennially*
Film "Sneaks" Annual	*Pierian*	*1972*
The Song List	*Pierian*	*1974*
Film Music: From Violins to Video	*Scarecrow*	*1974*

Work in Progress: *Remakes, Sequels and Series* (1979)

He says: "Always give first choice to the publisher who offers a contract!"

LITWAK, LEO E. 1924-
Born: May 28, 1924; Detroit, Michigan
Parents: Isaac and Bessie (Gastman) Litwak
Married: Divorced
Children: Jessica Litwak
Education: University of Michigan, 1943, 1945; Wayne State University, B.A. 1948; Columbia University, 1948-51
Career: Teacher of Philosophy at Washington University, St. Louis, MO. (1951-60). Teacher of literature and creative writing at San Francisco State University (1961-).
Address: 1933 Greenwich, San Francisco, California 94123

Writings:

To the Hanging Gardens	World	1964
Waiting for the News	Doubleday	1969
College Days in Earthquake Country	Random House	1971

Work in Progress: *The Dreamer*

He says: *"Waiting for the News* was set in Detroit and covers the period 1938-45. At present, I'm working on a book that is concerned with labor strikes in the early Thirties. This is a novel, also set in Detroit."

LOBDELL, HELEN B. 1919-Deceased
Born: May 14, 1919; Royal Oak, Michigan
Parents: Walter and Vanessa (Perry) Lobdell
Education: Fenn College, A.B.; Western Michigan University, M.A. 1957
Career: Teacher, writer

Writings:

Golden Conquest	Houghton Miflin Company	1953
The King's Snare	Houghton Miflin Company	1955
Captain Bacon's Rebellion	Macrae Smith	1959
The Fort in the Forest	Houghton Miflin Company	1963

Helen Lobdell taught first in Ohio and later in Michigan. Her interest in history is reflected in the historical fiction she has written with a special appeal to junior high readers.

LOCHLONS, COLIN see JACKSON, C[AARY] PAUL

LODGE, JOHN CHRISTIAN 1862-1950
Born: August 12, 1862; Detroit, Michigan
Parents: Edwin Albert and Christina (Hanson) Lodge
Education: Detroit schools
Career: John Lodge was a reporter on the *Detroit Free Press* for four years; he then became editor. From here he accepted the position as chief clerk in the Wayne County Board of Auditors. He was employed by the Dwight Lumber Company and the Chandler Radiator Company. In 1907 Mr. Lodge won the Senatorial race in his district. He served as alderman, and then as the first president of the nine-man council of Detroit. He became mayor of Detroit in 1972.

Writings:
I Remember Detroit   *Wayne State University Press*
        (written in collaboration with
        Milo Quaife)   *1949*

LONG, NAOMI CORNELIA see: MADGETT, NAOMI LONG

LOWE, BERENICE BRYANT see: LOWE, BERENICE J.

LOWE, BERENICE J. 1896-
Pseudonym: Berenice Bryant Lowe
Born: October 26, 1896; Flint, Michigan
Parents: Ralston S. and Jennie Adell (Pierce) Jones
Married: Stanley T. Lowe, Physician, ret.
Children: Majorie Lowe Newquist, Stewart Lowe and Sharon Lowe Davis
Education: Hope College, 1914-17; University of Michigan, A.B. 1918; M.A. 1927
Career: Teacher: Keene (N.H.) Normal School, Battle Creek High School, Kellogg School Phys. Ed.; Asst. U. of M. Freelance writer intermittently since 1924; speaker and housewife
Address: 225 W. Columbia Ave; Apt. 2, Battle Creek, Micigan 49015

Writings:
Hello, Michigan   *Singer*   *1939*
Everyday Play in French and

| English | Banks Upshaw | 1960 |
| Tales of Battle Creek | Miller Foundation | 1976 |

Work in Progress: *Changing Michigan;* Michigan Historical Division, Dept. of State. Co-author, Amy South. Completed Publishing date planned: 1977.

She says: "In 1951 I decided to 'rock myself into old age,' reading. The first subject to which I was attracted was the lake on whose bank I lived. Inasmuch as I was unable to find easily obtainable material, and felt that much was surely available, I began a search for it. Local history became an obsession and I have indulged in what was dubbed 'attic archeology' ever since. Talks and writing have pretty much been along that line these 25 + years. Sojourner Truth, black 18th century reformer, lived here. Many legends had been accepted about her life that needed clarification, so that delving into her truth also became a pet subject. My findings are in Michigan Historical Collections, U. of M., and on microfilm. Augmented local history is at Willard Library, Battle Creek, Michigan State Library and elsewhere. My collecting philosophy has been not to buy or sell but to beg and give away. This policy strictly adhered to, has greatly contributed to any success I may have had."

LUTES, DELLA THOMPSON ?-1942
Born: Jackson, Michigan
Career: Teacher, editor, writer

Writings:
Just Away
The Country Kitchen
Home Grown
Milbrook
Gabriel's Search
The Country Schoolma'am

Mrs. Lutes was born in Jackson, Michigan, and during her early life lived in Cooperstown. She began her career as a district teacher, later teaching in Detroit. She was an editor of the magazines *American Motherhood; Table Talk; Today's Housewife;* and *Modern Priscilla.* Her life on the farm gave the charming, homespun background she used with so much feeling in her essays, such as *The Country Kitchen* and *The Country Schoolma'am.*

LYMAN, MARILYN F. 1925-
Born: August 17, 1925; Detroit, Michigan

Parents: Ellis E. and Florence (Gowman) Smauder
Married: George F. Lyman
Children: Claudia Ann Sarkisian and George David
Education: Albion College; Wayne State University
Career: Writer, speaker
Address: 3886 Wedgewood Dr., Birmingham, MI 48010

Writings:

The Girl Who Knew Rule One	*Scholastic Books*	*1972*
That Face in the Mirror	*Scholastic Books*	*1974*

Work in Progress: I have just finished a 90,000 word book about a noted local person and a 60,000 word action novel for teens in the mail, making the rounds.

She says: "Since Planet Earth is a workshop, not a waiting room, I think being a writer is a privileged way to spend the years. Writers stay alive to what's going on around them; to how the world is developing at large; to needs and reactions of people close by. Using either end of the telescope to view Life, a writer can always find some aspect that may need his own particular work. Even if all the jottings and long-time efforts don't find a home with a publisher, the writer still gains, growing a new way with each new kind of communication he tries."

McBIE, JULIE see: BIEKKOLA, JULIE

McCOMBS, JUDITH 1939-
Born: January 20, 1939; Virginia
Parents: Charles and Thelma (Sutterlin) McCombs
Married: Ernst Benjamin, College Professor
Children: Cassandra, Daniel
Education: Ohio Wesleyan University, 1956-58; University of Chicago, B.A. and M.A. 1958-61
Career: Active in Wayne's Miles Modern Poetry Committee, 1969-74. Editor and co-founder *Moving Out,* Wayne's feminist literary arts journal, 1971-73. Michigan Council for the Arts Poet in the Schools, 1976-present. Instructor in English, Wayne State University, 1966-73. Instructor of English and creative writing, Center for Creative Studies College of Art and Design, Detroit, 1972-present. Many readings and conferences for literary and women's events, most recently at EMU, WSU, MSU, OCC
Address: 34015 Oakland, Farmington, Michigan 48024

Writings:

Sisters and Other Selves	*Glass Bell Press*	*1976*
Against Nature: Wilderness		

Work in Progress: Lyric poems and series of articles/books on how women nature writers conceive nature, concerning Atwood, Dillar, Piercy, Raine, Griffin

She says: "I've lived in almost all the states as a child, and in Ghana, West Africa, as a grown-up. I've traveled, backpacked in U.S. and Canada—with a 5-year old—salvaged one old building and rebuilt another, nursed babies, co-founded *Moving Out* (which is now a national success) and passed the editorship on to others; developed and taught courses on wilderness literature and women's literature as well as creative writing and English—will be doing science fiction and fantasy soon; have led writers' workshops for kids, community people, WSU and CCS college students, and elder writers. Published widely in little and feminist journals here and in Canada (+ 100 poems, 6 parables, 2 articles on Atwood and 2 on other subjects); anthologized in Bantam, Crowell, Dustbooks, Coach House and Bissett (the last two are Canadian) books. Focus on women's and nature and Canadian writing. As teacher and editor, like to get people writing and projects going; like to bridge fields."

McCORMICK, MICHAEL 1951-
Born: June 19, 1951; Haure-de-Grace, Maryland
Parents: John and Evelyn Mary (Davis) McCormick
Education: Michigan State University, B.A. 1972; University of Montana, M.F.A. 1974
Career: Subsistence farming
Address: 2876 N. Ramshorn, Fremont, Michigan 49412

Writings:
The Assassination of Poetry	*M.S.U.*	1972
The Blue Woman	*University of Montana*	1974

Work in Progress: Bibliography: Michael Hamburger (London)

He says: "To be a poet, one has only to surrender his freedom to those words which order the least amount of time and space necessary to live."

McCOY, IOLA FULLER 1906-
Pseud.: Iola Fuller
Born: January 25, 1906; Marcellus, Michigan
Parents: Henry and Clara Fuller
Married: Raymond McCoy, artist
Children: Paul Goodspeed

Education: University of Michigan, A.B., A.M.
Career: Librarian, U.S. Indian School, Santa Fe, New Mexico; Librarian, Dexter, Michigan Schools

Writings:

The Loon Feather	Harcourt Brace	1940
The Shining Trait	Duell	1943
The Gilded Touch	Putnam's	1958

Awards: Phi Beta Kappa, Avery Hopwood Award

McDOLE, CAROL see: FARLEY, CAROL

McGUIGAN, DOROTHY GIES 1914-
Born: November 12, 1914; Ann Arbor, Michigan
Parents: Charles G. and Jennie (Sturman) Gies
Married: Bernard Joseph McGuigan, deceased
Children: Michael John (attorney) and Cathleen Mary (writer)
Education: University of Michigan, 1932-36; A.B. cum laude Columbia University, 1936-37; 1939 M.A., Kings College, University of London, 1937-38
Career: Sales Promotion, Macmillan Publishing Co., 1938-42; Feature writer, Jack Starr-Hunt News Agency, Mexico, D.F., 1943-44; Overseas staff, England, France, Germany for American Red Cross, 1944-46; Feature writer, Germany for Stars and Stripes, 1946-49; Instructor, Written Communication, University of Michigan School of Business Administration, 1955-56; Editor, Program Director, University of Michigan Center for Continuing Education of Women, 1970-(current); Lecturer, University of Michigan, Department of English, 1974-75
Address: 470 Rock Creek Drive, Ann Arbor, Michigan 48104

Writings:

The Habsburgs (Foreign ed. published in England, France, Germany, Netherlands, Spain, and Jugoslavia)	Doubleday	1966
A Dangerous Experiment: 100 Years of Women at the University of Michigan	University of Michigan CEW	1970
A Sampler of Women's Studies (editor)	University of Michigan CEW	1973
New Research on Women (editor)	University of Michigan CEW	1974
Metternich and the Duchess	Doubleday	1975
(German edition)	Vienna: Molden Verlad	1977

New Research on Women and   University of Michigan
   Sex Roles   CEW   1976

Work in Progress: *Women In the Literary Trades In England, 1500-1700;* Novel based on Vienna Congress; Biography of Isabella of Spain; History of women's education in the Western world

Awards: Hopwood Awards in Creative Writing, fiction, essay, poetry—1933, 1934, 1935, 1936

McKEOWN, TOM 1937-

Born: September 29, 1937; Evanston, Illinois
Parents: Thomas S. and Ruth Ann (Fordyce) McKeown
Education: University of Michigan, B.A. & M.A. 1957-62
Career: Alpena Community College, 1962-64; Wisconsin State University (now the University of Wisconsin-Oshkosh) 1964-68; Stephens College (Missouri) 1968-74; University of Wisconsin (Stevens Point) 1976—Also West Shore Community College (summers-Michigan) 1973-76
Address: Box 82, Pentwater, MI 49449

Writings:

The Luminous River	Sumac Press	1974
Driving to New Mexico	Sunstone Press	1974
The House of Water	Basilisk Press	1974

Seven chapbooks, the latest being *Maya/Dreams,* Wisconsin Review Press, 1977. In addition to three books and seven chapbooks published in several hundred magazines including *The New Yorker, Saturday Review, The Atlantic Monthly, Harper's, The Nation, Commonwealth, The Harvard Advocate, The New York Times,* and *The Kansas City Star.*

Work in Progress: Two finished manscripts of poems, a third in preparation. One novel finished in second draft.

He says: "Interested in the archetypal and mythic in poetry as well as the music of words. Basically I am a nature poet; at times my work is fairly misanthropic. As I continue to write my work seems to become more metaphysical."

McKERCHER, BERNETH N. 1915-

Born: January 18, 1915; Milan, Michigan
Parents: Dr. Kenneth and Berthia (Blackmer) Noble
Married: Leonard McKercher, Pharmacist (deceased)
Children: Judith Novak and Patrick L. McKercher
Education: Eastern Michigan University, 1931-34; Life Certificate;

Eastern Michigan University, 1934-37, B.S., and Michigan State University, 1952-57, M.A.

Career: Elementary School Teacher (11 years); County Reading Consultant (3 years); County Superintendent (2 years); and Staff Instructor Michigan State University (13 years)

Address: 6140 Coach House Dr., East Lansing, Michigan

Writings:

What You See Is What You Get	MSU Press	1972
Dear Tom and Along Came Tim	Vantage Press	1972
People Shall Lead the Way	Vantage Press	1975

She says: "As an intructor for MSU, I also served as a student teacher supervisor. I find that these young people are a constant and challenging influence on my life. They make 'Chronological aging' very insignificant! I shall direct my tenth summer reading clinic this summer—promoted by MSU and local school systems. In these clinics I work both with teachers and children."

McLEAN, J. SLOAN see: GILLETTE, VIRGINIA M.

McLEAN, J. SLOAN see: WUNSCH, JOSEPHINE McLEAN

MADGETT, NAOMI LONG 1923-

Pseudonym: Naomi Cornelia Long; Naomi Long Witherspoon
Born: July 5, 1923; Norfolk, Virginia
Parents: Clarence M., Sr. and Maude S. (Hilton) Long
Married: Leonard P. Andrews, retired principal
Children: (Mrs.) Jill Whiterspoon Boyer
Education: Virginia State College; B.A. 1945; Wayne State University, 1954-55, M. Ed. 1956, 1967-68; University of Detroit, 1961-62
Career: Teacher, Detroit Public Schools, 1955-65, 1966-68; Research Associate, Oakland University, 1965-66; Associate Professor English, Eastern Michigan University, 1968-73; Professor of English, Eastern Michigan University, 1973-; Lecturer, University of Michigan, 1970
Address: 16886 Inverness, Detroit, Michigan

Writings:

Songs to a Phantom Nightingale* (Poetry)	Fortuny	1941

One and the Many* (Poetry)	Exposition	1956
Star by Star (Poetry)	Harlo	1965
(Revised edition)	Evenill, Inc. (reissued Lotus)	1970
Pink Ladies in the Afternoon (Poetry)	Lotus	1972
Success in Language and Literature/B (co-author text)	Follett	1967

*Reprints available through University Microfilms

Work in Progress: *Exits and Entrances* (Poetry) 1978; A College Guide to Creative Writing (text)

She says: "Poems have appeared in more than 70 anthologies in U.S. and four European countries, as well as numerous journals. Wrote and read an inaugural poem on the request of Mrs. William Milliken at the Inaugural Ceremonies in Lansing, January 1, 1975. Have participated since the program began in Poetry Readings in the Classroom now sponsored by Michigan Council for the Arts. Teaching specialization in creative writing and Afro-American literature. Daughter is also a poet and author of one book."

MAGOON, MARIAN W.

Born: Syracuse, New York
Education: Syracuse University, A.B.; University of Michigan, A.M.
Career: Teacher, Writer

Writings:
The Emperor's Nephew
I Smell the Devil (Co-authored with Elizabeth Carey)
Little Dusty Foot
Ojibway Drums

The following letter to a student library assistant in Livonia shows Mrs. Magoon's gracious, preceptive treatment of people: "I was born in New York State but have lived in Michigan for fifty years and regard myself as a Michigan woman. I graduated from Syracuse University with an A.B. and earned my A.M. at the University of Michigan. I have taught in Chelsea, Lansing, and Ypsilanti Central and finally at Eastern Michigan University where I taught for thirty-three years. I retired in Febrary, 1958 with the title of Emeritus Professor of English." Summers Mrs. Magoon lived alone on an island surrounded by an Ojibway Indian Reservation.

MAINONE, ROBERT FRANKLIN 1929-
Born: February 11, 1929; Flint, Michigan

Parents: Robert H. and Nell Claudine (Phillips) Mainone
Married: Carolyn Beryl (Bothwell) Mainone, teacher
Education: Michigan State University, 1947-51, B.S.; Michigan
 State University, 1951-52, B.S.F.; U.S. Air Force; Weather
 School, 1953; University of Utah, 1954-55; Michigan State Uni-
 versity, 1954-55, 1959, M.S.
Career: Jr. Curator, Detroit Zoological Park; Seasonal Ranger-
 Naturalist, National Park Service; Weather Observer, U.S. Air
 Force; Naturalist, Kalamazoo Nature Center; Interpretive Ecolo-
 gist; Michigan State University's Kellogg Bird Sanctuary.
Address: c/o Kellogg Bird Sanctuary, Michigan State University,
 Route 1, Augusta, Michigan 49012

Writings:

An American Naturalists' Haiku	Published (self)	1964
Parnassus Flowers	Published (self)	1965
Where Waves Were	Published (self)	1966
This Boundless Mist	Published (self)	1968
Shadows	Published (self)	1971
Young Leaves	Published (self)	1974
High On The Wind	Published (self)	1975

Work in Progress: Books of Haiku poetry

He says: "There are magic moments everywhere. . .awareness
growing. . .symbols falling together. . .if only to hint at these
wonders along a varied path. . .would this not be a life of high
endeaver?

> This spirit world. . .
> This universe. . .
> This atom dance!"

"My interest in haiku has taken me backpacking along Lake
Michigan from Frankfort to Leland; canoeing Michigan streams;
and to Japan to walk in places the classic Haiku poets walked."

MAINPRIZE, DONALD CHARLES 1930-

Pseudonym: Richard Rock
Born: August 28, 1930; Coleman, Michigan
Parents: James Raymond and Ople Smythe (Calkins) Mainprize
Married: Dories Olive; Pianist, composer, poet
Children: Daniel, Debra, Susan, and Edward
Education: Grand Rapids School of the Bible & Music; 1950-53,
 Pastor's Diploma; University of Oklahoma, 1958-60, B.A. (Writ-
 ing); Central Michigan University, 1966-68, M.A. (English)
Career: Pastor in Michigan and Oklahoma; Editor, Scripture Press
 Publications; Freelance writer; College teacher
Address: SR 79, Box 203, Houghton Lake, Michigan

Writings:

Christian Heroes of Today	Baker	1964, 1966
Enjoy the Christian Life	Zondervan, Key	1966, 1971
Good Morning, Lord	Baker	1974
Happy Anniversary, Don & Doris	Baker	1975
ABCs for Educators	Walch	1976
STARS STARS STARS (student poems)	Self	1977
Stonesville, U.S.A.	Self	1977
How to Enjoy the Bible	Self	1978

Work in Progress: *Fragments of Faith and Failure* (poems), *Bound to Love* (novel), *Marble and Mud* (novel), *Songs of the Spirit* (poems)

He says: "My creative work is confined to 5-7 A.M. and evenings. We have a building purchased and will start the Center for Creative Arts in July, 1978. Classes in leisure time writing will include poetry, fiction (novels, short shorts, and short stories), song writing, article and non-fiction book writing. You learn to write by writing, writing, and rewriting."

MALKUS, ALIDA SIMS 1895-Deceased
Born: 1895; Hampton, New York
Married: Hubert Malkus
Children: William and Hubert
Career: Writer, newspaper work, censor in Puerto Rico (during World War I)

Writings:
Pirate's Port
Eastward Sweeps the Current
Citadel of a Hundred Stairways
Little Giant of the North
The Story of Good Queen Bess
We Were There at the Battle of Gettysburg
Blue-Water Boundary
Meadows in the Sea

Alida Sims Malkus was born in Hampton, New York, but moved at an early age with her parents to Bay City, Michigan. Her father was a judge. At the age of thirteen, Alida was writing for the school newspaper and doing her own illustrating. In 1910 the family moved west, and Alida entered art school in San Francisco. She spent much time in New Mexico drawing the beauty of the West. Mrs. Malkus traveled extensively in Europe and the Americas. One book, *Blue-Water Boundary*, shows her love of the Great Lakes and the history of that area.

MALLOCH, DOUGLAS 1877-1938
Born: 1877; Muskegon, Michigan
Married: Helen (Miller) Malloch
Children: Dorothy and Jean
Career: Editor, writer

Writings:

Today	*n.d.*
Michigan My Michigan	*1902*
Come On Home	*1923*
The Heart Content	*1927*

Douglas Malloch, "Lumberman Poet," was born in Muskegon at a time when that city was becoming one of the world's great lumbering centers. He loved it forests, sawmills, and lumbering scenes. As a boy, he wrote his first poem, published in *The Detroit News.* This love for Michigan outdoors and talent for writing he combined, serving on the editorial staff of *The Muskegon Chronicle* from 1890 to 1930, when he became associate editor of the *American Lumberman* in Chicago. During these years his love for nature, especially trees, is reflected in much of his writing. One poem, "Memorials," commemorates the planting of a tree in honor of each member of the Chicago Rotary Club who fell in World War I. In 1944 Muskegon honored Mr. Malloch's memory by dedicating the Douglas Malloch Memorial Forest on U.S. 31, and a room in the Muskegon County Museum containing his desk, workshop equipment and part of his library. Present at the ceremony were his wife, Mrs. Helen Miller Malloch and his two daughters, Dorothy and Jean. His was the poetry of the simple and kindly things of life.

MANN, ETHEL E. (deceased)

Writings:

Living Lyrics	*1959*
Nature Fantasies	*1961*

A native of Cross Village, Michigan, Mrs. Mann lived in St. Ignace where she was in charge of the Handicrafters' Shop. She was active in local, civic, and state activities, such as the Michilimackinac Historical Society; Michigan Week Chairman for Mackinac County, 1959; Red Cross; Civic League; chairman for National Poetry Day in the Upper Peninsula; and many others.

MASON, PHILIP P. 1927-
Born: April 28, 1927; Salem, Massachusetts
Parents: Homer Philip and Mildred (Trask) Mason
Married: Henrietta Dow Mason

Children: Catherine, Susan, Stephen, Johnathon, and Christopher
Education: Boston University, B.A. 1950; University of Michigan, M.A. 1951, Ph.D. 1956
Career: Professor of History, Archivist at Wayne State University Libraries
Address: 8 Oxford Road, Pleasant Ridge, Michigan 48069

Writings:

Schoolcraft's Expedition to Lake Itasca: The Discovery of the Source of the Mississippi	*Michigan State University Press*	*1958*
The Literary Voyager	*Michigan State University Press*	*1958*
From Bull Run to Appomattox: Michigan's Role in the Civil War	*Wayne State University Press*	*1962*
Harper of Detroit, The Orgin and Growth of a Great Metropolitan Hosital	*Wayne State University Press*	*1964*
A History of American Roads	*Rand McNally*	*1967*
Prismatic of Detroit	*Edwards Brothers*	*1970*

Work in Progress: Indian Agency of the Upper Lakes, 1820-1860

MAY, GEORGE S. 1924-

Born: November 17, 1924; Ironwood, Michigan
Parents: Eslie and Louise (Smith) May
Married: Tish (Gerber) May
Children: Sally
Education: Gogebic Jr. College, 1943-44; Michigan Tech., 1944; University of Michigan, A.B., M.A., Ph. D., 1945-54
Career: Instructor in history, Allegheny College, 1948-50; Research Associate, State Historical Society of Iowa, 1954-56; Historic Sites Specialist and Editor, Michigan Historical Commission, 1956-66
Address: 962 Sherman, Ypsilanti, Michigan 48197

Writings:

James Strang's Ancient and Modern Michilimackinac	*W.S. Woodfill*	*1959*
Michigan Civil War History: An Annotated Bibliography	*Wayne State U. Press*	*1961*
Michigan and the Civil War Years, 1860-1866	*Michigan Civil War Centennial Commission*	*1964*
Let Their Memories be Cherished: Michigan Civil War Monuments	*Michigan Civil War Centennial Commission*	*1965*

Pictorial History of Michigan: The Early Years	Wm. B. Eerdmans	1967
Pictorial History of Michigan: The Later Years	Wm. B. Eerdmans	1969
A Michigan Reader: 11,000 B.C. to A.D. 1865 (with Herbert Brinks)	Wm. B. Eerdmans	1974
A Most Unique Machine: The Michigan Origins of the American Automobile Industry	Wm. B. Eerdmans	1975
R.E. Olds: Auto Industry Pioneer	Wm. B. Eerdmans	1977

Work in Progress: Revision of *Michigan: A History of the Wolverine State,* by Willis F. Dunbar

MEEK, FORREST B. 1928-
Born: June 11, 1928; Tustin, Michigan
Parents: Robert Burns and Electa (Gallup) Meek
Married: Jean (Grimes) Meek, Elementary Teacher
Children: Sally, Thomas, Nancy, and Charles
Education: Spring Arbor College, Assoc. Arts, 1950; Michigan State University, Bachelor Arts, 1953; Central Michigan University, Master of Education, 1966; University of Georgia, Master of Science program, 1968
Career: Two years in Army (Austria), 1 year driving truck, life insurance sales, Assistant Sup't of metal fabricating factory, 18 years high school teacher, auto and truck mechanic during summer vacations
Address: 2865 East Rock Rd., Clare, Michigan

Writings:

Michgan's Timber Battleground	Eerdmans	1976

Work in Progress: A history of Michigan's lumbering industry. Publication date expected to be 1982. I expect this to be a definitive work on the lumber industry.

He says: "Having taught history in the public schools of Lansing (Eastern), Grand Rapids (Kentwood), and in Clare, I know that many think the topic is a bore. Of course, this doesn't have to be true. History is actually the story of what people did according to an interpreter. The abilities of an interpreter therefore becomes the focal point. With my wide and varied background, I feel that my interpretations and researching skills have made and will continue to make a valuable addition to the record of what Michiganians have done.

"Many families have been able to use this book and trace their own families' part in the settling of Northern Michigan. I have several letters attesting to this important aspect.

"One lady from Saskatchewan was traveling in northern Michigan last summer. She and her husband are in their early nineties. They stopped in a book store in Petoskey and picked up a copy of my book. Since they were from Michigan originally, they bought it. Upon their return home, the lady began to read it. In my introduction I told about a mother who was deserted by a young husband in one of the lumbering towns long since abandoned. She could hardly believe her eyes, for there was the story of how her mother struggled to keep her four little children from starving to death in 1894, and she was one of those four who had been abandoned by the father.

"While this story may not be of much universal value, to me it is critical. If I have been able to help one son or daughter to better appreciate the heavy burdens the pioneering generation endured, then my efforts have been hugely successful and just as rewarding."

MIKOLOWSKI, KEN 1941-
Born: June 22, 1941; Detroit, Michigan
Parents: Herman and Opal (Lyon) Mikolowski
Married: Ann (Stroman) Mikolowski, an artist
Children: Michael and Molly
Education: Wayne State University, A.B. 1964
Career: Lecturer in poetry, University of Michigan Residential College; Editor, publisher, and printer of The Alternative Press with my wife and partner, Ann
Address: 3090 Copeland, Grindstone City, Michigan

Writings:
Thank You Call Again   *Perishable Press (Wisconsin)*1974
Poems in numerous literary magazines and anthologies

Work in Progress: *Little Mysteries and Big Enigmas*

He says: "I believe in poetry as immediate energy transference."

MILLER, HELEN TOPPING 1884-1960
Born: Fenton, Michigan
Married: Roger Miller, a newspaper editor
Education: Michigan Agricultural College (now M.S.U.) 1905
Career: Teacher, writer

Writings:

Sharon
Dark Sail
Sound of Chariots
Born Strangers
Cameo
Witch Water
Hollow Silver
Slow Dies the Thunder
Sing One Song
A Man Ten Feet Tall
Night Shade, (unpublished at the time of her death, Feb. 6, 1960)

Mrs. Miller began writing for children's magazines at the age of 10, and had published 400 short stories and 11 magazine serials. Most of her novels, fifty in all, dealt with Reconstruction days in the South. Her writing thus covers a span of more than half a century.

MILLER, ISABEL see: ROUTSONG, ALMA

MILLER, RITA A. 1930-
Born: August 21, 1930; Sacramento, California
Parents: Elmo and Frances (Syler) May
Married: Sidney E. Miller, Pharmacist
Children: Sidney II, Shawn, Barry, Steven, Tanya, Lura, Darren
Education: Currently working on B.F.A. degree at Grand Valley State College
Career: Wood sculpture-poetry presentations to schools and social groups, am included in the Writer-in-the-school project, sponsored by Michigan Council for the Arts, and a wood sculptor.
Address: 4385 Henry St., Muskegon, Michigan 49441

Writings:

Quick Blue Gathering (one of 4 poets)	Snake Grass Press *(Chapbook)*	*1977*
Second Cutting (one of 4 poets)	*Snake Grass Press (Chapbook)*	*1978*

Work in Progress: *House of Moon*—full length book; *Remus Poems*—full length

She says: "My philosophy is to celebrate life-the bad with the good—in whatever manner one can, by song, sculpture, painting or poetry."

MILLICENT see: JORDON, MILDRED ARLENE

MINER, O. IRENE 1906-
Born: 1906; Kewadin, Michigan
Parents: John and Carrie Frazine
Education: Western Michigan University, B.S.
Career: Teacher, writer

Writings:
True Book of Plants
True Book of Policeman and Fireman
True Book of the Post Office
First Book of the Earth
First Book of Talking and Listening

Irene Sevrey Miner attended East Jordan Public Schools and Muskegon Heights High School. She took her B.S. at Western Michigan and has taught school at Whitehall and Muskegon Heights. Mrs. Miner is a member of many professional organizations, and is founder and director of the Juvenile Writers' Workshop. She is a lecturer and world traveler. In 1960 she was named Muskegon Career Woman of the Year.

MINTY, JUDITH 1937-
Born: August 5, 1937; Detroit, Michigan
Parents: Karl and Margaret (Hunt) Makinen
Married: Edgar S. Minty
Children: Lora, Reed and Ann
Education: M.S.U.; Ithaca College, B.S.; Muskegon Community College; Thomas Jefferson College; Western Michigan University, M.A.
Career: Guest lecturer in Eng/poet-in-residence, College Arts & Science, Thomas Jefferson College, Grand Valley State College, 1973-77; Poet-in-residence, Central Michigan University, 1977-
Address: 310 W. Circle Dr., N. Muskegon, Michigan 49445

Writings:
Lakes Songs and Other Fears   *University of Pittsburgh*
                                  Press   1974

Work in Progress: Translations of contemporary French women poets, *Palmistry for Blind Mariners* (poems) and *Yellow Dog Journal* (poems), Short fiction

She says: "I participate in the poet-in-prison-pilot project state of Michigan, live on the Great Lakes in a sailboat in summer, and hermitize in upper peninsula of Michigan often in other seasons."

Awards: United States Award, International Poetry Forum, 1973; John Atherton Fellowship in Poetry, Bread Loaf Writer's Conference, 1974; Eunice Tietjens Memorial Award, *Poetry* magazine, 1974

MIZNER, ELIZEBETH HOWARD 1907-
Pseudonym: Elizabeth Howard
Born: August 24, 1907; Detroit, Michigan
Parents: Walter I. and Agnes (Roy) Mizner
Education: University of Michigan, A.B. in Ed. 1930; Wayne University, School library training, 1930-32; University of Michigan, A.M. in History, 1935
Career: History teacher (Shorter College, 1935-36) and writer
Address: 9692 West Bay Shore, Traverse City, Michigan 49689

Writings:

Sabina	Lothrop, Lee & Shepard	1941
Adverture for Alison	Lothrop, Lee & Shepard	1942
Dorinda	Lothrop, Lee & Shepard	1944
Summer Under Sail	William Morrow	1947
North Winds Blow Free	William Morrow	1949
Peddler's Girl	William Morrow	1951
Candle in the Night	William Morrow	1952
A Star to Follow	William Morrow	1954
The Road Lies West	William Morrow	1955
A Girl of the North Country	William Morrow	1957
The Courage of Bethea	William Morrow	1959
Verity' Voyage	William Morrow	1964
Winter on Her Own	William Morrow	1968
Wilderness Venture	William Morrow	1973
Out of Step With the Dancers	William Morrow	March, 1978

MULDER, DR. ARNOLD 1885-1959
Born: 1885; Holland Township, Michigan
Education: Hope College, A.B.; University of Chicago, Master's Degree
Career: Editor, professor, writer

Writings:
Americans from Holland
The Outbound Road
The Sand Doctor
The Kalamazoo College Story
Dominie of Harlem
Bram of Five Corners

Arnold Mulder was born in Holland Township on a farm. He

attended school in Holland and received his A.B. at Hope College. He did graduate work at the University of Michigan, but received his Master's degree at the University of Chicago. He was editor of several papers and magazines before becoming professor of English at Kalamazoo College. He served as head of the English Department from 1929-1953. Mr. Mulder was active in civic affairs and clubs, at the same time writing prolifically many magazines articles and books. One of the best known of these is *Americans From Holland,* a book for which he was decorated by the Government of the Netherlands. Arnold Mulder died March 28, 1959, at his home in Kalamazoo.

MURTON, JESSIE WILMORE
Born: Kirksville, Kentucky

Writings:

Christopher Cricket	
Make Believe Journeys	
Let's Write a Poem	
Frankincense and Myrrh	1939
Whatsoever Things are Lovely	1948
The Shining Thread	1950
A Child's Book of Verses	1952
Grace Notes	1960
Grandfather's Farm	1960

NELSON, J. RALEIGH 1873-1961
Born: 1873; Bement, Illinois
Education: University of Michigan, A.B. 1894, M.A. 1903
Career: Latin Teacher, Chicago, Illinois; Latin Department Chairman, Lewis Institute, 1900-1908; Faculty, College of Engineering, University of Michigan, 1908-1933; Professor of English, University of Michigan, 1936-43

Writings:
Writing the Technical Report
From Sunny Pastures (poetry)
Lady Unafraid (a biography of his mother when she taught the Ojibways)

Educated in Ann Arbor, J. Raleigh Nelson was distinguished for his service in writing and producing plays; lecturer for the University Extension Division; active in many civic and church services. During his years on the faculty of the University of Michigan, Mr. Nelson aided foreign students with language difficulties.

NERN, DANIEL D. 1926-
Born: February 8, 1926; Chicago, Illinois
Parents: William F. and Marie E. (DeHayes) Nern
Married: Margaret (Seemann) Nern
Children: Mark, Carolyn, and Danny
Education: Georgia Military Academy; University of Detroit
Career: Copywriter, *The Detroit Times;* Magazine Editor; Editor of Publications for an advertising firm

Writings:

Black as Night	*Beacon Press*	*1958*

Short stories in New Story, Northern Review, American Courier

NEVILL, JOHN 1901-1957
Born: 1901; San Antonio, Texas
Career: U.S. Marine Corp.; Reporter, *Greenville,* (Texas) *Evening Banner;* Sailor; Newspaper, *Detroit Free Press,* 1925-28; Public Service Council, Detroit Street Railways, 1944; Columnist and Feature Writer, *Sault Ste. Marie Evening News*

Writings:

Wanderings: Sketches of Northern Michigan Yesterday and Today	*Exposition Press*	*1955*
Miracle Bridge at Mackinac (Collaborator with David B. Steinman)	*Eerdmans*	*1957*

John Nevill was the son of a Texas Ranger. He quit school when he was sixteen years old to enlist in the Marine Corp., where he served for two years. After trying various occupations, he became a newspaper reporter in Texas and then worked on *The Detroit Free Press.*

While vacationing near DeTour, Michigan, in August, 1950, with his wife, daughter, and two dogs, he decided that he liked the area well enough to make it his permanent home.

He became feature writer and columnist for the *Sault Ste. Marie Evening News.* His column in that newspaper provided the material for his chief book, *Wanderings,* a potpourri of ramblings, fables, legends, and reports, with the Upper Peninsula as background. His writings are humorous, "folksy," sympathetic, and entertaining.

His untimely death as his book *Miracle Bridge at Mackinac* was going to press in 1957 was caused by injuries suffered when his home burned.

NEWTH, REBECCA 1940-
Born: September 21, 1940; Lansing, Michigan
Parents: William and Catherine (Messenger) Newth
Married: John Arthur Harrison, a librarian
Children: Gloria, John, Olivia
Education: Michigan State University, B.A. 1961
Career: Nursery school teacher
Address: 60 Boston Post Road, Guilford, Connecticut 06437

Writings:

Xeme (Poems)	Sumac Press	1971
A Journey Whose Bones Are Mine	Truck Press	1977

Work in Progress: A third book of poems

She says: "My poems are an attempt to find out about myself and other things and creatures. They are anti-musical, which means they cross and re-cross the essential music of our thought and language and heartbeat. I wish to celebrate even the sorrow. Writing poems is the only way I know to live deeply."

Awards: National Endowment for the Arts, 1971, for a poem published in Sumac Magazine

NEWTON, STANLEY 1874-1950
Born: 1874; Park Hill, Ontario, Canada
Career: Reporter, *Bay City Times;* Bay City Meat Company, 1900-05; Hammond, Standish & Co., Detroit, 1905

Writings:

The Story of Sault Ste. Marie	Sault News Co.	1923
(Reprint)	Black Letter Press	1975
Mackinac Island and Sault Ste. Marie		1909
(Reprint)	Black Letter Press	1976
Paul Bunyan of the Great Lakes	Packard & Co.	1946

Mr. Newton moved to Sault Ste. Marie in 1905 until he retired and moved to Florida where he died in 1950.

NIBBELINK, CYNTHIA 1948-
Pseudonym: Maggie Williams
Born: September 8, 1948; Iowa
Parents: William Nibbelink
Education: University of Iowa, B.A., M.F.A. 1971; Harvard University, Post-grad study; Oxford University, England, Post-grad

study

Career: Poet, folklorist

Address: 924 Coldbrook, N.E., Grand Rapids, Michigan 49503

Writings:
Animals (poetry)

Work in Progress: a novel

She says: "One perfect definition of poetry, not the only perfect definition, but a perfect definition is that it is the relaxation of the unconscious.

"Folklore is the poetry of history. Like poetry, folklore satifies certain psychological needs we all have, I think, to create, to hope and to sense the possibilities in each of us.

"I love history but it's more appealing to be a folklorist than a historian, dealing with data. I just love to go beyond that. And folklore is a way of celebrating our past, of taking a look at ourselves.

"I use simple language. I don't hunt around to use big words and I don't try to use lots of words of embellishment. I come from people who speak simply and directly, and I guess I'm comfortable speaking that way.

"It seems to me, anyway, that the finest art, whatever it might be—writing, music, artifact, whatever—has a certain simpleness about it which reaches out and touches the souls of everyone. It stands between you and me, between one culture and another. It brings the ocean to the land, so to speak."

NILES, GWENDOLYN 1914-

Born: March 11, 1914; Sanilac County, Michigan

Parents: A. Lynn and Hazel (Schwarzentraub) Niles

Education: Eastern Michigan University, B.S. 1940; University of Michigan, M.A. 1946; Attended Stanford, Columbia, etc.

Career: Teacher of English and literature in high school and college

Address: 1218 State, St. Joseph, Michigan 49085

Writings:

A Changing Sky	*Banner Press, Emory University, Georgia*	*1945*
The Singing of the Days	*Banner Press*	*1962*
The Silence of the Rose	*Branden Press, Boston*	*1970*

Work in Progress: Another collection of poems

She says: "I am editor of *Peninsula Poets,* official organ of the Poetry Society of Michigan, which keeps me quite busy. Since I have retired from teaching, I travel quite a little: Europe, Hawaii, California, etc."

NORTON, MARY BETH 1943-
Born: March 25, 1943; Ann Arbor, Michigan
Parents: Clark and Mary (Lunny) Norton
Education: University of Michigan, B.A. 1964; Harvard University, M.A. 1965, Ph.D. 1969
Career: Teacher, University of Connecticut, 1969-71; Associate Professor of History, Cornell University, 1971-
Address: History Department, Cornell University, Ithaca, NY 14853

Writings:

The British-Americans: The Loyalist Exiles in England, 1774-1789	Little, Brown	1972

Numerous scholarly articles

Work in Progress: A book on women in the Revolutionary War era, 1760-1800

She says: "My aim as a teacher and writer of history is to try to make the past come alive by examining the lives of real people, ordinary people in the past. At the moment, I find women's history the most exciting and rewarding field of research."

NYE, RUSSEL B(LAINE) 1913-
Born: February 17, 1913; Viola, Wisconsin
Parents: Charles H. and Zelma (Schimmeyer) Nye
Married: Kathryn Chaney, 1938
Children: Peter William
Education: Oberlin College, A.B. 1934; University of Wisconsin, M.A. 1935, Ph.D. 1940
Career: Assistant, University of Wisconsin, Madison, 1939-40; Instructor, Professor, Distinguished Professor of English, Michigan State University, 1940-

Writings:

George Bancroft: Brahmin Rebel	Knopf	1945
Fettered Freedom: Civil Liberties and the Anti-slavery Controversy	Michigan State University Press	1947
Midwestern Progressive Politcs	Michigan State University Press	1948

The Modern Essay	Scott	1953
A History of the United States	Pelican Books (London)	1956
William Lloyd Garrison and the Humanitarian Reformers	Little	1956
A Baker's Dozen: Thirteen Unusual Americans	Michigan State University Press	1957
Benjamin Franklin's Autobiography	Houghton	1958
The Cultural Life of the New Nation: 1776-1830	Harper	1960
Structure in Reading and Writing (with Wilma Ebbitt)	Scott	1961
The Diary of Benjamin Strang (Editor)	Michigan State University Press	1961
American Literary History, 1607-1830	Philadelphia Book Co.	1970
Crises on Campus	Bowling Green University	1971
New Dimensions in Popular Culture	Bowling Green University	
Society and Culture in America: 1830-1860	Harper	1974

Awards: Pulitzer Prize for biography, 1945 for *George Bancroft: Brahmin Rebel*

OLDENBURG, E. WILLIAM 1936-1974
Born: April 4, 1936; Muskegon, Michigan
Parents: William and Thress (Kroes) Oldenburg
Married: Jean (Dyk) Oldenburg Yonker, a medical technologist
Children: Jennifer Anne and William Ryan
Education: Calvin College, B.A., 1958; University of Michigan, Masters in English, 1960, Ph. D. 1966
Career: Teacher: Kalamazoo Christian High School, 1958-59; Calvin College, 1960-61; Grand Valley State College, 1965-74

Writings:

Amity Avenue and other poems	Metamorphosis Press	1971
Poems '67 to '72	Pilot Press Books	1973
Potawatomi Indian Summer	William B. Eerdmans	1975
E. William Oldenburg 1936-1974	Being Publications	1977
William Faulkner's Early Experiments with Narrative Techniques	University of Michigan	1966

His wife says: "Two years before his death, he worked toward a new publication of Grand Haven, Michigan, history with a fellow historian, Ron Kuiper. They used primarily intervieiwng techniques to gain knowledge of the social history of Grand Haven from the year 1900 to the present.

"Bill Oldenburg attempted to write with humor and honesty and to give the reader a refreshing awareness of the profound meaning of life. His Protestant Calvinistic background shows through strongly in his view of human conflict. Although writing of poetry, drama and fiction was his primary interest, he taught English on the college level and performed in live theater at Grand Valley State College, Grand Haven and Muskegon Civic Theaters and Hope College Summer Theater in Holland, Michigan. He served on the periodicals committee of "The Banner", the weekly publication of the Christian Reformed Church. He helped establish a Community Chapel in Grand Haven, Michigan, based on the relationship of evangelical Christianity to contemporary social issues and spoke weekly on the Grand Haven Radio Station, reproducing each chapel service. He followed American sports avidly, whether baseball, football or ice hockey, and enjoyed summer and winter fishing for relaxation."

ORR, MYRON DAVID
Born: Caro, Michigan
Parents: Fred H. and Katherine (O'Kelly) Orr
Married: Thelma Warner
Children: Sally Orr Putnam
Education: University of Michigan; Detroit College of Law; Columbia University; New York University
Career: Lawyer; English and History Professor, Alpena Community College; Author; Captain, United States Marine Corp.

Writings:

White Gold	Capper Harmon Slocum	1936
Cathedral in the Pines	Capper Harmon Slocum	1938
Citadel of the Lakes	Dodd, Mead	1952
Mission to Mackinac	Dodd, Mead	1956
The Outlander	Thomas Bouregy	1959

Dr. Orr, a "Fifth Generation Michiganite", has had over two hundred short stories and essays published in American, Canadian, and British publications.

Dr. Orr had a major heart attack in 1977.

OSBORN, CHASE SALMON 1860-1949
Born: January 22, 1860; Huntington County, Indiana
Parents: George Augustus and Margaret (Fannon) Osborn

Married: Lillian Gertrude Jones, May 7, 1881 (died February 4, 1948) Stellanova Brunt, April 9, 1949

Children: Ethel Louise, George Augustus, Lillian (dec.), Chase Salmon, Emily Fisher, Orren Chandler (dec.), Miriam Gertrude (dec.), Stella Brunt (adopted; adoption annulled April, 1949)

Education: Purdue University, B.S. 1880; Detroit College of Medicine, M.D. 1909; University of Michigan, L.L.D. 1911; Olivet College, 1911; Alma College, 1912; Northwestern University, 1922; Atlanta Law School, 1935; Wayne University, Sc.D. in Natural Science 1944

Career: Newspaper Work: *Lafayette* (Indiana) *Home Journal, Chicago Tribune, Florence* (Wisconsin) *Mining News, Miner and Manufacturer, Sault Ste. Marie News, Saginaw Courier-Herald;* Postmaster, Sault Ste. Marie, Michigan, 1889-93; State Game and Fish Warden, 1895-99; Commr. of Railroads for Michigan, 1899-03; Regent, University of Michigan, 1908-11; Governor of Michigan, 1911-12; Author

Writings:

The Andean Land (2 volumes)	*1909*
The Iron Hunter	*1919*
The Law of Divine Concord	*1921*
Madagascar, the Land of the Man-Eating Tree	*1924*
Short History of Michigan	*1926*
The Earth Upsets	*1927*
Following the Ancient Gold Trail of Hiram of Tyre	*1932*
Northwoods Sketches	*1934*

(With Stellanova Brunt Osborn)	
The Conquest of a Continent	*1939*
Schoolcraft-Longfellow-Hiawatha	*1942*
Hiawatha with Its Original Indian Legends	*1944*
Errors in Official U.S. Area Figures	*1945*
Northwoods Sketches	*1949*

Chase Salmon Osborn was a candiate for Vice-President of the United States; a candidate for the U.S. Senate; a member and chairman of many civic committees.

Because of his interest, many thousands of acres of Michigan land were given to various universities. He was also able to persuade the United States to add 40,000 square miles to the official area of Michigan.

Before his death, he lived in Sault Saint Marie and had a summer home in Poulan, Georgia. During these active years, Mr. Osborn was also writing, sometimes as sole author, again as co-author with Stellanova Brunt Osborn.

OSBORN, STELLANOVA 1894-

Born: July 31, 1894; Hamilton, Ontario, Canada
Parents: Edward and Rosa Lee Brunt
Married: Chase Salmon Osborn, 1949
Education: Collegiate Night School, Hamilton, Ontario, Canada, University of Michigan, A.B. Summa Cum Laude, 1922, A.M., 1930
Career: Secretary for North America, International Movement for Atlantic Union; Author; Lecturer

Writings:
(With Chase Salmon Osborn)

The Conquest of a Continent	*1939*
Schoolcraft-Longfellow-Hiawatha	*1942*
Hiawatha With Its Original Indian Legends	*1942*
Northwoods Sketches	*1949*

(Alone)

Eighty and On	
A Tale of Possum Poke in Possum Lane	
Balsam Boughs	
Jasmine Springs	
Polly Cadotte	
Beside the Cabin	
An Accolade for Chase S. Osborn (Editor)	*1940*
Iron and Arbutus	*1962*

In 1949, Stellanova Brunt married Chase Salmon Osborn, former governor of Michigan, and with him was co-author of many books.

Mrs. Osborn was secretary for North America of the International Movement for Atlantic Union, and traveled extensively in Europe and this continent in promoting the idea of world government.

Honors: Phi Beta Kappa, University of Michigan

OSOLINSKI, STAN JR. 1942-

Born: April 24, 1942; Detroit, Michigan
Parents: Stan and Anne (Monzo) Osolinski
Education: University of Detroit, B.A., 1963
Career: Elementary school teacher for 10 years; Seasonal naturalist for Huron-Clinton Metroparks; Currently free lance photographer, writer and speaker

Writings:

Michigan	*Graphic Arts Center*	*July, 1977*
Moments	*Valeron Corporation*	*July, 1977*

He says: "I have released the shutter of my camera in places as diverse as a mosquito-infested swamp forsaken by all but the marsh animals, or a public parking lot choked with the city's automobiles. Still other moments have been photographically saved by snapping along the pristine silence of a woodland trail at dawn or amidst the bustling activity of lunch hour at the school where I once taught.

"But the purpose has remained a constant: to record the beauty of the natural world wherever it may be discovered. Although I was the photographer, the true author of each scene was frost or sun, hoof or wing, water or earth.

"Mother Nature should be considered the director and sole dramatist; the camera-merely a silent spectator.

"I view my photography as an esthetic medium for conveying my concern and interest in nature. I would like to think the narrations I write. . .help to enhance that feeling in my audiences by wedding image and word to touch mind and heart."

OTIS, CHARLES HERBERT 1886-
Born: January 25, 1886; Nebraska
Parents: Willard D. and Louisa M. (Geiger) Otis
Married: Margaret Atwell Stone
Children: Cynthia Jane, James
Career: Professor Emeritus of Biology, Bowling Green State University (retired)

Writings:

Michigan Trees: A Handbook of Native and Most Important Introduced Species	University of Michigan Press	1915, 1931

Mr. Otis is one of Michigan's most distinguished men of science. He spends part of the year in Ohio and summers near Ann Arbor, Michigan, where his famous book has had many editions and is now in paperback. One of his hobbies is research in hybridization and genetics of the daylily.

OXHOLM, JOSÉ M. 1927-
Born: May 8, 1927; Guayanilla, Puerto Rico
Parents: Cristino and Maria Luisa (Lopez) Oxholm
Married: Alicia Oxholm
Children: María Luisa, Teresa, Nilda, José Jr., Judith, Nellie
Education: University of Puerto Rico, 1945-50; University of Michigan, 1952-53; Wayne State University, 1954-
Career: Medical technologist
Address: 19454 Woodbine, Detroit, MI 48219

Writings:

Rasgos de mi Mundo	Litografica Regma, S.A.	1966
Dos Puntos y Aparte	Litografica Regma, S.A.	1967
Hacia el Puerto	Imprenta El Soplon	1971
Alta Mar y Horizontes	Imprenta El Soplon	1972
Mago de Día	Imprenta El Soplon	1973
Acequias Nuevas, Aljibes Hondos	Imprenta El Soplon	1974
Dimensión de Angeles	Imprenta El Soplon	1976

Work in Progress: A new book of poetry; a family magazine *Days of Milk and Honey;* a new edition of *Puerto Norte Y Sur* (International magazine of poetry)

He says: "For me, poetry is a way of searching my soul, trying to solve the problems of identity brought by growing under two cultures. With my poetry, I talk to my true self.

"All the members of my family (wife and children) are involved in our publishing venture (Imprenta El Soplon). The children (10-13) have published for over 5 years, *Days of Milk and Honey,* a paper for children of all ages. Its main contributors have been so far Dr. Benjamin Spock, Senator Edward Kennedy, President Gerald Ford, Governor Ronald Reagan, Senator Eugene McCarthy, Nobel Prize Winner Norman E. Borlaugh, Governor Milliken, and many, many distinguished gentlemen and ladies.

"We started *Days* to better communicate with our children, to share experiences with them, to get them involved with living things, to help educate them out of the classroom.

"We started publishing our own books out of frustration. Our first two were published in Mexico and our time meant nothing to our editors; mistakes took a long time to correct. We do our own work now, completely by hand: printing, setting type, sewing, binding, etc.

We have a valuable collection of letters from great poets around the world, books, etc. The children could easily have an interesting exhibit of letters; just one sample: a four page handwritten letter by Dr. Benjamin Spock telling Maria how he was made honorary member of a tribe of Indians in Hominy, Oklahoma.

"We have many experiences to share. . ."

OXHOLM. JOSÉ M., JR. 1967-
Born: January 4, 1967; Detroit, Michigan
Parents: José M. and Maria Alicia Oxholm
Education: Burgess Elementary, 1972-75; St. Agatha Elementary, 1975-
Career: Student

Address: 19454 Woodbine, Detroit, Michigan 48219

Writings:

Lizards in My Pocket (poetry)   *El Soplon*   *1975*

Work in Progress: *Frogs are Company*

He says: "I'm co-editor of *Days of Milk and Honey,* our family magazine. I love to write about animals."

PACKARD, ROSALIE

Born: Detroit, Michigan
Parents: Dorothy (Braden) and Warren Packard II
Married: W.T.S. Digby-Seymour, a lawyer
Education: Mary Baldwin College, B.A., 1946; Wayne State University
Address: 8 Ennismore Gardens, London S.W.7, England

Writings:

Love in the Mist	*Constable (London)*	*1958*
	Houghton Mifflin (Boston)	*1959*
Love in Question	*Houghton Mifflin (Boston)*	*1961*
The Plastic Smile	*Constable (London)*	*1961*

She says: "I have contributed to *Colliers, Saturday Evening Post, The Ladies Home Journal,* and *The Spectator."*

PAHZ, CHERYL SUZANNE 1949-

Pseudonym: Cheryl Goldfeder
Born: January 29, 1949; Ypsilanti, Michigan
Parents: Morris Lee and Shirley Irene (Bender) McConnell
Married: James Alon Pahz, an Assistant Professor at Central Michigan University in Public Health Education
Children: Two
Education: University of Tennessee, B.S. in Special Educ., 1973
Career: Masters Degree student in Library and Information Science at the University of Tennessee

Writings:

The Girl Who Wouldn't Talk	*National Assoc. of the Deaf*	*1975*
Will Love Be Enough	*National Assoc. of the Deaf*	*1977*
Robin Sees a Song	*National Assoc. of the Deaf*	*1977*

Work in Progress: *Total Communication,* Charles C. Thomas, Fall, 1977

She says: "Writing is something that my husband and I do together. Up to this point, all of our publications have concerned the handicap of deafness—with a positive theme. We believe that handicapped persons are looking for respect and acceptance, not sympathy. Aside from writing, I have also illustrated our two children's books. Although we plan to continue writing books about deafness, we also hope to branch out into broader areas in the future.''

PARKER, BONNIE ELIZABETH
Born: Detroit, Michigan
Education: Wayne State University
Career: Writer

Writings:
Dark Tigers of My Tongue
Season of the Golden Dragon
Leopard on a Topaz Leash

Bonnie Parker has had her poetry published in many anthologies and in such magazines as *McCalls, Good Housekeeping, Country Gentlemen, Ideals, Farm Journal, P.T.A. Magazines,* and newspapers such as the *New York Herald Tribune, New York Times, Denver Post, Chicago Tribune, Detroit News.* Her poems have been read over radio and TV stations here and in Canada, Mexico, and Belguim.

Her hobbies are reading, oil painting, music, and above all poetry. She has been awarded prizes in nation-wide contests and speaking engagements in various states and been affiliated with numerous poetry associations.

PATYN, ANN see: CARLI, AUDREY

PAULSON, JACK see: JACKSON CAARY PAUL

PECKHAM, HOWARD 1910-
Born: July 13, 1910; Lowell, Michigan
Parents: H. Algernon and Harriet (Wilson) Peckham
Married: Dorothy Koth
Children: Stephen, Angela
Education: Olivet College, 1927-29; University of Michigan, A.B., 1931, M.A., 1933; Olivet College, Litt. D., 1975
Career: Editorialist, The Grand Rapids Press, 1935; Curator of Mss., Clements Library, University of Michigan, 1936-45; Direc-

tor, Clements Library, University of Michigan, 1953-77; Director, Indiana Historical Bureau, 1945-53

Address: 213 London Road, Hendersonville, NC 28739

Writings:

Introduction to Book Collecting	*Bowker*	*1946*
Pontiac and the Indian Uprising	*Princeton*	*1947*
Captured by Indians	*Rutgers*	*1954*
The War for Independence	*Chicago University*	*1958*
The Colonial Wars	*Chicago University*	*1964*
The Making of the University of Michigan	*University of Michigan Press*	*1967*
The Wm. L. Clements Library, 1923-73	*Clements Library*	*1973*
The Toll of Independence	*Chicago University*	*1974*
Indiana, a Bicentennial History	*Norton*	*1978*

FOR CHILDREN

Wm. Henry Harrison, Young Tippecanoe	*Bobbs Merrill*	*1951*
Nathanael Greene, Independent Boy	*Bobbs Merrill*	*1956*
Pontiac, Young Ottawa Leader	*Bobbs Merrill*	*1963*

Also, several edited works.

Work in Progress: *Historical Americana*

He says: "I find American History more fascinating than most fictions."

PERKINS, OWEN ADELBERT 1930-
Born: November 14, 1930; Royal Oak, Michigan
Parents: Owen Caster and Alice Rozena (Lemons) Perkins
Married: Grace Louise (Kidder) Perkins, Educator
Children: Glenn Stuart, Carol Kay, Janet Ruth, Jill Louise, Paul Owen
Education: Albion College, B.A., 1952; Michigan State University, M.A.T., 1968
Career: Secondary School Science teacher for 26 years; Girls gymnastic coach for past 10 years
Address: 2806 Linwood Ave., Royal Oak, Michigan 48073

Writings:

Royal Oak Michigan: The Early Years	*Golden Jubilee, 1971, Inc.*	*1971*
Buffum Family, Volume I	*Miran Publishers*	

Work in Progress: *Royal Oak Michigan: The Later Years; Buffum Family, Volume II*

He says: "I am interested in young people, their heritage, their future. I enjoy helping them use their physical and mental capabilities in learning gymnastic skills and applying them in competition. I enjoy nature and outdoor activities, especially collecting and studying lepidoptera and ornithology. I am presently chairman of the Royal Oak Historical Commission and past president of the Royal Oak Historical Society.

PERRY, WILL 1933-
Born: May 11, 1933; Morris, Illinois
Parents: Wilbur and Mary (Hrebik) Perry
Married: Patricia, an advertising director
Children: Stephen, Karen, Susan
Education: University of Michigan, B.A. in L.S.A., 1955
Career: Newspaper writer, 1958-68; Sports Information Director at the University of Michigan, 1968 to present
Address: 1540 King George Court, Ann Arbor, Michigan

Writings:

The Wolverines. . .A Story of Michigan Football	Strode	1974

He says: "The thought that 10,000 copies of a book relating the rich traditions of college football at the University of Michigan have been read is extremely rewarding."

PETERS, ARTHUR 1914-
Born: March 18, 1914; Detroit, Michigan
Parents: Albert E. and Birdsall (Lillibridge) Peters
Married: Margot Peters, a teacher and writer
Children: Henry, Albert, Marc, Claire
Education: University of Michigan, B.A., 1939; University of Wisconsin, M.A., 1961
Career: Teacher of English, Madison Area Technical College, Madison, Wisconsin
Address: 304 West Wilson, Apt. 5, Madison, Wisconsin 53703

Writings:

Abram Force: A Novel of the American Revolution	Lee-Howard Co.	1975

PETERS, T.R., SR. 1929-
Born: November 14, 1929; Detroit, Michigan
Married: Norman A. and Eleanor (Schneider) Peters
Married: Lillian (Lee) Peters, an artist and art teacher

Children: Jennifer, Thomas Jr., Sarah Jeanne

Education: Hillsdale College, B.A., 1954; Wayne State University, M.A., 1962; Twenty hours beyond M.A. in journalism and communications

Career: Ten years of professional writing for The Jam Handy Organization and The Detroit Free Press; Ten years of teaching at Wayne State University, Macomb Community College, and Grosse Pte. Schools; Author of business films, nationally published speeches, booklets, etc.

Address: 350 Moselle Place, Grosse Pte., Michigan 48236

Writings:

The Education of Tom Webber (Novel)	*Exposition-Banner*	1977
A Van Gogh Portfolio & Other Poems (Booklet)	*Privately published*	1967

Addresses published in *Vital Speeches of the Day, 1970-71*

Work in Progress: A second novel which will hopefully be completed in November, 1978

He says: "Ever since winning the Ewing Award for Creative Writing at Hillsdale College in 1954, I have been steadily and seriously involved in creative writing. Had it not been an economic necessity, I would have never entered business but spent a lifetime creating novels, stories, poems. The subconscious evolution of a book takes quite a long time for me—but once begun, I am capable of writing fast, fairly polished first drafts. After two self-edits, I consider my work ready for publication. My editor on my first published novel only changed three words in the book, and we quibbled over two of them. As a creative writer, I am more of an artistic craftsman than a word-magician. In early efforts, I had a rich, colorful style, but after studying works which I particularly admired (and which gained a vast reading audience), I deliberately concocted a simple, direct (clipped) style. Both my first novel and the one I am working on are set in Michigan.

"The first short story I ever tried to market, "Fanfare at Twelve", was a third selection by *Mademoiselle Magazine* (they published the other two) way back in 1953 while I was still in college. As a creative writer apprentice, I took 16 credit hours of Creative Writing at three schools under three different novelist professors, and they all singled out my work as outstanding and professionally publishable. Even so, it still took me many years to get a novel between hard covers. I did have experiences which were at once heartening and disheartening, however, when the first three major publishers I sent my novel to all wrote back personal, lengthy letters explaining that my book had passed one or two editors and had been recommended for publication--only to be declined by the Board or an Executive editor specializing in sales market potential. I

243

consider my work more literary (than pop market) which makes it all the more difficult to sell to a publisher.

"The novel I am now working on will be of particular interest to Michigan readers because, interspersing the plot which is in four segments (and all takes place in the Detroit area), will be narrative flashbacks of real state historical events which I feel were significant and have relevance to my plot. I have already researched this part of the book and am enjoying writing these!"

Awards: Ewing Award for Creative Writing, Hillsdale College, 1954; Consultant to The 1970 White House Conference on Children; "Vital Speeches Magazine" published the address "Experiment for the White House" which was made to the National Organization of Women Conference at Oakland University

PETERSON, MRS. CHARLES see: WILLIAMSON, MARGARET

PETERSON, WILFERD ARLAN 1900-
Born: August 21, 1900; Whitehall, Michigan
Parents: Peter H. and Elsie Marie (Gilbert) Peterson
Married: Ruth Rectore, a housewife and helper with my books
Children: Mrs. Gordon Thorpe, a teacher in Winston Salem, NC
Education: Extension courses from Michigan State University and the University of Michigan
Career: Copywriter, Editor, Creative Director and Secretary of the Board of Directors of the Jaqua Company, an ad agency in Grand Rapids
Address: 1721 Woodward Avenue, S.E., Grand Rapids, MI 49506

Writings:

The Art of Getting Along	Self	1949
The Art of Living	Simon & Schuster	1961
The New Book of the Art of Living	Simon & Schuster	1963
More About the Art of Living	Simon & Schuster	1966
Adventurers in Art of Living	Simon & Schuster	1968
Art of Living in the World Today	Simon & Schuster	1969
The Art of Living, Day by Day	Simon & Schuster	1972

Work in Progress: *The Art of Living Treasure Chest,* a paperback containing the essays from his first three books, Simon & Schuster, 1977

He says: "The idea of the Art of Living books is to provide in brief two page essays the Arts of the Good Life, a philosophy of life in brief, easy to read form. Thirty of these essays were published in *This Week Magazine* circulated through 42 big city Sunday papers to 14 million families. A million copies of my books are in print. Hallmark, since 1966, has put out an annual Art of Living Calendar containing condensations of essays from my books and have also used my material in cards and booklets.''

Awards: Advertising Man of the Year, 1963; GW Medal from Freedom Foundation, 1958

PIERCY, MARGE 1936-
Born: March 31, 1936; Detroit, Michigan
Parents: Robert and Bert Bernice (Bunnin) Piercy
Education: University of Michigan, A.B., 1957; Northwestern University, M.A., 1958
Career: Poet-in-residence, University of Kansas, 1971; Distinguished Visiting Lecturer, Massachusetts Foundation for Humanities and Council on Arts, 1974; Thomas Jefferson College, Fall, 1975; Women's Writing Center, Cazenovia College, New York, 1976; Fiction Writer in Residence, Holy Cross University, Worcester, 1976; Staff, Writers Conference, Indiana University, Bloomington, 1977; Butler Chair of Letters, State University of New York, Buffalo, Summer, 1977
Address: Box 943, Wellfleet, Massachusetts 02667

Writings:

Breaking Camp	Wesleyan University Press	1968
Hard Loving	Wesleyan University Press	1969
Going Down Fast	Trident	1969
Dance the Eagle to Sleep	Doubleday	1970
4-Telling	The Crossing Press	1971
Small Changes	Doubleday	1973
To Be of Use	Doubleday	1973
Living in the Open	Knopf	1976
Women on the Edge of Time	Knopf	1976
The High Cost of Living	Harper and Row	1978
The Twelve-spoked Wheel Flashing	Knopf	1978

THE POETRY LADY see: LAWTON, ETHEL CHAPIN

POITIERS, ANGELE see: FOX, HUGH

POST, MARIE J. 1919-

Born: February 8, 1919; Grandville, Michigan
Parents: Jacob G. and Jennie (Sietsema) Tuinstra
Married: R. Jack Post, an electronics retailer executive
Children: Judith, R. Jack Jr., Meredith, Douglas, Beth, Barbara
Education: Calvin College, B.A., 1941
Career: Teacher; Homemaker, Freelance writer; Painter; Reader; Conference Director
Address: 2105 E. Shiawassee Dr., S.E., Grand Rapids, MI 49506

Writings:
I Had Never Visited an Artist
  Before (poetry collection)   *Being*   1974

Work in Progress: Collection of 40 poems about St. Peter; Collection of light verse

She says: "In I-can't-tell-how-many-years of writing and of publishing I have found that poetry is human speech made musical. To be a 'successful poem' the lyrics must achieve an intensity of communication. No matter how difficult or 'heavy' the message I am expressing in a poem it has to perform itself beyond its difficulties, beyond the unphrasable but phrased emotion. The poem has to generate its own context. After finishing a poem I sometimes have no idea why I selected each phrase, why I thought it complete, what I intended to do with it and why it 'jells'. I am seldom concerned with the form, the poetic diction, allusions, metaphors, etc., because I have had rigorous training instructed forms, in the use of all these things so that they come naturally. This training in sonnet, ballad, the French forms, etc., I find indispensable to good poetry composition."

POWERS, WILLIAM 1930-

Born: July 31, 1930; Davenport, Iowa
Married: Sally
Children: Mary Amanda, Will, Matthew
Education: University of Illinois, B.A. 1956; M.A. 1957; Ph.D 1967
Career: Associate Editor, Henry Publication, NYC, 1959-61; Assistant Professor, University of North Carolina-Chapel Hill, 1967-71; Professor and Head of Humanities Department, Michigan Tech., 1971-75; Professor and Dean of Science and Arts, Michigan Tech.,1975-present
Address: 1013 E. 6th Avenue, Houghton, Michigan 49931

Writings:
Writer's Mind   *Prentice Hall*   1969

Work in Progress: *Writers and Readers,* Winthrop

He says: "I write poetry, fiction, scholarly pieces, and textbooks. Most of the poetry and fiction is midwestern in setting; in recent years generally shows Michigan's U.P."

POYER, JOE 1939-
Born: November 30, 1939; Battle Creek, Michigan
Parents: Joseph J. and Eileen (Powell) Poyer
Married: Susan (Pilmore) Poyer, Teacher
Children: Joseph J. III, Geoffrey Robert
Education: Kellogg Community College, A.A. 1959; Michigan State University, B.A. 1961
Career: Assistant Director of Public Information, Michigan TB Association, 1961-63; Proposal Editor, Pratt & Whitney Aircraft, 1963-65; Manager, Medical Communications, Beckman Instruments, Inc., 1965-67; Manager, Interdisciplinary Communications, BioScience Planning, 1967-68; Manager of Regulatory Affairs, Allergan Pharmaceuticals, 1969-72; Senior Project Manager, Allergan Pharmaceuticals, 1972-July, 1977
Address: Wallace, Aitken & Sheil, Inc., New York, New York

Writings:

Operation Malacca	*Doubleday*	
	V. Gollancz (British)	
	Pyramid	
	Sphere (British)	
	U.S.	*1968*
North Cape	*Doubleday*	
	V. Gollancz (British)	
	Sphere (British)	
	Pyramid	
	Forum (Danish)	
	Almqvist (Swedish)	
	Bruna (Dutch)	
	Oren Orlygur (Iceland)	*1969*
The Balkan Assignment	*Doubleday*	
	Pyramid	
	Almqvist (Swedish)	
	Orne Orlygur (Iceland)	
	V. Gollance (British)	
	Sphere (British)	
	Forum (Danish)	*1970*
The Chinese Agenda	*Doubleday*	
	Weidenfeld (British)	
	Futura (British)	
	Almqvist (Swedish)	
	Forum (Danish)	*1972*
The Shooting of the Green	*Doubleday*	

	Pyramid	
	Weidenfeld (British)	
	Futura (British)	
	Mondorri (Italian)	
	Shobo (Japanese)	
	Sphere (British)	1974
The Day of Reckoning	Weidenfeld (British)	
	Sphere (British)	
	Almqvist (Swedish)	
	Forum (Danish)	1976

Work in Progress: *The Contract,* V. Gollancz (British), Shere (British), Atheneum 1911 (Working title) Simon & Schuster, V. Gollancz (British), Sphere (British)

PRESS, SIMONE JUDA 1943-
Born: April 12, 1943; Cambridge, Massachusetts
Parents: Walter and Renee (Molino) Juda
Married: Steven Eric Press, a psychiatric social worker
Children: Corinna Nicole, Valerie Gabriella
Education: Universite de Lausanne, Cert. d'Etudes Franc. 1962; Bennington College, B.A. 1965; Columbia University, M.A. 1967
Career: Assistant Professor of English, Siena Heights College, 1973-present; Poetry Residencies, Michigan Council for the Arts
Address: 1109 W. Washington, Ann Arbor, Michigan 48103

Writings:

Thaw	Inwood/Horizon Press	1974

Poetry in numerous magazines such as *Boston After Dark, The New York Times, The Ann Arbor Review,* and *Green House.*

Work in Progress: *Pieces of Thunder* (poetry) and *A Poem Isn't Ready Until it's Done* (a book about teaching creative writing in a psychiatric setting.)

"It is one of my aims to make poetry more readily accessible to myself and others by paying special attention to its interrelationship with all facets of life, internal and external. At the elementary, high school, and college level as well as in the hospital environment, I have found that it is possible to create extraordinary pieces of art work and that the cultivation of the necessary and appropriate environment is essential. Along with the development of creative expression, both enthusiastic encouragement and critical skills are necessary for the shaping of any serious and important results.

"As for my relationship with my own writing, I'm not sure who is the leader and who is the follower; I go where it takes me and I take it with me wherever I go."

Awards: Michigan Council for the Arts MCA Poetry

Residencies:

A grant to work at the University of Michigan, Children's Psychiatric Hospital Inpatient School: April, 1976; Day Treatment School: May-June, 1977

A grant to work at Ypsilanti State Hospital (Residential and Community Assistance Schools), January, 1978

A grant to work at the Neuro-Psychiatric Insitute, University of Michigan Hospital, March, 1978

A grant to work at St. Norbert Elementary School (March, 1978) and Garden City Public Schools (May, 1978)

She says: "I am always involved in the writing of poetry and am particularly interested in the relationship between poetry and all the other arts (painting, dance, music) as well as the integration of writing in various educational settings. My own work has taken me to the teaching of poetry at public schools, colleges, and psychiatric hospitals. My philosophy basically consists of the belief that although poetry is a highly intense and specialized art form, it is easily integrated into daily life.

QUAIFE, MILO MILTON (1880-1959)

Born: October 6, 1880; Nashua, Iowa
Parents: Albert Edward and Barbara S. (Hine) Quaife
Married: Letitia (Goslin)
Children: Helen Elizabeth, Donald Lincoln, Dorothy Barbara, Mary Louise
Education: Grinnell College, Ph. B., 1903; University of Missouri, A.M., 1905; University of Chicago, Ph.D., 1908; Wayne State University, Litt. D., 1951
Career: Historian; Secretary, Burton Historical Collection, Co-founder, The Algonquin Club (for men interested in the history of the Detroit-Windsor area), 1934; Lecturer of history, Wayne State University and University at Detroit

Writings:

Condensed Historical Sketches for each of Michigan Counties	*J.L. Hudson Co.*	*1940*
Sixty Years: Six Decades in Growth & Development of Detroit and It's Environs, 1881-1941	*J.L. Hudson Co.*	*1941*
The Flag of the United States	*Grosset & Dunlap*	*1942*
(Editor) The American Lake Series, 10 Volumes	*Bobbs-Merrill Co.*	*1942-49*
Lake Michigan	*Bobbs-Merrill Co.*	*1944*
Michigan: from Primitive Wilderness to Industrial Commonwealth, co-authored with Sid-		

ney Glazer	Prentice-Hall	1948
I Remember Detroit, Co-authored with John C. Lodge	Wayne State U. Press	1949
This is Detroit: 1701-1951, Two Hundred & Fifty Years in Pictures	Wayne State U. Press	1951

Awards: Honorary President for Life: The Algonquin Club. Tribute of a published bibliography; *46 Years: The Published Writings of M.M. Quaife, 1910-1955.* Algonquin Club, 1956

QUIMBY, GEORGE IRVING 1913-

Born: May 4, 1913; Grand Rapids, Michigan
Parents: George Irving and Ethelwyn (Sweet) Quimby
Married: Helen Ziehm Quimby, artist
Children: Mrs. Sedna Q. Wineland, George Edward, John Emerson, Robert William
Education: University of Michigan, B.A. 1936, M.A. 1937; University of Chicago, 1938-39
Career: State Supervisor Louisiana WPA Archaeological Survey, 1939-41; Director Muskegon Museum, 1941-42; Asst. Curator of N. of Amer. Archaeology & Ethology Field Museum, 1942-43; Curator of Exhibits, Anthropology, 1943-54; Curator of N. Amer. Archaeology, 1955-56; Research Associate, 1965-present; Professor of Anthropoloy, University of Washington, 1965-present; Director of Burke Museum, University of Washington, 1968-present
Address: 6001-52nd Ave., N.E. Seattle, WA 98115

Writings:

Indian Life in the Upper Great Lakes	Univ. of Chicago Press	1960
Indian Culture and European Trade Goods	Univ. of Wisconsin Pr.	1966
The Dunaw Creek Site, A 17th Century Prehistoric Indian Village and Cemetery in Osceana County, Michigan	Field Museum Press	1966
Indians Before Columbus: Co-author	Univ. of Chicago Press	1947
Maritime Adaptations of the Pacific: Co-editor	Moulton: The Hague	1975
In the Land of the War Canoes: Kawkiutl Indian Life on the Northwest Coast (Co-editor)	Univ. of Washington Pr.	1974

Work in Progress: Book about Edward S. Curtis as a pioneer cinematographer among Northwest Coast Indians with co-author

He says: "I have had published mostly articles and monographs beginning in 1937. All of them deal with archaeology, ethnography and history in a humanistic context."

QUIRK, JOHN EDWARD 1920-
Born: August 15, 1920; Akron, Ohio
Parents: Robert Emmett and Ethel (Hall) Quirk
Married: Betty Goodwin
Children: John Goodwin, Kimberly Hall
Education: Wayne State University, United States Naval Academy, B.S., 1942
Career: Quirk and Hankins (sales engineering)
Address: 4993 Elm Gate Drive, Orchard Lake, MI 48033

Writings:

No Red Ribbons	Devin	1962
The Hard Winners	Random	1965
The Chocolate Bunny	Avon	1965
The Rookie	New American Library	1965
The Survivor	Avon	1965

RANDALL, DUDLEY 1914-
Born: January 14, 1914; Washington, D.C.
Parents: Arthur and Ada (Bradley) Randall
Married: Vivian Spencer
Children: Phyllis Sherron
Education: Wayne State University, B.A., 1949; University of Michigan, MALS, 1951
Career: Librarian, Lincoln University (Missouri) Librarian, Morgan State College (Maryland); Wayne County Federated Library, 1956-69; Reference Librarian, University of Detroit, 1969-75; Poet in Residence, University of Detroit, 1969-74; Founder, Broadside Press, 1965
Address: 12651 Old Mill Place, Detroit, MI 48238

Writings:

Poem Counterpoint	Broadside Press	1966
For Malcolm	Broadside Press	1967
Cities Burning	Broadside Press	1968
Love You	Paul Breman, Ltd.	1970
More to Remember	Third World Press	1971
The Black Poets	Bantam Books (editor)	1971
After the Killing	Third World Press	1973

Awards: Wayne State University Thompkins Award: 1962 and

RANKIN, CAROLINE (WATSON) 1864-1945
Pseudonym: Carroll Watson Rankin
Born: May 11, 1864; Marquette, Michigan
Parents: Jonas William and Emily (Wood) Watson
Married: Ernest Frederick Augustus Rankin
Children: Florence Imogene, Ernest Harvey, Eleanor Wood, Phyllis Spencer
Education: Taylor's Academy, Greenock, Scotland, 1 yr.; Kemper Hall, Kenosha, Wisconsin, 2 yrs.; Chicago Female College, 1 yr.
Career: Author

Writings:

Dandelion Cottage	*Holt*	*1904, 23, 31, 46, 51*
Reprinted	*Marquette County Historical*	
	Society	*1977*
The Girls of Gardenville	*Holt*	*1906*
The Adopting of Rosa Marie	*Holt*	*1908, 36, 43*
The Castaways of Pete's Patch	*Holt*	*1911*
The Cider Pond	*Holt*	*1915*
Girls of Highland Hall	*Holt*	*1921*
Gipsy Man	*Holt*	*1926*
Finders Keepers	*Holt*	*1930*
Wolf Rock	*Holt*	*1933*
Stump Village	*Holt*	*1935*

Her daughter Phyllis tells us: "Carroll Watson Rankin started writing and illustrating her stories as soon as she could hold a pencil. It was a delight to get a letter from her because it was invariably amusing as well as informative of what was going on around her. By the time she was fifteen she had stories published in various Sunday School papers and in *Waverly's Magazine.* At the age of sixteen, she responded to an advertisement in the *Mining Journal* seeking a bright boy to do reporting. Her response was that while she wasn't a boy, she was almost sure she was bright. She got the job and worked for the paper as their Society Editor.

"Also during this period before her marriage she gave drawing and painting lessons to private pupils.

"She continued writing short stories, anecdotes and articles for many magazines including *Youth's Companion, Harpers, Life, St. Nicholas, Bookman, Garden, Critic, Delineator, Leslie's, Lippincott's, Metropolitan, Everybody's* and *Munsey's.*

"She loved gardening. She had an artist's keen observation and delight in minute detail of form, color, and design in anything she encountered."

RANKIN, CARROLL WATSON see: RANKIN, CAROLINE CLEMENT

RANKIN, ERNEST HARVEY SR. 1888-
Born: January 6, 1888; Marquette, Michigan
Parents: Ernest F.A. and Caroline Clement (Watson) Rankin
Married: Agnes (Breslin)
Children: Ernest Harvey, Jr., Mary Carol, John Breslin, Eleanor Ann
Education: Marquette High School, 1907; School Railway Signaling, 1910-1911
Career: Railroad signal engineering, 1909-1954; Genealogist, secretary/treasurer and executive secretary; Marquette County Historical Society, 1955-69; Founder and editor; *Harlow's Wooded Man,* Quarterly, Marquette; County Historical Society, 1966-69
Address: 830 Tamalpais Avenue, Novato, CA 94947

Writings:

The Indians of Gitchie Gumee	Marquette County Historical Society	1966, 1975
A Brief History of the Marquette Iron Range	Marquette County Historical Society	1966
North to Lake Superior (co-editor)		

Contributed over 200 articles to various publications devoted to the history of Marquette, Marquette County, Lake Superior, and the people of the era and area, as well as book reviews on the Great Lakes.

He says: "Do not be afraid of work and keep the mind active." He has recently completed *A Rankin Family History* for the benefit of Rankin descendants, a task which spanned thirty years of research and writing. His grandfather, Edward Peter Rankin, brought his name and bride to Pontiac in 1844 and his family of eight was raised and lived in the Detroit area. His father left the family hearthside in 1885 and moved to Marquette.

RATIGAN, ELEANOR 1916-
Pseudonym: Virginia Wharton (among others)
Born: May 23, 1916; Denver, Colorado
Parents: William Thomas and Ida (Strickler) Eldridge
Married: William Ratigan; Writer
Children: Mrs. Patricia Ranger, Mrs. Anne Pelton, Shannon Ratigan
Education: University of Tennessee, 1934-35; Maren Elwood Pro-

fessional Writers College (Hollywood, California), 1940-44
Career: Writer, Librarian, and Editor
Address: 223 Park Avenue, Charlevoix, Michigan 49720

Writings:

Radio shows	KOA, Denver and NBC	'37-39
Deep Water	Lothrop, Lee & Shepard	1961
The Adventurers of Trudy and Flame Series: includes the Coming of Flame, Son of Flame, etc.	Dell Publishing Co., Dell Seal Books	1963-

Hundreds of articles and stories written for American national magazines including Canadian publishers

Mrs. Ratigan's husband has compiled this information and he proudly says: "Like many who were forced by illness to 'lay abed' (Robert Louis Stevenson, for instance) in childhood, Eleanor developed a love for books and music. She had a sharp ear and eye and could mimic the sound of any language without knowing the words. She could imitate anyone. In later school years she fancied herself as an opera prima donna and drive her sisters somewhat wild. She loved to dance, especially with her handsome Tennessee father, she was his girl to his death. She collected stamps during her illness, began a collection of famous signatures (now quite unusual), and carried away her first prize in poetry in her senior year of high school. Meanwhile, she and some bright girlfriends had formed a 'very sophisticated' poetry club which tended toward writing imitations of Dorothy Parker, Gibron et al. She still loves to recite *Gunga Din.*

"Since becoming a seasoned writer, Eleanor always has devoted much of her time to helping aspiring writers, young and old. She has tremendous enthusiasm and is a catalyst to boot. She makes things happen. She has taught several adult education courses in creative writing and her students always have found her challenging and inspirational.

"A dedicated and no-nonsense craftsman, she has been a tremendous editor; both for the neophytes and for those who have called for her help from the 'Ivory Towers of Academe.' "

RATIGAN, WILLIAM 1910-
Born: November 7, 1910; Detroit (Corktown), Michigan
Parents: B.J. and Bertie (Laing) Raitgan
Married: Eleanor (Eldridge), Librarian and writer
Children: Mrs. Patricia Ranger, Mrs. Anne Pelton, and Shannon
Education: University of Detroit, University of Chattanooga, B.A.; Michigan State University, M.A. 1961, Ph.D. 1963
Career: NBC network newsman; Director, Far Eastern Listening

Post; Supervisor, War Correspondents and Commentators, Pacific Theater of Operations; NBC Editor and Scriptwriter, United Nations Conference, San Francisco; Counselor and University Lecturer; Writer; Founder/proprieter, The Dockside Press, since 1954; Consultant, the Smithsonian Institute for technical developement of Great Lakes craft.

Address: The Dockside Press, Box 1, Charlevoix, MI 49720

Writings:

Hiawatha and America's Mightiest Mile	Eerdmans	1955
Young Mister Big	Eerdmans	1955
The Adventures of Captain McCargo	Random House	1956
Straits of Mackinac!	Eerdmans	1957
Triology of verse: The Blue Snow, Tiny Time Pine, The Adventures of Paul Bunyan and Babe	Eerdmans	1958
The Long Crossing	Eerdmans	1959
Highways Over Broad Waters	Eerdmans	1959
Soo Canal, (2nd edition)	Eerdmans	1968

Great Lakes Shipwrecks and Survivals:		
Bradley edition, Lake Michigan	Eerdmans	1960
Morrell edition, Lake Huron	Eerdmans	1969
Edmund Fitzgerald edition, Lake Superior	Eerdmans	1977
Encyclopedia Americana: summary of Paul Bunyan		

Professional books:

Conflicts with Counseling	Univ. Microfilms	1964
School Counseling, a View from Within	American School Counselor Assn.	1967
Theories of Counseling, (2nd edition)	McGraw-Hill	1972

Work in Progress: I never discuss my writing until a publisher accepts and puts it into public circulation in book form.

He says: "One of the favorite sidelights is that my writing about the North Country led to my being adopted as an Ottawa Chief of the Algonquin Nation and given the name *Opwa-Nan Iian Kano Tong,* Interpreter of Dreams.

"If I were to point out one way for beginners to learn to write, it would be to take other languages than English and try translating small passages (poetry was my selection) into American language. In my time I have done other things but they have always been peripheral to my writing—and I have never stopped writing, no matter what else.

"There is a joy in writing that I have never found in any other occupation. My first published short story came about a year and a half after marriage nad first child. It was a detective story for a 'pulp' magazine. They paid 1¢ a word, so my first check was $50.00. My wife and I were so excited we left Detroit and went to her hometown of Denver."

Awards: Intercollegiate Odes of Horace Poetry Prize; Chaparral Poetry Prize

REED, JAMES D. 1940-
Born: October 7, 1940; Jackson, Michigan
Parents: Clair and Esther (Bryden) Reed
Married: Christine Flowers Reed, Writer
Children: Phoebe, Alicia
Education: Albion College, 1958-60; Michigan State University, B.A., 1961; Stony Brook University, 1966-68; University of Montana, MFA, 1969
Career: Guggenheim Fellow-Poetry, 1970; Director MFA in writing program, 1970-75; Assistant Professor of English, University of Massachusetts, 1974; Staff Writer, *Sports Illustrated,* 1975-present
Address: Sports Illustrated, Time & Life Building, Rockefeller Center, New York, NY 10020

Writings:

Expressways, Poems	*Simon & Schuster*	*1968*
Whiskey Profiles	*Baleen Press*	*1970*
FatBack Odes	*Sumac Press*	*1971*

Work in Progress: *The Tower to Destroy:* a novel of the IRA, to be published by E.P. Dutton in 1978

He says: "The change from college teaching and writing poems to the emergency-war atmosphere of *Sports Illustrated,* where I write long, feature articles—and to the world of novel writing, is a huge quantum-leap. It will be interesting to see if these two worlds will ever meet in a single book."

REESER, CECILIA M. 1910-
Born: November 8, 1910; Petrel, Michigan
Parents: Julian and Louse (LaCasse) Draze
Children: Stanley Drobeck and Mrs. Betty Artress
Education: Ontonagon County Normal, 1929; Eastern Michigan University, B.S. (Spec. Ed.), 1957

Career: 32 years as teacher, 28 years as a consultant and teacher in special education

Address: Picture Bay Trailer Park, L'Anse, MI 49946

Writings:

Beauty Loves Company (poems)Carlton Press, Inc.	*1977*

Work in Progress: *Whoo-Whom* and *Raki Raccoon;* both for children and to be published by Carlton Press

She says: "To help children and adults help themselves and others—Everyone should be permitted to have freedom and to express his own individuality. This does not stop love, but clearly enhances it. Love is not a duty, it is not always beautiful but it should be freedom in depth which is shared with many in a variety of moods. I enjoy helping children and adults through these thoughts so that they grow and become individuals who understand and respect themselves and others."

She is a woman of many interests which includes photography, music, belly dancing, karate, welding, fishing, hunting, motorcycling, and flying. In 1972 she performed her first and only skydiving feat and is entered in the 1976 edition of the *Guinness Book of World Records* as the oldest woman skydiver.

Awards: Outstanding Woman—Ontonogon County, 1976 (one of ten). Presented to the Women's Club by Charles Willman, Judge of Probate.

REIMANN, LEWIS C. 1890-1961

Born: September 22, 1890; Stambaugh, Michigan

Married: Pearl

Children: Mrs. Lawrence F. Smith

Education: University of Michigan, B.A., 1916

Career: YMCA, 3 years; Director, Presbyterian Students activities, University of Michigan, 1920-27; Organizer and Director, University of Michigan Fresh Air Camp; Director, Canadian Canoe Treks; Owner, Northwoods Publishing Co.; Democratic candidate for 33rd District Michigan Senator, 1954, defeated; Author

Writings:

Between the Iron and the Pine	*Northwoods Publ. Co.*	*1951*
When Pine was King	*Northwoods Publ. Co.*	*1952*
Incredible Seney	*Northwoods Publ. Co.*	*1953*
Hurley-Still No Angel	*Northwoods Publ. Co.*	*1954*
The Lake Poinsett Story	*(Arlington, S.D.)*	*1957*
The Successful Camp	*Univ. of Mich. Press*	*1958*
The Game Warden and the Poachers	*Northwoods Publ. Co.*	*1959*

Mr. Reimann was best known at the University of Michigan as an athlete where he was tackle on the Fielding Yost's "Point-a-Minute" football team, 1914-15; and the Big Ten Wrestling Champion, heavyweight division, 1915.

RENDELMAN, DANNY 1945-
Born: November 25, 1945; Flint, Michigan
Parents: William F. and Beatrice J. (Winn) Rendleman
Married: Alice M. Rendleman
Children: Eliot F.
Education: Central Michigan University, 1963-68; University of Michigan-Flint, BGS, 1974; Goddard Collge (Vermont), MFA, 1978
Career: Assistant to Director, Right to Read Program (HEW), 1974-75; Instructional Associate, English Department, University of Michigan-Flint, 1975-
Address: 4382 Carrie, Burton, Michigan 48509

Writings:

Signals to the Blind, poetry	Ithaca House Press	1972
The Winter Rooms, poetry	Ithaca House Press	1975
Asylum, poetry	Red Hill Press	1977

Work in Progress: Book on poetry of Galway Kinnell; Several books of poetry in various stages.

He says: "I have no consistent theories about poetry. Current concern is with the roles of narration, syntax and diction in my own work and that of others. Also, although somewhat 'late' in the game. I'm finally understanding the value of revision. My next book may be several years off, as a result."

RENICH, HELEN T. 1916-
Pseudonym: Jill Renich
Born: July 29, 1916; China
Parents: Reuben Archer and Janet Slade (Mallary) Torrey, Jr.
Married: Frederick Charles Renich, Minister and writer
Children: Janet, Rosalie, Frederick, and Jacqueline
Education: Pyengyang, Korea, 1933-36; Wheaton College, 1936-41
Career: Founder and President of Winning Women (radio program); Speaker for *Between Us Women;* Author; Lecturer around the world; Home "Person", mother, grandmother, wife of an author and an unusual man
Author: 5 Cruser Street, Montrose, PA 18801

Writings:
Between Us Woman Series (4) Zondervan   *1965*

So You're a Teenage Girl	*Zondervan*	*1966*
To Have and To Hold	*Zondervan*	*1972*
Did You Marry the Wrong Man?		
(booklet)	*Living Life*	*1974*

Work in Progress: a number

She says: "Would enjoy more lives so I could do more things!"

RENICH, JILL see: RENICH, HELEN T.

RENNE, ANTHONY 1913-
Born: November 26, 1913; Ypsilanti, Michigan
Parents: Alex and Addie (Attix) Renne
Married: Geraldine Renne
Children: Theodore, Sherri, Sandra, Michael, and Jeanine
Education: Wayne State University, LLB, 1940
Career: Legal officer and Judge Advocate, United State Marine Corps. 3½ yrs.; Assistant Prosecuting Attorney, Oakland County, 1957-61; General practice of law specializing in criminal defense trial work, 1961-present
Address: 5095 Parview, Clarkston, MI 48016

Writings:
| *The Pig-Tailtwister* | *Exposition Press* | *1977* |

Work in Progress: Engaged in writing sequel to first novel.

He says: "In *The Pit-Tailtwister,* I attempted to use the factual information from actual criminal cases which I handled over a long period of years, either as Assistant Prosecuting Attorney, or as defense counsel. The events related in the book, about various crimes, are authenic. The romantic episodes, and the humorous episodes in the book are fictitious.

"I wanted to create a story that would discourage the 'would-be criminal', by showing how the character in my book, Carl Dorski, lives in a constant state of fear and anxiety for his freedom. By the same token, I wanted to illustrate how the average professional criminal learns that he cannot trust his friends, and perhaps cannot even trust himself, or his own personal instincts.

"On the other side of the picture, I also attempted to make the book worthwhile for the average 'businessman' to read, as it might prove helpful to the 'honest businessman' to learn about the tactics used by professional criminals in burglaries, safe-cracking, counterfeiting, and other crimes involving trickery.

"With the above objects in mind, I attempted to accomplish these purposes in a story that would be fast moving, and interesting, and entertaining for the reader. I believe I have accomplished what I set out to do in *The Pig-Tailtwister.*

"In writing my first book, I also came to the conclusion that the public has been bombarded with stories, movies, television shows, for a long time, in which the central hero character is a policeman, policewoman, private detective, or international spy. I felt that the public must be getting bored with so many of the same type of stories, and I thought that it was time that someone write a book presenting the 'other side of the coin' from the standpoint of professional criminal, as the central character, not particularly as a hero, but more as a figure who thinks, talks, and acts like a real human being, subject to the usual weaknesses, fears and anxieties of ordinary people, in like cirumstances of our present generation.

"I do not regard my book as a 'literary gem', it is simply a story about a 'criminal' who tries to cope with the problems of 'easy money', and staying out of jail.

"Last of all, I might add that I feel somewhat proud to be a native of Michigan, and that I can, at least, make a very small contribution to the literary heritage of the State of Michigan."

RICHEY, DAVID JOHN 1939-
Pseudonym: John Davey; Richard Johnson
Born: July 22, 1939; Flint, Michigan
Parents: Lawrence and Helen (Millhouse) Richey
Married: Kay Lynn Richey
Children: Kimberley, Stacey, David Jr., Guy
Education: Flint Institute of Barbering, Barber diploma, 1961; Mott Community College, 1972
Career: Full-time freelance outdoor-travel writer/photographer
Address: 6767 Miller Road, Buckley, MI 49620

Writings:

Getting Hooked on Fishing with J. Knap	Pagurian Press	1974
A Child's Introduction to the Outdoors	Pagurian Press	1976
Steelheading for Everybody	Stackpole Books	1976
Trout Fisherman's Digest	DBI Books	1976
The Brown Trout Fisherman's Guide	Hawthorn Books	1978
How to Catch Trophy Freshwater Gamefish	Outdoor Life Book Club	1978
Dardevle Guide to Fishing	Dorrance Co.	1978
The Small Boat Handbook	T.Y. Crowell	1979
Shakespeare Guide to Fishing		

the Great Lakes   *Shakespeare Co.*
Sea Run with Paul Bernsen

Work in Progress: Editing *Outdoor Life's* "Guide to Fishing the Midwest", and other magazine assignments. No books at this time.

He says: "My work involves a great deal of travel which gives me great pleasure. It enables me to see things many people never have a chance to experience. I love writing and photography and this vocation offers me a chance to dispense my knowledge to readers. It is a very gratifying experience."

ROBERTS, HOMER 1912-
Born: 1912; Onaway, Michigan
Education: Presque Isle Normal, B.S., M.A.
Career: Teacher: rural school near Rogers City, Garden City, 6 yrs, Redford Union (biology and AV Director), retired; Naturalist and program director, boy's camp, 19 yrs., Director, Nature Counselors' Training Camp, 11 yrs., Past president of Detroit and Michigan Audubon Societies
Address: P.O. Box 65, Hale, Michigan 48739

Writings:

Enjoying Birds in Michigan	*Michigan Audubon Society*	*1952*
An Introduction to Ornithology		
Illustrator	*Michigan Audubon Society*	*1955*
Building for Birds		

ROBERTS, WILLO DAVIS 1928-
Born: May 29, 1928; Grand Rapids, Michigan
Parents: Clayton R. "Bill" and Lealah (Gleason) Davis
Married: David Roberts, Photojournalist
Children: Kathleen, David, Christopher, Larrilyn Linquist
Education: Pontiac Senior High School (Pontiac, Michigan), 1946
Career: Author
Address: Rt. 1, Box 98-A, Granite Falls, Washington 98252

Writings:

Murder at Grand Bay	*Arcadia House*	*1955*
The Girl Who Wasn't There	*Arcadia House*	*1957*
Murder Is So Easy	*Vega Books*	*1961*
The Suspected Four	*Vega Books*	*1962*
Nurse Kay's Conquest	*Ace Books*	*1966*
Once A Nurse	*Ace Books*	*1966*
Nurse At Mystery Villa	*Ace Books*	*1967*

Shroud of Fog	Ace Books	1972
Devil Boy	New American Library	1970
Return to Darkness	Lancer	1969
The Waiting Darkness	Lancer	1970
Shadow of a Past Love	Lancer	1970
The House at Fern Canyon	Lancer	1970
The Tarot Spell	Lancer	1970
Invitation to Evil	Lancer	1970
The Terror Trap	Lancer	1971
King's Pawn	Lancer	1971
The Gates of Montrain	Lancer	1971
The Watchers	Lancer	1971
The Ghosts of Harrell	Lancer	1971
Inherit the Darkness	Lancer	1972
Nurse in Danger	Ace Books	1972
Becca's Child	Lancer	1972
Sing a Dark Song	Lancer	1972
The Nurses	Ace Books	1972
The Face of Danger	Lancer	1972
Dangerous Legacy	Lancer	1972
Sinister Gardens	Lancer	1972
The M.D.	Lancer	1972
The Evil Children	Lancer	1973
The Gods in Green	Lancer	1973
Nurse Robin	Lennox Hill	1974
Didn't Anybody Know My Wife?	Putnam's	1974
White Jade	Doubleday	1975
White Jade	Popular Library	1976
Key Witness	Putnam's	1975
Expendable	Doubleday	1976
The View From the Cherry Tree	Atheneum	1976
The Jaubert Ring	Doubleday	1976
Act of Fear	Doubleday	1977
Don't Hurt Laurie!	Atheneum	1977
Cape of Black Sands	Popular Library	1977
House of Imposters	Popular Library	1977

Work in Progress: A series of 8 (with an option for 4 more) novels for *Popular Library*—gothic family sagas, to be followed by a historical romance for Popular Library

She says: "I began writing as a small child, love what I do, and have worked with a number of beginning writers to help them toward publication. I am on the executive board of the Pacific Northwest Writers Conference, the largest in the country, and will conduct a workshop in Tacoma in July, 1978. I led a two-day workshop on Popular Fiction at Stanford in July, 1977, and am active in various writers' organizations—Seattle Freelances, Mystery Writers of America, Science Fiction Writers of America, and lead a local workshop group in Snohomish County where I live. I do a fair amount of speaking in various schools (both in Washington and California) about writing and enjoy working with young people.

"Though I have been gone from Michigan for some time, I have many friends and relatives there, and many fond memories. And, of course, Michigan gets into my books once in a while; I can't think of a more perfect place for a child to grow up than in the woods and lake country in both upper and lower Michigan. I'll always love it."

Awards: *View From the Cherry Tree* is one of the nominees for the Mark Twain Award (in Missouri schools); the winner will be chosen by popular vote of the school children in January, 1978

ROCK, RICHARD see: MAINPRIZE, DONALD CHARLES

ROETHKE, THEODORE (1908-1963)
Pseudonym: Winterset Rothberg
Born: May 25, 1908; Saginaw, Michigan
Parents: Otto Theodore and Helen Marie (Huebner) Roethke
Married: Beatrice Heath O'Connell
Education: University of Michigan, A.B., 1929, M.A., 1936; Harvard University, 1930-31
Career: Educator and poet; English Department, Lafayette College, 1931-35; Pennsylvania State University, 1936-43; Bennington College, 1943-46; University of Washington, 1947-62 and Poet-in-residence, 1962

Writings:

Open House	Alfred A. Knopf	*1941*
The Lost Son and Other Poems	Doubleday & Co.	*1948*
Praise to the End!	Doubleday & Co.	*1951*
The Waking: Poems 1933-1953	Doubleday & Co.	*1954*
Words for the Wind	Doubleday & Co.	*1958*
I Am! Says the Lamb (juvenile)	Crowell-Collier	*1961*
Party at the Zoo (juvenile)	Doubleday & Co.	*1963*
The Far Field	Doubleday & Co.	*1965*
On the Poet and His Craft: Selected Prose of Theodore Roethke, Ed., R.J. Mills	U. of Washington Press	*1965*
The Collected Poems of Theodore Roethke	Doubleday & Co.	*1966*
Selected Letters of Theodore Roethke. Ed., R.J. Mills	U. of Washington Press	*1968*
Selected Poems of Theodore Roethke. Ed., Beatrice		

Roethke	Faber	1969
Straw for the Fire	Doubleday & Co.	1972
Dirty Dinky and Other Crea- tures: Poems for Children	Doubleday & Co.	1973

Awards: Guggenheim Fellowship, 1945, 1950; Tietiens Prize, 1947; Levinson Prize, 1951; Ford Foundation Fellowship, 1952; The National Institute of Arts & Letters, 1952; Honorary Membership: International Mark Twain Society; Pulitzer Prize for Poetry, 1953 *(The Waking);* Fulbright Grant, 1955; Borestone Mountain Awards, 1958; Edna St. Vincent Millay Award, 1959; Bollingen Award, 1959; Longview Award, 1959; Pacific Northwest Writers Award, 1959; National Book Award, 1959; Shelley Award Winner, 1962; Honorary Doctorate of Letters Degree, University of Michigan, 1962; Phi Beta Kappa

ROGERS, FRANCES (1888-1974)
Born: 1888; Grand Rapids, Michigan
Education: Public and Private schools in Grand Rapids; The Art Institute, Chicago, Wilmington, Delaware; Boston Museum of Fine Arts
Career: Illustrator and cover designer for books and leading magazines until 1933; Writer, adult and juvenile

Writings:

Picture Puzzle Posters, co-au- thor: Alice Beard	Ray Long and Richard Smith	1933
Heels, Wheels, and Wire	Stokes	1936
3rd edition		1966
Fresh and Briny, co-author: Alice Beard	Stokes	1936
5000 Years of Glass, co-author: Alice Beard	Stokes	1937
Big Miss Liberty	Stokes	1938
5000 Years of Gems and Jewelry	Stokes	1940
Indigo Treasure	Stokes	1941
Old Liberty Bell, co-author: Alice Beard	Stokes	1942
Paul Revere: Patroit on Horse- back, co-author: Alice Beard	Stokes	1943
Birthday of a Nation, co-author: Alice Beard	Lippincott	1945
Jeremy Pepper, co-author: Alice Beard	Lippincott	1946
Mr. Brady's Camera Boy	Lippincott	1951
Fire Engine Boy	Lippincott	1953
Lens Magic	Lippincott	1958

Painted Rock to Printed Page	*Lippincott*	*1960*
5000 Years of Stargazing	*Lippincott*	*1964*
The History of a Small Town		
Library	*Vanguard*	*1974*

ROMERO, DOROTHY LANKIN see: WITTON, DOROTHY

ROMIG, WALTER (1905-1977)
Born: December 29, 1905; New York, New York
Parents: Arthur J. and Phobie (Lawrence) Romig
Married: Madeleine (Collins); Librarian (retired)
Children: Mary, Thomas, Teresa Romig Heil
Education: Sacred Heart Seminary (Detroit, Michigan), A.B., 1927; Mt. St. Mary Seminary (Norwood, Ohio); Post graduate
Career: Writer and Religious Editor

Writings:

The Man in the Mirror (poetry)	*J.V. Sheehan Co.*	*1928*
Who's Who in Detroit	*Walter Romig & Co.*	*1935-36*
The American Catholic Who's		
Who	*Walter Romig & Co.*	*1937-71*
The Catholic Bookman		*1937-40*
The Guide to Catholic Litera-		
ture, 6 Volumes	*Walter Romig & Co.*	*1940-60*
The Book of Catholic Authors,		
5 Volumes	*Walter Romig & Co.*	*1942-*
Negro Catholic Writers	*Walter Romig & Co.*	*1945*
Josephine Van Dyke Brownson	*Gabriel Richard Press*	*1955*
Michigan Place Names	*Walter Romig & Co.*	*1965*

Awards: Catholic Library Association conferred Honorary Membership, 1957; for the following publications: *The Book of Catholic Authors, The Guide to Catholic Literature,* and *The American Cathlic Who's Who;* Honorary Degree: St. Bonaventure University (Olean, New York); L.H.D., 1960; Award of Merit by the Historical society of Michigan, 1973; First Annual *Walter Romig* Award conferred posthumously on Mr. Walter Romig by the Sacred Heart Seminary College (Detroit), December 11, 1977

RORKE, MARGARET (CURRY) 1915-
Born: November 1, 1915; Ann Arbor, Michigan
Parents: Robert J. and Anna (Ludolph) Curry
Married: William Craig Rorke, Executive Secretary-Credit Bureau of Saginaw

Children: Robert Craig and Margaret Ann
Education: University of Michigan, B.A., 1938, J.D., 1942
Career: Attorney
Address: 1882 Lathrup Rd., Saginaw, MI 48603

Writings:

My Ego Trip	Exposition Press, Inc.	1976
The Detroit Free Press	Judd Arnett column	Bi-weekly

Contributor of verse for the Saginaw News editorial page—22 years

She says: "May you enjoy the 'trip'! while reading this poetry which reaffirms the goodness of traditional values as she brings to mind the hopes and cares of every family."

ROSE, ELINOR K. (Living)

Born: Edon, Ohio
Parents: D.T. and Bertha Laura (Twichell) Kiess
Married: Dana Rose, (deceased) Asst. Vice-Pres., Michigan Bell Telephone Co.
Children: Stuart Rex, Douglas Dana, and Bruce Geoffrey
Education: Hillsdale College, A.B., B.S.; Ohio State University
Career: Freelance writer and professional speaker
Address: 25560 Dundee Road, Royal Oak, MI 48070

Writings:

Relax, Chum	Five Oaks Press	
Sugar and Spice	Five Oaks Press	
Rhyme & Reason	Simon & Schuster	1967
Echoes From The Moon, Antho-logy; co-editor	Hot Apples Press	

Daily syndicated light verse for newspapers, 25 years; Published in *Reader's Digest, Good Housekeeping, Christian Herald, Saturday Evening Post, McCall's, Quote, The Writer, Writer's Digest, Wall Street Journal, Good Reading.*

Work in Progress: Syndicated copy must be prepared approximately six weeks in advance.

She says: "The light-verse quatrain is more difficult to write than most people realize because so much has to be said in so little space and because the rules for rhyme and meter are so precise. The last line is the most important, either because it has a twist or because the idea is buttoned up in some manner.

"I believe humor can help us all live with frustration more comfortably—and letters from readers agree. Also a sturdy belief in religion (I am a Methodist), my country, and people contribute to a blithe outlook on life.

"While my family has been the central point, I've throughly enjoyed professional contacts with other writers and find it exhilarating to do humor programs for audiences.

"I'm a member of the Detroit Press Club, Detroit Women Writers, and the Board of Trustees of Hillsdale College."

Awards: Alumni Achievement Award, Hillsdale College, 1955; Writer of the Year Award, Detroit Women Writers, 1959; National Achievement Award Kappa Kappa Gamma, 1968; Michigan Council for the Arts program in schools, 1977

ROTHEBERT, WINTERSET see: ROETHKE, THEODORE

ROUTSONG, ALMA 1924-
Pseudonym: Isabel Miller
Born: November 26, 1924; Traverse City, Michigan
Parents: Carl John and Esther (Miller) Routsong
Married: Bruce Brodie (divorced)
Children: Natalie, Joyce, Charlotte, Louise
Education: Western Michigan University, 1942-44; Michigan State University, B.A., 1949
Career; U.S. Navy, Hospital Apprentice, 1945-46; Columbia University, editor, 1968-71; Writer
Address: 155 Bank Street, New York, New York 10017
Writings:

A Gradual Joy	Houghton	1953
Round Shape	Houghton	1959
A Place for Us	Bleeker Street Press	1969
republished as: Patience and		
Sarah	McGraw-Hill	1972

Of Interest: Active in the gay liberation movement since 1970.

RUGGLES, GLENN I. 1930-
Born: October 20, 1930; Grand Blanc, Michigan
Parents: Beryl and Christina (Munro) Ruggles
Married: Margaret
Children: Scott, Julie, Tim, Suzy, Angela, Marissa
Education: University of Detroit, B.S., 1959, M.S., 1965
Career: Teacher, Walled Lake Central High School, 1959-
Address: 2531 Watonga, Union Lake, Michigan 48085

Writings:

Something From Nothing	Privately published	1976
Film: The River's the Same	Co-produced with Robert	

Work in Progress: Book dealing with Michigan Lumber Camps to be published by Hillsdale Press; A current film and book project in Oakland County is beginning to develop; Possible future projects in book form which have been researched although no cohesive text has been developed as yet: 1. Lake Macatawa War; 2. Soper fraud and; 3. Early Grist Mills of Michigan

He says: "My work focuses on folk history, emphasizing the 'average' settler who seems to get lost in the big history books. Grand Traverse region has been my chief focus, but a project in Oakland County is beginning to develop." His interests have resulted in the following involvements:

Past President, Commerce Township Area Historical Society

Former Board Member, Commerce Township Historical Commission

Past Board Member, Oakland County Pioneer and Historical Society

He personally researched the first historical marker in Antrim County which was the Elk Rapids Blast Furnace (1873) and erected the marker in 1973. He then wrote a fifteen page booklet on the history of the furnace.

Awards: Grant from the Michigan Council for the Arts for the production of the film, *The River's the Same,* 1975; Award for *The River's the Same;* 1976 Award of Merit (Historical Society of Michigan)

RUSSELL, ANNE DORA 1931-

Born: January 7, 1931; Daleville, Alabama

Parents: Rev. C.G. and Bertha (Ingram) Roberson

Children: John, television news reporter, Shirley, teacher of emotionally impaired

Education: Alabama State College, B.A., 1958; Northwestern University, Summers, 1961 & 62; Wayne State University, Summer, 1967; University of Michigan, M.S. Ed., 1969; Pre-Doctoral Candidate presently

Career: Business/English teacher, Coppinville, Alabama High School, 1958-62; Subsitute teacher, Pontiac, 1962-63; Secretary, University of Michigan Medical School, 1963-64; Director of Health-Welfare & Housing, Pontiac Urban League, 1964-65; Business/English teacher, Pontiac, 1965-71; Assistant Principal, Pontiac Central High School, 1971-present

Address: 1158 Dudley Street, Pontiac, Michigan 48057

Writings:
Blacks in Pontiac, Volume 1   Privately published   1975

Blacks in Pontiac, Revised   Privately published   1977
Articles in the *Alabama State Teachers Association Journal* and
The Crisis

Work in Progress: *Builders of Detroit,* currently writing book and
looking for publisher. Anticipate publication in 1978

She says: "My writing has been a labor of love, and it has sparked
the interest of indivduals as well as institutions.

"Creative ability should be used as a means of inspiration to others,
as well as to the personal responsible for its being. *Blacks in Pontiac* has not only caught the interest of individuals, but colleges,
universities, and public libraries throughout the State of Michigan.

"If you have an idea, push it forward and go through with it. The
results are sometimes surprising."

SAGENDORPH, KENT (1902-1958)
Born: April 23, 1902; Jackson, Michigan
Parents: William Kent and Ethel May (Abbott) Sagendorph
Married: Ruth D. (Howard)
Children: Mary Lou and Wallace K.
Education: University of Michigan, Air Corps Flying School, 1922-
Career: Writer, 1926-; Lecturer & Author for U.S. Air Force; Tech-
nical Material for aviation trade magazines, more than 300 arti-
cles, 20 years; President, Veteran's Flying Association (during
WW II, Lt. Colonel); Editor, *Inside Michigan*

Writings:
Adult-

Thunder Aloft: U.S. Air Power Today	*Reilly & Lee*	*1942*
Stevens Thomson Mason: Misunderstood Patroit	*Dutton*	*1947*
Michigan: The Story of the University	*Dutton*	*1948*
Charles Edward Wilson American Industrialist	*General Electric*	*1949*

Juvenile-HIS Dan Perry Adventure Stories

Radium Island	*Cupples & Leon*	*1938*
Beyond the Amazon	*Cupples & Leon*	*1938*
Sin—Kiang Castle	*Cupplies & Leon*	*1938*

SANDBURG, HELGA 1918-
Born: November 24, 1918; Maywood, Illinois

Parents: Carl and Lilian (Steichen) Sandburg
Married: George Crile, Jr., Physician
Children: John Carl Steichen and Karlen Paula Polega
Education: Michigan State College, 1939-40; University of Chicago, 1940
Career: Secretary to father, Carl Sandburg, during adolescent and adult years, often while employed elsewhere; Dairy Goat Breeder, 1944-51; Secretary in Manuscripts Division and for The Keeper of the Collections, Library of Congress, Washington, D.C., 1952-56; Administrative Assistant for The Papers of Woodrow Wilson, Woodrow Wilson Foundation, 1958-59; Author, poet and lecturer
Address: 2060 Kent Road, Cleveland Heights, Ohio 44106

Writings:

The Wheel of Earth	*McDowell, Obolensky*	*1958*
Measure By Love	*McDowell, Obolensky*	*1959*
The Owl's Roost	*Dial Press*	*1962*
Sweet Music	*Dial Press*	*1963*
Blueberry	*Dial Press*	*1963*
Joel and The Wild Goose	*Dial Press*	*1963*
Gingerbread	*Dial Press*	*1964*
Bo and the Old Donkey	*Dial Press*	*1965*
The Unicorns	*Dial Press*	*1965*
Above and Below, co-author: Geo. Crile Jr.	*McGraw-Hill American Wilderness Series*	*1969*
To a New Husband	*World Publishing Co.*	*1970*
Anna and the Baby Buzzard	*Dutton*	*1970*
Children and Lovers	*Harcourt Brace Jovanovich*	*1976*
A Great and Glorious Romance	*Harcourt Brace Jovanovich*	*1978*

Work in Progress: a sequel to *A Great and Glorious Romance: The Story of Carl Sandburg and Lilian Steichen*

Awards: *Virginia Quarterly Review* Prize for Best Short Story, 1959; Borestone Mountain Poetry Award, 1962; Grant from Finnish American Society and from *Svenska Institute* for travel in Finland and Sweden, 1961; American Specialist, State Department's Bureau of Cultural and Educational Affairs; lecturer and conducted seminars in Great Britain and Europe, 1961; *Chicago Tribune* Poetry Award, 1970; Seventh Annual Kansas Poetry Contest, 2nd prize; Triton College Second Annual "All Nations Poetry Contest", 1975; Triton College Third Annual "All National Poetry Contest", 1976

SARETT, LEW (1888-1954)
Born: May 16, 1888; Chicago, Illinois. Raised in Marquette and Benton Harbor, Michigan

Parents: Rudolph and Jeanette (Block) Sarett
Married: Margaret (Husted), died 1941; Juliet (Barker) second
wife, died 1945; Alma (Johnson) third wife, Professor and author
Children: (with first wife) Lewis Hastings Sarett and Helen Sarett
Stockdale
Education: University of Michigan 1907-08; Beloit College, A.B.
1911; Harvard University, 1911-12; University of Illinois, LL.B
1916
Career: Forest ranger, woodsman, and wilderness guide, Professor, University of Illinois, 1914-20; Professor, Northwestern
University 1920-1953; Poet, writer, and lecturer, Visiting Professor, University of Florida 1951-54

Writings:

Many, Many Moons	*Holt*	*1920*
The Box of Gold	*Holt*	*1922*
Slow Smoke	*Holt*	*1925*
Wings Against the Moon	*Holt*	*1931*
Collected Poems	*Holt*	*1941*
Covenant with Earth, Edited by		
Alma Sarett	*Univ. of Florida Press*	*1956*
Textbooks with W.T. Foster:		
Basic Principles of Speech	*Houghton Mifflin*	*1936*
2nd edition	*Houghton Mifflin*	*1946*
3rd edition, revised by Alma		
Sarett	*Houghton Mifflin*	*1958*
4th edition	*Houghton Mifflin*	*1966*
Modern Speeches on Basic		
Issues	*Houghton Mifflin*	*1939*
Speech: a High School Course		
with James H. McBurney, re-		
vised in 1947, 1951, 1956	*Houghton Mifflin*	*1943*

He says: "A few of us set out to devote our lives to re-creating for
others the beauty of wild America; to writing much and to speaking
much of American backwoods and frontiers, of wolves and deer
and bear, of loggers and voyageurs and Indians.

"I have written about these simple folk of earth because I have
lived with them, I know, I find pleasure in their compainship, and
my spirit belongs to them.

"If these poems, therefore, convey to others a slight measure of
the wild beauty of America, of her mountain ways and forest life,
and if in some degree it gives others pleasure, I shall be glad. If it
does not thus succeed—it was Walter Savage Landor who said,
'There is delight in singing, though none hear beside the singer.' "

Said about him: ". . .even though Lew was born in Chicago and
lived most of his life in Illinois, he thought of Michigan as his home
state."

Alma Johnson Sarett, November 6, 1977

Awards: Helen Haire Levinson Prize, 1921; Poetry Society of America Award, 1925; Honorary Litt. D.; Baylor University, 1926; Chicago Foundation for Literature Award, 1934; Honorary L.H.D., Beloit, 1945; Lew Sarett Collection, Library Archieves, Northwestern University, 1956; Lew Sarett Wildlife Sanctuary and Nature Center, Benton Harbor, Michigan, 1965

SAVAGE, JOAN see: WEISMAN, JOAN

SCAGNETTI, JACK 1924-
Born: December 24, 1924
Parents: Quinto and Albina (Tardella) Scagnetti
Children: Kimberly and Craig
Education: Southwestern High School 1943, Detroit
Career: Sports editor, Detroit high school newspaper (Southwestern) Sports; writer and police reporter, suburban Detroit weekly, 5 years.; Editor suburban Detroit weekly, 2 years; Copy Director, automotive advertising agency, 1 year; Public Relations Director, private Detroit athletic club, 8 years; Director, So. California chain of 17 bowling centers, 7 years; Editor, *Popular Hot Rodding* magazine, 2 years; Editorial Director, Argus Publishers, 2 years; Free-lance writer/photographer since 1968; Author of more than 800 magazine articles; Literary Agent, 1974-present
Address: 5643 Farmdale Avenue, North Hollywood, California 91601

Writings:

Famous Custom & Show Cars (2nd printing)	E.P. Dutton	1973
Golf for Beginners	Grosset & Dunlap	1973
Five Simple Steps to Perfect Golf	Nash Publishers	1974
Cars of the Stars	Jonathan David	1974
The Intimate Life of Rudolph Valentino	Jonathan David	1975
Movie Stars in Bathtubs	Jonathan David	1975
The Life and Loves of Gable	Jonathan David	1976
Laurel & Hardy Scrapbook	Jonathan David	1976
Bicycle Motocross	E.P. Dutton	1976
Soccer	Harvey House	1977
Racquetball, The Game and How to Play It	Lion Books	1977

He says: "I combine a career that involves full-time multiple writing—author, magazine feature writer/photographer (mostly on sports, automotive, and movie subjects) and publicity and promotion work plus a limited, selected work for referral writers who use me as their literary agent.

"I was a resident of Detroit from 1927 to 1958."

SCANLON, MARION STEPHANY (d. 1977)
Born: Lanesboro, Minnesota
Parents: Cornelius and Margaret (Rafferty) Scanlon
Education: Ripon College, B. Ph.; University of Minnesota; graduate study in Medical School; University of Wisconsin, M.S. postgraduate study; University of Michigan, postgradue study
Career: Professor of health education, Marygrove College

Writings:

Wiggley Nell	Edwards	1949
Calm and Cool was Penguin Row, a Ferry-Boat I'd Like to Ride	Edwards	1953
Seven Frisky Lambs	Edwards	1954
Trails of the French Explorers	Naylor	1956
Pudgie Pat's Pets	Edwards	1958
Freddie the Froggie	Edwards	1959
Three Little Clouds	Denison	1959
Mister Roberto R. Robot	Edwards	1960
Little Johnnie Trout	Denison	1962
Hygiene for College Freshman	Edwards	1963
Sports and Ballroom Dancing for College Freshman	Edwards	1963
White Beaver		1974

Honors: Avery Hopwood award for drama, The University of Michigan, 1942; National League of American pen women, third place for juveniles, 1964

SCHMOCK, HELEN H. 1909-
Pseudonym: Helen H. Cloutier, Steve Bell
Born: March 17, 1909; Manistique, Michigan
Parents: Henry H. and Carrie Olive (Little) Hargreaves
Married: John W. Schmock
Children: John H. & Charles H. Cloutier, John, Richard, Robert Schmock
Education: University of Los Angeles, B.A.; University of Minnesota; Northern Michigan University; Michigan State University;

University of Illinois; Western Michigan University; Central Michigan University, B.S., M.A.

Career: Librarian, Chinchilla Rancher, Union Musician, Beautician, Radio WESK Womens Director, Dancing School owner/operator, Housewife

Address: 301 E. Court Apt. 712, Ludington, Michigan 49431

Writings:

Sim Barton	Pageant	1952
Isle Royale Calling	Dodd, Mead	1957
Reprinted	Eerdmans	1966
Honey Babe		
Murder—Absolutely Murder	Chicago Paperback House	
Venus of Lesbos		
Adventures of Mournful Mouse (9 books)		
The Many Names of Lee Lu	Albert Whitman	1960

Work in Progress: *I Smiled before Christmas,* with an agent

She says: "We are again in the thro's of moving—My IBM is still packed—. My husband and I are 'ham radio operators' W8GJX and W8VHQ and met over the air. We talked for three years before we ever met personally.

"We have been hotel living in Manistee for fifteen months and have just moved into a retirement complex, 'Longfellow Towers.'

"Expect some new work evolving from retirement this coming year."

Honors: First women member of the Quarter Century Wireless Association, 1954. In 1979 she will be eligible for certification as the first women amateur radio operator in the world to have fifty years of continuous licensed operation in the amateur bands.

SCHOOLCRAFT, HENRY ROWE (1793-1864)

Born: March 28, 1793; Albany County, New York

Parents: Lawrence, Manager of Glass Factory, and Margaret Anne Barbara (Rowe)

Married: Jane (Johnston); one-half Chippewa Indian; educated in Europe, died 1842; Mary E. (Howard) second wife

Children: William Henry (died at age 3), Jane Susan Anne (Howard), and John Johnston; Adopted daughter: Alice Schoolcraft Wright

Education: Union College, (at age 15); Middleberry College, 1813

Career: Explorer: southern Missouri and Arkansas, 1817; Cass expedition, 1820; western Lake Superior, 1831; source of Mississippi, 1832; Indian Agent, Lake Superior tribes, 1822; Served in the Michigan Territorial Legislature, 1828-32; Superintendent of

Indian Affairs for Michigan, 1836-41

Writings:

A View of the Lead Mines of Missouri	Wiley & Co.	*1819*
Travels in the Central Portion of the Mississippi Valley	Collins & Hannay	*1825*
Narrative of an Expedition Through the Upper Mississippi to Itasca Lake, the Actual Source of this River	Harper & Bros.	*1834*
Reprinted as: Expedition to Lake Itasca editied by Philip P. Mason	Mich. State Univ. Press	*1958*
Indian Legends from Algic Researches (the myth of Hiawatha, Oneota, the Red Race in America) and Historical and Statistical Information Respecting the Indian Tribes of the United States	Harper & Bros.	*1839*
Reprint	Mich. State Univ. Press	*1956*
Alhalla, or the Lord of Tallagega, a Tale of the Creek War with some selected Miscellanies chiefly of early date	Wiley & Putnam	*1843*
Plan for the Investigation of American Ethology	E.O. Jenkins	*1846*
Notes on the Iroquois	E.H. Pease & Co.	*1847*
Oneota: The Indian in his Wigwam	Graham	*1848*
Personal Memoirs of a Residence of Thirty Years with the Indian Tribes on the American Front	Lippincott, Grambo & Co.	*1851*
Historical and Statistical Information Respecting the History, Condition and Prospects of the Indian Tribes of the United States, 6 Volumes	Grambo & Co.	*1855-57*
Summary Narrative of an Exploratory Expedition to the Source of the Mississippi River in 1920: Resumed and Completed by the Discovery of its origin in Itasca Lake in 1832	Lippincott, Grambo & Co.	*1855*

Literary Voyager (magazine) information on Indian ceremonies, supersititions, songs and legends

He says: ". . .life is, at best, but short, and he only lives well who does something to benefit others."

From a letter to George Johnston, Grand Traverse Bay, August 31, 1844. Said about him, "In the 1820's and '30's, Schoolcraft frequently served as Superintendent of Indian Affairs, and by 1850 he had become a recognized authority on Indian lore. Drawing upon this extensive knowledge, he was able to fill out his stories with details that made them more readily understandable to readers of English.

Today when students of Indian culture record legends, they attempt to make an exact translation. Schoolcraft did not merely translate, he interpreted. The result is a story form that is loosely knit, often poetic, highly romantic—and thoroughly American."

John Bierhorst, *The Fire Plume,* Dial Press, 1969

Also said about him, ". . .curiously unheroic, conventionally pious, a little prim, self-consciously the literary man who could never rid himself of the sentimental and pedantic language of the second-rate New York poets of the period, a little pompous with certainly a touch of the schoolmaster. . .a romantic, courageous. . .a good observer of other people."

H.R. Hays, *Explorers of Man,* Crowell-Collier, 1971

And finally, "Henry Rowe Schoolcraft is not only one of the most versatile and brillant but one of the most human characters in the history of America."

Chase S. and Stellanova Osborn, *Schoolcraft—Longfellow—Hiawatha.* Jacques Cattell Press, 1942

Noteworthy: Considered among the first to do anthropogical observations. Leader in the education and cultural life of the territory. Helped to found: State Historical Society of Michigan, 1828; Michigan Territorial Library, 1828; Algic Research Society, 1832; Inspiration for Longfellow's *The Song of Hiawatha;* ". . .for without your books, I could not have written mine"; Regent of the University of Michigan, 1837-1841.

SCHRADER, PAUL 1946-
Born: July 22, 1946; Grand Rapids, Michigan
Parents: Charles and Joan (Fisher) Schrader
Education: Calvin College, B.A., 1968, U.C.L.A., M.A., 1970
Career: Screenwriter of Taxi-Driver, Yakuza, Obsession, and Rolling Thunder; Writer and Director of Blue Collar, and Hardcore
Address: Burbank Studios, Burbank California

Transcendental Style in Film   *Univ. of California Press*   *1971*

SCHULTZ, GERARD (1902-1974)
Born: February 11, 1902; near Herman, Missouri
Parents: Rev. George C. and Helene (Meier) Schultz
Married: Jennie L. Schultz, Teacher (retired)
Children: John L., Gerard, Jr., Dan F.
Education: Elmhurst Academy, 1921; Knox College, A.B., 1925;
(Magna cum Laude); University of Minnesota, M.A., 1928
Career: Teaching fellow, History Department, University of Minnesota, 1925-28; Teacher and Writer, 30 years

Writings:

A History of Miller County, Missouri	*1933*
The Early History of the Northern Ozarks	*1937*
History of Warren County, Iowa	*1953*
History of Marshall County, Iowa	*1955*
A History of Michigan's Thumb	*1964*
Revised as : The New History of Michigan's Thumb	*1969*
Walls of Flame	*1972*
Treasure Map of the Great Lakes Region	

Since the death of her husband, Jennie L. Schultz, has carried on the final distribution of his books which are now out of print. She is undertaking the enormous task of sorting his papers, many of which are valuable. He was a meticulous and accurate researcher and most agree that he left a rich and valuable legacy.

SCOTT, HERBERT 1931-
Born: February 8, 1931; Norman, Oklahoma
Parents: Herbert Hicks and Betty (Pickard) Scott
Married: Shirley Clay Scott, Teacher
Children: Herbert A., Megan E., Rannah S., Erin L., Kyla M.C.
Education: Fresno State College, B.A., 1964; University of Iowa, MFA, 1966; Lake Forest College, Univ. of Oklahoma, College of Sequoias, and Fresno City College
Career: Worked in grocery business, 1953-64; Instructor in English, Southeast Missouri State College, 1966-68; Associate Professor of English, Western Michigan University, 1968-present
Address: P.O. Box 2615, Kalamazoo, MI 49003

Writings:

Disguises	*Univ. of Pittsburgh Press*	*1974*
The Shoplifters' Handbook	*Blue Mountain Press*	*1974*
Groceries	*Univ. of Pittsburgh Press*	*1976*

The Third Coast: Contemporary
   Michigan Poetry, Co-editor   *Wayne State Univ. Press*   *1976*
"Our Appetites in Our Eyes"
   30 minute color video tape   *Western Michigan Univ.*   *1977*

Work in Progress: a book of poems and a novel

Honors: Creative Writing Fellowship, University of Iowa, 1964-66; National Endowment for the Humanities Fellow at Boston University, 1976; Poet in Residence on the American Wind Symphony's Bicentennial Tour, August, 1976

SCOTT, VIRGIL J. 1914-

Born: August 1, 1914; Vancouver, Washington
Parents: Charles E. and Elda T. (Swift) Scott
Married: Justine Bittikofer Scott, Professor (ret)
Children: Mrs. Nancy Hoffman, Mrs. Catherine Williams, Mrs. Gary Miller, David A. Scott
Education: Ohio State University, A.B., M.A., Ph. D. 1935-45
Career: English teacher, Franklin High School, Franklin, Ohio, 1937-41; Instructor: Ohio State University, 1941-45; University of Minnesota, 1945-47; Professor, Michigan State University, 1947-77; retired
Address: 62 W. Sherwood, Williamston, MI 48895

Writings:

The Dead Tree Gives No Shelter	Morrow	*1947*
The Hickory Stick	Morrow	*1948*
The Savage Affair	Harcourt Brace	*1958*
I, John Mordaunt	Harcourt Brace	*1964*
The Kreutaman Formula	Simon & Schuster	*1974*
Walk-In	Simon & Schuster	*1976*
Studies in the Short Story		
(Textbook)	Holt	*1949, 60, 68, 70, 76*

Work in Progress: *Fair Game* (a novel)

Awards: Ohioanna Award, 1948 for *The Hickory Stick;* Nominated for Edgar Award by Mystery Writers of America for *The Kreutman Formula*

SEAGER, ALLAN (1906-1968)

Born: February 5, 1906; Adrian, Michigan
Parents: Arch and Emma (Allan) Seager
Married: Barbara (Watson); died 1966; Joan (Rambo)
Children: (with first wife) Mary, Laura
Education: University of Michigan, A.B., 1930; Oriel College, Osford (Rhodes Scholar), B.A., 1933, M.A., 1947

Career: Assistant Editor, *Vanity Fair;* Teacher of English Bennington College, 1944; Professor English, University of Michigan, 1945-68; Novelist, short stories, translator, biographer

Writings:

Equinox	*Simon & Schuster*	*1943*
The Inheritance	*Simon & Schuster*	*1948*
The Old Man of the Mountain	*Simon & Schuster*	*1950*
Amos Berry	*Simon & Schuster*	*1953*
Hilda Manning	*Simon & Schuster*	*1956*
Death of Anger	*McDowell-Obolensky*	*1960*
A Frieze of Girls	*McGraw-Hill*	*1964*
The Glass House	*McGraw-Hill*	*1967*

"Mr. Seager set his novels in the pleasant rural midwest, but dramatized dark psychological tensions and themes of social protest. Critics praised his wit and craftsmanship."
                        The New York Times, November 10, 1977 (Obituary)

"Once", he wrote of himself, "I would have hesitated to say that the novel is the conscience of the middle class, but when I remember of my own *Equinox, The Inheritance* and *Amos Berry,* I discover that I believe it."

Awards: Guggenheim Fellowship, 1966; National Foundation on the Arts and the Humanities, 1966

SECRIST, MARGARET C. 1905-
Born: October 29, 1905; Andover, Ohio
Parents: Lyle S. and Eva (Howe) Peck
Married: John H. Secrist (deceased), Professor, Wayne State University
Education: Oberlin College, A.B., 1927; Wayne State University, M.A., 1964
Career: High school teacher, Detroit, Michigan; Poet, Staff of Detroit Women Writer's Conference; Speaker, Detroit Adventure, 1965
Address: Box 185, Andover, OH 44003

Writings:

Trumpet Time	*Alan Swallow*	*1958*
Before Flight	*Branden Press*	*1965*
All These	*Branden Press*	*1972*
Ville D'Etroit	*Penman Pub.*	*1967*
Anthologies:		
That Eager Zest		*1961*
Echoes From the Moon		*1976*
Chap Book: Women of the Re-volution	*Spoon River Quarterly*	*1977*

Work in Progress: Poems and novelette

She says: "As I grow older, my poetry grows less lyric. The light touch disappears. Satire appears instead. Nevertheless, life with all its wonders continues to fascinate me. My work has gone from the pastoral to portraiture as is seen in my Chap Book published last December. A poet can still 'go around the world by the old Marlborough Road.' (Thoreau)"

Awards: Detroit Women Writer's Award, 1959, 1968

SEESE, ETHEL GRAY 1903-
Born; September 13, 1903; near Brandenburg, Kentucky
Parents: David Clarence and Mary Emily (Bruner) Gray
Divorced
Children: Charles Scott Roberts, Jr., David Howard Roberts, Perry Gray Seese, and Carol Nadine
Education: Meade County High School, 1922; Lab & X-ray Training, Kentucky, 1937; Wayne State University
Career: X-Ray Technician, City of Detroit, 25 yrs.
Address: P.O. Box 90, Lake Ann, MI 49650

Writings:
Psychic Hinge   *Golden Quill*   1974

Anthlogies: Ten Detroit Poets, Five Black and Five White; Echoes of the Moon

Work in Progress: Two poetry books for children, ages 2 to 7 and 8 to teen; Also book of Haiku and near-Haiku

She says: "My faith in Christ has been the sustaining factor of my life. I work with the Traverse State Hospital as foster grandparent for the neglected boys, and work with the R.S.V.P. I am listed in *Who's Who in Poetry* and *The Worlds Who's Who of Women*, also in the upcoming *International Biography*."

Awards: Third World Congress of Poetry for Peace, June 1976

SHARPE, ERNEST JACK see: SHARPSTEEN, ERNEST JACK

SHARPSTEEN, ERNEST JACK (1880-1976)
Pseudonym: Ernest Jack Sharpe
Born: July 8, 1880; Wyoming, Michigan
Parents: Washington Irving and Amelia Adelaid (Anderson) Sharpsteen
Married: Serece Doreene (Kinnedbrew)

Education: Grand Rapids Public Schools
Career: Circus Performer, Clown; Vaudeville actor, Director, Playwright; Free-lance writer; Founder, Jugville and Newt Publications

Plays:

Red Thread of Guilt	T.S. Dennison & Co.	1927
Lifting Jimmy's Jinx	T.S. Dennison & Co.	1927
A Rural Belle	T.S. Dennison & Co.	1927
His Wife's First Husband	T.S. Dennison & Co.	1928
The Wage		1913
The Tempter		1913
The Prospector		1913
Fugitives	Central Play Co.	
A Soul's Awaking		
The Infidel	Central Play Co.	
The Call of the Mountains	Central Play Co.	
Joggin' Along with Jed		
Girl Who Paid	Central Play Co.	
Hate		
The Rat	Central Play Co.	1924

Poetry:

Adventures of Windy	Patterson Printing	1944
Bugle, the Smart Dog	Patterson Printing	1944
One Life-Autobiography and Verse	Dean Hicks co.	1950
Narratives of Nature	Adams Press	1960
Memories of Yesteryear	Adams Press	1960
Tall Tales of Newaygo Newt	Pryamid Publishers	1962
(Folk character originated by E. Jack Sharpe)		
Verse to Live By	Pyramid Publications	1965
Jack Squires, A Scout with Kit Carson	Newt Publications	1965
Century Wit and Humor	Patterson Printing Co.	1966
Remembering: New Narrative Poems About the Good Ole Days	Adams Press	1966
The Wonders of Nature	Adams Press	1972
Michigan: Its Emblem and Environments	Adams Press	1973

E. Jack Sharpe willed his estate to the White Cloud Public Library which has since been renamed the E. Jack Sharpe Public Library.

Awards: Oustanding Friend to Libraries, Michigan Library Association, 1972

SHIEFMAN, VICKY 1942-
Born: June 29, 1942; Detroit, Michigan
Parents: Saul and Emma (Goldman) Shiefman
Education: University of Chicago, B.A., 1964; New York University, M.A., 1974
Career: Teacher of early childhood
Address: 260 W. 21st Street, New York, New York 10011

Writings:

Mindy	*Macmillan*	*1974*

Work in Progress: several

She says: "I still think of myself as a Michigander. In fact, I have a hard time voting in New York because it still doesn't seem real that I live here. Also, I've spent a good deal of time on the West Coast, as well as the East Coast, and each convinces me that I am truly a Midwesterner. It has something to do with rhythm, the pace by which one lives one's life, measures one's words—space, how you think homes should be, like apartments always seemed too cramped and there's no storage—emphasis, like the West Coast aims for style, newness, relaxation while the East energizes work and the Midwest combines work and play with an emphasis on family. I also valued the community feeling which I loved and also chafed under in the Detroit Jewish community; other places are more spread out and anonymous. I know people all over the world feel and long for the same things. Still there is a definite sense of place and while others jokingly label Midwesterners boring, I like that quality which I see as full of steady, unchanging, family values and that slower place. I'm glad I grew up in Detroit."

SHOWERS, PAUL C. 1910-
Born: April 12, 1910; Sunnyside, Washington
Parents: Frank L. and M. Ethelyne (Walker) Showers
Children: Paul and Kate
Education: University of Michigan, A.B., 1931
Career: Newspaper copy editor, The Detroit Free Press, 1937-40; The New York Herald Tribune, 1940-42; Yank (Army) Magazine, 1943-45; New York Sunday Mirror Magazine, 1946; New York Times Sunday Department, 1946-76; New York Times Sunday Magazine, 1963-76; Free-lance writer, 1961-
Address: 261 Hicks Street, Brooklyn, New York 11201

Writings:

Find Out by Touching	*Crowell*	*1961*
In the Night	*Crowell*	*1961*
Listening Walk	*Crowell*	*1961*
Look at Your Eyes	*Crowell*	*1962*

How Many Teeth	Crowell	*1962*
Follow Your Nose	Crowell	*1963*
Columbus Day	Crowell	*1965*
Your Skin and Mine	Crowell	*1965*
Drop of Blood	Crowell	*1967*
How You Talk	Crowell	*1967*
Before You Were Born	Crowell	*1968*
A Baby Starts to Grow	Crowell	*1969*
Indian Festivals	Crowell	*1969*
What Happens to a Hamburger?	Crowell	*1970*
Fortune Telling for Fun	Newcastle	*1971*
Use Your Brain	Crowell	*1971*
Sleep Is For Everyone	Crowell	*1974*
Where Does the Garbage Go?	Crowell	*1974*
The Bird and the Stars	Doubleday	*1975*
The Moon Walker	Doubleday	*1975*
A Book of Scary Things	Doubleday	*1977*
Me and My Family Tree	Crowell	*In production*

Work in Progress: A book about small-town life in Michigan the time of World War I (not a children's book). Two more books for the Crowell Let's Read and Find Out Series

He says: "From 1937 until my retirement in 1976 I was a newspaper copy editor, doing occasional stories for magazines *(The New Yorker, Time Sunday Magazine)*. This work did not allow time for full-length books. Now I have the time and have begun writings."

SINCLAIR, JOHN 1941-
Born: October 2, 1941; Flint, Michigan
Parents: John A. and Elsie Dudley (Newberry) Sinclair
Married: Leni
Children: Marion Sunny, Celia
Education: Albion College, 1959-61; University of Michigan (Flint College), A.B. 1964; Wayne State University, 1964-65
Career: Founder, Detroit Artists' Workshop, 1964-67; Editor, *Work* magazine and *Change* magazine; General Editor, Artists' Workshop Press; Co-editor, *Guerrilla* magazine; Columnist and contributing editor, *Fifth Estate,* 1965-69; Associate editor, *Ann Arbor Argus,* 1968-70; Founder, *Detroit Sun* newspaper, 1967; Arts Editor, Editor-in-Chief, *Detroit Sun,* 1975-76; President and Board Chairman, Rainbow Multi-Media Corp., 1972-74; President/Creative Director, Strata Associates, 1977; Co-Producer, Ann Arbor Blues and Jazz Festivals, 1972, 1973, 1974
Address: 689 Virginia Park, Detroit, Michigan

Writings:
This Is Our Music (poetry)	Artists' Workshop Press	*1965*

Fire Music: a record (poetry)	*Artists' Workshop Press*	*1966*
The Poem for Warner String-		
fellow	*Artists' Workshop Press*	*1966*
Meditations: A Suite for John		
Coltrane	*Artists' Workshop Press*	*1967*
Music and Politics (essays)	*World Publishing*	*1971*
Guitar Army (essays)	*Douglas Books/World Pub.*	*1972*

Poems and essays appear in numerous anthologies

Work in Progress: Biography of Coleman A. Young, *The Hard Core: Selected Poems 1964-77; Revisions-Another Look at Modern Music* (essays)

He says: "My writing is derived from the African-American cultural tradition, particularly from the work of the great African-American song lyricists Little Walter Jacobs, Sonny Boy Williamson, Jimmy Reed, Chuck Berry, Smokey Robinson and Don Robey, and from the jazz rhythms of John Coltrane, Charlie Parker, Cecil Taylor, Theonious Monk, Sonny Rollins, Gene Ammons, Charles Mingus, Miles Davis, Ornette Coleman and their peers in modern music. LeRoi Jones (Ameer Baraka), A.B. Spellman, James Baldwin, Billie Holiday and Toni Morrison—among thousands of others—have taught me intelligence and its rhythmic applications. That I am of Scotch-Irish-English descent only underscores the effect of the African-American cultural tradition in shaping my work. I must also name the poets Ezra Pound, Charles Olson, Robert Creeley, Michael McClure, Allen Ginsberg, William Burroughs, Jack Kerouac, Henry Miller; the exhilarating experience of inhabiting the City of Detroit; and the three years I spent as a prisoner of the State of Michigan as prime forces in my life to date."

SMITH, ABBIE WHITNEY 1919-
Pseudonym: Abbie Whitney
Born: July 7, 1919; Manitoba, Canada
Parents: Willard Armes and Jennie (Flanders) Whitney
Married: Ferrell Karl Smith, a manufacturing engineer
Children: Theryn Karla Falkowski and Shelia Ann Rundquist
Education: Muskegon Heights High School, 1937
Career: Writer
Address: 2061 Columbus Ave., Muskegon, MI 49441

Writings:
Patchwork of Poems		*1976*
The Freelanders (a novelette	*Western Producer*	
published in 13 segements)	*Magazine*	*1974-75*

Poems published in Bardic Echoes, Peninsula, Poets, Hyacinth and Biscuits, etc.

Work in Progress: *The Freelanders* (as a full length novel) *The Kansas Tanners*

She says: "Though I was born in Canada, I have spent all but four years of my life in Michigan. Mother was born in Nunica, Michigan and Father in Manhattan, Kansas. *The Freelanders* is a story of their homesteading life in Canada and *The Kansas Tanners* is a pioneer story based on the lives of my Whitney great grandparents. It was a long running thing with a new teacher in school, when asked the usual questions, 'How did you all get together?' meaning my father, mother, and me.

"I'm an old-fashioned gal with a modern outlook. Up to a point."

SMITH, KAY (Catherine R.) 1925-
Pseudonym: Angela Adams, Vickie Andrews
Born: February 21, 1925; Philadelphia, Pennsylvania
Parents: Thomas G. and Mary Katherine (McGough) Rabbitt
Married: Joseph Earl Smith Jr., corporation president
Children: Cecily Alison, Joseph Earl III, Deirdre Leigh, John Davidson, Jared Thomas Quintin
Education: Chestnut Hill College, B.A. (Literature), 1947
Career: Women's editor, "The Germantown Courier," newspaper weekly, 1947-48; Reporter and feature writer, Philadelphia Bulletin, 1948-53; Philadelphia Correspondent, New York Herald Tribune, 1948-53; First Writer-in-Residence, Michigan Council for the Arts, 1970; Director, Writers' Conference Oakland University, 1965-68; Speaker, Oakland University and Wayne State University; Director, Bicentennial Writers' Workshops, 1976; Chairman, Bi-centennial Commission of Bloomfield Township, 1976; Member and past president, Detroit Women Writers; Member, Literature Panel Michigan Council for the Arts, 1976; Member, Planning Commission, Bloomfield Township, 1975-; Ad Hoc Committee of the Oakland County Cultural Commission, 1976-; Civic contributions: speaker, fund raiser, promotion campaigner for The Hope Ship United Foundation, Millage proposals
Address: 668 Ardmoor Drive, Brimingham, MI 48010

Writings:
Bloomfield Blossoms   *Alden Press*   1976
Freelance contributor of newspaper and magazine articles since 1951

Work in Progress: History of Bloomfield Township (completed and in process of publication); *Tocqueville and Beaumont's Three Weeks in Michigan 1831;* Novel on Revolutionary War Theme

She says: "I've never wanted to be anything but a writer nor have I ever even thought of another career as predominant even though I'm a stockbroker and day-trade in the market (for kicks—that giant roulette wheel in the sky). My philosophy is that for the first half of your life you put things in and for the second half you put things out. My four ambitions were/are to: Read the dictionary through; read all of Shakespeare; read the Bible through; and write a good novel. With the first three almost completed I've now turned my entire attention to the fourth. It's time to stop putting in and to leave something to the coming generations. I very much enjoy speaking engagements and do a minimum of two a week. My current subject is the History of Bloomfield Township and Bloomfield Hills, Michigan, and my slide talk is very well received as was my book on that history, *Bloomfield Blossoms,* which has been a bestseller in area bookstores since it publication."

Awards: State of Michigan Award for Creativity in Conference Planning for the 1967 Writers' Conference Oakland University. Only woman every appointed to a Township Board of any kind in Bloomfield

SNEIDER, VERN 1916-

Born: October 6, 1916; Monroe, Michigan
Parents: Fred and Matilda Dorothy (Althaver) Sneider
Married: Barbara Lee Cook, deceased; June (Schudel) Clark
Children: Stepson, Timothy S. Clark
Education: Notre Dame University, A.B., 1940; Princeton University, Graduate studies, 1942
Career: Assistant Credit Manager, then Credit Manager, Sears, Roebuck & Co., 1940-41; U.S. Army, Private to Captain, 1941-46; Professional Writer, 1946-
Address: 426 North Macomb Street, Monroe, MI 48161

Writings:

The Teahouse of the August Moon	Putnam	1951
A Pail of Oysters	Putnam	1953
A Long Way From Home	Putnam	1956
The King From Ashtabula	Putnam	1960
West of the North Star	Putnam	1969

Television: U.S. Steel Hour, Robert Montgomery Presents, Playhouse of Stars, Alcoa Hour, GE Theatre
Magazines: Saturday Evening Post, Holiday, Antioch Review, American Sportsman, Argosy, Ford Times, The Writer

Work in Progress: *The Structures of Fiction,* a technique book for writers

Honors: Friends of American Writers Award, 1952, for novel *The Teahouse of the August Moon*

SNELLER, DELWYN LEE 1945-

Born: March 21, 1945; Holland, Michigan
Parents: Bernard and Charlotte (Vander Schaaf) Sneller
Married: Jereen Evon (Bergman) Sneller
Children: Michelle Robin, Emily Dawn, and Leslie Anne
Education: Holland Christian High School, 1963; Hope College, B.A., 1967; Michigan State University, M.A., Ph. D., 1972
Career: Graduate Assistant, Michigan State University, 5 yrs.; Professor and Director of Creative Writing, Brescia College; Employee, Haworth Industries; Owner, 10 acre vineyard of French hybrid wine grapes, hopefully, will establish a winery
Address: 1794 Vans Blvd., Holland, MI 49423

Writings:
Secret and Silent in the Earth   Stone Country Press   1976
Numerous poems and several scholarly articles in literary journals.

Work in Progress: *Earth's Way of Laughing* (poetry); *My Best Days* (religious poetry)

He says: "I am listed with the Michigan Creative Writers in Schools Program. I enjoy factory work and farming the vineyard, because they keep me fit for loving and writing. To avoid blurry crowds of editors an stampedes of significant new writers, I am turning more and more to writing religious (Christian) poetry, an old genre presently overlooked. Most everything is work, but poetry works, and it is one business a man cannot will to his children."

SNODGRASS, WILLIAM DEWITT 1926-

Born: January 5, 1926; Wilkensburg, Pennsylvania
Parents: Bruce Dewitt and Helen (Murchie) Snodgrass
Married: Camille
Children: Cynthia, Russell Bruce, Kathy Ann Wilson (step-daughter)
Education: Geneva College, 1943-44, 1946; State University of Iowa, B.A., 1949, M.A., 1951; MFA, 1953
Career: English Department: Cornell University, 1955-57; University of Rochester, 1957-58; Wayne State University, 1959-67; English and Speech Departments, Syracuse U., 1968-present
Address: R.D. #1, Erieville, NY 13061

Writings;
Heart's Needle	*Alfred A. Knopf*	*1959*
Gallow's Songs	*Univ. of Mich. Press*	*1967*

After Experience	Harper and Row	1967
In Radical Pursuit	Harper and Row	1975
Six Troubadour Songs	Burning Deck	1977

Work in Progress: *The Fuhrer Bunker, Boa* Edition, 1977

Awards: Ingram-Merrill Award, 1958; Hudson Review Fellowship in Poetry, 1959; Longview Literary Award, 1959; Yaddo, Saratoga, NY, Resident, 1959-61, 65; Poetry Society of America, Special Citation, 1960; National Institute of Arts and Letters, Grant, 1960; Pulitzer Prize in Poetry for Heart's Needle, 1960; Guiness Poetry Award (Great Britain), 1961; Ford Foundation Grant for Study in the Theatre, 1963-64; Miles Modern Poetry Award, 1966; National Council on Arts, Sabbatical Grant, 1966-67; National Institute of Arts & Letters, Member, 1972; Guggenheim Fellowship, 1972-73; Academy of American Poets, Fellowship, 1973; Bi-centennial Medal, William & Mary College, 1976

SPENCER, ZANE A. 1935-

Born: May 21, 1935; Murray, Kentucky
Parents: James H. and Patsy L. (Jones) Story
Married: Robert J. Spencer; Elementary Principal
Children: Mark J., Michael R., Matthew D., Leeann K.
Education: Eastern Michigan University, B.A., M.A., 1975
Career: Freelance writer and teacher
Address: 2173 W. Reid Road, Flint, Michigan 48507

Writings:

Elementary Enrichment Program	Mott Publishers	1969
Flair, Creative Writing, grades K-8	Educational Service	1972
Prevent, Safety in grades K-8	Educational Service	1975
150 Plus, early education source book	Fearon Publishers	1976
Cry of the Wolf (young adult novel)	Westminister Press	1977
Writing With Sound and Fun	Media Materials	1977
Following Directions: First Things First	Media Materials	1977
Body in Elevator M (reluctant reader)	Oddo Publishers	pending

Work in Progress: *Hooray for Holidays,* Media Materials; *Stamped Runaway,* Scholastic

She says: "My writing has provided one of the greatest personal challenges of my life. It has brought tears and frustration as well as great moments of elation and tremendous personal satisfaction. Through creative writing I have learned the value of discipline and the necessity of perfecting my craft. And I am still learning. . .still standing on the edge, hoping I can fly."

SPOONER, ELLA BROWN JACKSON (1880-1963)
Born: December 3, 1880; Denver, Colorado
Parents: S.M. Jackson and Rachel Moriah Brown Jackson
Married: Charles Cutler Spooner, Professor of Mathematics, Northern Michigan University (after whom Spooner Residence Hall is named)
Education: Presbyterian Academy; Northern Michigan College, 1911
Career: Music Teacher; Organist; Author

Writings:

Clark and Tabitha Brown	*Privately Published*	*1927*
2nd edition	*Exposition Press*	*1957*
The Brown Family History: Tracing the Clark Brown Line (100 copies)	*The Laurel Outlook*	*1929*
This Broad Land (poems)	*Exposition Press*	*1949*
From Mount to Shore (poems)	*Exposition Press*	*1951*
Way Back When	*Exposition Press*	*1953*
A Lullaby of Names	*Exposition Press*	*1956*
Tabitha Brown's Western Adventures	*Exposition Press*	*1958*

Honors: Honorary member of the International Mark Twain Society, 1952

STABLEY, FRED W. 1915-
Born: September 7, 1915; Dallastown, Pennsylvania
Parents: William H. and Lottie M. (Ness) Stabley
Married: Alma R. Stabley, Housewife
Children: Fred Jr. and Susan
Education: Penn State University, B.A., 1937; Michigan State University, M.A., 1956
Career: Supervisor in school for juvenile delinquents; Insurance salesman; Taxi driver; Newspaper reporter; Assoicated Press editor; City editor; Public Relations man in Pennsylvania state government; General news editor, Michigan State University; Sports information director, Michigan State University
Address: 412 Rosewood, East Lansing, Michigan 48823

Writings:

Spartan Saga	*Michigan State University*	*1971*
The Spartans	*Strode Publishers Inc.*	*1975*

He says: *"Spartan Sage* is an encyclopedia of MSU sports from their beginnings in the 1860's. Some of its contents are complete event results, list of all-time letterwinners, chronology, brief history of each sport, 162 illustrations, Big Ten, NCAA, Olympic performers, All-Americans. (264 pages)

"The Spartans is a story of Michigan State football from its start in 1896. Included in the narrative are details of many games, human interest appearances, comprehensive records and statistics in an appendix, more than 120 illustrations. (313 pages)."

STADTFELD, CURTIS K. 1935-
Born: April 9, 1935; Remus, Michigan
Parents: Lawrence and Dorothy (Merritt) Stadfeld
Married: Susan
Children: Peter and Christopher
Education: Michigan State University, B.A., 1957; Eastern Michigan University, M.A., 1969
Career: Reporter, Michigan newspapers, 1959-61; St. Louis Post-Dispatch, 1961-66; Director, Information Services, Eastern Michigan University, 1966-71; Associate Professor, English, Eastern Michigan University, 1971-present
Address: Eastern Michigan University

Writings:
From the Land and Back	Scribner's	1972
Whitetail Deer: A Year's Cycle	Dial	1974

Published fiction in Family Circle, MS., Yankee, & non-fiction in Audubon.

Work in Progress: Rather confusingly at work on two novels and a non-fiction book

He says: "I own a farm near Remus, and much of both my fiction and non-fiction centers around the relationship of man and the land."

Awards: 1977 National Magazine Award for excellence in reporting on Michigan's PBB disaster entitled "Cheap Chemicals and Dumb Luck" in the January 1976 issue of AUDUBON magazine.

STARK, ANNE CAMPBELL see: CAMPBELL, ANNE

STARK, GEORGE WASHINGTON (1884-1966)
Born: February 22, 1884; Detroit, Michigan

Parents: Nicholas and Isabelle (Wharry) Stark
Married: Anne (Campbell), Poet
Children: George Winter, Alison Jean Wilson, Richard Campbell
Education: Eastern High School (Detroit), 1903; University of Michigan, 1904; Wayne State University, Honorary degree, 1946
Career: Newspaper columnist: *The Detroit Free Press,* 1905-1914; *The Detroit News,* 1914-1958; Managing Director, Detroit Historical Society (first and only president; Official Historiographer, City of Detroit, 1943-66

Writings:

In Old Detroit	*Arnold-Powers*	*1939*
City of Destiny	*Arnold-Powers*	*1943*
Two Heads are Better, co-authored with Anne Campbell	*Alved*	*1947*
Seventy-five years in public Service: Detroit News	*The Detroit News*	*1948*
Detroit at the Century's Turn	*Wayne Univ. Press*	*1951*
Detroit: An Industrial Mercale		*1951*
The Huron Heritage (Huron Portland Cement Co.)		*1957*
Made in Detroit, co-authored Norman Beasley	*Putnam*	*1957*
The Best Policy (Standard Accident Insurance Co.)	*Powers*	*1959*

He was "born on Detroit's lower East Side when it was known as a neightborhood of 'lace curtain Irish' families, the son of a lumber schooner skipper.

In his 'Town Talk' column in *The Detroit News,* Mr. Stark became recognized as almost the official voice of Old Detroit. His encyclopedic knowledge and love of the city had been recognized in 1947 when he was named city historiographer, a title Mr. Stark described many times as his proudest distinction."
The Detroit News, January 29, 1966 (Obituary)

STIEBER, CAROLYN 1923-
Born: July 6, 1923; Cincinnati, Ohio
Education: University of Chicago, B.A., 1944; University of Pittsburgh, M.A., 1954
Career: Michigan State University Political Science faculty, 1957-present; Ombudsman, Michigan State University, 1974-present
Address: 231 Lexington, East Lansing, MI 48823

Writings:

The Politics of Change in Michigan	*Michigan State Univ. Press*	*1971*

Work in Progress: Articles on the University as a political system and metropolitan consolidation—various approaches

She says: "My full-time job now is to serve as 'Complaint Department' for 43,000 students, but I am continuing to teach courses on state politics in my department."

STILES, MARTHA BENNETT (Living)

Born: March 30; Manila, Philippine Islands
Parents: Forrest Hampton and Jane (McClintock) Wells
Married: Martin Stiles, Chemistry Professor
Children: John Martin
Education: College of William and Mary; University of Michigan, B.S., 1954
Career: Writer' First children's story, *Humpty Dumpty's Magazine,* November, 1957; First short story; *Virginia Quarterly Review,* January, 1959; Taught writing, Ann Arbor, YMCA
Address: 2580 Newport Road, Ann Arbor, MI 48103

Writings:

The Strange House at Newbury-port	*Dial Press*	*1962*
One Among the Indians	*Dial Press*	*1963*
Darkness Over the Land	*Dial Press*	*1966*
Dougal Looks for Birds	*Four Winds Press*	*1972*
James the Vine Puller	*Carolrhoda*	*1975*

Reviewer of opera and/or books for local newspapers: The Ann Arbor News, The Detroit Free Press, The Michigan Free Press. Articles in horse magazines, Stero Review, Esquire, New York Times, Mankind. Short Stories: Georgia Review, New Orleans Review, Seventeen. Light verse: Perspectives in Biology & Medicine, Green's Magazine, Worm Runner's Digest.

Work in Progress: A mystery of the Dark Ages in France, working title, "The Star In the Forest," to be published by Four Winds Press in 1978.

She says: "Except for picture books and light verse, I write to learn. Picture books and verse I write to pleasure myself."

Awards: Hopwood Awards, University of Michigan, 1956 and 1958. Hornbook: Notable Books of 1966

STIRLING, ANTHONY see: CAESAR, EUGENE LEE

STONE, NANCY Y. 1925-
Born: December 15, 1925; Crawfordsville, Indiana
Parents: William Foster and Mary Emma (Engel) Young
Married: William Royal Stone, Graphic Designer
Children: John Conrad and Emily Foster
Education: Antioch College, B.A., 1948; Western Michigan, M.A., 1970
Career: Worked on Ohio newspapers as Antioch co-op student; Wrote advertising and promotion, Sequoia Press (husband's firm); Teach Children's Literature, Western Michigan University, at present; Free lance writer; Author of children's literature, since 1966; Script writer for multi-image slide show of Kalamazoo history for Bicentennial
Address: 2219 Sycamore Lane, Kalamazoo, MI 49008

Writings:

Whistle Up the Bay	*Wm. B. Eerdman's*	*1967*
The Wooden River	*Wm. B. Eerdman's*	*1973*

Work in Progress: A new juvenile novel, also historical, is finished and currently being typed for submission to my publisher.

She says: "Since I consider myself primarily a children's writer, I guess my philosophy is that my readers deserve the very best I have in me to give. And I am no longer annoyed or threatened by those who say 'You write for children? When are you going to write for adults?' The implication that I'd better grow up and do something worthwhile is simply amusing now, in an age when adults find their greatest literay joys in *Lord of the Rings* and *Watership Down* while children are exploring this world in worlds such as *Go Ask Alice* and *Sounder.*

"Although I was born in Indiana, I have lived in Michigan since infancy and consider myself a true Wolverine. Both my published works are Michigan historical novels for children. Michigan has a fascinating history and as I work on each book, I find myself spending an inordinate amount of time on the research."

STONEHOUSE, FREDERICK 1948-
Born: August 21, 1948; New Brunswick, New Jersey
Parents: Frederick and Martina (Mortensen) Stonehouse
Education: Northern Michigan University, B.S., 1970, M.A., 1977
Career: Free lance writer, scuba diver, and Operations and Training Officer for 107th Engineer Battalion, Michigan Army National Guard

Writings:

Great Wrecks of the Great		
Lakes	*Harboridge Press*	*1973*

Isle Royale Shipwrecks	*Harboridge Press*	*1973*
Marquette Shipwrecks	*Harboridge Press*	*1973*
Isle Royale Shipwrecks	*Avery Color Studios*	*1977*
Marquette Shipwrecks	*Avery Color Studios*	*1977*
Went Missing	*Avery Color Studios*	*1977*

Work in Progress: Continued research in the area of Lake Superior shipwrecks

He says: "To live is to dare, to get up off your collective posteriors and do something! The watchword is adventure."

STURTZEL, JANE LEVINGTON COMFORT 1903-
Pseudonym: Jane Annixter
Born: June 22, 1903; Detroit, Michigan
Parents: Will Levington and Ada (Duffy) Comfort
Married: Howard A. Sturtzel (Paul Annixter), author
Education: Detroit Public Schools, Canadian Public Schools, Venice, California Polytechnic High school, Private tutoring by English Teacher grandmother and author father
Career: Author; writing began in father's study at age 9 with an essay every day! Short stories in American and British periodicals in the early twenties.
Address: 2581 Bonita Way, Laguna Beach, California 32401

Writings:

From these Beginnings (under the name of Jane Levington Comfort)	*E.P. Dutton*	*1937*
Time Out for Eternity, started collaborating with husband in 1954	*E.P. Dutton*	*1938*
The Runner	*Holiday House*	*1956*
Buffalo Chief	*Holiday House*	*1958*
Horns of Plenty	*Holiday House*	*1960*
Windigo	*Holiday House*	*1963*
The Great White	*Holiday House*	*1966*
Vikan the Mighty	*Holiday House*	*1969*
White Shell Horse	*Holiday House*	*1971*
Ahmeek	*Holiday House*	*1970*
Sea Otter	*Holiday House*	*1973*
Trumpeter	*Holiday House*	*1974*
Wapootin	*Coward, McCann*	*1976*
Monkeys and Apes	*Franklin Watts*	*1976*

Work in Progress: *The Year of the She-Grizzly,* to be published by Coward, McCann in 1978

She says: "In writing for young people the necessity for clear thinking and simple language is a continous challenge. It seems to us that two writers working together increase the dynamics of both. For nature stories there is, of course, a great deal of research, but transforming culled facts into the flesh and blood of a story is the big job every time. We love this work. There is never an end to it."

SUMMERS, JOHN A. see: LAWSON, HORACE L.

SWARTHOUT, GLENDON 1918-
Born: April 8, 1918; Pinckney, Michigan
Parents: Fred H. and Lila E. (Chubb) Swarthout
Married: Kathryn Swarthout, author
Children: Miles Hood Swarthout
Education: University of Michigan, A.B., 1939, A.M., 1946; Michigan State University, Ph. D., 1955
Career: Sgt., 3rd Infantry Division, Italy France, 1943-45; Professor of English, University of Michigan, University of Maryland, Michigan State University, Arizonia State University, 1946-62
Address: 5045 Tamanar Way, Scottsdale, Arizona 85253

Writings:

Willow Run	T.Y. Crowell	1943
They Came to Cordura	Random House	1958
Welcome to Thebes	Random House	1962
Where the Boys Are	Random House	1960
The Cadillac Cowboys	Random House	1964
The Eagle and the Iron Cross	New American Library	1966
Loveland	Doubleday	1968
Bless the Beasts and Children	Doubleday	1970
The Tin Lizzie Troop	Doubleday	1972
Luck and Pluck	Doubleday	1973
The Shootist	Doubleday	1975
The Melodeon (with Kathryn Swarthout, the following)	Doubleday	1977
The Ghost and the Magic Saber	Random House	1963
Whichaway	Random House	1966
The Button Boat	Doubleday	1969
TV Thompson	Doubleday	1972
Whales to See The	Doubleday	1975

He says: "My forebears came via covered wagon from upper New York State in 1836 and settled in Livingston County, south of Howell, where some of the Chubb farm still remains in the family. The swarthouts followed the same path in the same year and settled northeast of Pinckney. 'Swarthout Road' there is named after them. My great grandfather, Ephraim B. Chubb, served in the 10th

Michigan Cavalry, Company K, during the Civil War, seeing action in Kentucky and Tennessee.''

SWARTHOUT, KATHRYN 1919-
Born: January 8, 1919; Columbus, Montana
Parents: L.H. and Lona Blair (Cox) Vaughn
Married: Glendon Swarthout, author
Children: Miles Hood Swarthout
Education: University of Michigan, A.B. 1940; Michigan State University, M.A. 1956
Career: Author
Address: 5045 Tamanar Way, Scottsdale, Arizona 85253

Writings:
(with Glendon Swarthout)

The Ghost and the Magic Saber	Random House	1963
Whichaway	Random House	1966
The Button Boat	Doubleday	1969
TV Thompson	Doulbeday	1972
Whales to See The	Doubleday	1975

SWARTZ, HARRY 1911-
Pseudonym: Not for publication
Born: June 21, 1911; Detroit, Michigan
Parents: Issac and Anne (Srere) Swartz
Married: Eve (Sutton); Art Director-Textbooks (retired)
Children: Mark Sutton
Education: University of Michigan, A.B., 1930, M.D., 1933
Career: Clinical Asst. Allergy, New York University, 1937-40; Flower and 5th Avenue Hospital, New York, 1940-42; Asst. Chief Allergy Clin., Harlem Hospital, 1946-48; Adj. Prof. of Medicine and Chief Allergy, New York Polyclin Medical School and Hospital, 1957-72; Asst. Attending Physician, Inst. Allergy, Roosevelt Hospital, 1946-72; Consultant
Address: APDO 752, Cuernavaca, Morelos, Mexico

Writings:

Allergy: What it is & What To Do About It	Rutgers Univ. Press	1949
2nd edition	Frederick Ungar	1962
Your Hay Fever & What To Do About It	Funk & Wagnalls	1951
2nd edition	Frederick Ungar	1964
The Allergic Child	Coward McCann	1954
2nd edition	Frederick Ungar	1965
Laymans Medical Dictionary	Frederick Ungar	1955

The Allergy Guide Book	*Thomas Nelson*	*1956*
2nd edition	*Frederick Ungar*	*1966*
Your Body (juvenile)	*Whitman*	*1962*
Simplified Medical Dictionary	*Medical Economics*	*1977*

Work in Progress: *The Drug Guide,* Medical Economics, 1977; *Drugs Affecting Laboratory Tests,* Medical Economics Book Division, 1978

He says: "The future of our species lies in genetics. I'm a strong adovcate of Edward O. Wilson's *Sociobiology.*

TALBOT, FANNIE SPRAGUE 1873-1957
Born: May 4, 1873; East Leroy, Michigan
Parents: Elliott and Marie Hannah Sprague
Married: Robert, clothier in Battle Creek and Chicago
Education: High School, Battle Creek
Career: Newspaper woman
Activities: DAR, Women's League, Federation of Women's Clubs, Poetry Society of Michigan

Writings:

Poems	*Gorham Press*	*1910*
Nosegay	*Torch Press*	*1946*

"Old Days and Old Ways at Meadowbrook" (Series of articles published by Battled Creek Inquirer and News, 1950-53)

TALLAFIERRO, GABRIEL see FOX, HUGH

TAYLOR, DAWSON 1916-
Born: November 14, 1916; Detroit, Michigan
Parents: George M. and Florence (Dawson) Taylor
Married: Mary Ellen Connolly
Children: Ellen Denise (Mrs. Patrick Martin), Mary Christine, and Dawson
Education: University of Detroit, A.B., 1936, L.L.D., 1939
Career: Admitted to Michigan Bar, 1942; Practicing attorney in State of Michigan, 1942-43; Dawson Taylor Chevrolet, Inc., Detroit, President, 1957-69; Book editor, National Enquirer, Lantana, Fla., 1969-; Military service: U.S. Navy, 1942-45, served in Pacific; became lieutenant, junior grade, received Navy Unit Commendation
Address: National Enquirer, Lantana, FL 33462

Writings:

The Secret of Bowling Strikes	Barnes	*1959*
The Secret of Holing Putts	Barnes	*1960*
The Making of the Pope	Barnes	*1961*
Your Future in the Automotive Industry	Rosen	*1962*
Your Future in Automotive Service (with James Bradley)	Rosen	*1971*
The Masters: Profile of a Tournament	Barnes	*1973*
St. Andrews: Cradle of Golf	Barnes	*1974*
Winning Bowling (with Earl Anthony)	Contemporary	*1978*
Inside Golf	Contemporary	*1978*
Alphabetical Animals in Rhythmetical Rhyme	*(completed but not sold)*	

Member: American Society of Composers, Authors and Publishers with fourteen songs published. *Stars Over my Shoulder* and *They Said You'd Come Back Running* on Dinah Washington's last album *Tribute to Dinah; I Turn the Corner of Prayer* with text by Dylan Thomas in Mormon Tabernacle repertoire and performed on national radio network, CBS; *I Will Bring you a Rainbow* with lyrics by Steve Allen recorded by John Cacavas and Orchestra

TEFFT, BESS H. 1913-1977
Born: October 6, 1915; Hillsdale, Michigan
Parents: Elmer B. and Violetta (Greenshaw) Hagaman
Married: Robert F. Tefft
Children: William W. and Robert M.
Education: Hillsdale College, 1937
Career: Editor of Washtenaw County (Michigan) Farm Bureau News; Taught creative writing in the adult education program of the Ann Arbor Public Schools; Member of the Saline School Board, 1956-65; one of the founders of the University of Michigan's International Hospitality Program; member of the Detroit Women Writers Club and of the Ann Arbor Writers Club.

Writings:
Ken of Centennial Farm	Follett	*1959*
Merrie Maple	Dutton	*1958*

TERRY, ROBERT WILLIAM 1937-
Born: October 5, 1937; Port Jefferson, New York
Parents: Isaac and Lillian Terry
Children: Steven James

Education: University of Chicago; M.A. 1966; Ph.D. 1973 Colgate-Rochester Divinity School; B.D. 1964 Cornell University; B.S. 1959

Career: Instructor (part-time), University of Windsor, 1967-1968; Faculty (part-time), University of Detroit, 1968-1971; Associate Director, Detroit Industrial Mission, 1967-1972; Partner in Neely, Campbell, Gibb, Terry and Associates; Senior Partner in Organizational Leadership, Inc., present; and Non-resident faculty, University of Oklahoma, Human Relations Department, present.

Address: 512 S. Main St., Adrian, Michigan 49221

Writings:

For Whites Only	*Eerdman's*	*1970*
Revised Edition		*1976*

Work in Progress: *Action from the Boundary: A Historical study of Detroit Industrial Mission, 1956-1970; White Male Club*

THERON, HILARY see: AMOS, WINSOM

THOMAS, PETER 1928-
Pseudonym: Simon Pederek (in Ghana only)
Born: May 11, 1928; Gloucester, England
Parents: Archibald Donald and Lucy Anne (Packer) Thomas
Married: Mary Eunice Thomas
Education: County Major Scholar to Magdalen College, Oxford, (Honors English School); B.A. 1950; M.A. 1954; Hampshire Drama School, Bournemouth, English LGSM 1956
Career: Senior Master/Headmaster at schools in England 1954-57 and in Ghana 1958-60; Founding member of the English Department at the University of Nigeria 1960-65; visiting lecturer at the University of Utah 1965-68; Junior Fellow at Mackinac College 1968-69; Professor at Lake Superior College 1969-
Address: 620 Sheridan, Sault Saint Marie, Michigan 49783

Writings:

Poems from Nigeria	*Vantage Press*	*1967*
Sun Bells	*Unicorn Hunters Press*	*1974*
Revealer of Secrets	*African Universitie's Press*	*1975*

Work in Progress: *Articles on Christopher Okigbo, Children's books of C.S. Lewis and J.R.R. Tolkien, American Mountain Men as Fact and Myth, American Indian as Myth and Memory*

He says: "Strongly influenced by C. S. Lewis and J.R.R. Tolkien, I believe, like Joseph Campbell, in seeking "Myths to Live By." Hence, the wedding of myth to landscape in my poems and the concentration on myth or fantasy in my scholarly work."

He has taught creative writing in W. Africa and the U.S., is the founding editor of *The Woods-Runner* at LSSC, and Senior Herald of the Unicorn Hunters there: an association of writers and artists who believe that the life of the spirit, as expressed in imaginative literature and art, is the most humanizing pursuit any of us can engage in. One of his favorite readings is chapter 13 in Steinbeck's *East of Eden,* in which the great novelist proclaims his faith in "the free, enquiring mind" and the many "glories" of insight and understanding by which a man's true value may be reckoned.

THOMPSON, ELIZABETH ALLEN see ALLEN, ELIZABETH

THOMPSON, JAMES W. 1935-
Pseudonym: Elethea Altemese
Born: December 21, 1935; Detroit, Michigan
Education: University of Detroit; Wayne State University; New York University; The New School for Social Research
Career: Choreographer of Ice Art, Alaskan Winter Carnival, Fairbanks, 1955; Assistant Director of Restoration Arts Theatre, Detroit, 1959-61; Member of *Umbra Magazine;* Aframerican Literary Magazine, New York City, 1961-66; Dancer Clifford Fears Dance Company, Stockholm, Sweden, 1967; Aristic Consultant and executive assistant of the Harlem Cultural Council; Participant in new Black Poets in America at the Apollo Theatre; Dance Editor and critic for *The Feet,* New York City, 1969-71; Poet-in-residence at Antioch College, 1971-72; Consultant to Thirteen College Consortium's "Seminars on Communication Skills," sponsored by Clark College in Atlanta, GA; Poet-in-residence in schools in regions one, five, Southfield and Bloomfile Hills via a grant from the Michigan Council for the Arts "Writers in the Schools" program; Artist and Instructor for the Clifford Fears Dance Theatre, Detroit, 1975-76; Poet-Lecturer, 1977
Address: P.O. Box 07243, Detroit, MI 48207

Writings:

First Fire	*Paul Breman, Ltd.*	*1970*
Fire In The Flesh	*Fire Publications*	*1977*

Work in Progress: Motor City Solo & Where The Blues Were: Time is a Body

He says: Regarding his return to Detroit: "I'm glad to be here at this time. I can see a tremendous renaissance, a renaissance that has nothing to do with the Renaissance Center. Although it is physical, too, this rebirth is basically spiritual and intellectual.

"I've decided the best way to reintroduce myself to this city on a basic level is through the schools. Under the sponsorship of the Michigan Council for the Arts, I've worked in elementary, junior, and senior high schools introducing students to Aframerican poetry."

He sees his role as that of a modern "griot," revising and restoring essentials of Aframerican culture through his method of teaching: Contrast-Cohesion-Continuum, developed during his tenure with the Thirteen College Consortium's "Seminars." This extremely flexible interdisciplinary method has been utilized in his presentation: The Praise Song—Aframerican Poetry Past & Present, Oral & Literary.

TIPTON, JAMES 1942-

Born: January 18, 1942; Ashland, Ohio
Parents: James Robert and Ruth (Burcher) Tipton
Married: Lynn Ellen (Johnson) Tipton
Children: Jennifer Lynn and James Daniel
Education: Purdue University, B.A. 1964, M.A. 1968
Career: Alma College, English Professor
Address: 7088 N. Winans Rd., Alma, MI 48801

Writings:

Convent Pieces	Goliards Press	1969
Sentences	Granium Press	1970
Matters of Love	Granium Press	1970
Bittersweet	Cold Mountain Press	1975
Michigan Poetry	Wayne State Univ. Press	1976

Work in Progress: *The Third Coast: Contemporary Michigan Fiction Alive at the End of the Journey*

TOMPERT, ANN 1918-

Born: January 11, 1918; Detroit, Michigan
Parents: Joseph and Florence (Pollitt) Bakeman
Married: Robert Tompert, case worker
Education: Siena Heights College, A.B. '38
Career: Teacher, 1938-59
Address: 141 Loretta Road, Marine City, MI 48039

Writings:

What Makes My Cat Purr?	Whitman	1965
When Rooster Crowed	Whitman	1968
The Big Whistle	Whitman	1968

Maybe a Dog Will Come	*Follett*	*1968*
A Horse for Charlie	*Whitman*	*1970*
The Crow The Kite and The Golden Umbrella	*Abelard-Schuman*	*1971*
Fun For Ozzie	*Steck-Vaughn*	*1971*
Hyacinth, The Reluctant Duck	*Steck-Vaughn*	*1972*
It May Come in Handy Some-day	*McGraw-Hill*	*1975*
Little Fox Goes to the End of the World	*Crown*	*1976*
The Way Things Were, an Autogiography of Emily Ward	*Newport Press*	*1976*
Little Otter Remembers and Other Stories	*Crown*	*1977*
The Clever Princess	*Lollipop Power, Inc.*	*1977*
Badger on His Own	*Crown*	*1978*

She says: "After reading *Little Women* when I was twelve years old, I always dreamed of being a writer like Jo. I didn't put forth any serious efforts to make my dream come true, however, until 1960. Then I worked for three years before selling my first story to *Jack and Jill* magazine. All my published work is in the Juvenile field although at one time I was sure that I would someday write the Great American Novel.

"All my stories are first put down in longhand as I cannot compose on the typewriter. It seems to me to be some kind of monster standing between me and what I wan to say.

"I write for children because I was a child once and I just never grew up!"

TORGERSEN, ERIC 1943-
Born: October 6, 1943; Huntington, New York
Parents: John and Elizabeth (Elsbeck) Torgersen
Divorced
Education: Cornell University, A.B., 1964; University of Iowa, M.F.A., 1969
Career: U.S. Peace Corps Volunteer, Ethiopia, 1964-66; Instructor, Quincy College, Quincy, Illinois, 1968-70; Professor, Central Michigan University, 1970-
Address: Route 2, Shepherd, MI 48883

Writings:

The Carpenter	*Salt Mound Press*	*1969*
At War With Friends	*Ithaca House*	*1972*
Ethiopia	*Hanging Loose Press*	*1977*

Work in Progress: My Blindness

He says: "I have always considered myself predominantly a poet, but reaction to my just-published novella, *Ethiopia,* has encouraged me to work harder at fiction."

TOROSIAN, JEANNE WYLIE 1913-
Born: February 24, 1913; Cincinnati, Ohio
Parents: Clarence Raymond and Elizabeth (Shaw) Wylie
Married: Edward Torosian (deceased)
Education: Northwestern University, B.S., 1933; Wayne State University, M.S., 1936
Instructor: Speech Correction, Wayne State University, Creative Writing, Wayne State University; Creative Writing, Michigan State University at Okaland, Expository and Creative Writing, University of Utah
Address: 1251 Country Club, Estes Park, CO 80517

Writings:
Face to Face (novel)   Morrow   *1952*
Short stories in Atlantic Monthly, O'Henry Memorial Short Story Collection, Good Housekeeping, Ladies' Home Journal, McCall's Magazine, Maryland Quarterly.

She says: "My work in progress, *A Long Look Home,* which is a book of poems with water color illustrations, is being prepared as my unique contribution to the good earth and the survival of all its creatures. If and when it is published, all proceeds will go to the cause of ecological sanity. I am particularly gradified by my work in the field of conservation and especially pleased to receive the Governor's award as the Utah Conservationist of the Year, 1970. My hobbies are water color painting, hiking, bowling, golf, skiing, and cloud watching."

TRAVER, ROBERT see: VOELKER, JOHN DONALDSON

TRELOAR, JAMES ARTHUR 1933-
Born: March 29, 1933; Iron Mountain, Michigan
Parents: Wilbert H. and Caroline (Anderley) Treloar
Married: Elizabeth (Halverson), Teacher
Children: Stephen, David, Rebecca, Timothy
Education: Northern Michigan University, B.A., 1955
Career: Reporter: *Marquette Mining Journal,* 1952-55; *Benton Harbor News-Palladium,* 1958-64; *Detroit Free Press,* 1964-67; *Detroit News,* 1968-present
Address: 691 Kings Highway, Wyandotte, MI 48192

Writings:

Educational Vacations	*Gale*	*1973*

He says: "I'm pursuing a personal interest in family history and genealogy, and would like to help create a national repository for family history that could serve as a data bank for future historians."

TROJANOWICZ, ROBERT C. 1941-
Born: May 25, 1941; Bay City, Michigan
Parents: Chester R. and Loretta (Duffy) Trojanowicz
Married: Susan E. (Schell)
Children: Eric, Elise
Education: Michigan State University, East Lansing, B.S., 1963, M.S.W., 1965, Ph. D., 1969
Career: Professor Criminal Justice
Address: School of Criminal Justice, Michigan State University, East Lansing, Michigan 48824

Writings:

Juvenile Delinquency: Concepts and Control	*Prentice-Hall*	*1973*
	(Second Edition)	*1978*
Criminal Justice and the Community (with Samuel L. Dixon)	*Prentice-Hall*	*1974*
Community based Crime Prevention (with John M. Trojanowicz and Forest M. Moss)	*Goodyear*	*1975*

Work in Progress: *The Environment of the First Line Supervisor* (with John M. Trojanowicz) Prentice-Hall, 1978

TURCO, LEWIS, 1934-
Pseudonym: Wesli Court
Born: May 2, 1934; Buffalo, New York
Parents: Luigi and May (Putnam) Turco
Married: Jean Houdlette Turco
Children: Melora Ann, Christopher Cameron
Education: University of Connecticut, B.A., 1959; University of Iowa, M.A., 1962
Career: Instructor of English, Cleveland State University, 1960-64; Assistant Professor, Hillsdale College, 1964-65; Professor, State University of New York, College at Oswego, 1965-present
Address: 54 W. 8th Street, Oswego, NY 13126

Writings:

First Poems	*Golden Quill Press*	*1960*

The Sketches	American Weave Press	1962
Awaken, Bells Falling	University of Missouri	1968
The Book of Forms	E.P. Dutton	1968
The Inhabitant	Despa Press	1970
The Literature of New York	N.Y. State English Council	1970
Procoangelini: A Fantography	Despa Press	1971
Poetry: An Introduction through Writing	Reston Publ. Co.	1973
The Weed Garden	Peaceweed Press	1973
Courses in Lambents	Mathom Publ. Co.	1977
A Cage of Creatures	Upland Poetry Pamphlets (Potsdame, N.Y.)	1978
Curses and Laments	Song Magazine	1978

He says: "My philosophy of writing may be found in an essay, 'Sympathetic Magic,' in *American Poets in 1976*, ed. William, Heyen, Bobbs-Merrill, 1976."

UMSCHEID, CHRISTINA-MARIE 1946-

Pseudonym: Christina-marie
Born: January 28, 1946; Weiden, West Germany
Parents: Alfred R. and Barbara Betty (Schmidt) Hoffman
Married: Stephen M. Umscheid
Children: Joyell Marie, Heidi Ann
Education: St. Louis Board of Education, Practical Nursing, Technical, 1966; Meramec Community College, St. Louis, MO, Associate, 1969
Career: "While studying nursing, I have continued to write and study poetry and have published continually since my high school years."
Address: 149 Washington St., Petoskey, MI

Writings:

Portraits	Snow Owl Press; Harbor Springs, Inc.	1977

Work in Progress: *Recrossings; The Book of Aislinn—Book One; Faces*

She says: "I write mainly from the female's viewpoint, using fantasy or tales to create an image, a personality or an emotion. My poems crystallize from my German fairytale heritage (such as Grimm Brothers) and from the Bible as well as many more modern writers (such as D.H. Lawrence, Hesse, Tolkien, Edgar A. Poe, to name a few)."

UNGER, JOAN 1931-

Born: July 10, 1931; Detroit, MI
Parents: Foster W. and Genevieve (Muller) Hass
Married: Steven Edward Unger, sales
Children: Diane, Gary
Education: University of Michigan, R.N., 1952
Career: Nursing—hospital, office, nursing home staff and director of nursing, home care, private duty, commercial department store
Address: 12866 Sutherland, Rd., Brighton, MI 48116

Writings:

Creative Candlecraft	*Grosset & Dunlap*	*1972*

Work in Progress: *How to Survive in the Hospital*

She says: "I enjoy a variety of creative hobbies and crafts, as well as working with and helping people. Out of this, has come my philosophy for life (although that sounds a very presumptuous title for it)—I believe we are here to help others, to leave the world a little better place because we lived. I believe women are innately creative, so endowed by the Creator, as evidenced by their unique biological function of creativity. These creative urges are expressed in myriad ways, contributing immeasurably to the betterment of family and society. Writing, teaching, caring for the sick are some of the ways I express my creativity."

VACHON, JINGO VIITALA 1918-

Born: May 29, 1928; Toivola, Michigan
Parents: Erkki and Elina (Makinen) Viitala
Married: Stanley Vachon, retired
Children: Erik, Clara, John, Phillip, Pamela, Victor, Helmi
Education: Misery Bay School, 8th grade diploma 1931
Career: Housewife and mother
Address: Toivola, MI 49965

Writings:

Taller Timber Tales	*L'Anse Sentinel*	*1973*
Sagas from Sisula	*L'Anse Sentinel*	*1975*
Finnish Fibbles	*L'Anse Sentinel*	*1978*

Work in Progress: *"Saltfish and Peasoup"* and *"Anni of Sisula"*

She says: "I am a frustrated song writer. I know that I am a much better composer and lyricist than I am an author—then how come my books sell and I don't get anywhere with my songs?! I have had poetry published since I was 14 and painted portraits for some years. Now I do my own cartoons to illustrate my stories. I used to sing publicly with my own guitar but I now sing at home and bang my 12 string. I spend my spare time hiking and backpacking in the woods—love-love-love animals and nature.

"As far as my simply country philosphy goes, I believe that each human individual should have rights—equally, no matter how poor and lowly, no matter how great and powerful. Both have their own purpose in this world; we all have equal value in the scheme of things. I believe that there is a purpose to every living thing on this earth. We are woven together in a vast, intricate network of relationships but I think or believe that man has thrown a monkey wrench into this system and sometimes I wonder if it will every run smoothly again??? I'm not a fatalist, just a realist who is also an idealist.

VAN DOMMELEN, DAVID B. 1929-

Born: August 21, 1929; Grand Rapids, Michigan
Parents: Henry and Thelma Almira (Brown) Van Dommelen
Married: Michal Bonstedt Van Dommelen, librarian
Children: Erica, Dorn
Education: Harrington Interior Design Institute, Interior Design Diploma, 1952; Michigan State University, B.A., 1956, M.A., 1957
Career: Teacher, Warren Consolidate Schools, 1957-59; Professor University of Maine, 1962-64; Pennsylvania State University, 1959-62, 1964-present
Address: 1981 Highland Drive, State College, PA 16801

Writings:

Design at Work: Its Forms and Functions (with Edward Adams and George Pappas)	Penn. State Univ.	1961
Decorative Wall Hangings: Art with Fabric	Funk & Wagnalls	1962
Walls: Enrichment and Orna- mentation	Funk & Wagnalls	1965
Designing and Decorating Interiors	John Wiley & Sons	1965
New Uses for Old Cannonballs	Funk & Wagnalls	1966
Doughboy Letters	(Private publication)	
	VDI Press	1977

Work in Progress: Allen H. Eaton: Dean of American Crafts, Pennsylvanian Crafts

He says: "My work as a writer and designer is aimed at enriching the lives of the average family and individual through art in the home. For 13 years I taught in home economics but now teach as a professor of art education. At present my main thrust is craft development in South America where I have acted as a craft consultant to the Colombia government and private craft organizations. I am a weaver and stitchery craftsman and exhibit my work throughout the United States and South America."

VANDER HILL, CHARLES WARREN 1937-
Born: September 20, 1937; Nyack, New York
Parents: L.J. and J.M. (Fisher) Vander Hill
Married: Joy, Elementary Teacher
Children: Jon Charles, Sara Lynn
Education: Hope College, B.A., 1960; University of Denver, M.A., Ph. D., 1967
Career: Grand Rapids Junior College, 1963-65; Hope College, 1966-68; Ball State University, 1965-66, 1968-present
Address: 306 Normandy Drive, Muncie, IN 47304

Writings:

Gerrit J. Diekema	*Eerdmans*	*1970*
Settling the Great Lakes Fron-tier: Immigration to Michigan, 1832-1924	*Michigan Historical Commission*	*1970*
American Society in the Twen-tieth Century (with Dwight Hoover)	*Wiley*	*1972*
A Michigan Reader: 1865 to the Present (with Robert Warner	*Eerdmans*	*1974*

Work in Progress: Research on the history of the family, particularly the immigrant family in the middle west

He says: "My hobbies are fly fishing and fly typing, jogging, and cross-country skiing."

VANDER MOLEN, ROBERT 1947-
Born: April 23, 1947; Grand Rapids, Michigan
Parents: Robert and Marjorie (Mollo) Vander Molen
Education: Michigan State University, B.A., 1971; University of Oregon, M.F.A., 1973
Career: Billposter for a circus in Canada, ranch hand in Montana, babysitter in San Francisco, foundry worker in Three Rivers, part-time instructor at Grand Rapids Junior College
Address: 2215 Ducoma Dr., Grand Rapids, MI

Writings:

Blood Ink	*Zeitgeist Press*	*1967*
The Lost Book	*Zeitgeist Press*	*1968*
Variations	*Zeitgeist Press*	*1970*
The Pavilion & Other Poems	*Sumac Press*	*1974*
Along The River & Other Poems	*New Rivers Press*	*1977*

Work in Progress: *Of Helping a Strangler*

He says: "I have been writing poetry since I was 15. Gradually I discovered that for my taste the best poetry is fictional rather than non-fictional, is sense-oriented rather than intellectual, tends to be mind-association (or a pseudo stream of consciousness) rather than that seeemingly deliberate image-block business. Lastly, poetry that contains certain facets of Romanticism interests me, poetry that deals with such stuff as the individual, the dare, the dream /fantasy, the hope/future, etc. And this is what I try to do in my work."

VARICK, ROSE see: BIRD, DOROTHY MAYWOOD

VIRCH, PATRICIA J. 1926-
Pseudonym: Pat Virch
Born: September 29, 1926; Murdo, South Dakota
Parents: William and Laura (Larsen) Draeger
Married: Niron L. Virch, Telephone Engineer
Children: Margaret, Rosemary, William, Julie
Education: Independent study in Norway, Switzerland and New England
Career: Homemaker and mother from 1946 to 56, then study of folk arts and began teaching Norwegian Rosemaling in 1965, conducted seminars in 17 states since 1970. Awarded Norwegian Medal of Honor by the Vesterheim Museum of Decorah, Iowa in 1974. Taught Early American Decorative arts since 1967.
Address; 1506 Lynn Ave., Marquette, MI 49855

Writings:

Traditional Norwegian Rose-maling	Nordic Publishers	1970
Traditional Norwegian Rose-maling Folio I	Nordic Publishers	1972
Traditional Norwegian Rose-maling Folio II	Nordic Publishers	1973
Rosemaling in the Round	Nordic Publishers	1976
Decorated Tinware-An Early American Folk Art	Nordic Publishers	1977

Work in Progress: Additional books on folk arts

She says; "I am a true folk artist as I have no formal art training. I try to offer as clearly as possible insight into the charming simplicity of folk decoration. The books I have written are pure How-to-do-it in Norwegian folk art and Early American folk art. I hope to encourage people to create their own Heirlooms of Tomorrow-Today. Thus they will spend leisure time in productive and satisfying way; to leave pleasure giving monuments instead of just the granite markers in well tended cemeteries. I use adaptations of the old folk decorations in their traditional forms and apply them to our reproductions of old pieces or functional new pieces of woodenware and tinware, I am, of my own choosing, a folk artist, not a fine artist. But I feel I am a fine craftsman producing useful objects in this 20th century."

VIS, WILLIAM RYERSON 1886-1969
Born: August 17, 1886; Drenthe, MI
Parents: Ryer and Nancy Vis
Married: Alice Taylor
Children: Vincent Almon Vis
Education: University of Michigan, M.D., 1916
Career: Practicing physician in Internal Medicine for 52 years in Grand Rapids
Address: 1709 Breton Rd., Grand Rapids, MI 49506

Writings:

Saddlebag Doctor	*Eerdmans*	*1964*

VOELKER, JOHN DONALDSON 1903-
Pseudonym: Robert Traver
Born: June 29, 1903; Ishpeming, Michigan
Parents: George Oliver and Annie (Traver) Voelker
Married: Grace Taylor (8-2-30)
Children: Elizabeth (Mrs. Victor N. Tsaloff); Julie (Mrs. H. Jordon Overturf); Grace (Mrs. Ernest Wood)
Education: Northern Michigan College, 1922-24; University of Michigan, L.L.B., 1928
Career: Marquette County, Michigan prosecuting attorney, 1934-52; State of Michigan, Supreme Court Justice, 1957-60; Author since early depression days, mostly stories in "little" magazines such as Story, Prairie Schooner, Hinterland, etc., etc.
Address: Deer Lake Road, Ishpeming, Michigan 49849

Writings:
(All under pseudonum Robert Traver)

Troubleshooter	*Viking*	*1943*
Danny and the Boys	*World Publishing*	*1951*
Small Town D.A.	*World Publishing*	*1954*
Anatomy of a Murder	*St. Martins Press*	*1957*
Trout Madness	*St. Martins Press*	*1960*

Hornstein's Boy	St. Martins Press	1962
Anatomy of Fisherman	McGraw	1964
Laughing Whitefish	McGraw	1965
The Jealous Mistress	Little, Brown & Co.	1968
Trout Magic	Crown	1974

Asked why he publishes so infrequently he replied: "During the fleeting hours of trout season I can barely find time to sign my Social Secruity checks let alone write books and stories."

VUGTEVEEN, VERNA see: AARDEMA, VERNA

WAGNER, LINDA WELSHIMER 1936-
Born: August 18, 1936; St. Marys, Ohio
Parents: Sam and Esther (Scheffler) Welshimer
Children: Douglas, Thomas, and Andrea
Education: Bowling Green State University, B.A., B.S. in Education, 1954-57, M.A., 1959, Ph. D., 1963
Career: Teacher of English in Michigan and Ohio schools, at Bowling Green and Wayne State Universities, since 1968; professor of English and Associate Chairperson of English Department at Michigan State University
Address: 1620 Anderson Way, East Lansing, MI 48823

Writings:
The Poems of William Carlos Williams	Wesleyan U. Press	1964
Denise Levertov	Twayne	1967
Intaglios: Poems	South & West	1967
The Prose of William Carlos Williams	Wesleyan U. Press	1970
Phyllis McGinley	Twayne	1971
T.S. Eliot	McGraw-Hill	1974
William Faulkner: Four Decades of Criticism	Michigan State U.	1973
Ernest Hemingway: Five Decades of Criticism	Michigan State U.	1974
Hemingway and Faulkner: Inventors/Masters	Scarecrow Press	1975
Introducing Poems (with David Mead)	Harper & Row	1976
Interviews with William Carlos Williams	New Directions Press	1976
A Reference Guide to Ernest Hemingway	G.K. Hall	1977
Robert Frost: The Critical		

Heritage	Burt Franklin	1977
A Reference Guide to William		
Carlos Williams	G.K. Hall	1977

Work in Progress: *John Does Passos: Architect of History; Poems for Isadora* (long sequence of poems)

She says: "I teach writing, criticism, and literature classes at Michigan State, believing that all three are inter-related—must be inter-related—and the same conviction shows in my own writing."

WALKER, LOUISE JEAN (1891-1976)
Born: February 10, 1891; Jackson, Michigan
Education: Albion College, A.B., 1917; Columbia University, M.A., 1924; studied at University of Michigan, University of Colorado, and Miami University
Career: Teacher of high school English in Indiana and Michigan; Associate Professor of English, Western Michigan University; visiting Professor at New Highlands University, Las Vegas, New Mexico

Writings:

Legends of Sky Hill	Eerdmans	1959
Red Indian Legends	Odhams Press Limited,	
	London	1961
Woodland Wigwams	Hillsdale	1964
Beneath the Singing Pines	Hillsdale	1967
Daisy Strikes on Saturday Night	Eerdmans	1968

More than 160 articles and stories for such magazines as *Children's Activities, Highlights for Children, Journal of American Folklore, American Nature Magazine, Your Personality, Out Dumb Animals, The English Journal,* and others

Miss Walker started her writing career shortly after she began teaching. While living in Charlevoix, Michigan, she became very interested in the Chippewa Indians and their legends which she felt should be preserved. It often took six weeks to get the story of one legend from an Indian squaw. She gather 64 legends and the material for her books in northern Michigan, Wisconsin, and southern California. In June, 1961, Miss Walker retired from Western Michigan University after 37 years of teaching there. She died in 1976.

WALKER, MILDRED 1905-
Born: May 2, 1905; Philadelphia, Pennsylvania
Parents: Walter and Harriet (Merrifield) Walker

Married: Ferdinand Ripley Schemm
Children: Margaret Ripley Hansen, George, and Christopher
Education: Wells College, New York, B.A., 1926; University of Michigan, M.A., 1934
Career: Advertising copy writer with John Wanamaker Co. in Philadelphia, 1926-27; Professor English Literature, Wells College, 1955-68

Writings:

Fireweed (Avery Hopwood Award)	*Harcourt*	*1934*
Light from Arcturus	*Harcourt*	*1935*
Dr. Norton's Wife	*Harcourt*	*1938*
The Brewers' Big Horses	*Harcourt*	*1940*
Unless the Wind Turns	*Harcourt*	*1941*
Winter Wheat	*Harcourt*	*1944*
The Quarry	*Harcourt*	*1947*
Medical Meeting	*Harcourt*	*1949*
The Southwest Corner	*Harcourt*	*1951*
The Curlew's Cry	*Harcourt*	*1955*
The Body of a Young Man	*Harcourt*	*1960*
If a Lion Could Talk	*Harcourt*	*1970*
A Piece of the World	*Harcourt*	*1972*

Born in a parsonage in Philadelphia, Mildred Walker came to Michigan 1927 when she married Dr. F.R. Schemm, a young surgeon. It was here in a lumber town on Lake Superior that she wrote short stories, verse, and novels, most of which she burned. Her first novel, *Fireweed,* with its background of a Lake Superior mill town, relects a Michigan influence.

Miss Walker spent a year in Japan as a Fulbright scholar and 23 years as a resident of Great Falls, Montana. After her husband's death she moved to Grafton, Vermont.

WALKINSHAW, LAWRENCE HARVEY 1904-
Pseud.: Larry
Born: February 25, 1904; Calhoun County, Pennfield Township
Parents: Beatson Charles and Eva Marie (Grinnell) Walkinshaw
Married: Clara May Cartland
Children: James Richard and Wendy Anne Schake
Education: Olivet College, 1924-25; University of Michigan, D.D.S., 1929
Career: Dentist (retired 1968)
Address: 1145 Scenic Drive, Muskegon, MI 49445

Writings:

The Sandhill Cranes	*Cranbrook Institute*	*1949*
Cranes of the World	*Winchester Press*	*1973*

Some 300 articles on birds and animals

Work in Progress: *Summer Kirtland's Warbler Studies; Life History of the Field Sparrow* (mss. complete); *Ezra Grinnell Genealogy* (mss. complete); *Walkinshaw Genealogy;* A manscript on world crane bibliography

He says: "I believe in God and Jesus Christ. Our world, its inhabitants, its perfect and complete organization, could have been produced only by God. I believe in work, in accomplishing things and completing them. I believe in people and their ability. I feel there are times we need to help those less fortunate than we, that we can serve them at times, and that we can aid the young. I thus worked with Boy Scouts for 40 years and with the Battle Creek Lions Club of which I was president. I have also worked with the S.W. Michigan Dental Society, Wilson Ornithological Society and the Ridge Audubon Society at Wales, Florida. I am happy to see boys like two of my grandsons and prior to that, my son, become Eagle Scouts—they finished something they started."

WARNER, ROBERT M. 1927-
Born: June 28, 1927; Montrose, Colorado
Parents: Mark Thomas and Bertha (Rich) Warner
Married: Jane Bullock
Children: Mark Steven and Jennifer Jane
Education: University of Denver, 1945; Muskingum College, B.A., 1949; University of Michigan, M.A., 1952, Ph. D., 1958
Career: High school teacher in Colorado, 1949-50; U.S. Army, 1950-52 at University of Michigan, and Director of Michigan Historical Collections, Professor of History and Library Science, 1957-
Address: Bentley Hisorical Library, University of Michigan, Ann Arbor, MI 48109

Writings:

Profile of a Profession, A History of the Michigan State Dental Association	*Wayne State U.*	*1964*
The Modern Manuscript Library, (with Ruth Bordin)	*Scarecrow*	*1966*
A Michigan Reader, 1965-the present, (with C. Warren Van- der Hill)	*Eerdmans*	*1974*

He says: *"My field of writing is primarily professional and scholarly writing in the areas of local history and archival adminstration."*

WARSAW, IRENE 1908-
Born: November 26, 1908; Kawkawlin Township, Bay County, MI
Parents: Herman A. and Augusta (Malzahn) Warsaw
Education: Bay City Central High School, 1925; Writers' Conferences and workshops at Middlebury College, Vermont, at University of Indiana, University of Vermont, and University of Colorado
Career: Secretary; Trust Officer and Vice-President of Peoples National Bank & Trust Co. (retired, 1974)
Address: 888 N. Scheurmann Rd., No. D-24, Essexville, MI 48732
Writings:

A Word in Edgewise (humorous poetry)	Golden Quill Press	1964
	6th printing	1975

Poems published in some 75 magazines and papers, some of which are: Saturday Evening Post, Christian Science Monitor, The Atlantic, and The New York Times Magazine.

Work in Progress: poems for magazines and contests

She says: "I frequently act as judge for contests and have been on the staffs of various writers' conferences and conventions as lecturer or panelist. I very frequently address 'lay' groups on poetry, telling about experiences with editors and illustrating points of technique and about the struggle for publication. I speak mostly on humorous poetry. People enjoy it and I have concentrated more on humor, with the result that I have had more humorous poems published than serious ones. I would classify most of my humor as satire dealing with life's incongruities and human foibles and frailties. Many of my poems have been called epigrammatic. I am a member of the National League of American Pen Women, Detroit Women Writers, Poetry Society of Michigan, Pennsylvania Poetry Society, and the Poets Study Club of Terre Haute."

Awards: Bay City Central High School of Fame, 1975; many prizes and awards in national and state poetry contests.

WASHBURNE, HELUIZ CHANDLER 1892-1970
Born: January 25, 1892; Cincinnati, Ohio
Parents: Charles Colby and Julia (Davis) Chandler
Married: Carleton W. Washburne, professor and writer
Children: Margaret (Mrs. James C. Plagge); Beatrice (Mrs. John E. Visher); Chandler
Education: attended School of Industrial Arts and Women's School of Design, both in Philadelphia, Pennsylvania
Career: home fashion advisor with Carson, Pirie, Scott & Co., department store in Chicago, 1928-30; travel columist, *Chicago Daily News,* 1940-42; author of books for children, 1930-60

Writings:

Letters to Channy: A Trip Around the World (Junior Literary Guild)	Rand McNally	*1932*
Stories of the Earth and Sky, with husband and Frederick Reed (Junior Literary Ghild)	Appleton	*1933*
Little Elephant Catches Cold	Whitman	*1937*
Little Elephant's Christmas	Whitman	*1938*
Little Elephant's Picnic	Whitman	*1939*
Fridl, a Mountain Boy	Winston	*1939*
Rhamon, a Boy of Kashmir	Whitman	*1939*
Land of the Good Shadows: The Life Story of Anauta, an Eskim Woman (with Anauta Blackmore)	John Day	*1940*
Little Elephant Visits the Farm (with Anauta Blackmore)	Whitman	*1941*
Children of the Blizzard (Junior Literary Guild)	John Day	*1952*
Tomas Goes Trading	John Day	*1959*
Articles for Britannica Junior Encyclopedia		

Mrs. Washburne wrote for children and some of her books were about children in other lands. Vacationing in Saugatuck, Michigan, during summers provided an opportunity for much of this writing. She lived in Italy, Mexico, and Cambodia, she frequently visited Europe, in her lifetime she also visited China, Japan, Korea, India, Russia, the Near East, New Zealand, Africa, South America, and Australia.

Letter to Channey was published in England and Poland; *Children of the Blizzard* was published in Denmark, Germany, Sweden, Japan, and England.

WEAVER, CLARENCE LAHR 1904-
Born: November 5, 1904; Delaware, Ohio
Parents: Charles Oscar and Maggie Jane Betts (i.e. Betz) Weaver
Married: Gertrude Viola Pratt, 1904-70 (poet and author of *The Emporor's Gift,* Nelson, 1969)
Children: Eleanor Janet Hogan, Kenneth Harmon, Charles Albert, and Carol Lynne Benton
Education: Ohio Wesleyan University, B.A. 1926; Western Reserve University, B.S. in Library Science 1934; University of Michigan, M.S. in Library Science 1959
Career: Copy and layout with *Lakeside Press,* 1926-31; landscape gardening and dairy farming, 1931-34; head of catalog and order

department and assistant editor of publications for the Ohio State Historical Society, 1934-46; chief of catalog and order department of Grand Rapids Public Library until 1969 now retired.
Address: 1036 Emerald Ave., N.E. Grand Rapids, MI 49503
Writings:

With All My Love (poetry)	Quickening Seed Press	1936
A Bard's Prayers	Bardic Echoes Brochures	1967

Joint complier of County History Materials of the State of Ohio, 2 editions, 1936, 1945

Work in Progress: editing *Bardic Echoes,* a quarterly of poetry 1960-; a collection of my own poetry

He says: "As editor I have endeavored to give the amateur, that is the beginner, a show place, if he has something original to say, in a creative manner, even though the form of presentation may be imperfect, and at the same time offer him a hint or two toward improvement. As a poet I have originated the weave pattern which has been well accepted by many in the poetry field as a valid form with a useful place in the poet's repertoire for creative expression in the modern milieu. The weave pattern is a five line stanza done with a syllable count of 9-11-13-11-9."

WEBBER, GORDON, 1912-
Born: October 25, 1912; Linden, Michigan
Parents: Roy Eugene and Dorothea (Boyd) Webber
Children: Jacqueline, Dorothea, and Laura
Education: Jamestown College, Jamestown, North Dakota, A.B., 1933, University of Michigan, M.A. Journalism, 1936
Career: Writer, producer, associate creative director and manager of creative department, Benton & Bowles Advertising, script writer, television news writer, editor with National Broadcasting Company; lecturer at various colleges and universities; most recently on staff of Parsons School) of Design teaching writing
Address: 7 East 86th St., New York City, NY 10028

Writings:

Years of Eden	Little, Brown & Co.	1951
The Far Shore	Little, Brown & Co.	1954
	Bantam Books	1955
	Victor Gollanz, London	1955
What End But Love	Little, Brown & co.	1959
"I Remember Mama"	TV Series	1950-55

Films: "The Endless War"-documentary for Senate Amendment to End the War Committee. "The Jogger"-winner of CINE Golden Eagle and Edinburgh Film Festival certificates

Work in Progress: Novel—*The Great Buffalo Hotel* set in a northwest college town

He says: "Get up every morning and do some useful work. Try to love more than you hate; but hate who and what deserves to be hated. Preserve as long as you can your sense of wonder and mystery."

WEESNER, THEODORE 1935-
Born: July 31, 1935; Flint, Michigan
Parents: William and Margaret (McInnes) Weesner
Married: Sharon Long
Children: Ted, Anna, Steve
Education: Michigan State University, B.A., 1959; University of Iowa, M.F.A., 1965
Career: Writer
Address: 7 Orchard Drive, Durham, NH 03824

Writings:

The Car Thief	Random House	1972
A German Affair	Rnadom House	1977

Work in Progress: *Annaliese* (a novel), Random House, *Have You Seen This Man?*, Summit books, Simon & Schuster, (a non-fiction novel)

He says: "I am a realist. There is something in the term 'neo-realism' which implies an intense realism, and as both writer and reader this is where my interest lies. Stated otherwise, while some writers write about what might or could happen, I write about what has happened. But I am not a reporter.

"I have some writer-friends who are realists like myself, and some writer-acquaintances who are not. Friendship with non-realists doesn't go far. As if they were Republicans all along. They are certain, they will tell you, of their point of view; I know in the center of my stomach that I am right.

"I have written a realistic account of the confused realities of a sixteen year old boy stealing cars. I have also written a realistic account of the implications of a young man's sexual drive transferring from flesh to creativity. Everyone liked the first novel, but no one like the second. I was surprised.

"Now I am writing a non-fiction novel. It is an account of the Oakland County, Michigan, child murders. With my wife and three children, I am living in Oakland County while I do the work. Most people believe that crimes really happen only to people in the newspapers; I am going to show that they happen to ordinary folks like you and I. Really."

Awards: *Car Thief* earned the Great Lakes Colleges Award for the best new novel of 1972

WEGNER, ROBERT E. 1929-
Born: March 1, 1929; Cleveland, Ohio
Parents: Ernst R. and Esther (Streblow) Wegner
Education: Michigan State University, B.A., 1950; Western Reserve University, M.A., 1952, Ph. D., 1955; State University of Iowa, 1952-53
Career: Assistant Professor of English, Wilmington College, 1955-57; Professor of English, Alma College, 1957
Address: 9650 Pinegrove Rd., Vestaburg, MI 48891

Writings:

The Poetry & Prose of E.E. Cummings	*Harcourt*	*1965*
"I'm Going Down to Watch the Horses Come Alive," a story reprinted in The Age of Anxiety	*Allyn*	*1972*

Work in Progress: *The Kingdom of Bancroft Winkeler,* a novel; short stories

He says: "Timeless awareness as over against time-ridden chronology that seems to hold most fiction in thrall is what intrigues me as creative process; how to achieve the former without sacrificing a sense of progression. It is a continuous challenge."

WEISMAN, JOAN 1921-
Pseudonym: Joan Savage
Born: February 6, 1921
Parents: Louis and Mae (Rugowitz) Savage
Married: Norman Weisman (deceased)
Children: Sarah Mae and Samuel K.
Education: Wayne University, 1941-43; B.A. in Education; Wayne State University, 1974-75; M.A. in Human Development
Career: Most of my life has been spent teaching at the pre-school level. I was with Head Start for 10 years. After my husband died in 1973, I continued my interest in human development but concentrated on adulthood and aging rather than children. I have a Specialist Certificate on Aging from the University of Michigan-Wayne State University Institute of Gerontology. At present I am teaching a class of elderly people at Highland Park Community College. We are exploring their family histories and it is from tap-

ing their recollections that *Christmas Memories* was evolved. At Wayne State College of Lifelong Learning I am teaching one course in Child Development and another in Aging and Society. **Address:** 29260 Franklin Road, #514, Southfield, Michigan 48034

Writings:

Hurray for Bobo	*Childrens Press*	*1957*
The Bad of the Quicksand	*Campus Publishers*	*1976*

Work in Progress: *Christmas Memories* (edited recollections of a group of elderly Southern black people), Broadside Press, 1978; *A Princess Must Grow* (a filmstrip for children showing non-sexist career choice and an introduction to hospital), Program Resources, 1978; *Some People Are Old* (a book about aging for young people), Program Resources, 1978

She says: "People are usually surprised when then find my interests are children's literature, pre-school education and gerontology. For me, the three fit together very comfortably. Juvenile books and children were my first loves. Now, I am interested in seeing how the elderly are depicted in children's books and am committed to including positive images of old people in my own writing. *Christmas Memories*, the reminiscences of early childhood taped in my Highland Park senior adult class, will be prepared as a juvenile book. When I asked the students if their grandchildren knew these tales and they answered negatively, I felt these recollections would be a wonderful contribution to their grandchildren and to all children.

"*Some People Are Old* is a factual presentation of aging for children. *A Princess Must Grow* depicts an elderly woman as an interesting working person. Long ago I wrote *Hurray for Bobo* and it showed successful integration and co-operation between the generations.

"When I want to tell children a little about dinosaurs *(The Bad and the Quicksand)* or about integration and co-operation or about choosing a career *(A Princess Must Grow)*, I usually prefer to tell a story. It is simply a preference because I know that the world is full of children who are happy to read lists of facts, even a phone book.

"My children are grown now, and I am no longer working in pre-school but the children I have known, mine and hundreds of others, always inspire me. Little Bobo was a Chinese boy I knew in nursery school in New York City. My children, when they were very young, romped on the bed and once our daughter announced they were going to be extinct if they fell into the bad of the quicksand. Children's confusion about 'old' partly inspired *Some People Are Old.* Mother and daddy are old, big sister is old—what are they to think about grandparents and great grandparents?"

WEXSTAFF, BERNICE 1898-
Born: June 28, 1898; Charlevoix, Michigan
Parents: Loren Engene and Mary (Ward) Crandell
Married: Arthur C. Wexstaff, dry cleaner
Children: Robert Eugene
Education: Charlevoix High School, Alma College
Career: Writer, part time musician, and business woman
Address: 230 Antrim Street, Charlevoix, MI 49720

Writings:

The Black Panther of the Great Lakes	Eerdmans	1957
Haunt of High Island	Eerdmans	1958
Belvedere Club	Private Club publication	
Church of God	Private Church publication	

Work in Progress: *The Old Dixie Highway-1926 and Now*

She says: "I do historical research on many topics including the old Dixie from Canada to Key West. Rex Beach, author, was born in northern Michigan but never recognized there until this year, 1977, when I rpesented his credentials on the occasion of his 100th birthday anniversary September 1st. I am also interested in politics on both the local and national level and work on grass-roots opinions on national legislation for the Monitor Poll based in Washington, D.C. I am a member of the Daughters of the American Revolution and concerned about the future of our American Republic and the democratic processes inasfar as my family has been here since 1634."

WHITE, PAULETTE CHILDRESS 1928-
Born: December 1, 1948; Hamtramck, Michigan
Parents: Norris and Effie (Storey) Childress
Married: Bennie White, Jr., a postal employee and professional artist
Children: Pierre, Oronde, Kojo, Kala, and Paul
Education: Ecorse Public Schools, 1966; Center for Creative Studies, 1967
Career: Writer and homemaker
Address: 2554 S. LaSalle Gardens, Detroit, Michigan 48206

Writings:

Love Poem to a Black Junkie	Lotus Press	1975
Short story in Essence Magazine, January 1977		

Work in Progress: a series of short stories that may evolve into a novel or a collection

She says: "My birth as a writer has been slow and painful, yet it has been equally joyful in the discovery and realization that I have to offer something unique, as person, as black person, as women person; that I may be one of a small but wealthy tradition of black women writers. Writing for me has been a process of search and definition. That which I had searched to define has grown from some early overwhelming dilemmas to the probing of a world within. I am writing about myself now—and primarily for myself. If I am ever done with me, life may just lead me back out to write and worry about a larger world. Other than writing, my interests are family, friends, all creative people, reading and the visual arts."

WHITE, WILLIAM 1910-

Born: September 4, 1910; Paterson, New Jersey
Parents: Noel D. and Beccia (Firkser) White
Married: Gertrude Mason
Children: Roger W. and Geoffrey M.
Education; University of Tennessee, A.B., 1933; University of Southern California, M.A., 1937; University of London, (England), Ph. D., 1953; also attended University of California and University of Dijon, France
Career: Newspaper stringer, reporter, feature writer, correspondent, copy editor with *Chattanooga Times; Inc., Hartford Courant, Los Angeles Examiner, Detroit Free Press, Los Angeles Times;* edited 15 weeklies in the Detroit area; Professor at Whitman College, Mary Hardin-Baylor College, Ohio Wesleyan University, California State University at Long Beach, University of Southern California, University of Hawaii, University of Rhode Island, and Oakland University
Address: 25860 W. 14 Mile Rd., Franklin, MI 48205

Writings:

A Henry David Thoreau Bibliography, 1908-1937	Faxon	1939
A.E. Housman: The Parallelogram, the Amphisbaena, the Crocodile	Jake Zeitlin	1941
John Donne since 1900	Faxon	1942
D.H. Lawrence: a Checklist, 1931-50	Wayne State U.	1950
This is Detroit, 1701-1951: 250 Years in Pictures (with M.M. Quaife)	Wayne State U.	1951
Sir William Osler: Historian and Literary Essayist	Wayne State U.	1951
John Ciardi: A Bibliography	Wayne State U.	1959
Walt Whitman: An 1855-56 Notebook (with Harold Blodgett)	Southern Illinois U.	1959

A.E. Housman: A Centennial Memento	Oriole	1959
A.E. Housman to Joseph Ishill: Five Hundred Unpublished Letters	Oriole	1959
W.D. Snodgrass: A Bibliography	Wayne State U.	1960
Karl Shapiro: A Bibliography	Wayne State U.	1960
Walt Whitman: The People and John Quincy Adams	Oriole	1961
	revised	1962
Ernest Hemingway: Guide to a Memorial Exhibition	Wayne State U.	1961
George Orwell: A Selected Bibliography (with Z.G. Zeke)	Boston Linotype Print	1962
Wilfred Owen, 1893-1918: A Bibliography	Ken State U.	1967
By-line: Ernest Hemingway	Scribner's	1967
	London	1968
	Bantam	1968
	Penguin	1970
	Bombay	1970
translated into 13 foreign languages		
Walt Whitman's Journalism: A Bibliography	Wayne State U.	1969
The Merrill Studies in The Sun Also Rises	Merrill	1969
The Merrill Guide to Ernest Hemingway	Merrill	1969
The Merrill Checklist of Ernest Hemingway	Merrill	1970
Edward Arlington Robinson: A Supplementary Bibliography	Kent State U.	1971
Walt Whitman in Our Time: Four Essays	Wayne State U.	1970
Walt Whitman in Europe Today (with Roger Asselineau)	Wayne State U.	1972
Ernest Bramah: Kai Lung: Six	Non-Profit Press	1974
Nathanael West: A Comprehensive Bibliography	Kent State U.	1975
The Bicentennial Walt Whitman: Essays from The Long Islander	Wayne State U.	1976
Walt Whitman: Daybooks and Notebooks, (collected writings of Whitman)	New York U.	1977
The Serif Series: Bibliographies		

and Checklists, (General Editor)	Kent State U.	1967-75
Annual Bibliography of English Language and Literature for the Modern Humanities Research Association		
Walt Whitman Review (Editor)	Wayne State U.	1955-

Work in Progress: *Walt Whitman: Variorum Edition of Leaves of Grass; Ernest Bramah; The Aphorisms of Kai Lung; Walt Whitman: The Critical Reception; Walt Whitman: Journalism*

He says: "Let me quote from *Who's Who in America:* With a certain intelligence, sesitivity (but not too much), an optimistic temperament, experience (what you learn from books and your own coming and going), a sense of humor (so you won't take yourself too seriously), energy, good health, and lots of luck, you may succeed in doing what you set out to do, get a little recognition and some satisfaction; you may even make some money, though that's not important, only pleasant. If your keep busy enough and have the love of one wife and a few good friends, you may find pleasure in life and forget the corruptibility of man."

WHITNEY, ABBIE see: SMITH, ABBIE WHITNEY

WIDDER, KEITH R. 1943-
Born: August 16, 1943; Sheboygan, Wisconsin
Parents: Hugo and Marie (LeMahieu) Widder
Education: Wheaton College, Wheaton, ILL, A.B., 1965; University of Wisconsin, Milwaukee, M.A., 1968
Career: Teacher-librarian, Brookfield East High School, Brookfield, Wisconsin, 1968-71; Lecturer, University of Wisconsin-Parkside, 1969-71; Museum Curator, Mackinac Island State Park Commission, Mackinac Island, Michigan
Address: 126 Centerlawn, East Lansing, MI 48823

Writings:
Reveille Till Taps	Mackinac Island State Park Commission	1972
Dr. William Beaumont: the Mackinac Years	Mackinac Island State Park Commission	1975
Mackinac National Park, 1875-1895	Mackinac Island State Park Commission	1975
At the Crossroads: Michilmackinac, During the American Revolution (co-authored with David A. Armour)	Mackinac Island State Park Commission	1977

He says: "I think historical narratives should include ample illustrations that are closely related to the text. Publications for the general public should be regarded as exhibits of the subject under consideration."

WIDICK, B.J. 1910-
Born: October 25, 1910; Yugoslavia
Married: Barbara K. Widick
Children: Marshall and Brian
Education: University of Akron, B.A. 1933; Wayne State University, M.A. 1963
Career: Newspaperman, 1933-37; CIO Research Director, UAW activist and staff member, 1946-60; Wayne State and Columbia Universities; Labor correspondent of *The National Magazine,* 1959-77
Address: 560 Riverside Drive, New York, NY 10027

Writings:

UAW and Walter Reuther (with Irving Howe	*Random House*	*1949*
Labor Today: Triumphs and Failures of Unionism	*Houghton-Mifflin*	*1964*
Detroit: City of Race and Class Violence	*Quadrangle Books*	*1972*
Auto Work and Its Discontents	*Johns Hopkins U. Press*	*1976*

He says: "As a social critic, I conceive of my function as a writer to ask the tough questions. So few people do that today. This is not the road to financial or other success, but it is rewarding for such a function does assist people to come up with better answers than the old cliches."

WIEGAND, WILLIAM 1928-
Born: June 11, 1928; Detroit, Michigan
Parents: Jack J. and Kathryn (Diener) Wiegand
Education: University of Michigan, A.B., 1945, A.M., 1950; Stanford University, Ph. D., 1960
Career: Instructor, Harvard University, 1960-62; Assistant Professor, Assoicate Professor, and Professor of English and Creative Writing, San Francisco State University, 1962-
Address: Department of Creative Writing, San Francisco University, 1600 Holloway Ave., San Francisco, CA 94132

Writings:

At Last, Mr. Tolliver	*Rinehart*	*1950*
The Treatment Man	*McGraw*	*1959*

The School of Soft Knocks	*Lippinott*	*1968*
Student's Choice (anthology		
with R. Kraus)	*Merrill*	*1970*
In War Time (introduction to the		
reprint of a novel)	*College & University Press*	*1978*

Work in Progress: Another novel

WILLIAMS, MAGGIE see: NIBBELINK, CYNTHIA

WILSON, HOLLY
Born: Duluth, Minnesota
Married: Frederick W. Wilson, a doctor
Children: Mary and Ann
Education: University of Michigan
Career: moved to Marquette, Michigan, after the death of her father; after her marriage she lived in Topeka, Kansas, and Clifton Springs, New York; in 1959 the Wilsons moved to Traverse City, Michigan

Writings:

The King Pin	*1938 (Hopwood Award)*
Deborah Todd	
Caroline Unconquered	
Snowbound in Hidden Valley	
Always Anne	
The Hundred Steps	
Stranger in Singaman	

Mrs. Wilson's writings reflect her love of Michigan and her understanding of young people.

WINN, JOSEPHINE
Born: Erie, Pennsylvania
Married: Otis Winn, an architect
Education: Chicago Art Institute, studied voice in Rome, Italy, for two years
Career: lived in Detroit, writing

Writings:

Each Day's Proud Battle	*Putnam's*	*1961*
"The Hugging Sister" (short		
story) in the anthology, Amer-		
ican Accent		*1954*

WITHERSPOON, NAOMI LONG see: **MADGETT, NAOMI LONG**

WITTON, DOROTHY
Born: Stanton, Michigan
Married: Luis Romero, a Mexican forestry engineer
Education: Public Schools in Detroit, the University of Michigan, (with study under Roy Cowden, famous literary coach) and Gorham Munson's Writing Classes at the New School for Social Research in New York
Career: Grew up in Detroit, worked on the *Michigan Daily* at the University of Michigan, book reporting, and writing
Address: Mexico

Writings:

Crossroads for Chela	*Messner*	*1956*
Treasure of Acapulco	*Messner*	*1963*

ghost writing, articles for the Greenwich Village Weekly; short stories; series for The American Girl

Mrs. Witton, after her marriage, became a citizen of Mexico. Concerning her writing, she says that writing for teen-agers gives her the greatest satisfaction because she hopes through them to contribute to the understanding between the young people of two countries.

WOLFF, MARITTA 1918-
Born: December 25, 1918; Grass Lake, Michigan
Parents: Joseph and Ivy (Ellis) Wolff
Married: Leonard Stegman, jewelry business man
Children: Hugh
Education: University of Michigan, B.A. 1940
Career: author

Writings:

Whistle Stop (Avery Hopwood Award)	*Random*	*1941*
Night Shift	*Random*	*1942*
About Lyddy Thomas	*Random*	*1947*
Back of Town	*Random*	*1952*
The Big Nickelodeon	*Random*	*1956*
Buttonwood	*Random*	*1962*

Maritta Wolff wrote her first novel, *Whistle Stop,* in her senior year at the University of Michigan and at that time critics likened her to Farell, Steinbeck, and Caldwell. *Whistle Stop* and *Night Shift* were made into movies.

WOODFORD, ARTHUR MacKINNON 1940-

Born: November 23, 1940; Detroit, Michigan
Parents: Frank B. and Mary-Kirk(MacKinnon) Woodford
Married: Margaret Holmes, housewife
Children: Mark Holmes and Amy MacKinnon
Education: University of Wisconsin, 1958-60; Wayne State University, B.A., 1963; University of Michigan, AMLS, 1964
Career: Librarian, Detroit Public Library, 1964-72; Personnel Director, Detroit Public Library, 1972-74; Assistant Director, Grosse Pointe Public Library, 1974-77; Director, St. Clair Shores Public Library, 1977-
Address: 23279 S. Rosedale Court, St. Clair Shores, MI 48080

Writings:

All Our Yesterdays: A Brief History of Detroit (co-authored with father, Frank B. Woodford	Wayne State U.	1969
Detroit and Its Banks: The Story of Detroit Bank and Trust	Wayne State U.	1974

Work in Progress: A history of the United States Lake Survey Research on the Battle of Lake Erie, 1813; Research on Johnson's Island, a military prison at Sandusky, Ohio, 1861-1865

He says: "I am a member of the American Library Association Michigan Library Association, U.S. Naval Institute, Great Lakes Maritime Institute, Algonquin Club of Detroit and Windsor, and the Primatic Club of Detroit. My hobbies include reading, bridge, tennis, and model ship building."

WOODFORD, FRANK BURY 1903-1967

Born: February 27, 1903; Detroit, Michigan
Parents: Fred V. and Florence (Bury) Woodford
Married: Mary-Kirk MacKinnon
Children: Susan and Arthur
Education: Hillsdale College, 1921-23; Wharton School, University of Pennsylvania, B.S., 1925
Career: Reporter and Chief Editorial Writer, *Detroit Free Press,* 1931-62; Deputy City Treasure, Detroit, 1962-67

Writings:

A Telescope on Mars	(privately printed)	1925
Lewis Cass, the Last Jeffersonian	Rutgers University	1950
Yankees in Wonderland (monograph)	Wayne State U.	1951
Mr. Jefferson's Disciple	Michigan State U.	1953
We Never Drive Alone	Automobile Club of MI	1958

Gabriel Richard (with Alfred Hyma)	Wayne State U.	1958
Introduction to Mighty Mac	Wayne State U.	1958
Law Day U.S.A.	State Bar of Michigan	1961
Father Abraham's Children	Wayne State U.	1961
Alexander J. Grosebeck: Portrait of a Public Man	Wayne State U.	1962
Harper of Detroit (with Philip P. Mason)	Wayne State U.	1964
Parnassus on Main Street: A History of the Detroit Public Library	Wayne State U.	1965
All Our Yesterdays: A Brief History of Detroit (with son, Arthur M. Woodford)	Wayne State U.	1969

Mr. Woodford died at his home in Detroit on June 17, 1967

WOODS, JOHN 1926-
Born: July 12, 1926; Indiana
Parents: Jefferson Blount and Doris (Underwood) Woods
Married: Emily Carol
Children: David and Richard
Education: Indiana University, B.S. 1949, M.A. 1961
Career: Professor English, Western Michigan University, 1955-
Address: English Department, Western Michigan University, Kalamazoo, MI 49081

Writings:

The Deaths at Paragon, Indiana	Indiana U. Press	1955
On the Morning of Color	Indiana U. Press	1961
The Cutting Edge	Indiana U. Press	1966
Keeping Out of Trouble	Indiana U. Press	1968
Turning to Look Back: Poems 1955-70	Indiana U. Press	1972
Striking the Earth	Indiana U. Press	1976
Bone Flicker	Juniper Books	1973
Thirthy Years on the Force	Juniper Books	1977

Work in Progress: *Free Fall,* a book of poems; *Collected Poems and Prose* (probably 1980); *Medicine,* short fictions

He says: "I don't have anythink as grand as philosophy, although might informally have enough working theory to get through a poem."

WRIGHT, ELIZABETH P. (WEIL) 1905-

Born: February 5, 1905; East Lansing, Michigan
Parents: Charles L. and Ella (Bass) Weil
Married: Hayden L. Wright, a draughtsman
Children: John North and Albert Lockwood
Education: University of California, 1923-25; Radcliffe College, B.A., 1927; St. Lawrence University, 1934-37; Western Michigan University
Career: Secretary to the Dean, St. Lawrence University, 1931-37; teacher, Riversdale Girls School, 1937-39; Grier School, 1939-40; Port Huron High School, 1940-41; Director of Education, Kambly School for Retarded, 1968-73; semi-retired

Writings:
Shakespeare's Own "Endangered Species"   *privately printed for environmental cause)*

Work in Progress: *Temper of the Times,* a study of pre-Civil War conditions; *We are Six Bird Songs,* legends, music, illustrations; *Letters of K4,* Secret Service agent in Detroit area investigating Lindbergh kidnapping; *I Sum up for the Defence,* re: Hauptmann

She says: "My creative work is that of an amateur and should make no pretensions to being classical. It is only poetry in the sense of being an expression of intense feeling with analogous images/metaphors. I think I have read and loved so much good poetry the rhythms may have stayed in my mind and be built in. I think finding the familiar—our soul, perhaps God, the ideal in old or new, is happiness and can be attained by courageous trial of the new. . .you'll discover a truth—its goodness or badness. . .or by steadfast adherence to the old. The motive and honesty are what count. To me, that we enjoy and suffer mean that God has prepared a place for us. Education is helping the uninitiated to enjoy their minds, bodies, and external world. This is it today."

WUNSCH, JOSEPHINE McLEAN 1914-

Pseud.: J. Sloan McLean
Born: February 3, 1914; Detroit, Michigan
Parents: John F. and Georgiana (Grant) McLean
Married: Edward S. Wunsch, a lawyer
Children: Katherine (Mrs. Donald Remsen), Elizabeth (Mrs. Ralph Gordon), and Edward, Jr.
Education: University of Michigan, B.A. 1936; Wayne State University
Career: Wife, mother, author
Address: 830 Bishop Rd., Grosse Pointe, MI 48230

Writings:

Flying High	McKay	*1962*
Passport to Russia	McKay	*1965*
Summer of Decision	McKay	*1968*
The Aerie, a collaboration with Virginia Gillette under pseud- onym	Nash	*1974*
	Danish rights	*1976*

Work in Progress: 2 adult suspense novels

She says: "I have been Women's Editor of the *Michigan Daily* at the U. of M. followed by a stint of publicity work in New York. I worked on the *Free Press* a year and a half and was married in 1940. I have three children and three grandsons. I have published fiction and non-fiction nationally in magazines. We are a sports-minded family and were "Skiers of the Week" at Aspen. I still play in the Detroit Women's Golf Association. My husband sailed in 30 Mackinac Races—also several ocean races. He is a third generation lawyer in Detroit."

YERIAN, MARGARET A.
YERIAN, CAMERON JOHN
Born: Urbana, Ohio; Durand, Michigan
Parents: Chauncey P. and Margaret (Chase) Forward; Wilson D. and Myrtle (Smith) Yerian
Married: Cameron John Yerian, writer and editor; Margaret A. Yerian, writer and editor
Children: Phoebe A. and Cameron scot
Education: Both of them: University of Michigan (under-graduate and graduate work)
Careers: Television producer/director, writer, editor; Writer, editor, book designer
Address: Box 1101, Ann Arbor, MI 48106

Writings:
(each is co-authored by Margaret and Cameron Yerian)

When I Go to Bed	*Whitman*	*1967*
ABCs of Aerospace	*Elk Grove Press*	*1971*
ABCs of Hydrospace	*Elk Grove Press*	*1971*
My Little Counting Book	*Whitman*	*1971*
Rainbows and Jolly Beans	*Elk Grove Press*	*1971*
Creative Activities, a 20 vol. set (editors)	*Children's Press*	*1977*

Work in Progress: Margaret and Cameron Yerian are currently working on early childhood materials and also multi-media materials in the area of effective education.

They say: "We are concerned with writing and publishing for

children because we feel that they are our most important resource."

YOUNG, ALBERT JAMES 1939-

Pseud.: Al Young
Born: May 31, 1939; Ocean Springs, Mississippi
Parents: Albert J. and Mary (Campbell) Young
Married: Arlin Young, a textile designer
Children: Michael James Young
Education: University of Michigan, 1957-61; Stanford University, (on Fellowship) 1966-67; University of California, B.A. in Spanish 1969
Career: Lecturer in Creative Writing, Stanford U. 1969-76; active writer, editor, and lecturer throughout U.S.
Address: 514 Bryant Street, Palo Alto, CA 94301

Writings:

Dancing (poems)	Corinth Books	1969
Snakes (novel)	Holt	1970
	Sidgwick & Jackson, London	1970
	Dell	1972
The Song Turning Back into Itself	Holt	1971
Who Is Angelina? (novel)	Holt	1976
	NAL/Signet	1977
Yardbird Lives! (anthology edited with Ishmael Reed)	Grove Press	1978

He says: "I grew up in Michigan and there will always be something of the romantic but practical Midwestern in my work. I regard my work as both a practical and a spiritual activity; its purpose is to share what I have learned about being human in such a way as to strike responsive chords in the hearts of my readers."

Awards: Stenger Fellowship, 1966; Joseph Henry Jackson Award, 1969; Guggenheim Fellow, 1974; NEA Writing Fellow, 1975

ZARIF, MARGARET MIN'IMAH

Pseudonym: (formerly Margaret Boon-Jones)
Born: Detroit, Michigan
Parents: William E. and Manie C. (Bascome) Boone
Children: Michael Douglas Jones
Education: Hillsdale College, 1940-42; Wayne State University, B.A., 1944; Oberlin College, M.A., 1947; University of Cape

Coast; University of Toledo; University of Ibadan
Career: Instructor & Director of Christian Education, Allen University, South Carolina; Director of Xnt. Education, St. James, Cleveland, Ohio; Teacher, Toledo, Ohio and Virginia Public Schools; presently kingergarten teacher, Detroit, Michigan
Address: 6550 Scotten Ave., Detroit, MI 48210

Writings:

Martin Luther King, Jr., A Picture Story	Childrens Press	1968
To Be Somebody	Vantage	1976

Ghost writer of pamphlets for the National Association of Sickle Cell Disease

Work in Progress: Childrens' books about scientist and engineers for curriculum at Latch-Key school and a new nursery; Children's book on a global theme

She says: "I am a staff writer for the *Bilalian News,* a newspaper for the World Community of Islam in the West (WCIW). Some of my favorite activities involve Afro-American Museum, Your Heritage House, and Wali Muhammad Masjid #1."

ZOLOTOW, CHARLOTTE 1915-

Pseudonym: Charlotte Bookman; Sara Abbot
Born: June 26, 1915; Norfolk, Virginia
Parents: Louis J. and Ella (Bernstein) Shapiro
Married: Maurice Zolotow, a writer
Children: Stephen and Crescent
Education: University of Wisconsin
Career: Editor, 1939-44 and 1962-70, Harper & Row; Editorial Direcotr, Jr. Books, 1970-76, Harper & Row; Vice-President and Associate Publisher, Jr. Book Department, Harper & Row, 1976
Address: 29 Elm Place, Hastings-on-Hudson, NY 10706

Writings:

The Park Book	Harper	1944
But Not Billy	Harper	1947
The City Boy and the Country Horse	Wonder Books	1952
The Magic Word	Wonder Books	1952
The Storm Book ('52 runner-up, Caldecott Medal)	Harper	1952
Indian, Indian (Herald Tribune Honor Book)	Golden Books	1952
The Quiet Mother and the Noisy Little Boy	Lothrop	1953
One Step Two	Lothrop	1955
Not a Little Monkey	Lothrop	1957

Over and Over	Harper	1957
Do You Know What I'll Do?	Harper	1958
The Bunny Who Found Easter	Parnassus	1959
Aren't You Glad	Golden Books	1960
Big Brother	Harper	1960
The Little Black Puppy	Golden Books	1960
In My Garden	Lothrop	1960
The Man with the Purple Eyes	Abelard	1961
The Night When Mother Went Away	Lothrop	1961
The Three Funny Friends	Harper	1961
Mr. Rabbit and the Lovely Present (runner-up, Caldecott Medal)	Harper	1962
When the Wind Stops	Abelard	1962
The Quarreling Book	Harper	1963
The Sky Was Blue	Harper	1963
Thomas the Tiger	Lothrop	1963
The White Marble	Abelard	1963
I Have a Horse of My Own	Abelard	1964
The Poodle Who Barked at the Wind	Lothrop	1964
A Rose, a Bridge, and a Wild Black Horse	Harper	1964
When I Have a Little Girl	Harper	1965
Someday	Harper	1965
Big Sister and Little Sister	Harper	1966
If It Weren't for You	Harper	1966
All That Sunlight	Harper	1967
The Hating Book	Harper	1967
I Want to Be Little	Abelard	1967
Summer Is	Abelard	1967
When I Have a Son	Harper	
A Father Like That	Harper	1968
My Friend John	Harper	1968
The New Friend	Abelard	1968
The Sleepy Book	Lothrop	1968
A Day in the Life Of Yani	Crowell	1969
The Old Dog	Coward	1969
A Week in the Yani's World	Crowell	1969
A Day in the Life of Latef	Crowell	1970
A Week in Latef's World	Crowell	
Flocks of Birds	Abelard	1970
Here We Are	Crowell	
River Winding	Abelard	1970
Where I Begin	Coward	1970
Wake Up and Goodnight	Harper	1971
You and Me	Macmillan	1971

The Beautiful Christmas Tree	Parnassus	1972
Hold My Hand	Harper	1972
William's Doll	Harper	1972
Janey	Harper	1973
Overpraised Season	Harper	1973
My Grandson Lew	Harper	1974
The Summer Night	Harper	1974
The Unfriendly Book	Harper	1975
When the Wind Stops (new edition)	Harper	1975
It's Not Fair	Harper	1976
May I Visit	Harper	1976
Someone New	Harper	1977

Work in Progress: *Early Sorrow, an Anthology*

She says: "A good picture book, I think, must be honest and unpretentious and direct. Whether it is funny or poetic (or both) there should be some universal truth or feeling in it, and what Margaret Wise Brown called the 'unexpected inevitable'. I love children's books because the author or artist dips into the freshness and originality of children, and these qualities are open to an infinite variety of theme and treatment.

"My children and their friends have often reminded me of things from my childhood which have become the theme of a book. Sometimes it is a kind of double exposure-an adult awareness of a phenomenon and the memory of what it seemed to me as a child or seems to the children around me."

ZUCKER, JACK 1935-

Born: January 23, 1935; Brooklyn, New York
Parents: Morris and Elsie (Wachtel) Zucker
Married: Helen Zucker, an art critic for the *Birmingham Eccentric*
Children: Laurie and Elizabeth
Education: City College of New York, B.A., 1957; New York University, M.A. 1961
Career: Garden Country Day School 1959-61; Ohio State U. 1961-62; Newark State College (now Kean State College) 1962-65; Babson College, Mass. 1965-68; Marietta College, O. 1968-70; Phillips Academy, Mass. 1970-76; Roeper City & Country School, Bloomfield Hills, 1976-present
Address: 624 S. Fox Hills Dr., Bloomfield Hills, MI 49013

Writings:

Critical Thinking (with Ira Konigsberg)	Macmillan	1968

Articles in Andover Review, Ann Arbor Review, Gissing Newsletter, Independent Schools Bulletin; poems in Literary Reveiw, Es-

quire, *Southern Poetry Review, Trace III-IV, California Review, Folio,* in additional literary magazines and in anthologies

Work in Progress: *To Nat, Wherever He Is* to be published by K-Tdid Press, 1978; more poetry

He says: "I am a Jewish ethnic poet, not because I am religious or nationalistic, but because I believe that a good deal of poetry, and mine particularly, goes back to early memories and places."

Awards: Gretchen Warren Award and Masefield Award for Narrative Poem; *To Nat, Wherever He Is* has been a runner-up in several national contests

SOURCES CONSULTED

American Book Trade Directory, 22nd. ed. Ed. & comp. by Jacques Cattell Press., R.R. Bowker, 1975.

Author's and Writer's Who's Who. Hafner, 1971.

Authors of Books for Young People. Scarecrow Press, 1964.
—First Supplement, 1967.

Bailey, Leaonead Pack. Broadside Authors and Artists: An Illustrated Biographical Directory. Broadside Press, 1974.

Biographical Dictionaries Master Index, 1975-76: A Guide to More Than 725,000 Listings in Over Fifty Current Who's Whos and Other Works of Collective Biography. Ed. by Dennis LaBeau and Gary C. Tarbert., Gale Research, 1975.

Birmingham (Mich.) Eccentric, July 10, 1975.

Books in Print. R.R. Bowker, 1948-1977.

Contemporary Authors: A Bio-Bibliographical Guide to Current Authors and Their Works. Vols. 1-64. Gale Research, 1962-1976.

Contemporary Literary Criticism. Gale Research, 1973-1977.

Cumulative Book Index. H.W. Wilson, 1928-1977.

Current Biography. H.W. Wilson, 1940-1976.

Detroit (Mich.) Free Press, August 22, 1976.

Detroit (Mich.) News, October 17, 1962.

Directory of American Poets. Poets & Writers, 1977.

Directory of Michigan Publishers. Michigan Library Association (Reference Section), 1975.

Encyclopedia of American Biography. Harper, 1974.

Goodrich, Madge Knevels. A Bibliography of Michigan Authors. Richmond, Va.: Richmond Virginia Press, 1928.

Green Bay (Wisc.) Press Gazette. Clipping, n.d.

Harpers Magazine, August, 1971.

Hilbert, Rachel M., ed. Michigan Authors. Michigan Association for School Librarians, 1960.
—Michigan Poets, with Supplement to Michigan Authors 1960. Michigan Association for School Librarians, 1964.

Hopkins, Lee B. Books Are By People. Citation, 1969.
—Pass the Poetry, Please. Citation, 1972.

The Junior Book of Authors. 2d ed. Ed. by Stanley J. Kunitz & Howard Haycraft. H.W. Wilson, 1951.

Lania, Leo. Hemingway: A Pictorial Biography. Viking, 1961.

Leaders in Education. 5th ed. Ed. by Jacques Cattell Press. R.R. Bowker, 1974.

Literary Market Place, 1976-77. R.R. Bowker, 1976.

The McGraw-Hill Encyclopedia of World Biography. McGraw-Hill, 1975.

Michigan in Books. vol. 2, 1960 to vol. 13, 1977. Michigan State Library.

More Junior Authors. Ed. by Muriel Fuller. H.W. Wilson, 1963.

New York Times. July 17, 1971; January 6, 1973.

Something About the Author. Vol. 1-10. Gale Research, 1971-76.

Telephone Directories, various cities.

Third Book of Junior Authors. H.W. Wilson, 1972.

Twentieth Century Authors. Ed. by Stanley J. Kunitz. H.W. Wilson, 1942.

—Supplement, 1955.

200 Contemporary Authors. Ed. by Barbara Harte & Carolyn Riley. Gale Reseach, 1969.

U.S. Library of Congress

    The United States Catalog: Books in Print Jan. 1, 1928. 4th ed. H.W. Wilson, 1928.

    A Catalog of Books Represented by Library of Congress Printed Cards issued to July 31, 1942.

    —Supplement: Cards issued Aug. 1, 1942 to Dec. 31, 1947.

    The Library of Congress Author Catalog: A Cumulative List of Works Represented by Library of Congress Printed Cards, 1948-52.

    The National Union Catalog: A Cumulative Author List Representing Library of Congress Printed Cards and Titles Reported by Other American Libraries, 1953-57.

    —1958-62.

    —1963-67.

    —1968-72.

    —1973.

    —1974.

    —1975.

    The National Union Catalog: Pre-1956 Imprints. Masell, 1972.

Webster's Biographical Dictionary. G. & C. Merriam, 1969.

The Writers Directory, 1974-76. St. Martin's, 1973.

—1976-78. (1976)

Who Was Who in America. Marquis, 1966.

Who's Who in America. Marquis, 1950.

Who's Who in the Midwest. 9th ed. Marquis, 1964.

ADDENDUM

HOBBS, J. KLINE 1928-
Born: May 9, 1928; Battle Creek, Michigan
Parents: Joe W. and Elizabeth L. (Kline) Hobbs
Education: Michigan State University, B.A. 1949; Columbia University, M.A. 1951; Western Michigan University, M.L.S. 1974
Career: Resident artist at Olivet and Kalamazoo Colleges; Freelance writer, director and actor in Michigan and New York. Recent Projects: Researcher/writer exhibition catalogue Black American Art exhibition Battle Creek Civic Art Center, 1977. Director Riverlight Poetry Fair, videotaped reading series, Battle Creek Civic Art Center, 1977. Co-director Immigrant Oral History Interviews, Battle Creek Public Library/CETA, 1977-78. Director Regional Theatre for Regional Playwrights Conference, Kalamazoo College, 1978.
Address: 657 E. Michigan Ave., Battle Creek, MI 49017

Writings:

Of Pickles and Purple Peacocks	Michigan State U.	1948
The Hypocritical Satellites	Michigan State U.	1949
Pedants Delusions	Columbia University	1951
Notes on a Hypothetical Second Coming	Olivet College Writers Conference	1964
This Was Planned to be a Choral Drama	Resident Professional Co. at Kalamazoo College	1978
"Notes on a Hypothetical Second Coming" Under Covers	Stovepipe Press	1976
Modern American Lyrics: the Best of Contemporary Poetry	Young	1963
Forty Salutes to Michigan Poets	PSM/MCA	1976
Under Covers	Stovepipe Press	1976
Diary of the Ultimate One Night Stand . . . and that Other Quest	Expedition Press	1979

Work in Progress: *Business of Theatre, Films and Broadcasting* (Resource Book); *Arrivals and Departures* (poetry chapbook); *You Should Have Seen What Was Playing Here Last Month* (Play)

He says: "Much of my creative work has been focused on personal liberation in terms of sexual as well as racial and ethnic identity."

STEINHARDT, HERSCHEL S. 1910-

Born: May 21, 1910
Parents: Abraham and Zelda Steinhardt
Children: Dr. Joyce N. Garber and Mrs. Judie E. Goldstein
Education: Hunter College, 1947-48; New School For Social Research, 1938-39; Wayne State University, 1928-29
Career: In order to learn about plays, worked as an usher at the Bonstelle and Schubert Theatres; Playwright at Federal Theatre, under Emmet Lavery. Writing career interrupted periodically by family responsibilities but has presently been resumed full-time.
Address: Southfield, MI 48075

Writings:

Sons of Men	Bookman Associates	1958
A Star in Heaven	New Voices	1965
"Voice of the Bell"		
Song of the Street		
Before the Morning		
The Power of the Dog		
Man On Earth		

Ten (10) one-act plays published; other one-act plays produced in New York, Holland, Germany and South America. *"Voice of the Bell"* was broadcast throughout the U.S. Four full-length plays are making the theatrical rounds. *Song of the Street* is scheduled for production this fall at Paul Robeson Theatre, Detroit, MI.

Work in Progress: *Make a Noise in the World,* a play in three acts; *The Last Roundup, From Pillar to Post, The Red Ball*

He says: "The late John Gassner, Sterling Professor of Playwriting at Yale, wrote: 'Herschel Steinhardt's plays are vivid examples of soundly constructed playwriting characterized by sympathetic attitudes toward representative characters of common life.' "